# The Complete Idiot's Reference Card

## Catholicism's Timeline

### Before the Common Era (B.C.E.)

| | |
|---|---|
| 8000–3000 | Catholicism's tribal roots grow out of earth-based farming communities in the Near East. |
| 1200 | Judaism creates its Jewish identity and settles in Israel. |
| c. 347 | Plato, the most influential philosopher of the ancient age, and proponent of the split between mind and body, dies. |
| 332 | Greeks occupy Israel. |
| 322 | Aristotle, philosopher, student of Plato, and founder of a tradition of systematic logic, dies. |
| 400–100 | The Old Testament is organized. |
| 63 | Romans occupy Israel. |

### The Common Era (C.E.)

| | |
|---|---|
| c. 0 | Jesus is born. |
| c. 30–33 | The Public Life of Jesus: he preaches, performs miracles, and gathers followers. |
| c. 33 | Jesus is crucified. |
| 50–180 | The New Testament is written and organized. |
| c. 64 | First systematic persecution of Christians by the Roman Emperor Nero. St. Peter and St. Paul are martyred. |
| 70 | The destruction of the temple at Jerusalem completes the split between Christians and Jews. |
| c. 107 | St. Ignatius of Antioch, the first writer to use the term *Catholic,* dies. |
| c. 270 | St. Anthony of Egypt goes into the desert and begins the tradition of Catholic monasticism. |
| 313 | Constantine issues the Edict of Toleration for Catholics, which ends the persecution of Catholics by the Roman Empire. |
| 325 | The Council of Nicaea, the First Ecumenical Council (or council of the whole church), formally declares the divinity of Jesus. |
| c. 420 | St. Jerome, whose translation of the Bible from Hebrew to Latin became the standard for the Catholic Church, dies. |
| 430 | St. Augustine of Hippo, author of *The City of God* and most influential theologian of the early church, dies. |
| 431 | The Council of Ephesus declares Mary is the mother of God. |
| c. 461 | St. Patrick, missionary to Ireland, dies. |
| 476 | The western half of the Roman Empire falls. |
| c. 547 | St. Benedict of Nursia, founder of the Benedictine Order, which became the foundation for Western monasticism, dies. |
| 632 | Muhammad, founder of Islam, dies. |
| 711–1492 | The armies of Islam occupy Spain. |
| 754 | St. Boniface, missionary to Germany, dies. |

*tear here*

ALPHA

## Catholicism's Timeline (continued)

| | |
|---|---|
| 800 | Charlemagne is crowned Emperor of the Romans. |
| 1054 | The Orthodox Church separates from the Catholic Church. |
| 1095–1291 | The Crusades take place. |
| 1221 | St. Dominic de Guzman, founder of the Dominican order and advocate of the Rosary, dies. |
| 1226 | St. Francis of Assisi, champion of the poor and founder of the Franciscan order, dies. |
| 1231 | Pope Gregory IX authorizes the Medieval Inquisition. |
| 1274 | St. Thomas Aquinas, master logician, philosopher, and theologian of the church, dies. |
| 1380 | St. Catherine of Siena, doctor of the church and mystical writer, dies. |
| 1431 | Joan of Arc is burned at the stake. |
| 1479 | The Spanish Inquisition is established. |
| 1492 | Columbus claims the New World for God and Spain. |
| 1517 | Martin Luther openly challenges the church's authority. |
| 1531 | Our Lady of Guadalupe appears in Mexico. |
| 1534 | Henry VIII declares the independence of the Church of England. |
| 1542 | Pope Paul III establishes the Roman Inquisition. |
| 1545–1563 | The Council of Trent condemns the Protestants and reforms the Catholic Church. |
| 1556 | St. Ignatius of Loyola, founder of the Jesuit order and author of *Spiritual Exercises*, dies. |
| 1565 | St. Augustine, Florida is founded, becoming the first Catholic community in the present-day United States. |
| 1582 | St. Teresa of Ávila, doctor of the church, writer, mystic, and reformer, dies. |
| 1618–1648 | The Thirty Years War between Catholic and Protestant states in Europe, the last and largest of the religious wars. |
| 1634 | The Catholic colony of Maryland is established. |
| 1790 | John Carroll becomes the first bishop consecrated in the United States. |
| 1806 | The Holy Roman Empire is dissolved. |
| 1834–1860 | Anti-Catholic feeling in the United States reaches its peak. |
| 1854 | The doctrine of Mary's Immaculate Conception is declared. |
| 1870 | Vatican Council I declares papal infallibility. |
| 1907–1967 | Priests are required to take oath against modernism. |
| 1960 | John Fitzgerald Kennedy becomes the first Catholic elected U.S. president. |
| 1962–1965 | Vatican Council II takes place. |
| 1978 | Pope John Paul II, the first non-Italian pope since 1523, is elected. |
| 1980 | Dorothy Day, founder of the Catholic Worker, dies. |
| 1995 | Cardinal Bernardin appoints the first woman pastoral coordinator to head up a Chicago parish. |

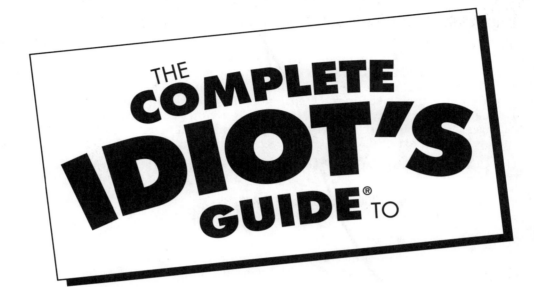

# THE COMPLETE IDIOT'S GUIDE® TO

# Understanding Catholicism

*by Bob O'Gorman, Ph.D.*
*and Mary Faulkner, M.A.*

alpha
books

Macmillan USA, Inc.
201 West 103rd Street
Indianapolis, IN 46290

A Pearson Education Company

**Publisher**
*Marie Butler-Knight*

**Product Manager**
*Phil Kitchel*

**Managing Editor**
*Cari Luna*

**Acquisitions Editor**
*Amy Zavatto*

**Development Editor**
*Suzanne LeVert*

**Production Editor**
*Christy Wagner*

**Copy Editor**
*Heather Stith*

**Illustrator**
*Brian Moyer*

**Cover Designers**
*Mike Freeland*
*Kevin Spear*

**Book Designers**
*Scott Cook and Amy Adams of DesignLab*

**Indexer**
*Brad Herriman*

**Layout/Proofreading**
*Darin Crone*
*Donna Martin*

# Contents at a Glance

# Contents

# Foreword

The underlying idea behind "idiot" in Greek (*idiotes*) is "a private individual" not holding public office. This usage got extended to mean "common person," the lay man or woman who is not a professional, not a specialist. Snobs later downgraded private, common, lay individuals into what most people think idiot means: imbecile, dunderhead.

This book rescues and re-elevates the term so that it is no longer an insult. In fact, it applies to most of us, since most are not professionals or specialists in Catholic life and thought. For that matter, it applies to virtually all of us, since it is almost impossible to be informed about the whole range of topics in this book. We are all common, lay people in respect to some themes. (All right, I'll exempt the up to half-dozen producers of single-author encyclopedias of Catholicism. It's their job to match the knowledge, skills, ambition, and industry of Bob O'Gorman and Mary Faulkner here.)

The authors succeed admirably in teasing us into the many chambers of the house Catholic, taking us toward the beginnings of the many Catholic trails, tantalizing us with the glimpses of what the Catholic vision is all about, and letting us sense the Catholic sensibility.

They have their own *shtick,* their own ways of getting attention and accenting favored themes. They acknowledge the influence of Andrew M. Greeley and Virgilio Elizondo, for instance. That means that they do not dwell on the grim, downside of Catholic life. They communicate, in the midst of the realism about life and church, a sense of exuberance and an impartation of hope. That's all to the good in an age when Catholicism often gets lumped with "organized religion" as some sort of grumpy, tyrannizing force.

Professionals, specialists, in knowledge of things Catholic, they are also expert at telling stories, holding attention, and ministering to a hungry Catholic (and surrounding) world, where many "prefer" or "identify with" Catholicism but have a hard time gaining access to knowledge of what it's all about. This book is about "what it's all about."

Professor Martin E. Marty

Professor Martin E. Marty is the Fairfax M. Cone Distinguished Service Professor (Emeritus) of the History of Modern Christianity Divinity School, University of Chicago.

The best way of introducing this marvelous book, which I know will enrich the lives of anyone who reads it, is by exploring it in terms of why I love being a Catholic. This is the religion of my parents and ancestors, and it connects me with the very origins of my life and existence.

Being a Catholic is great fun, and this book celebrates the fun of this religion. Jesus started his public ministry with the feast at Cana—enjoying himself with family, friends, and other guests. Throughout his life, he loved going to the festivals in Jerusalem and having a good time with anyone and everyone. Mexican Catholicism is festive. It allows us to experience in very vivid ways the deepest mysteries of our faith, of God's love for us, of the life of Jesus, the Son of God made human for us, Mary, the sorrowful mother, and the saints who were sinners like us but achieved great virtue. For every mystery of the faith, there is a festive and elaborate celebration allowing us to enter into the mystery as if it was taking place in our own back yard.

Catholicism is colorful, it's sensual, it's emotional, it's dramatic, and it's fun. As this book helps you see, you can take part and benefit from the great celebrations of the faith like Guadalupe, Christmas Posadas, Midnight Mass, Ash Wednesday, Holy Week rituals, Day of the Dead, and many others. These popular festive celebrations allow everyone and anyone to enter into a collective mystical experience of the sacred as it is present among us here and now today.

The book tells you how Catholics have so many ways of being in touch with God throughout the day wherever we happen to be. Medals, holy cards, scapulars, rosaries, holy water, candles, home shrines, and other simple things put us in immediate contact with God, just like the picture of a loved one in my wallet helps to put me in their presence even when they are far away or even gone to heaven. These simple objects allow us, as the book points out, to touch God and feel God's touch even when we don't know much about God.

I love being a Catholic because much more than a religion, it seems to be a large, extended family, or as the book says, a tribe! We find ourselves at home wherever we go in the world, and even though the language and some of the details may be different, the basic symbols are the same and we immediately recognize ourselves to be among family. When people travel or migrate to other countries, we can immediately find a religious home in a local Catholic Church.

I love being a Catholic because our Catholic story, as this book does such a good and balanced job of saying, is so human and divine at the same time. Human because of the many crazy, stupid, weird, and even cruel things we have done, as well as the many heroic acts and movements of charity, mercy, and compassion. Through all this weakness, I see all the good and beautiful things the church has done throughout history and continues to do today: orphanages, lepresoriums, schools, universities, hospitals, community-organizing, social justice initiatives, visitation of the sick, aid to immigrants, and on.

*The Complete Idiot's Guide to Understanding Catholicism* is wonderful and stimulating. It is brief while exposing substantial matter in an attractive way. I am honored to have been asked to introduce this book, which will definitely reach many more people than some of the best theological works or even the official catechism of the Catholic Church. It is written in a simple and attractive way, it is easy and exciting to read, and the authors have managed to distill and condense very technical matter into a very cohesive book.

Father Virgilio Elizondo
The Mexican American Cultural Center, San Antonio, Texas

# Introduction

In almost every way, the history of the Catholic Church is the story of Western civilization, and for 1,200 years, all Christians shared its story. Today, there are over a billion Catholics worldwide, making it the largest denomination in the world. For most of its 2,000-year history, it has been wrapped in mystery. Its rituals and prayers were chanted in Latin. Its statues, candles, incense, and many other practices have enthralled many and frightened some. However, in the early 1960s, a radical change occurred within the church, and since that time, it has uncloaked some of its own mystery and opened itself to the world.

In telling the story of the church, we are clearly telling two stories: one that existed when the twentieth century began and one that exists as the twenty-first century dawns. We talk about the church from both the perspective of the church that many older Catholics remember and the perspective of the emerging church.

We look at the church from many angles: its history and vision, its unique character, and the similarities and differences among Catholics. The book is about the people and their beliefs. It's about their prayers and practices. It's about the contemporary world and the challenges that the church faces in the future.

Who are Catholics and how are they different from the rest of the folks? Answering this question engages the paradox of being unique and belonging to a world community. This is a delicate matter for Catholics, because in the past they have claimed that theirs is the only true religion. We have not made that claim for Catholicism; however, we have acknowledged that to be Catholic is to be different. The purpose of this book is to discover what is unique and what is different about being Catholic.

Sacraments are at the heart and soul of what it means to be a Catholic, and we look at them in detail in this book. To be Catholic is to see, hear, taste, touch, and smell the presence of God. For Catholics, this experience happens through the sacraments, which is the most distinguishing mark of Catholicism. Catholics have a tradition of prayers and practices, statues, medals, rosaries, and more that is part of their everyday life. This rich collection has been accumulating for some 2,000 years and comes from many cultures.

Perhaps the most recognizable Catholic figure is Mary. She is often the face of Catholicism to the world. The relationship between a Catholic and Mary embodies a special emotional bond or grace itself. The book explores the many roles of Mary and what she means to Catholics.

Catholics are everywhere. However, they have some particular gathering places where you are more apt to find them. The neighborhood parish is one of them. This is where Catholics come together on a weekly basis to celebrate the Mass. During the week, they participate in a number of social, recreational, educational, and outreach activities centered there. Catholic parishes are led by priests, sisters, and other professional church ministers. You'll meet this special group of people in this book.

Another characteristic of Catholics is their sense of unity, their tribal nature. Catholics belong to a neighborhood community and a worldwide church. The Catholic Church is a highly structured institution with a lot of people managing it. For Catholics, there is a sense of connection to the worldwide community, and this sense brings into being the vision that we are all God's people.

Catholic unity has a powerful potential to influence the world. Perhaps at no other time in history is this influence more apparent than with the present pope, John Paul II. His tireless world travels have symbolized religious truth for many. His presence magnifies the witness of the "body of Christ" all over the world. Electronic communication through television, the World Wide Web, and newswires, along with global travel, has made fulfilling the mission of the church to announce the presence of God throughout the world a greater possibility than in any other era.

This book tells the Catholic story from its beginning with the tongues of fire on the feast of Pentecost to its present-day position in the modern world. It explores the church's rich mysticism and its varied forms of spirituality, as well as highlights its traditional and contemporary theologies.

In this book, we focus more on the story of the faith of the people than the institutional story. You get an inside glimpse of the everyday practices of Catholics: their prayer life, the rich history of the saints, and the way they live out the holy seasons of the year from the springtime of Easter to the autumn of All Souls' Day and the winter renewal of Christmas. We trace the church's rituals back to their roots in the earth itself.

Today Catholicism comes in many shapes and sizes. It's grown beyond the old stereotypes, yet the character of being Catholic is still very much intact. As we pass along our knowledge and stories to the next generation, we look at the challenges the church will face and the resources it has to survive and remain meaningful to the people and faithful to Jesus.

# What You'll Discover in This Book

The book is divided into six sections:

**Part 1, "What's a Catholic?"** provides a profile of Catholics and a peek at their practices and prayers. You'll get inside the workings of the Vatican and learn all about the church's revolution, Vatican II.

**Part 2, "Putting the 'Ism' in Catholicism: Becoming Catholic, Becoming Different,"** explores the roots of Catholicism in the earth, the Bible, and in Jesus, and Catholicism's emergence as a religion.

**Part 3, "The Sensuous Side of Catholicism: How Catholics Experience God,"** lets you in on the way Catholics taste, touch, hear, smell, and see God through their sacramental practices and how Catholics experience Jesus. In this part, you'll learn all about Mary and Catholics' relationship to her.

**Part 4, "Imagination and Prayer,"** takes you into the world of Catholics, their statues and holy cards, their liturgical cycle of seasons, their Rosary, their sacred music, their contemplative life, and most important, the Mass.

**Part 5, "Catholic Identity: What Makes a Catholic?"** looks at the center of Catholic life: its parishes and its schools and charities. You'll find out about key Catholic teachings and who determines them. You'll meet the hierarchy of the church as well as its foot soldiers.

**Part 6, "The Church's History,"** begins with a visit to the Roman Empire and looks at important people who had a hand in shaping the early church. You will see the church grow and struggle through the Middle Ages. You'll hear all about the miracle that brought Catholicism to the New World and meet a new generation of Catholics who carry the vision into the future.

In the appendixes, we have included information that will provide you with some interesting and useful details. There is a glossary for you to quickly check terms used in the book. There is a list of the books and sources we have drawn from and others that you might find helpful for further reading. There is a chart of religious symbols that show how Catholic rituals connect to the elements of the earth. Finally, we have included a list of fascinating but lesser known popes the Church has had, as well as a story on an alleged female pope.

# Helpful Hints for the Reader

Throughout the text, you will find helpful and interesting information to spice up your journey through Catholicism.

### Saints Preserve Us

In these boxes, you'll learn the stories of some well-known and not-so-well-known saints, their feast days, and who and what they watch over.

### Epiphanies

These boxes offer a quick study of interesting Catholic tidbits. Use this information as a resource to impress your Catholic friends.

### For Heaven's Sake!

This information is designed to help keep you on the straight and narrow and alert you to common misunderstandings about the church.

**Your Guardian Angel**

The Catholic Church is known for its mysterious practices. These boxes contain suggestions for the reader on how to easily participate regardless of whether you are a believer, along with helpful tips.

**S'ter Says**

The Catholic religion has a language of its own. Information provided in this sidebar will give you a quick grasp of terms that may be new to you.

## Our Gratitude List

We've got a lot of people to thank. Some of the ones who were indispensable were Linda Roghaar, our agent; Suzanne LeVert, our primary editor; Jim Mallett, our religious editor; and Dan O'Gorman, our historical editor. We had great technical help from Dean Caskey, our personal photographer, and Valerie Harrell, who did our graphics, Cherri Kowalchuk and Matt Lohmeier, our Gen X'ers, and Scott Weiss, who untangled the computer. We had special consultation from Margaret Ann Crain, Jack Seymour, Joe Glab, Sheila Bourelly, and Lynne Westfield. Our perspectives in writing this book were greatly influenced by two people who have made major contributions to the study of Catholicism, Andrew M. Greeley, professor of Social Science, University of Chicago, and Virgilio Elizondo, founder of the Mexico-American Cultural Center, San Antonio, Texas.

Our families and friends helped us, too, including Mary Lou, Tim, John, Lucile (who prayed a lot), Elizabeth, Susan, John, Martha Leigh, Dorothy, Lilyleone, Noris, Claudia (for picking up the slack at the office), Paul Dokecki and Bob Newbrough (for patience and support), The Ladies of Nashville Circle, and Darby.

Our thanks also go to all the words and thoughts of others both written and spoken that have worked their way into this book.

## Special Thanks to the Technical Reviewer

*The Complete Idiot's Guide to Understanding Catholicism* was reviewed by an expert who double-checked the accuracy of what you'll learn here, to help us ensure that this book gives you everything you need to know about Catholicism. Special thanks are extended to Rev. James K. Mallett, Pastor of Christ the King Church, Nashville, Tennessee.

## Trademarks

All terms mentioned in this book that are known to be or are suspected of being trademarks or service marks have been appropriately capitalized. Alpha Books and Pearson Education, Inc., cannot attest to the accuracy of this information. Use of a term in this book should not be regarded as affecting the validity of any trademark or service mark.

# Part 1

# What's a Catholic?

*A pop image of Catholics that exists in the world of movies, television, and books: the Irish cop, the spunky nun, and a priest who refuses to break the seal of confession all make interesting characters and plots. Nostalgic remembrances, stereotypes, prejudice, and just plain curiosity surround this somewhat mysterious religion. Candles, incense, processions, statues, and visions of Mary … We'll look at what is fact and what is fiction regarding Catholics and their practices.*

*In addition to the romanticized version of a Catholic, there also exists an image of the Catholic as a political, social, and economic force in society. In most cities, there is an abundance of Catholic institutions: schools, hospitals, homes for the aged, and other vital social agencies. The church exists in many countries and among many nationalities. It has a colorful mix of cultures that are not always part of the common Catholic image.*

*A massive renovation occurred at a council of church leaders called Vatican II. During this four-year process, the church underwent a radical and comprehensive renewal. Now, let's take a look at all this and more.*

# Chapter 1

# Can You Judge a Catholic by the Cover?

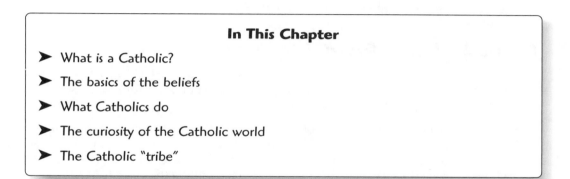

**In This Chapter**

➤ What is a Catholic?

➤ The basics of the beliefs

➤ What Catholics do

➤ The curiosity of the Catholic world

➤ The Catholic "tribe"

Can you identify Catholics by how they look, what they believe, or how they act in the world? One way of answering this question is to point to the great diversity that exists within the religion. Yet Catholicism also exists as a distinct culture. There is an "insider and outsider" character to it, which is captured by the language, rituals, songs, and beliefs of the religion, that serves to make Catholics distinct from other groups. Probably the best answer to the question "Can you judge a Catholic by the cover?" is to say sometimes yes and sometimes no.

This chapter outlines some of the ways individual Catholics are different from one another as well as some of the ways they are alike. By doing so, it will give you an idea of who Catholics are today.

## Why You Might Be Interested

Have you ever wanted to know more about this religion whose leader, the pope, has diplomatic relations with almost every country in the world and who receives weekly visits by heads of state? His frequent trips draw dramatic crowds everywhere he goes, from Uganda to Uruguay, from Paris to Papua, New Guinea.

Every cityscape reveals churches, hospitals, schools, office buildings, and cemeteries that are statements of the Catholic presence in the culture. When you were in school, you probably encountered this religion in your World History class, because the history of the Catholic Church is a major part of the history of the Western World. All Christian religions share a common history with the Catholic Church for their first 1,100 to 1,500 years.

Catholicism is a religion with a high media profile. Hardly a week goes by that there is not something about it in the newspaper or on the television. From protests to papal appearances, it makes the front pages of newspapers all over the world. In the United States during the 1960s, men and women in Roman collars and black and white habits stood with civil rights protesters in Alabama. In the 1970s, they blocked the passage of "the White Train" that carried nuclear material across the country. Every January, Catholics walk up the steps of the Lincoln Memorial to protest the Supreme Court's decision legalizing abortion. Let's find out more about this fascinating faith that has held so many people together for so long.

## Catholics Here, There, Everywhere

Perhaps you're reading this book because you were baptized a *Catholic* as a child but never practiced your religion. Perhaps you practice but don't fully understand the richness of your religion's culture and traditions.

Or maybe you're reading this book because you aren't Catholic but your daughter is about to marry one, or your boss has invited you to attend her son's baptism, or you're attending a Catholic funeral. What is it like to enter this religious world? Will you be expected to participate? If so, how? What will be the meaning of the ceremonies you'll be witnessing? What will it be like to mingle with these people in their own world? Catholicism has produced majesty, controversy, and sometimes fear. This book will help you separate fact from fiction and prejudice from truth and be more at ease with your encounters with this denomination.

Catholics are the largest single denomination of any religious group within the Unites States population, and the second largest group is made up of former Catholics. Think about it for a moment. How long would it take you to name five Catholics that you personally interacted with in the last 24 hours? Even if you aren't Catholic, when you go back through your family tree, chances are you'll find Catholic blood. Catholics are everywhere.

**S'ter Says**

**Catholic** means "universal" or "one" and refers to the fact that the Catholic Church is found all over the world and all its members follow a set of common beliefs.

## You're So Catholic If ...

➤ You have a St. Christopher medal in your car.

➤ You tip your hat when you pass a Catholic Church.

➤ You know more than 15 recipes for preparing tuna fish.

➤ You bury a statue of St. Joseph upside down in your yard when you are selling your house.

➤ You can name all of Ethel Kennedy's kids.

➤ You name your first daughter "Mary."

➤ You reach in your pocket for your handkerchief to cover a sneeze, and your rosary falls out.

➤ You still think twice about ordering a steak on Friday.

➤ You refer to other religions as "non-Catholic."

➤ You have mistakenly genuflected before taking your seat in the theater.

➤ You put J.M.J. at the top of your expense report before turning it in to your boss.

➤ You make the sign of the cross before shooting a basket.

➤ You suffer from free-floating guilt.

➤ You have a Maryknoll calendar on your desk.

➤ You have braided palm leaves stuck behind the corner of the crucifix in your bedroom.

➤ You have pinned a tissue to the top of your head to go to church.

➤ You know the difference between a C-rated movie and an X-rated one.

➤ You have ransomed a pagan baby.

➤ You know that a spiritual bouquet isn't something you buy at the neighborhood florist.

# What You Have to Believe

Throughout this book, we'll be discussing and exploring the various religious concepts and practices of the Catholic faith in some detail, including the ones mentioned in this chapter. In short, however, the basis of Catholicism is a belief in God as present in the world and a belief in God in a larger sense, as bigger and more inclusive than the creation over which he reigns and in which his presence resides. This is stated as God immanent (God present within human existence, all of creation) and God transcendent (God beyond the limits of human experience and creation). Catholics' devotional life centers on reinforcing God's availability and presence to his people.

In addition, a list of characteristics Catholics would have in common (although these characteristics are not necessarily unique to Catholics) would include the following:

➤ The belief in the physical incarnation of God as Jesus Christ

➤ A shared history of their church and common traditions

➤ A hierarchical governing structure with obedience to the pope regarding matters of faith

➤ The use of prescribed rituals called sacraments and a strong commitment to Holy Communion

➤ A belief in Mary, the mother of God, as intercessor and reverence for the saints

➤ A rich tradition of spirituality and contemplative prayer, monasticism, and religious orders

➤ The use of statues, pictures, and other religious and artistic symbols and a shared tradition of music

➤ A deep appreciation for both faith as a set of beliefs that are not approached through pure reason and reason as a means of faith

➤ An emphasis on community as an essential ingredient of the faith journey

➤ A social doctrine based on the dignity of the human person

➤ A sense of responsibility for social justice and outreach

**Your Guardian Angel**

Pray to Mary for help and guidance. Catholics believe that Mary has a special influence with God and that she acts as an intercessor, or go-between, and can get prayers answered.

Besides a lot of standing and kneeling during ceremonies, one of the distinguishing characteristics of Catholic religious life is its use of sacraments, statues, incense, sacred music, rosaries, candles, processions, and colorful priestly robes. These and many other traditional practices symbolize, celebrate, and reinforce the belief in God's absolute presence in the human faith journey. *Genuflection,* a practice of going down on one knee before taking one's seat in church in order to acknowledge the presence of Jesus, is one practice that might surprise a visitor. For instance, a Baptist woman who was engaged to marry a Catholic man was invited by her prospective mother-in-law to attend Mass. She had never been inside a Catholic church, and was trying to take it all in as she followed her mom-to-be up the aisle. Suddenly, without any warning, the mother-in-law stopped and genuflected before entering the pew. The visitor fell over her, knocking her down, and both of them spilled out across the floor. What an introduction to an already formidable situation!

Catholics believe that the faithful departed, as well as the living, are members of the church body. For this reason, Catholics pay respect to and seek the counsel of saints, especially Mary, who is the mother of Jesus and, therefore, has a particularly high place of honor. Catholics believe that a fellowship exists among the church's current members on earth, all members who have gone before, and those yet to come. Catholics have a rich tradition of mysticism, which means a personal religious encounter that usually occurs during prayer or meditation. During these encounters, a few people report visions of Christ, Mary, angels, or saints. However, mysticism is simply a time of being silent with God, and visions don't constitute the norm for Catholics. Catholic experiences for the most part are communal and happen in the context of organized church services.

The Catholic Church believes in both grace (God's presence in our life) and our own good nature. Redemption does not come through belief in God alone; faith and good works are necessary as well. The beliefs and traditions of the Catholic Church change as time goes on. For example, the Catholic understanding of heaven, hell, sin, and redemption is much softer now than it once was and is one of the areas where you will find a lot of different views expressed. We will go into this subject in greater detail at a later time in the book.

## The Richness of Catholic Tradition

*Tradition* means more than just a long history; it refers to the faith experience of the many people who make up the Catholic Church over a long period of time. It combines what has been discerned, received in revelation, lived, and handed down by the faithful members over the years. Catholic tradition, although it may appear to move slowly, is not static (fixed); it is always dynamic (in process). Tradition is open to new scholarly work of theologians, new witness of prophetic voices of the people, and the insight of the leadership.

**Your Guardian Angel**

If you're attending a Catholic service for the first time, be aware that Catholics **genuflect,** which means they go down on one knee just before taking their place in the pews to show respect for the altar.

**For Heaven's Sake!**

Guard against the presence of sin in your life! To be a good Catholic, you must avoid sin, but Catholicism has not been a "hell scared" religion for a long time. The present focus is on God's love and availability to the people—not on his judgment.

Although the church sometimes finds itself at odds with the world of science as science challenges church doctrine, its comprehensive approach fosters the belief that science and the arts also lead to God. The physical body is seen as sacred, rather than in opposition to the spiritual. God's spirit is seen as active throughout creation. Creation is believed to be essentially good because it is reflective of the divine.

**S'ter Says**

**Tradition** refers to both the process of handing down the faith to others and the material that has been handed down. Tradition refers to the scriptures, church doctrines, writings of the church teachers, and the liturgical life of the church down through the centuries; additionally, tradition refers to the everyday customs and practices of the church.

# Aren't All Catholics the Same?

If you ask any Catholic what he believes, you will hear as many different answers as people you have asked. Beliefs, like people, come in a lot of different shapes and sizes. Beliefs are about faith, and faith is a process. Catholic beliefs exist on a wide spectrum and must be considered on different levels. Although most Christians hold very similar beliefs, one of the differences between Catholics and other Christians is the Catholics' faith in the church itself. Catholics believe that the church has the divine authority to discern God's will and is the guardian of the basic truths of the religion. It represents the continuation of Jesus' presence as the active mediator of redemption.

The Catholic Church believes that God is the creator and that Jesus is the son of God who was born on earth, preached God's message, and brought God's love to the people. Jesus died and rose from the dead. Catholics believe that the church is the continuation of Jesus' presence through the Holy Spirit and that the church holds the authority, through its leaders, the pope and the bishops, to teach and continue to discern the will of God. There is faith that life continues after death. Catholics believe the Bible contains sacred revelation from God forming the basis of their beliefs and morality.

Although these beliefs have formed the essential fiber of Catholicism throughout its 2,000-year history, a reform movement called Vatican II, held in the middle of the twentieth century, radically altered how modern Catholics interpret these beliefs and act upon them. The emerging Catholicism is characterized by the following:

➤ A shift in emphasis from the institution of the church to the people

➤ Reconnecting to the foundation of Catholicism in scripture

➤ Greater participation by the members in the services and ceremonies

➤ Embracing the whole world: its people, their beliefs, culture, social and economic concerns, and an emphasis on world peace

➤ Cooperation with other religions and respect for the validity of their beliefs

➤ A call for an end to anti-Semitism and for a true respect for Judaism

➤ Valuing the role of the individual Catholic layperson as an emissary of Catholic values in society

➤ An end to discrimination of all kinds, recognition of the innate dignity of all people and of all of creation, and the upholding of the individual conscience as the norm for morality

# What You Have to Do

Catholics define their beliefs as much through their actions as by their verbal statements. For example, Catholics celebrate their central belief of God's presence in Jesus by attending weekly Mass.

Although the media portrays Catholics as all following a prescribed set of beliefs, the focus within the Catholic Church has shifted toward a personal sense of responsibility. The incubator for this sense of responsibility is Catholic schooling. Reading, writing, and arithmetic taught to the tune of a hickory stick. Values, heritage, and Catholic sensibility are instilled. The *liturgical* calendar reflects the seasons and cycles of the year and connects religious services with the events of one's life. Daily reminders of saintly ancestors model Catholic ideals of faithfulness to God.

# Mass on Sunday

It is the tradition among Christians to follow the Biblical commandment: "Keep holy the Lord's day." This tradition perhaps stems from the sacred story about the creation of the world in which God designates one day for rest. *Mass* is the term used to describe the Catholic church services. It is required to attend Mass on Sunday. (Mass is explained in detail in Chapter 16, "The Mass: The Catholics' Big Dinner Party.")

Indeed, one of the things that distinguishes Catholic practice is the obligation to attend Mass weekly (and on six other holy days during the year). This obligation is a very serious one, sometimes described as an obligation "under pain of sin," and for years it was considered a grave sin to miss Mass. In past years, no amount of effort was seen as too great for a Catholic to get to church on Sunday. For example, one Catholic who grew up in the 1950s remembers summer vacations in the far reaches of Canada. The family would get up before dawn to travel many miles by boat to attend services at the tiny log church tucked in the pine forest beside the water. Missing Sunday Mass was not an option, even while on vacation.

**S'ter Says**

**Liturgical** is the word the Catholic Church uses to describe church practices such as hymns, prayers, and services.

Even though the percentage of Catholics fulfilling their Sunday obligation has slipped from 60 percent to 40 percent over the past 30 years, it is still significantly higher than the national average for other Christians in the United States. Attending Sunday Mass is still considered an important part of being Catholic.

# Parochial School on Monday

Although not as serious an obligation as weekly Mass attendance, going to *parochial school* certainly puts you one rung up on the Catholic ladder. Catholic schools give

### For Heaven's Sake!

Don't forget to go to Mass! Sunday obligation describes the church law that Catholics are to attend Mass on Sunday. You can meet the obligation for Sunday Mass if you go on Saturday evening.

### S'ter Says

**Parochial schools** are private schools run by the parish church.

form and meaning to Catholic life. In addition to the religious values, many people, including some non-Catholics, are attracted by the sense of discipline and order these schools provide.

The Catholic school not only inculcates manners and respect, but also a sense of loyalty and identity to a particular way of life—part of being a special "tribe." The wardrobe is immediately identifiable: boys in shirts and ties and girls in jumpers.

At the high point of the glory days of Catholic parochial education, 1967, almost one out of every two Catholic churches boasted having its own school. Presently, there are 8,500 Catholic grade schools and high schools educating more than 2,700,000 youth.

## A Saint for Every Day of the Year

Catholics have a saint and a prayer for every day and all occasions. Saints are people who have lived exemplary Catholic lives and who the church declares worthy of special honor. Their goodness and holiness have been witnessed by others and ruled on by the church through a special process. The saints have been chosen and assigned to represent particular values. Their lives hold up a model for good living.

Most of us turn to prayer when we need something. For children especially, God can sometimes seem impersonal and distant, like the big boss. To approach him can sometimes feel intimidating. Saints are friends of God who have proven their sincerity and reaped the rewards of their good lives. They are in heaven and have the power to help us. It never hurts to have friends in high places, and it is often smart to have someone speak on your behalf. Saints offer intercession.

Patron saints are believed to have influence over certain situations because of some special circumstances of their lives. For example, Jerome Emiliani, born in 1481, was an abandoned prisoner of war miraculously set free after praying to the Virgin Mary. He then dedicated his life to caring for abandoned children and established orphanages. By doing so, he became the patron saint of orphans. Catholics traditionally name their children after saints.

Many Catholics will choose a particular saint as their patron because they feel a connection to this person. There are saints for many diverse matters. Some watch over funeral directors, gallstones, uncontrolled gambling, garage workers, gardeners, and glandular disorders. Some saints are remembered for particular causes. St. Anthony is the patron saint of lost objects; St. Jude is the saint for impossible cases. On

February 3, Catholics have their throats blessed in honor of St. Blase, who was a philosopher and a physician. On his intercession, a child was healed of a throat ailment. Since then, those in similar situations have sought his aid.

### Saints Preserve Us

**St. Maria Goretti, July 6, Patron of Youth**

St. Maria Goretti was born on a small farm in Italy in 1890. She was happy, good, open-hearted, and serious beyond her years. In her parents' words, she was a prayerful and obedient child. Alexander, a neighborhood thug, began to harass Maria. She rebuffed his unwarranted advances. Six months later, he attacked her. She fought off his advances, and when she would not yield to him, he stabbed her. In the hospital, she forgave him and prayed for his repentance. Maria died of her wounds a short time later. She was made a saint in 1950. Apparently Maria's prayers were effective. After eight years of being unrepentant and imprisoned, Alexander had a complete change of heart. He was later released for good behavior and became a lay brother, working for the church. He testified at the inquiry process that led to Maria Goretti's canonization. She is the patroness of youth, and her story is told to many a Catholic boy and girl in school. Her feast day is July 6.

On October 4, the feast of St. Francis, animals are blessed because he loved all of nature. A well-known prayer of young women seeking husbands is short and to the point: "Dear St. Anne, please send me a man." Everyone has a favorite saint. Perhaps you are named for one—Catholics are given the name of a saint at baptism—or perhaps it is the life story or virtue of the saint that attracts you. When the day of your particular saint comes around, you celebrate it in a special way. Catholic devotion to saints reaches beyond the church into all cultures. Everyone knows about St. Valentine's Day and St. Patrick's Day, and the ever-popular Santa Claus is old St. Nick, a bishop of Myra who handed out goodies to the needy.

### For Heaven's Sake

In Catholic school, lack of respect for your teacher is not an option. Many Catholics today have experienced learning ABCs and p's and q's from zealous nuns not afraid to strike the hands of their students with rulers.

## Follow the Rules Everyday

Certain requirements go along with membership in the Catholic Church, and Catholics are often identified by those requirements. Up until about 30 years ago, all Catholics tended to march to the same beat. The statistics on Catholics using birth control and their stand against abortion differed substantially from non-Catholics. That is not as true any more. Not too long ago, you could spot a Catholic in a restaurant at the end of the work week because he always ate fish on Friday. That's not the case any longer. However, popular images of being Catholic persist, and a vast number of Catholics elect to continue to observe many of these practices that were rules for many years.

Modern-day Catholicism has begun to shift away from the authoritarian model on which it was once based toward a religion offering many more choices. For example, many spiritual practices that once were mandatory are now optional.

Obeying a set of laws guaranteed your status as one who lived a moral life. This more mechanical form of morality is giving way to a creative model. Yet not every Catholic is comfortable with this change. The old model meant going by the rules to avoid sin rather than exploring options to find the best way to effect good. The new model is based in finding a loving response.

Science and technology present new challenges about the basic dignity and right to life that did not exist previously. Examples of today's moral challenges include surrogate parenthood, in vitro fertilization, organ transplantation, life support systems, and dying with dignity. Catholics are presented with political/moral issues such as abortion, capital punishment, nuclear weapons, and AIDS.

### Epiphanies

In 1995, 49 percent of Catholics considered themselves pro-choice on the matter of abortion, and 41 percent considered themselves pro-life. Three years later, those figures were nearly reversed, with 48 percent of Catholics calling themselves pro-life and 41 percent calling themselves pro-choice. This shift mirrored the national shift in the same direction. Catholic beliefs are not all that different from the culture at large.

It used to be that the church made decisions about these types of issues and the followers simply obeyed the rules. The moral baton has been passed, and people must now work to resolve these issues in the context of the church's faith structures, regulations, and rules. Catholics use prayer, meditation, and reflection on the teachings of the church as a way of coming to decisions and establishing moral priorities.

# Catholic Ways

Community is a major part of what it is to be a Catholic. Within the community is an understanding of the importance of connecting to others less fortunate and extending an invitation to all to be included. This sense of community among Catholics produces a characteristic respect for their leaders and their tribal laws.

## Bingo, Raffles, and Pancake Breakfasts

In order to support their institutions, Catholics conduct many fund-raising events, such as bingos, raffles, and breakfasts, which not only provide an opportunity to raise money but also offer churchgoers some good times and community spirit. Although many think of church as a place you show up on Sunday, most Catholic parishes have a social structure that is as important as worship. In the original communities established in the early years of the Catholic Church, the religion highly emphasized its identity as a new family for its members. Meetings were held in homes, and meals were shared. Today this tradition can be played out in a different way: the pancake breakfast.

A Catholic may spend all Saturday with the Boy Scouts, for example, as they shop for the ingredients, deliver them to church, set up the chairs, cover the tables with white butcher paper, wrap the silverware in napkins, and stack the plates. Bright and early Sunday morning, the families of the Scouts are in the kitchen frying sausages, waiting for the crowd to show up. And show up it does. Between the 9:30 A.M. and 11:00 A.M. Masses, long lines of parishioners talk as they wait for their turn at the table. The priest moves in and out, working the crowd.

### For Heaven's Sake

Don't think being a Catholic means blind obedience. Just following the rules won't do it. You have to use your moral judgment.

These regular occasions provide opportunities for parishioners to check up on each other, to renew relationships, and to meet the new people in the parish. The next week's Sunday bulletin will tell how much money the church raised, but the real reward of such breakfasts is the development and nurture of the church family. This activity and others like it remain a distinctive mark of Catholic communities and strengthen "tribal" bonds.

## Charity Away from Home

In addition to supporting the membership of the local parish through social activities, Catholics have always had a strong tradition of social outreach. A common practice among Catholics growing up in the 1950s was to "ransom pagan babies" by saving money to send to foreign *missions*. Politically incorrect as such terminology is today,

**13**

**S'ter Says**

**Missions** are operated by the Catholic Church worldwide for the purpose of serving the poor and spreading the Gospel message.

the underlying message was about developing a social conscience and reaching out to others. Missions are churches, schools, hospitals, and other services operated by the church to bring the word of God and serve the poor.

Catholics have always understood that outreach was as much about offering material and physical comfort as it was about religious concerns. The Catholic presence as a social support system is impressive. Catholic hospitals, orphanages, refugee resettlements, homes for the elderly, and immigration services are vital to the world community. Catholic Relief Services is a major worldwide charity that has an impressive presence in war-torn areas and provides services to refugees.

Although these major forms of social outreach are a function of the institutional structure of the church, the individual Catholic participates in outreach by a number of "second collections." Second collections not only support missions, but also educate the parish about charity as a faith expression. This idea is reinforced by sermons on those particular Sundays. A focus on charity encourages Catholics to examine deeper issues of justice. This justice orientation has resulted in significant statements by the leadership of the church on matters such as disarmament, the economy, ecology, and racism.

## Dazzled by Habits, Collars, and Other Funny Clothes

There is no doubt about who the religious tribal leaders are because their dress sets them apart from the crowd. The structure of male leadership in the Catholic Church is hierarchical. At the top is the bishop of the diocese, designated by the color purple. When the bishop presides at Mass, he walks down the aisle holding a large gold-plated shepherd's staff called a *crosier* and wearing a tall pointed hat called a *miter* (with a purple skullcap underneath).

**Your Guardian Angel**

When your pet is sick, call on St. Francis. Animal lovers and ecologists call St. Francis their patron because he had an extraordinary relationship with animals and all of nature.

The priest's color is black. He is most easily recognized by his Roman collar, which is a white, two-inch-wide band at the throat. If the priest is a monsignor, who is a notch up the ladder, he will have purple piping on his robe and on his collar.

Although the distinctive dress of nuns has become modernized in current times, most people think of them as still wearing the black habits with white collars. Many nuns still choose to wear these traditional outfits. Stiffly starched collars and exotic headdresses defined that venerable religious order, The Daughters of Charity, as "God's Geese."

Monks' clothes have not changed for centuries. The Franciscans, for example, still wear brown robes with the characteristic pointed hoods and rope belt just as they and their founder, St. Francis, did in the 1100s. At that time, his clothes were those of a beggar, and he wore sandals, as do the modern-day Franciscans.

Religious dress both sets the leaders apart and enchants Catholics, who can then see leaders as different from the ordinary. This manner of dress connotes both timelessness and otherworldliness, setting the leaders apart from the affairs of the world, and it speaks of their spiritual availability.

## *Marry Another Catholic*

The customs and taboos a people follow set them apart from others. For Catholics, one of the strongest customs has been marrying their own, and the strongest taboo has been against marrying outside the faith. Although this practice is much less important to most Catholics today than it was a generation ago, the point is that to be Catholic means to live up to a particular set of expectations. If a Catholic married a non-Catholic but wanted the church to recognize the marriage, they had to be married by a priest in a Catholic ceremony and the non-Catholic had to promise to raise the children Catholic. The Catholic spouse was obligated to pray for their partner's conversion to the Catholic faith. Today, non-Catholic spouses are not obliged to make any promise, and the bishop may permit these marriages to be held in a non-Catholic church.

In more recent years, church teaching encourages its members to honor other religious beliefs and practices. Although tribal expectations and taboos still exist in Catholicism as they do in any religious group, as in the case of birth control and abortion, the choice to follow them is much more an individual decision. We talk more about these issues in Chapter 19, "The Teachings of the Church: More Than Just the Party Line." There is a concern among some of the tribe as the laws and teachings are weakened and people become more personally responsible for decisions. They raise the question: Will the tribe survive?

## The Classic Definition

Having looked at the beliefs and practices as they play out in everyday life, let's now consider a textbook definition of the Catholic Church. Just what is the Catholic Church? Let's begin with the word "church." The Catechism, the official book of definitions of the Catholic Church, says church is a convocation or assembly of people, gathered together for religious purposes.

The Catholic Church is a specific Christian denomination that declares its religious purpose to be to follow the teachings of Jesus Christ. The word "catholic" means universal. Catholics understand this to mean that God invites all people all over the Earth to be a part of his community of followers. Universal also means that these people

**15**

### S'ter Says

**Ecclesiastical** is a term used to describe church stuff. Like "civil" describes things that relate to government, ecclesiastical describes things that belong to an established institutional church.

profess a unified faith, a common set of beliefs and practices. This unity is maintained through an *ecclesiastical* structure, under the leadership of the pope.

There are three primary ways the word church is used:

➤ Church is a building where the members gather for religious services, as in "We went to church to pray."

➤ Church describes the group of people gathered together to support one another on the religious journey, as in "The church sent flowers to Mrs. O'Dwyer who is in the hospital."

➤ Church is the governing authority that unites all the parishes throughout the world, as in "The Catholic Church has declared a new saint."

The word *catholic* was first used by Ignatius of Antioch around the year A.D. 110. It is from the Greek word *katholikos,* which means universal or whole. Ignatius was suggesting that the church should be one body or membership, just as it was when Jesus Christ was alive and his followers were one.

*Christ the King Catholic Church, Nashville, Tennessee.*

*(Courtesy of H. L. [Dean] Caskey)*

Augustine, a Church theologian writing in the 400s, used the word *Catholic* to mean all membership, present everywhere, as one church. Over the next several hundred years, the term began to be used to distinguish what was considered the "one true church" from groups who had separated from it. Today the term *Catholic* refers to the fact that this religion teaches the same doctrine everywhere, and it includes all classes of people.

Now that you've had a look at some Catholic beliefs and practices, we will go on to look at the variety of people and cultures in the Catholic Church.

---

### The Least You Need to Know

➤ The Catholic Church is the largest single denomination in Christianity.

➤ A major rebirth happened to the church in the middle of this century.

➤ There is diversity of thought within the Catholic religion.

➤ Catholics value and connect to their ancestors through a practice of honoring the saints.

➤ Outreach, charity, and social justice are central to Catholicism.

➤ Catholicism is both a culture and a religion; it is tribal.

# Chapter 2

# The People: Many Faces, Many Flags

Right from the beginning, the mission of the Catholic Church has been to make the religion available to all people. As we learned in Chapter 1, "Can You Judge a Catholic by the Cover?" "catholic" means "universal," and that term describes the church very well. The Catholic Church includes many nationalities and exists in almost every country in the world.

## Would I Know One If I Saw One?

The church draws on a rich cultural heritage. Beyond the stereotypical image of a Catholic lies a diverse palette of cultural expressions of the religion. Particularly since Vatican II, the church has encouraged all cultures to include their unique music, art, dance, dress, and values in the Mass and other religious services. This process is called *indigenization*. It has resulted in expressions of Catholicism that differ greatly from those that many "traditional" Catholics are accustomed to. These expressions may surprise you.

### S'ter Says

**Purgatory** had traditionally been thought of as a place, like hell, where people spend time to suffer for their sins and are later released to heaven. More recently, the pope has clarified that purgatory is the condition of the soul of a person who at the time of death has not completely repented for wrongdoing.

### Your Guardian Angel

Pray for the dead! The prayers and good works of the living can help shorten the time that the deceased spends in purgatory. Thus Catholics have the practice of praying for the poor souls in purgatory. Modern theology has toned down the idea of purgatory, although it remains part of church doctrine.

## An Irish Catholic Wake

Perhaps no other cultural tradition carries more mystique than the Irish wake. Although the tradition has changed somewhat, many Irish Catholic families still observe it. In the "old country" of Ireland, the wake took place between the time of death and the time the body was carried to the church, which was usually the evening before the day of burial. Neighboring women gathered at the house, washed the body, and dressed it. They placed a crucifix on the breast and entwined rosary beads in the fingers of the dead one. They also tied the two big toes together, which they believed would prevent the deceased from returning as a ghost. They placed a pair of boots at the feet to help the deceased walk through *purgatory*. The deceased was laid out on a wooden slab supported by four kitchen chairs, and covered with a linen sheet, except for the face, hands, and toes. Candles were lighted and placed in candlestick holders around the body.

The women who prepared the body led the mourning. Muffled sobs or loud wailing, depending on the dimension of the loss, filled the house and could be heard outside as well. For example, a dead parent who left a large family might elicit more crying than the passing of an elderly one. Neighbors would arrive. Their task was to pull the mourners away from the deceased and console them.

In the meantime, men of the village would order the coffin and bring the supplies for the wake: bread, meat, all types of food, whiskey, stout, wine, pipes, tobacco, and snuff. Once the house was full of visitors, a plate of snuff would be passed around for all to take a pinch. Pipes were filled with tobacco, and food and drinks were served. The clocks were stopped as a mark of respect. All mirrors were turned to the wall or covered. Salt was sprinkled around to ward off the evil spirits who, it was believed, might steal the soul of the dead. The bed of the deceased person was taken out immediately and burned.

A woman attended the corpse by sitting beside it all evening. As the neighbors entered, they made their way to the side of the body, knelt down to recite a few prayers, and expressed sympathy to the family. Guests exchanged remarks about the deceased, and then wandered into another room where food and drink was laid out. The men gathered in the kitchen or outside. The corpse was in the parlor, kept separate from the celebration that was going on. Visitation lasted until midnight. The rosary was recited several times, led by an important person in the community, a teacher, for example. Most of the visitors left at midnight. Close neighbors remained until morning drinking tea or whiskey and relating stories of times passed with the deceased.

The next morning as the body was lifted, the four supporting chairs were kicked over, and the body left the house feet first. The corpse was placed in a wooden box, shouldered by the men, and carried to the church. The family walked behind the pallbearers, behind them came the men carrying spades, and behind them followed the rest of the family and relatives. As they neared the church, the priest approached wearing special death vestments embroidered by the women. Chanting and sprinkling holy water, he turned, leading the way to the church.

After Mass, the coffin was carried to the graveyard and set down into the ground and covered. Mourners passed by, placing a stone on the casket. Relatives and a few neighbors returned to the house where things were put back in order.

The practices of the Irish wake in the United States today are much more refined than those held in the old country. Typically they are no longer held in the home, but in the funeral parlor. But once again, they become major opportunities for the community to gather and tell stories. An Irish funeral home will typically provide a main room for the casket and several anterooms for the gathering of relatives and friends so that they can do the business of mourning and storytelling. In the United States, Irish Catholics pray and say the rosary in the funeral home, and then the body is moved to the church for a funeral Mass and burial the next day.

## A Mexican Cemetery

In the Mexican Catholic culture, death is seen as a part of the cycle of life, and it is met with humor and joy as well as sorrow, a contrast to a somber or tragic view of death held by many people in other cultures. The dead are honored during a time of celebration known as the Day of the Dead.

### For Heaven's Sake!

Don't be afraid of ghosts! There are many different cultural understandings of death. Many folks believe that the souls who have passed are very much present. It is not unusual for people with this understanding to see ghosts, and for them ghosts are not frightening, but are truly the spirits of their loved ones. To have a visit from the spirit world is an occasion for celebration.

Part of the Mexican celebration of the Day of the Dead includes eating special bread. Here is a recipe:

## Pan de Muerto
## (Bread of the Dead)

### (A Folk Recipe)

Mix together:

2 cups of flour

$\frac{2}{3}$ cup sugar

1 teaspoon and a pinch of salt

1 TB. anise seed

2 packages dry yeast

Combine in a saucepan:

$\frac{2}{3}$ cup milk

$\frac{2}{3}$ cup water

$\frac{2}{3}$ cut butter

Set aside for later:

5 eggs

$4\frac{1}{2}$ cups flour

Ingredients for glaze:

$\frac{1}{2}$ cup sugar

$\frac{1}{3}$ cup orange juice, fresh-squeezed and strained

2 TB. grated orange peel

Set oven at moderate (350°) and pre-heat. Mix dry ingredients, adding warm liquid, and beat. Gradually blend in remaining flour. Sprinkle flour on a board and knead dough for about 10 minutes. Let it rise in a greased bowl, setting it in a warm place for 1 to 2 hours, until it doubles in size. Punch dough down and make into shapes of skulls and figures. Let it rise again for about one hour. Bake at 350° for 40 minutes. Boil the glaze ingredients for about 2 minutes, and apply to warm shapes.

In Mexico and in many parts of the southwestern United States, markets are filled with bright orange marigolds, candy skulls, and figures of skeletons that are sold to grace home altars and graves. Every home, as well as many of the businesses and public buildings, has altars. In some towns in Mexico, the church builds an altar in the town square for "homeless" spirits. Families buy *Pan de Muerto* (bread of the dead) and other edibles that they place on the altar and serve to visitors. This is a time to gather at the local cemetery and clean the graves. Flower petals are strewn between the cemeteries and homes to show the spirits the way. Their favorite foods await them on the altars.

The Day of the Dead is the time for the whole family to come together for a celebration. During these two days, Catholics believe that the spirits of the dead return and spend several hours with the family. The family tells stories to share the events of the past year with the spirit of the loved one.

The celebration serves as a reminder that death comes as a natural part of life. It also dispels fear of death by poking fun at it. Skeletons are used as decorations, and the children play with them. There are sugar skulls to eat with one's own name written on them. A favorite game is to write a humorous obituary of a prominent townsperson and then read it out loud. Everyone enjoys a good laugh. The next day there is a Mass said for the dead.

The Day of the Dead festivities combine pre-Christian and European Catholic traditions. It occurs at the same time of the year as an old Aztec celebration of death, and dates back to pre-Christian Druid religion. Today, in the United States, Catholics honor the dead in two days of religious celebration. *All Saints Day,* on November 1, the souls of the dead who are believed to be in heaven are remembered. On November 2, All Souls Day, the souls of all the departed who are believed to be in Purgatory are remembered.

## *An African-American Mass*

Although African Americans make up a small percentage of the Catholic population in the United States, they have unique celebrations and worship services, and their cultural statement is strong. With the renewal of Catholic liturgy in the middle of this century, particular ethnic expression of the Mass was encouraged, offering quite a contrast to the uniformity that was the custom.

If you attend a Catholic African-American Mass, expect to participate in a two-hour ceremony. African-American spirituality celebrates a sense of God's presence everywhere, and it is met with a powerful emotional response. Sunday Mass is a family gathering, which brings together the gifts of all the people. Musically, hand

### **For Heaven's Sake!**

Check your local newspaper to find out if there are any Day of the Dead celebrations in your part of the country. You might find them at a local museum or cultural center. You might use this day to visit the cemetery where someone you love is buried. You might honor them with a small altar at home on which their picture is displayed.

### **Your Guardian Angel**

Get your marigolds early! Marigolds are called **flor de muerto,** or flower of death, and Mexican Catholics use them to decorate altars and graves at the feast of the Day of the Dead. Some say the flowers smell of incense and bones. Others say the cycle of life and death is shown in the marigolds' bright orange color, which is reminiscent of the sunrise and sunset.

### S'ter Says

**All Saints Day** is also known as the feast of All Hallows. The night before became known as All Hallows Eve, or Halloween. So when the "spooks" come to your door, they are honoring an old tradition as well as having a good night of fun.

### Your Guardian Angel

Learn more about the African-American branch of the Catholic family by reading one or more of the several African-American Bibles available. These Bibles feature devotions that celebrate the social experience and cultural heritage of black Christians. Many have illustrations that depict Jesus and the apostles as Africans.

clapping, tambourines, drums, and foot tapping set the tone. Everybody—the choir, the readers, the priest, and the servers—all move in the African rhythms that have been held sacred for generations. The congregation praises the Lord with body and soul. Several choirs made up of people of different ages join in song. The music varies from traditional hymns to spirituals to contemporary songs. It is an expression of the African-American soul: alive and spontaneous.

The priest delivers the gospel, speaking to the people with drama and passion. He usually talks about things that reflect the lives of the people: black pride, racism, poverty, and social and family values. Responses from the people punctuate the message: "Hallelujah! Thank you, Jesus!" Hands wave throughout the church. At the sign of peace, the time during the Mass when worshippers exchange handshakes, parishioners and the priest move throughout the church, greeting and hugging every member.

Often, members of the congregation furnish the art displayed in the church, which reflects their lives and experiences. African colors of red, black, and green adorn the altar and are worn as vestments by the priest as a sign of black pride and solidarity with the African people. Although the celebration typically lasts two hours, the parishioners generally remain after the service to visit and conduct church business. The rich cultural heritage of the African-American people is expressed within the honored traditions of Catholicism.

## A Rural Catholic Parish

When the Spanish arrived in the area now known as New Mexico, they found the native people living in permanent earth structures made of mud bricks in villages all along the Rio Grande. The Spanish called these settlements *pueblos* and named each of them for a saint who then became the patron saint of the village. Nineteen of these pueblos (considered parishes) still exist, and each one boasts a Catholic church. Over the years, the Native American people have adapted Christian practices and symbols to their native beliefs, creating a unique cultural blend of both religions.

The Southwestern Catholics regularly offer Masses on Christmas, New Year's Day, the Birthday of Mary, and Candlemas Day (the day on which the Church blesses the candles that will be used for the year). On St. Joseph's feast day and on the feast days of the patron saints, these parishes hold native dances and ceremonies as part of the religious feasts. The dances are prayers, not performances. One in particular, called the Deer or Matachina Dance, is a traditional, symbolic animal dance and is performed at San Ildefonso Pueblo on January 23. The night before the feast, *luminarios* (paper sacks partially filled with sand and containing a candle) glow, and their soft light illuminates the village.

In the large plaza, the Catholic church stands at one corner and an adobe-style *kiva,* a traditional native temple, stands in another. Fiesta *vespers* are held in the church at sundown. Afterward, people gather around juniper fires burning in the town square. They hold an all-night vigil in honor of the feast day. The medicine man, in traditional dress, makes a brief appearance, preparing the space for the festivities that will soon follow. Men dressed in traditional Native American costumes drum and chant.

**S'ter Says**

The word **vespers** means "evening star," and Catholics use this term to describe prayers traditionally said at sundown. Vespers are the sixth of seven prayers said throughout the day and night in the Catholic Church.

At first light of day, figures appear on the horizon of the hill just outside of the town. They seem to be walking on stick legs, and they wave heavy antlers over their heads. They are the deer men. They descend in a noisy procession accompanied by painted and feathered costumed dancers. The drums accompany ancient songs that honor the deer and buffalo. A Mass is offered in the church as part of the ceremonies.

## The Taos Pueblo Catholic Church

Taos Pueblo is said to be one of the oldest towns in the United States, populated continuously since the 1400s. The Native Americans in Taos have created a religious system that combines their own deeply spiritual beliefs with Christianity in a way that works for them.

In the center of the village sits the Catholic church that the villagers still refer to as the "new" church, even though it was built more than 150 years ago. The church has no electricity, but is lit by gas lamps along the walls. In the center of the altar in the place where you would usually find a crucifix is a large statue of the Earth Mother. She is dressed in a beautiful satin gown, the color of which changes to match each season. In the spring, for instance, she wears green. The other statues and the altar are draped in a similar fabric. A large casket covered with matching cloth stands at the side of the altar. The casket is where Christ resides and is a reminder to the congregation, which is mostly Native American, that Christ died for them, and it serves to remind the congregation that a lot of them died for Christ, too.

*San Jose de Gracia*
*Catholic Church in Las*
*Trampas, New Mexico.*

*(Bob O'Gorman and*
*Mary Faulkner)*

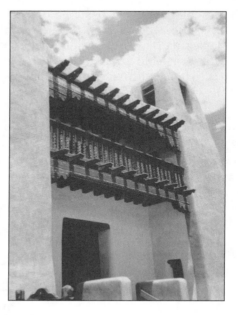

# So Where Would I Find a Catholic?

You can find Catholics everywhere. In its long history, Catholicism has become a global religion. Although there are certain regions that have high Catholic populations, there are no countries that do not include Catholics in their populations.

## The Americas: Close to Home

There are several lively Catholic centers in North and South America. The Catholic Church in Canada, for instance, exists under two separate but parallel hierarchies: French-speaking and English-speaking. Overall, Catholics account for about 45 percent of the total Canadian population, about 12.5 million people. Half of all Canadian Catholics live in the province of Quebec; French-speaking Catholics comprise the majority of the population there.

Further south, Mexico City became a diocese of the Catholic Church in 1530. A very Catholic country, with 90 million Catholics (93 percent of the population), Mexico's unique history makes its relationship with the Catholic Church interesting. In 1820, Mexico won its independence from Spain, which conquered it in 1521. When it overthrew Catholic Spain, Mexico also overthrew the rule of the Catholic Church. The Catholic Church was not allowed to operate with full legal rights after the war of independence. Only as recently as 1992 have Mexico and the Vatican established full diplomatic relations.

### Epiphanies

Did you know there is a French colony still in existence off the coast of Newfoundland? It consists of two groups of islands called Saint Pierre and Miquelon. Together they are one of the smallest Catholic communities in the world. The colony consists of three parishes, one bishop, two priests, and seven sisters. They had 89 baptisms in 1996. The total population of the colony is 7,000 people, and 6,000 of them are Catholics. Catholicism was introduced there in 1689.

Another heavily Catholic nation to the south is Nicaragua in Central America. Its 4 million Catholics make up about 90 percent of the total population. The history of Catholicism in Nicaragua goes back to the Spanish conquest in 1524.

Cuba's relationship with Catholicism began in 1514, and Cuba today has a Catholic population of 4.8 million, which comprises about 44 percent of the total population. When Communist Fidel Castro took control of the government in 1959, he nationalized Catholic schools and expelled more than 100 priests. The recent visit of the pope has highlighted the Cath-olic presence on this island and invigorated the church. In response to the popularity of this visit, the government has improved its relationship with the church.

The Caribbean nation of the Dominican Republic has been a Catholic country since Columbus arrived there in 1492. Today the Catholic population of seven million represents about 90 percent of the total population, and Catholicism is the state religion.

The largest Catholic population in the world lives in the South American nation of Brazil. First cele-

### Your Guardian Angel

Spanish-speaking communities in the United States are served by the Institute of Hispanic Liturgy, a national organization of liturgists, musicians, artists, and pastoral agents. It publishes liturgical material and promotes the development of liturgical spirituality among Hispanics. The Mexican-American Cultural Center in San Antonio, Texas is a center where Hispanic leadership is developed and cultural materials are available.

brating the Mass in 1500, Brazil is a country in which a significant number of clergy and lay Catholics have been active in movements for social reform. More than 135 million Catholics, making up 86 percent of the population, call Brazil home.

Because of the tightly woven relationship between the colonial governments and the church in Latin America, politics and religion have remained closely connected. As a result, many church leaders, both clerical and lay, take an activist role in the politics of Latin Americans.

Compared with Brazil, the United States has a relatively small Catholic population of just 61 million people, or 22.7 percent of the total population. Here's where most U.S. Catholics live:

➤ Los Angeles has 3 million Catholics, making up 30 percent of the population.

➤ Chicago has 2.3 million Catholics, representing 41 percent of the population.

➤ New Orleans has 500,000 Catholics, making up 35 percent of its population.

➤ Boston has two million Catholics, representing 53 percent of its population.

➤ New York City has 2.3 million Catholics, which is 45 percent of its population.

➤ El Paso has 600,000 Catholics, which represents 76 percent of the population.

**For Heaven's Sake!**

Don't make the mistake of thinking all Catholics look alike or come from the same part of the globe. Remember the word "catholic" means universal. The religion is worldwide. Less than 25 percent of its membership lives in the United States.

## The Rest of the World

Here is a random selection of Catholic populations around the world.

| Country | Catholic History | Catholic Population | Percent of Population |
|---------|------------------|---------------------|------------------------|
| Belgium | Introduced to Catholicism as early as the year 325. It was a Catholic land from about 730. | 8.3 million | 84 percent |
| Iceland | An island republic first visited by Irish hermits in the 700s. Catholicism was officially accepted about the year 1000. | 3,000 | 1 percent |
| Ireland | This island received Catholicism from St. Patrick in the middle of the 400s. | 4.5 million | 75 percent |
| Philippines | The Spanish introduced Catholicism in 1564. | 60 million | 84 percent |

| Country | Catholic History | Catholic Population | Percent of Population |
|---|---|---|---|
| Uganda | Catholic missionaries arrived in 1879. In its short history of Catholicism, 22 of its first converts were martyred. These people were declared saints in 1964. | 8.7 million | 43 percent |
| Australia | The first Catholics in the country were Irish convicts sent by the British. | 5.3 million | 29 percent |
| Israel | It all began here. | 94,000 | 1.5 percent |

## *Worldwide Catholic Population by Continents*

There are one billion Catholics in the world, or about 18 percent of the world's population. Nearly one in every five people in the world is Catholic.

➤ Africa: 12.9 percent

➤ Asia: .04 percent

➤ North America: 23.9 percent

➤ Central America: 85.5 percent

➤ South America: 87.3 percent

➤ Europe: 41.3 percent

➤ Oceania: 27 percent

As you can see, Catholicism comes in many colors, shapes, and sizes. There is also a great diversity in how it is practiced. In the following chapter, we'll look at some well-known Catholics who represent a wide range of spiritual expressions.

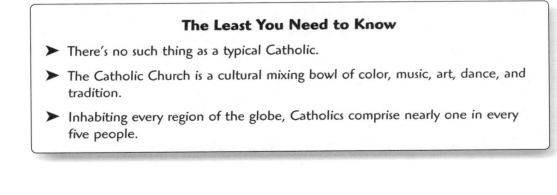

### The Least You Need to Know

➤ There's no such thing as a typical Catholic.

➤ The Catholic Church is a cultural mixing bowl of color, music, art, dance, and tradition.

➤ Inhabiting every region of the globe, Catholics comprise nearly one in every five people.

# Chapter 3

# Catholicism: It's a Big Tent

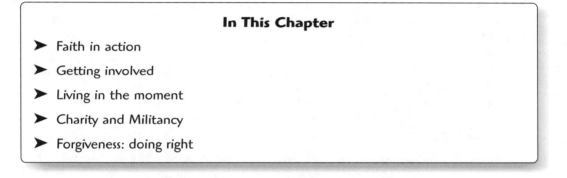

**In This Chapter**

➤ Faith in action

➤ Getting involved

➤ Living in the moment

➤ Charity and Militancy

➤ Forgiveness: doing right

Spirituality is the heart of religion. It is both the way we believe and how we express our beliefs through action. We have selected some well-known Catholics who represent a variety of spiritual positions. Beneath their unique spiritual expressions lies a communal base, a common ground upon which they all stand. For a church that is often characterized by an image of strict uniformity, these diverse approaches to Catholic life show that quite the opposite is true. In this chapter, we'll explore that diversity with you by introducing some famous Catholics and their contributions.

## From Bishop Sheen to Dan Berrigan

Two very important characteristics of the Catholic Church are its logical side and its passion for justice. During the 1950s, the leadership of the church focused on the reason side of the equation; in the 1960s, there was a radical shift into the realm of social justice. The Catholic leaders of these times reflected these trends.

## The Good Ambassador

In the mid-1950s, a common topic of conversation at work and in the grocery store centered on Bishop Sheen's talk the evening before on his phenomenally popular television show, *Life Is Worth Living*. Mingling religious ideas with secular life, Sheen had an audience of millions. He became a kind of pop culture icon for the Catholic Church and established himself as the best-known and most popular Catholic in 1950s America.

Through his television show, he moved Catholicism into mainstream American life, as well as redefined the church within the larger society by telling Catholic stories that had continuity both with other Christian communities and with Judaism. He made the social and political world of Catholics part of the American mainstream. His aim was to mediate between rather than divide denominations. He was responsible for many people choosing to become Catholic: Claire Booth Luce, Henry Ford II, and violinist Fritz Kreisler, among others, converted to Catholicism under Bishop Sheen's influence.

**Your Guardian Angel**

Pray for world peace! In the 1950s, it was common for Catholics to pray for the conversion of Russia at the end of every Mass. Catholics still pray for world peace regularly.

Sheen's approach to faith always provoked thought. He popularized philosophy. He took on a mission to preach against the evils of atheistic communism, and he focused Catholic spirituality in the 1950s on that mission. Working with his sharpest tools—logic, reason, and humor—he was the premiere anticommunist.

In England, Sheen had met and was inspired by G. K. Chesterton, a Catholic who held weekly radio broadcasts in the 1930s and 1940s on the BBC touting the Catholic Church as the center of reason in the modern world. Sheen saw reason as the best cure for family and social difficulties and the breakdown of morality in the culture. In his carefully crafted talks, he made philosophic reasoning work for the world, not just for the university.

## Religious Outlaw

Much to the surprise of both Catholics and the public, the turbulent 1960s revealed a liberal, activist side of Catholicism. For many, the spiritual awakening during this time continued through the next several decades and is still a vital part of their religious expression. At the center of this awakening was Daniel Berrigan, a *Jesuit*. He was one of the first clerics in the church to draw the media's attention to what he considered to be an important moral dimension to the political protest against the United States' role in the Vietnam War. In 1968, he and his brother Philip, also a priest, stormed the building housing draft records in Catonsville, Maryland. Using homemade napalm, he torched hundreds of files within 10 minutes.

He was sentenced to three years in prison, but he went underground for several months until federal authorities arrested him on Block Island, located off of the coast of Rhode Island. He used his time on the lam to publicly teach and lecture, showing up at various war protests. His every move made sensational news. He even managed to slip out a side door at Cornell University after giving a speech to a crowded auditorium with FBI agents sprinkled throughout the audience. What was the trick that allowed him to pull off such a feat? He hid in a larger than life papier-mâché puppet of an apostle. After 18 months in prison, Berrigan was paroled in 1972.

Dan Berrigan's radical leftist beliefs created great controversy within the Catholic Church. He pushed the church's theory of just war to the limits, and many say he pushed it past the limits. The church has a theory that limited war is acceptable only under a certain set of circumstances. We talk more about this in Chapter 20, "The Teachings of the Church: More Than Just the Party Line." Berrigan has written that "the death of a single human being is too great a price to pay for the vindication of any principle."

To this day, the political activism of Dan Berrigan and others is seen by some Catholics as a positive outgrowth of the true principles of the church and by others as totally inappropriate radicalism. Indeed, those who are incensed by such politics consider clerics like the Berrigans to be traitors hiding behind the religious collar. Those who agree with their motives and their methods consider them to be brave saints. Regardless of where you come down on the issues, the Berrigans focused Catholic spirituality in the 1970s on confronting injustice.

**S'ter Says**

**Jesuit** is the common name for a religious order of priests and brothers in the Catholic Church. The official name is the Society of Jesus, and hence the initials after a member's name are "S.J."

**For Heaven's Sake!**

Express yourself in a way that's right for you. Your spirituality is highly individual, and not all Catholics express their religion the same way. Some Catholics are activists working for political change, some lead quiet, prayerful lives in monasteries and convents. Some Catholics are conservative and some are liberal. There is not a "one-size-fits-all" form for Catholic spirituality.

# From Cesar Chavez to Clarence Thomas

Although theology and church beliefs are often defined in the Vatican chambers and universities, the average Catholic learns his religion in the home and transmits it by the way he lives in the real world. Two Catholic men, both from poor beginnings, developed very different ways of expressing their spirituality and helping their fellow workers during two different political eras (one in the 1960s and one in the 1990s). One chose the way of self-reliance, and the other chose community action.

## Grapes of Wrath

Cesar Chavez was born in 1927 in Yuma, Arizona. His family worked its small farm until 1939, when unpaid taxes forced them into the migrant labor stream. The year 1952 found Chavez working in a lumberyard in the San Jose barrio called Sal Si Puedes, which means, ironically, "get out if you can." There he met a Catholic priest who worked with migrant farm laborers. This priest immersed Chavez in the social activism side of the Catholic Church, particularly the pope's teachings on the right of labor to organize. Chavez also came under the influence of a community organizer who taught him how to apply the church's social philosophy to the community around him.

**Your Guardian Angel**

Look for the union label on all your grapes! Chavez and the many others who worked with him fought a long and hard battle to get better pay and working conditions for the migrant laborers who picked crops. They formed a union. You can join in the support of the dignity of the workers by buying union grapes.

In 1962, Chavez began organizing California's migrant workers into a union. His strategy was economic boycott. In 1968, Chavez led a boycott of table grapes. The response of the church and community groups in boycotting supermarkets who carried nonunion grapes resulted in contracts for the union for 85 percent of the table grapes market. Although his methods were political and economic, Chavez espoused a fundamental and absolute affirmation of the dignity of the human person and a firm commitment to nonviolence. He based his philosophy on the teachings of Jesus, St. Francis, Gandhi, and Martin Luther King Jr.

Chavez himself was a deeply religious man, thanks in large part to the influence of his mother. Fasting and daily Mass accompanied his protests. He named one of his largest marches a *peregrine* (pilgrimage, a religious term signifying the holy walk of a people). In addition to the union banner and the United States flag, he and his followers carried banners depicting the Mexican Lady of Guadalupe and the Aztec eagle.

His actions on behalf of justice gave new meaning to the concept of spirituality to his generation and the ones that followed. This spirituality consisted of a profound conviction of the absolute value of each individual, a firm commitment to nonviolence, and untiring work on behalf of the dispossessed.

## Dirt Poor in Georgia to the Supreme Court

Despite growing up in poverty and facing racial oppression, Clarence Thomas, who is now a Supreme Court justice, took advantage of the sacrifices that his family made for him to receive a good education. Thomas's family sent him to Catholic schools whose teachers taught him that with hard work and self-reliance, he could overcome the obstacles of discrimination. In the end, he would, but the road was never easy. Although he entered a Catholic seminary, he dropped out because of intolerable racial remarks made by classmates at the time of Martin Luther King's death.

### Epiphanies

There are many biblical references to the poor, and it is clear that the God of the Scriptures loves the poor, but not the condition of poverty. God's people, especially the leaders, are given the responsibility to care for the poor. They are a necessary part of bringing God's reign, and are a constant reminder that God's will is not yet fully accomplished. Their presence reminds the faithful of the responsibility we have for one another. The help of the poor is the hope of the church.

Thomas attended the Jesuit Holy Cross College, graduating cum laude, and was elected to Alpha Sigma Gnu, the Jesuit national honor society. From there, he received his law degree from Yale University, and then went on to serve the government in legal positions under conservative Republican administrations at the state and national levels. He was nominated and approved as a justice of the United States Supreme Court, October 16, 1991.

Thomas's conservative views on public policy evolved from his grandfather's self-reliance and independence. His grandfather was anti-welfare, holding that, "Man ain't got no business on welfare as long as he can work." Thomas's independence of spirit and strong belief in hard work and self-reliance articulate an American belief that everyone can succeed and speak to the spiritual belief that humans can overcome the odds and excel.

# From Bing Crosby to Madonna

Spirituality does not exist solely in the realm of academics, intellectuals, and politicians. Indeed, for most modern Americans, the media has the greatest effect on our religious imagination. Music, television, and film provide much of today's spiritual message. During the 1950s, some singers sang songs about the importance of living right. During the 1990s, the message was a different one, but it was a message just the same. Two of the most popular singers of these eras had one thing in common: being Catholic.

# The Good Priest

Harry Lillis, better known as the singer and actor Bing Crosby, was born in 1903 in Tacoma, Washington, graduated from Gonzaga High School in Spokane, and received an honorary doctorate from Gonzaga University. His first recording was "I've Got the Girl" in 1926, which began his career as a top pop vocalist for the next 50 years. He starred in 55 films and earned three Academy Award nominations. He won best actor in 1945 for his portrayal of a priest, Father O'Malley, in *Going My Way*.

**Your Guardian Angel**

Rent a video to catch a glimpse of the social history of the Catholic Church. Many films made in the 1940s and 1950s portray the pre-Vatican Catholic life in America. Check your video store classics.

*Going My Way* was the top box office draw of the year, and the film earned nine nominations and seven awards, including the award for Best Picture. The immensely popular film and its songs made a deep impression on the Catholic imagination in the 1940s and on the public's imagination of Catholics as well.

In this magical version of priestliness, Father O'Malley solves every problem great and small, from the finances of St. Dominic's to the threat of street gangs—and he does so with a cool nonchalance. The film's presentation of a nonsexualized version of male power created a paradigm for priests for generations to come. His black clerical dress topped with a straw hat created a mixture of religious restraint and jauntiness. Father O'Malley was a priest and a real okay guy at the same time.

The spirituality of the film and the music celebrates a hope-filled belief that right acting and right thinking will produce right results. To borrow from the old poem, "God is in his heaven and all is right with the world." The spirituality is focused on the accomplishment of goals as a virtue rather than the journey. It shows a world in which reason, order, and logic will prevail. Virtually everyone knew the songs from this movie by heart, particularly, "Would You Like to Swing on a Star?" The songs spoke of delayed gratification while exploring the basic themes of self-improvement through education—this "you can do" thinking was both personally and culturally uplifting.

# Wild Child, Modern Mystic, Existentialist

Madonna Ciccone, the rock star better known by her single first name, Madonna, was born near Detroit in 1958. She was the third of eight children. Her mother died of cancer when she was six years old, creating a void she has never filled. She says of herself, "I always considered myself an utterly motherless child." And probably no one, including Madonna herself, would argue that she also was a wild child. In the tradition of the Church *mystics* who explore that void through prayer and meditation, Madonna explores it through her art.

Madonna earned a scholarship to study dance at the University of Michigan. After two years, she struck out for New York and joined acclaimed dance troupes. She switched from dance to music, and in 1982, Warner Brothers signed her to a recording contract. Since that time, her music, her videos, her books, and her public appearances have created a great deal of controversy and made her one of the most well-known and provocative performers of the time.

In creating her art, Madonna enters and moves through a forbidden world where eroticism and religion meet. She brings the darkest part of her soul forward and puts it in the public's face. Is her work discomforting? Yes. Interesting? Absolutely. Fear-producing? Of course. Her work is also, by its very nature, distasteful to some and intriguing to many. Her uncharted expedition to the dark waters of the human soul dramatizes how dangerous truth can be, and she dares us to explore it. She reminds us that joy and pain are intertwined.

Madonna's Catholicism is reflected throughout this mystical journey. She says about Catholicism, "it's very sensual, and it's all about what you're not supposed to do … forbidden stuff … the confessional … heavy green drapes … stained glass windows … the rituals … the kneeling … there is something very erotic about all that."

Madonna grew up in what she calls a "very strict" Catholic household, and she attended Mass every morning before school. At the age of 17, she broke away from this regime, leaving both her family and the church behind. However, she soon found out that "The church pretty much stays with you. I have never stopped being a religious person." Today, she is drawn back into the silence of the church. The candles, the incense, the smells, and the rituals of Catholicism are grist for her videos. The church offers her a real sense of solitude and tranquility. In her own words, she says, "I reek of Catholicism."

Before a performance begins, you can find Madonna in a circle with her dancers and crew, leading them in prayer, urging them to treat one other with compassion,

**S'ter Says**

**Mystic** comes from the Greek word meaning mystery. The term describes a person whose prayer life includes meditation from which he or she gains spiritual understanding and new insight.

**For Heaven's Sake!**

Sexuality and spirituality are not two separate things. Although many religious thinkers over the ages have tended to separate the physical body from the spiritual soul, we know today that it is all one. Today's spirituality mends the soul/body separation that has characterized much of the church's teachings. Today's spirituality sees sex as very much a part of the human story and therefore part of the human spirit.

**Your Guardian Angel**

Try composing your own prayer. For a long time Catholics relied solely on prayers they memorized as children. Today's Catholics are more adventurous in their prayer life, creating prayers to fit the moment.

kindness, and respect, reminding them that there is already too much pain in the world. Madonna believes that prayer is found in the way we relate to one another.

Mystics don't take others' word for what God is like or what spirituality is. They go inside and find it for themselves. Madonna is an artistic mystic. She relentlessly explores through her music and dance. The mystical message Madonna offers for the millennium explores the erotic connection between sexuality, spirituality, and religion. For her, the church is both very sensual and mysterious. Her spirituality is of self-reflection. In her corner of the Catholic tent, you can find people who are looking within, redefining God and religion, and forging a new relationship between them.

# From Mother Teresa to Mother Angelica

Representing a spirituality of volunteerism with a clear vision and a clear message, Mother Teresa demonstrated a long tradition of serving the poor. A very different approach is Mother Angelica's concern for the loss of religious clarity in times of confusion and change.

## A Saint in the Making

Agnes Gonxha Bojaxhiu, better known as Mother Teresa, was born in 1910 in Macedonia. She was the daughter of an Albanian grocer. By the age of 12, Agnes had developed a special interest in overseas missions and realized her vocation was to help the poor. She joined an order of sisters that ran schools in India. For 17 years, she was a teacher and principal at a Catholic high school in Calcutta. Responding to a spiritual call to serve Christ in the slums among the poorest of the poor, she asked the pope for permission to start a religious order devoted to this charity. Although she began with 12 members, there are now over 4,000 Missionaries of Charity worldwide.

Mother Teresa's first act was to establish The Home for Dying Destitutes. Finding a woman half-eaten by maggots and rats lying in front of a Calcutta hospital, she sat with her until she died. It was then that she made her mission the act of caring for the human cast-offs that the world wanted to forget. During her lifetime, she created a global network of homes for the poor from Calcutta to New York, including one of the first hospices for AIDS victims. Today, her order operates more than 500 missions in more than 100 countries.

*Mother Teresa, winner of the Noble Peace Prize, worked with the dying in the streets of Calcutta.*

*(Courtesy of Photofest/Icon Archives)*

Mother Teresa's life and work is not without controversy. In 1994, British television produced a documentary entitled *Hell's Angel: Mother Teresa of Calcutta* that accused her of taking donations without questioning where they came from, including the likes of Haitian dictator Jean-Claude Duvalier. Inside the church, there were concerns that Mother Teresa did not bother to examine the social causes of poverty, but instead chose to direct her attention to bandaging up the victims of an unquestionably oppressive system of economics and politics. An article raising the question of the difference between charity and justice led with the headline "Mother, Why Are They Poor?"

In her defense, Mother Teresa did not see that it was her job to ask "Why?" Her spirituality was based in charity and love rather than politics. It was of the heart, not of the mind or intellect. She was charismatic, and she crossed all political boundaries. More important, she commanded the attention of all religious denominations and all classes of people. She inspired hundreds, both high-born and common, to join in her work at her hospice for the dying in India.

## *Radical and Right*

The largest religious cable broadcasting network in the world, Eternal Word Television Network (EWTN), resides in Irondale, Alabama. With more than 1,600 affiliates, the network reaches 54

**Your Guardian Angel**

Take a stand! The issues of charity and justice are closely linked. Many find they are drawn to work at the level of charity by taking care of the poor. Others are drawn to seeking justice through changing the social structures. They are two sides of a coin.

million homes in 34 different countries. The dynamo in front of the camera is Mother Angelica, a nun dressed in full Benedictine habit who, in best *Tonight Show* style, interviews a different guest every night. The network also broadcasts a Mass everyday, complete with the Latin *Tantum Ergo* (a favorite Catholic hymn) as well as a live recitation of the Rosary. The network also features a full series of lectures by priests and showcases Catholic events, especially the travels of the pope.

The mission of Mother Angelica is to present strict, hard-line Catholic belief. She is determined to uphold and highlight a traditional, conservative understanding of Catholic doctrine, culture, and discipline. She not only sees her mission as one of bringing the "true light" of *faith* to the common person, but she also wants to expose the liberal tradition of Catholicism, which she considers negative. She attacks personal speculation about religious beliefs. She cites what she considers to be liturgical abuses and doctrinal deviations. According to Mother Angelica, "The faithful need a solid and unambiguous doctrinal foundation upon which to build their Christian lives." She believes that she serves the people who are marginalized by the current trends in Catholicism.

**S'ter Says**

In the Catholic religion, **faith** has many aspects. One meaning of the word "faith" describes the way in which a person responds to Christ in their daily life. Faith is the presence of God within (grace) and the interior presence of the Holy Spirit moving the heart and turning it to God.

Mother Angelica's philosophy and approach has upset members of the Catholic leadership, but she fails to back down even in the face of some bishops, whom she characterizes as "wolves, preying upon people brought up to obey." In responding to one angry bishop who questioned "by what authority do you operate?" she responded, "I own the network."

The spirituality she represents appeals to those desiring a solid and unambiguous doctrinal foundation on which to build their religious lives. They are tired of questions, and they want answers. She expresses a side of Catholicism that has always been present in the church, albeit somewhat uncomfortably so: absolute certainty. It responds to a basic human condition that longs for assurance.

# From Ted Kennedy to Pat Buchanan

Catholics also express and experience their spirituality through both political ideals and practical politics. Indeed, Catholics have never been strangers to the political arena. Entering the ring from two different corners are two born and bred Catholic politicians, each with a passion and a mission, each playing their mission out in very different ways.

# The "Bleeding Heart"

Senator Edward M. Kennedy (Ted) was born in Boston in 1932, the youngest of the nine children of Joseph and Rose Kennedy. He was first elected to the U.S. Senate in 1962 when he took over the seat formerly held by his brother John F. Kennedy, who had been elected president of the United States in 1960.

For more than 35 years, Ted Kennedy has stood for the best in democratic liberalism, consistently supporting social programs for the poor, such as welfare, universal health insurance, and civil rights. In these efforts, he represents a Catholic tradition of social consciousness.

### Epiphanies

John Fitzgerald Kennedy, the only Catholic elected to the presidency of the United States, broke an enduring stereotype of Catholics as being unthinking, superstitious, clannish, and separatist. Prior to Kennedy, a Catholic could not expect to sit in the chair that administers the highest office of the United States, indeed of the world. One of the key battles to overcome was the lack of public acceptance and the fear that Catholics could not be trusted because of their loyalty to the pope and to Rome. In a memorable 1960 speech before the greater Houston Ministerial Association, Kennedy called upon the best in Catholic intellectual thought to show that good Catholic beliefs did not interfere with good citizenship.

Today, Ted Kennedy has become the patriarch of the Kennedy clan and continues to lead this powerful political and cultural family. The media spotlight that continues to shine on Ted Kennedy and his family reveals not only the family's glamour and influence, but also reveals their Catholic faith, particularly at times of tragedy and death.

As prominently displayed as his banner of liberalism and Catholic family heritage is his personal vulnerability. He reveals a Catholic characteristic of embracing what it means to be human by asking forgiveness and understanding. The Kennedy legacy has revealed a Catholic spirituality of endurance, faithfulness, loyalty, and of giving back to society, as well as human frailty and vincibility.

**For Heaven's Sake!**

Do something, because faith without works is dead! Catholics have a strong believe in putting their faith into action. You might even want to show a commitment to living your faith in the world by running for political office.

# Fighting for the Soul

Patrick Buchanan was a speech writer in the Nixon administration, and during the Reagan Administration, he rose to political prominence as a TV commentator on *Cross-Fire* where he represented the conservative position. In the 1990s, he ran for the Republican presidential nomination and attracted the most right-wing element of the party. He holds an uncompromising stand against abortion. Additionally, he is a proponent of United States isolationism in such matters as international trade agreements. In a recent book, he stated that the United States should not have joined the Second World War.

Born in 1938 in Washington, D.C., Patrick Buchanan did his undergraduate work at Catholic Jesuit Georgetown University before serving as a senior advisor in the Nixon administration. He attended four summits with President Nixon, including the one held during Nixon's historic trip to China in 1972. During the 1980s, Buchanan served as President Ronald Reagan's communication director, which allowed him to attend the Reagan-Gorbachev summit in 1986.

Buchanan's skills as a communicator expanded when he became a syndicated columnist. He has published several books in which he expresses his conservative political philosophy. He has been a formidable candidate for nomination at the Republican presidential convention for several years.

Buchanan focuses his politics and his faith on his moral principles. "There is a religious war going on in this country," he explained. "It is a cultural war as critical to the kind of nation we shall be as the cold war itself, for this war is for the soul of America." The religious war to which he refers is between people who hold very different ideas of what is sacred and what is ultimately true and good.

Buchanan is a deeply conservative Catholic who was imbued early on with the religion of his stern father. In his own words, he calls himself a "soldier in the war for America's soul." He is determined to preserve the American workers' standard of living by protecting the borders against illegal immigration. He favors trade protection. He is a pro-life conservative. He calls forth a strong populace base.

Buchanan presents a militant Catholic spirituality in the tradition of the Jesuits by whom he was educated. His spirituality encompasses respect for law and order, adherence to certain principles, and esteem for the rules. He presents a clearly drawn line between right and wrong. He is against privilege and identifies with the plight of the common man.

This chapter has shown how a variety of Catholic beliefs are played out in the public arena. The next chapter explains more about how these beliefs are shaped. You'll learn about the church's structure and guiding principles.

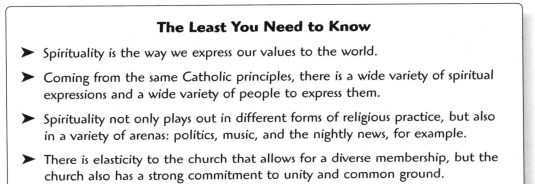

### The Least You Need to Know

➤ Spirituality is the way we express our values to the world.

➤ Coming from the same Catholic principles, there is a wide variety of spiritual expressions and a wide variety of people to express them.

➤ Spirituality not only plays out in different forms of religious practice, but also in a variety of arenas: politics, music, and the nightly news, for example.

➤ There is elasticity to the church that allows for a diverse membership, but the church also has a strong commitment to unity and common ground.

# Chapter 4

# The Vatican: The Church That's a Country

### In This Chapter

➤ Meet the Church's Leader

➤ Learn whether the pope can make a mistake

➤ Explore Vatican City

➤ Understand the church's organizational structure

The Catholic Church is a study in contrasts. It consists of more than a billion members throughout the world, but it has the ability to speak with one voice. It is made up of thousands of individual churches, but these houses of worship all follow the same faith. How is this unity accomplished? That's the focus of the chapter, which starts by introducing you to the leader of this massive organization: the pope.

## Just Who Is the Pope?

Pilgrims from all over the world travel to fill the square outside of this man's window every day and wait hours to catch a glimpse of him. Dignitaries from every country request an audience with him. On his worldwide visits, millions of people gather to cheer and witness his presence. Seldom does a week go by that there isn't international coverage on his whereabouts or pronouncements.

Who is the man that commands this much attention? It is the pope, the leader of one of the biggest and most complex organizations in the world: the Catholic Church. In

Latin, the word *pope* means papa or father. The pope is the spiritual father or head of the church. He is the focal point of unity among its members and has diplomatic relations with every country in the world.

*Pope John Paul II was the first non-Italian man elected pope in almost 500 years. This popular pope comes from Poland.*

*(Courtesy of Photofest/Icon Archives)*

All of this attention and power in the hands of one man may seem extraordinary. It may seem less so when you consider that Catholics believe that he is the physical representative of Christ on Earth and that his office is the storehouse for the truths of the church.

### S'ter Says

**Vicar of Christ** is a title given to the pope and all bishops with reference to the claim that they stand as representatives of Jesus Christ and act with his authority in the Church.

Since the ninth century, *pope* has been the designated title of the bishop of Rome, *Vicar of Christ,* a title he shares with all other bishops. Catholics have traditionally claimed St. Peter as the first of the Roman bishops and trace the succession of popes in a direct line back to this apostle. They believe the authority of the church rests on the commission given by Jesus to Peter found in Matthew 16:18–19:

You are Peter, and upon this rock I will build my church, and the gates of hell shall not prevail against it. I will give you the keys of the kingdom of heaven, and whatever you bind on earth will be bound in heaven, and whatever you loose on earth will be loosed in heaven.

Catholics believe that the pope is infallible. Papal *infallibility* means that the pope cannot make a mistake when defining a doctrine, or formal belief, of faith or morals for the Catholic Church. The pope speaks infallibly only when he claims to be using his authority according to the established process, when he speaks in regard to official beliefs of the church, and when he speaks about articles of faith or morals.

The pope works with the bishops in a shared decision-making process called collegiality. The pope, in communion with the bishops, is the highest teaching authority of the church. Together they make up what is known as the *magisterium*, which is the church's teaching authority. Collegiality is one of the most important pronouncements of the Second Vatican Council. It turned upside down the old way of looking at church hierarchy.

In reality, the pope seldom uses his power of infallibility. The last time an infallible doctrine was declared was in 1950 when Mary's assumption into heaven was proclaimed an article of faith, which Chapter 12, "Who Is Mary?" discusses in more detail. In other words, rather than being some mystical power of the pope, infallibility means the church allows the office of the pope to be the ruling agent in deciding what will be accepted as formal beliefs in the church.

## What's His Address?

The pope, bishop of Rome, resides in the Vatican. Vatican City is the smallest sovereign state in the world, covering an area no larger than 108.7 acres. The Basilica (or church) of St. Peter is the focal point of Vatican City and is the mother church of Catholics and the largest church in the Christian world. About 1,000 people live in the Vatican, and another 4,000 work there every day. In addition to being the home of the spiritual leader of the Catholic Church, the Vatican has an enormous library of sacred books and a vast collection of religious art.

**S'ter Says**

**Infallibility** is a gift of the Holy Spirit to protect the church's teachings from error. Papal infallibility is the church belief that when the pope defines a doctrine of faith and morals that must be held by the whole church, the Holy Spirit grants him infallibility. **Magisterium** is from the Latin word for "teacher" and refers to the teaching function of the church.

**Your Guardian Angel**

When traveling to Italy, don't miss St. Peter's Basilica, the largest church in the world. Other points of interest in the Vatican are the Sistine Chapel, an astronomical observatory, and the Vatican library, with many rare manuscripts. Swiss Guards, who wear a distinguished colorful striped uniform designed by none other than Michelangelo himself, protect the Vatican.

St. Peter's Basilica in
Rome, Christianity's
largest church, is the
Mother church of
Catholics.

*(Courtesy of Alinari/Art
Resource, New York)*

At one time, the small city-state of the Vatican comprised several states in central
Italy known as the Papal States. Although the size of the Vatican is now greatly reduced, it still maintains the accoutrements of a large country. The Vatican issues its
owns stamps and coins, and there is a remnant of the papal army represented by colorful Swiss guards who maintain a vigil that at least symbolically guards the pope.

### S'ter Says

The **College of Cardinals** is a
collection of cardinals that offers
counsel to the pope, elects new
popes, and governs the church in
between popes. There are approximately 130 members of the
college.

## Smoke Signals

The pope is elected by the *College of Cardinals* during
a council called to order no sooner than 15 days and
no later than 20 days after the death of his predecessor. A cardinal is a bishop of high rank appointed by
the pope. All cardinals under the age of 80 are eligible
to take part in the election. Election is permitted by a
voice vote, but the usual manner is the tradition of
secret ballot.

Ballots that fail to produce the necessary two-thirds
majority are burned in a small stove inside the counsel chambers, along with straw that will make dark
smoke. The dark smoke announces to the waiting
crowds that a pope has not yet been elected. When
the necessary majority is acquired, the ballots are
burned without straw, producing the white smoke
that signifies election of the pope.

# The Big Church and the Little Church

At the base of the organizational structure of the Catholic Church is the local diocese, which is under the direction of the bishop. A diocese is a group of parishes under the direction of the priest, called the pastor. Provinces, or archdioceses, join dioceses throughout a country. They are under the direction of an archbishop. Over all of this is the central administration of the church, the Vatican.

| Structure | Geographical Divisions |
|---|---|
| Pope | Vatican |
| Cardinals | Provinces or Archdioceses |
| Archbishops | Dioceses |
| Bishops | Parishes |
| Priests | |

The parish is the whole church as far as most Catholics are concerned. The various types of parishes include large suburban parishes, poor inner-city parishes, urban neighborhood parishes, and rural parishes. Additionally, ethnic parishes serve new immigrant groups in their native languages and customs.

At the center of a typical parish, you'll find the church itself, which is often named for a saint, such as St. Michael or St. Elizabeth. Various styles of architecture are represented in churches across the country from tiny little chapels to huge cathedrals. The church is the center of Catholics' faith life. They attend Mass there on a regular basis, they are married there, their children are baptized there, and family funerals take place there.

**Your Guardian Angel**

Resolve issues at the local level. Catholics are advised to conduct their business first with the parish priest, before going to the bishop.

Next to the church, you might find a rectory, or house where the priests live. Many Catholic parishes also have parochial school buildings. Parochial means "belonging to the parish" and is used to describe Catholic schools. If this school is conducted by a religious order of sisters, there will probably be a house for them on the parish property, too.

Another building you might find in a parish today is the parish center. This center is where the people gather: scouts, the Knights of Columbus, and prayer and scripture study groups. The center also provides a place for lectures or films. It contains the parish library and a full kitchen where weekly parish dinners happen. Some parishes use their center for homeless people in cold weather and offer the use of the building for community meetings such as Alcoholics Anonymous. Many parishes offer complete sports programs, so you might also find a basketball court and sports field for baseball or football.

# Rules and Regulations

As we discussed in Chapter 1, "Can You Judge a Catholic by the Cover?" the basis of Catholic morality is life in Christ, and the primary knowledge of Christ comes from the scriptures. This morality involves, among other things, the observance of the Ten Commandments. In the fulfillment of these commandments, special emphasis is placed on what is called the twofold law of love of God and neighbor, which Jesus said was the most important commandment. Other important sources for Catholic teaching come from the Bible's Sermon on the Mount, where Jesus pointed out the basics of moral behavior.

## *The Ten Commandments*

Collectively, the Ten Commandments are also called the Decalogue, which comes from the Hebrew phrase meaning "10 words." Taken from the Old Testament scriptures Exodus 34:28 and Deuteronomy 4:13; 10:4, the Ten Commandments are believed to have been given to Moses by God on Mount Sinai.

### For Heaven's Sake!

Don't get caught up in the rules! Remember, love is the first law, and motivates one toward good. "You shall love the Lord your God with all your heart, with all your soul, with all your mind, and all your strength." (Mark 12:30, Deuteronomy 6:5) Likewise, "Love your neighbor as yourself." This is the basis for the whole moral law.

### Epiphanies

Basilica means "king's hall" in Greek, and Catholics use the word to describe a Catholic church that has a specific historic significance and that continues to play a role in the religious life of a particular region. In addition to the major basilicas located in Rome, the Catholic Church honors other significant churches with this title. Major basilicas in North America include Mission Dolores in San Francisco, California; the Cathedral of St. Augustine in St. Augustine, Florida; Sacred Heart Basilica on the campus of Notre Dame in South Bend, Indiana; the Basilica of Notre Dame in Ottawa, Canada; and the Basilica of Notre Dame in Quebec, Canada.

The requirements set down in the commandments are not unique to the Jewish people; they can also be found in other texts of the ancient Near East. Nowhere, however, are they so clearly and concisely stated or expressed so personally and as intimately as having been given by God as laws to live by. As described in the scriptures, God gives the Ten Commandments directly to the Jewish people in his own voice. It is said that they were written by God's own hand on two tablets of stone, the first containing the commandments that directly refer to our relationship to God and the second governing our relations with one other. The Ten Commandments constitute the foundation of Christian law and ethics.

Here are the Ten Commandments as they appear in Catholic teaching:

1. I am the Lord your God. You shall not have strange gods before me.
2. You shall not take the name of the Lord thy God in vain.
3. Keep holy the Sabbath.
4. Honor your father and your mother.
5. You shall not kill.
6. You shall not commit adultery.
7. You shall not steal.
8. You shall not bear false witness against your neighbor.
9. You shall not covet your neighbor's spouse.
10. You shall not covet your neighbor's goods.

The Ten Commandments play an important role in a Catholic's life. One of the first tasks of a young Catholic is not only to memorize them, but also to understand what it means to live by them.

### Epiphanies

**The Code of Hammurabi**

As king of Babylon in 1792 B.C.E., Hammurabi founded an empire. His code of laws is one of the most celebrated of ancient codes. The laws are generally humanitarian. However, one severe feature is the nature of the punishment that follows the dictum, "an eye for an eye" literally. The code of Hammurabi precedes the Old Testament scripture. It is one of the few surviving sets of laws from the ancient Middle East.

## The Six Precepts

In addition to the Ten Commandments, the church has six rules, called *precepts,* for membership:

1. Attend Mass on Sunday and on the six other established holy days of obligation.
2. Observe the fast days as established by the church.
3. Confess any grave sins at least once a year.
4. Receive communion at least once a year, preferably during the Easter season.
5. Contribute to the support of the church.
6. Observe the church's laws concerning marriage.

**S'ter Says**

The term **canon** comes from the Greek word *kanon,* which means a "measuring stick of life." It is used to describe the rules governing the church, or church law.

## The 1,752 Canons

From the very earliest times up to the present, the church has compiled a complex system of rules called *Canon Law.* These rules are compiled and reviewed regularly. As of the current revision, there are 1,752 canon laws. Canon law functions in service of the people. It defines internal structures and describes the rights and obligations for its members in relationship to their religious life. Canon law provides the operational principles and structure of the church.

Canon Law affects the everyday Catholic by regulating how the faith should be lived. For example, Canon Law regulates how and when marriages take place, sets the rules for fasting, states the requirements for church attendance, and establishes the process by which leaders and teachers are chosen. For the most part, canon is church law, not moral law, which is contained in the Ten Commandments.

## The Eight Beatitudes

The spirit of the church laws is expressed in the beatitudes, which lie at the heart of the church's teachings. They provide examples of Jesus' love for the people and provide a map for Christian life. They sustain hope and proclaim the blessings and re-wards of life in Christ. The beatitudes teach that true happiness is not found in riches or well-being, fame, power, or material achievement, but in our good relations with one another. The following beatitudes are taken from the New Testament of the Bible in Matthew (5:3–12) and are Jesus' teachings from the Sermon on the Mount:

➤ Blessed are the poor in spirit, for theirs is the kingdom of heaven.

➤ Blessed are those who mourn, for they shall be comforted.

➤ Blessed are the meek, for they shall inherit the earth.

➤ Blessed are those who hunger and thirst for justice, for they shall be satisfied.

➤ Blessed are the merciful, for they will receive mercy.

➤ Blessed are the pure in heart, for they shall see God.

➤ Blessed are the peacemakers, for they shall be called the children of God.

➤ Blessed are those who are persecuted for righteousness' sake, for theirs is the kingdom of heaven.

➤ Blessed are you when people revile you and persecute you and utter all kinds of evil against you falsely on my account. Rejoice and be glad, for your reward is great in heaven, for in the same way they persecuted the prophets who were before you.

As we began this section, we pointed out that Jesus came to bring us the law of love that he expressed as love of God and neighbor. And this is the basis of all Catholic rules and regulations. With all of the laws and even the beatitudes, the individual ultimately stands responsible for his or her actions.

## Conscience, Virtue, and Grace

Catholics believe that moral conscience is present at the heart of a person, assisting in each person's choices by approving those that are good and denouncing those that are not. Catholics believe that when you listen to your conscience, you hear God speaking, and that voice is your conscience. The church teaches that it is important for every person to be present enough to hear and follow the voice of the conscience. Prudence results when we choose actions that conform to what our inner moral compass suggests. The church teaches that we have the right and responsibility to make our personal moral decisions. A person must not be forced to act against what he or she determines to be the right action for themselves. The church also requires that the conscience be educated and sees this as a lifelong process.

A virtue is the habit of doing the right thing. Virtues are developed through practice. In addition to the virtues we develop, there are virtues that are characteristic of our soul, the Holy Spirit of God within us. They lead us toward good and help steer us away from things that will harm us. The church calls these faith, hope, and love. These three virtues support us in the development of all others.

➤ By faith we intuitively understand that there is a God and actively seek to know and do God's will.

➤ Through hope we desire God regardless of the circumstances of our life at any given moment.

➤ Charity allows us to experience God's love, love ourselves, and love our neighbors.

Here are four key virtues we acquire through practice. They develop our inner compass:

➤ Prudence is following our "inborn" common sense.

➤ Justice is respecting other's rights and working for the common good.

➤ Courage ensures firmness in our pursuit of good.

➤ Temperance moderates our pursuit of life's pleasures, assuring balance.

Catholic spiritual life is formed in acquiring and honing these virtues. Catholic spirituality involves the practice of them in everyday interactions in the community with family, friends, and the society as a whole. To be a practicing Catholic means following these principles to the best of one's ability. The emphasis is on practice! The church is the people of God striving to live according to spiritual principles. To do this requires grace.

There are many definitions of grace. In the broadest sense, you could say grace is the gift of God's faithfulness to us. It is reflected in God's constant and unfailing love for us even when we fail to get it exactly right.

We've looked at the heart of the Catholic Church and the organizational structure that holds that core in place. In the next chapter we'll look at a shift in this organizational structure and some new challenges Catholics have been given to live their religious principles.

---

### The Least You Need to Know

➤ The Catholic Church expresses its unity through the office of the pope.

➤ The doctrine of infallibility is seldom evoked.

➤ The church is administered from a central headquarters with a worldwide network.

➤ The local parish is the seat of activity for church members.

➤ The church bases its moral laws on the Bible and tradition.

# Chapter 5

# The '60s: Seeds of Revolution

## In This Chapter

➤ The Catholic Church throws open the windows, and a lot of people catch cold

➤ Galileo forgiven: faith and science talk

➤ The church gets a new name

➤ The 1960s: the sexual revolution and church politics

➤ How we lost a few of our favorite things

Before getting any further into our exploration of Catholicism, let's take a look at what many consider the most formative event in the life of the church, the church council called Vatican II. Although you'll learn much more about the history of the church in Part 6, "The Church's History," right now it's important to understand this pivotal event that took place in 1960. During that year, the pope summoned the church leaders to begin to reform and update church policy and practice. Although many leaders of this revolution viewed this as a golden time for Catholicism, others resisted, preferring that it never happen.

The 1960s molded a new Catholicism. The tension between liberals and conservatives that began at that tumultuous time in history continues to characterize Catholicism today. This chapter tells the story behind this tension.

# The Stillness Before the Storm

Just as the bland sweetness of Wally and Beaver Cleaver represented the surface of America of the 1950s on television, growing up Catholic in the 1940s and 1950s had a similar innocence and order to it. It probably involved attending a Catholic grade school, which was most likely located right across the street from the public school. Other than a brief encounter at the crosswalks, the Catholics didn't mix much with the public school kids. Catholic schools were named things like Visitation, Incarnation, and Resurrection. They had their own ball teams, textbooks, library, and, of course, their own church.

Girls wore blue jumpers and white blouses for school. They kept their heads covered while they were in church, pinning on a tissue with a bobby pin in the absence of a proper scarf or hat. They always wore dresses to church and wore gloves on Sunday. Boys wore shirts and ties to school and suit coats to Mass. The sisters who taught school wore starched habits and long ropes of rosary beads that jangled (giving fair warning of their arrival) as they glided down clean, waxed corridors. The answers to all moral questions were neatly contained in the *Baltimore Catechism,* the little paperback book that held all the rules and beliefs of the church. Every Catholic child memorized it.

The popular images of this time in history were merely a thin veneer covering issues of social, political, and spiritual unrest that emerged in the 1960s. For better or worse, the world would never be the same again.

## *Vatican II: A Radical Departure and a Rebirth*

Characterized by Woodstock, political assassination, and America's seemingly endless and controversial involvement in Southeast Asia, the United States of the 1960s was in the throes of cultural and social revolution. As if the political questions being raised were not enough to shake the very ground of being, the Catholic Church chose this moment to come together to raise many of the same issues in the arena of religion that were being asked in the political world. Pope John XXIII, elected in 1958, called a *council* to update the church and to open it up to the modern world.

**S'ter Says**

A **council** is an assembly of representatives from the whole church called together by the pope to make decisions. The preceding council, Vatican I, was held from 1869 to 1870.

Ironically, Pope John XXIII was regarded as a transitional pope, someone who would fill the space between Pope Pius XII, a scholarly and aloof man, and the next strong leader yet to emerge from the ranks. Although Pope John XXIII's time at the helm was indeed short—an all-too-brief five years—the church soon realized this very energetic man with an instinctual connection to the people and a far-reaching vision for the church was to occupy a particularly crucial place in history. He was possibly the most popular pope of modern times, perhaps of any time, and he consistently demonstrated such warmth, simplicity, and charm that he won the hearts of Catholics, Protestants, and non-Christians alike.

The Second Vatican Council, or Vatican II, opened on October ll, 1962. By this time, the pope knew of his own fatal illness. His death came more than three years before the council ended. The council continued, and the changes that were effected are still unfolding, influencing, and changing the face of Catholicism in the post-modern world.

## *Lighting the Council Fires*

As the Catholic Church moved into the second half of the twentieth century, it found itself in perhaps the most powerful position in its history in terms of numbers of followers, influence on the international scene, and respect. And yet, it found itself too often locked in old battles, fighting against false beliefs and confronting the influence of Protestantism; these issues had been the focus of past councils. Vatican II was the first council called for the purpose of initiating change from within rather than combating heresy, pronouncing new dogma, or marshaling the church against hostile forces.

More than 900 million Catholics were living at the time of Vatican II, making it the world's largest religion. The revolution begun by Pope John XXIII with Vatican II put into motion ideas and forces that would come to affect a major portion of the world's population.

Church councils are rare; there had been only 20 in the nearly 2,000 years of Catholic history. Simply by summoning Vatican II to renew the Catholic Church, Pope John caused a major impact. Although councils are rare, revolutions in Catholicism are even more rare. The last one of any consequence happened more than 400 years ago and resulted in a major split when Protestantism was born (you'll read more about that in Part 6). In the 1960s, Pope John's historic mission was aimed at revitalizing the church's spirit, not only to bring the mother church of Christendom into closer touch with the modern world, but also to end the division that had fractured Jesus' message for four centuries.

By stretching out his hand in friendship to non-Catholic Christians, calling them "separated brethren," Pope John made history. He showed us that the walls that divided Christians could be broken down and that it was possible to align the church's life with the worlds of science, economics, and politics. Under his leadership, the church was to become more Catholic and less Roman, making a huge leap toward that distant and elusive goal of Christian unity. The church's revolution brought it into the world and onto the front pages of newspapers, often outranking the secular concerns of the day. The church's monolithic and absolutist character was forever changed.

### Your Guardian Angel

Do justice, love kindness, and walk humbly. A prophetic message from the past given to the Jewish people by Micah is as pertinent to the church today as it was then: "What does Yahweh require of you but to do justice and to love kindness, and walk humbly with your God?" (Micah 6:8)

Prophets have always existed and are part of religious history. We know their names from the Old Testament: Isaiah, Amos, Micah, and Elijah to name a few. Their voices often alerted the leaders to look where they were going; they cried out for change. In the 1960s, a revived spirit cried out for change and was heard. Perhaps the most revolutionary mark of Vatican II was the tacit acknowledgement of Catholicism's modern-day prophets. It recognized that those who had difficulty with the church, even those who had left it, may well have had good reasons for doing so.

Pope John invited the bishops to Rome to speak freely. He encouraged what he called "holy liberty." The bishops, who had long considered the pope as the sole source of power and authority in the church, discovered that they, and not just the pope, constituted the leadership of the church.

Pope John's unique gift of perception opened the way for change in the church. Most Protestant and Catholic clergymen and theologians, as well as many non-Christians, agree that Catholicism is a much stronger, more effective, and more positive influence today than it was when World War II ended. The church had finally begun to recognize and address the problems that had cut off much of its communication with the modern world.

### Epiphanies

A story that captures the spirit of the changing times in both the arena of politics and religion involves Jacqueline Kennedy's visit to Pope John XXIII. He asked his secretary what would be the proper way to address her. The secretary replied: "Mrs. Kennedy or just Madame, since she is of French origin and has lived in France." Waiting in his private library, the pope went over the options, trying to decide which one to use: "Mrs. Kennedy, Madame; Madame, Mrs. Kennedy." Then the doors opened, and the First Lady entered. He stood up, extended his arms, and cried "Jacqueline!"

In the five years of the council, church leaders pounded out a new definition of the church and a new way for the church to relate to the world. Catholics, who for more than 500 years had come to believe that the eternal truth resided only inside their religion, now found themselves in a new church that admitted that truth may indeed be found elsewhere as well. A major goal of Vatican II was to create a church less focused on its institutional structure and more focused on its people. Vatican II invited all church members to become full participants. The institutions and structures of the church, triumphantly expressed in buildings, fine liturgical vestments, and the reigning hierarchy, gave way to a church of the people.

Indeed, the old understanding for the church had focused on its institutional structure. It was guided by the image of the church as "the perfect society," self-sufficient, independent, and separate from the world around it.

Vatican II heralded a new model of church. "People of God" became the defining image. This image is from the Old Testament covenant relationship between God and his creation. The council understood this image to refer to the whole human race. Internally, the church shifted from seeing itself as a hierarchical institution that organized and ruled people to church as a community of people with co-responsibility. The hierarchy still exists as the organizational structure, but its purpose is to empower the people.

Externally, the church shifted from seeing itself as the only means of salvation to developing its relationship to the larger community—the whole people of God. It began to take down many of the walls that existed between Catholics and the rest of the world. In doing this, the council examined the following areas of the church:

➤ Liturgy: the prayers, songs, and the Mass

➤ The role of the laity: from spectators to participants

➤ The role of the church in the political and social world

➤ Religious freedom and respect for other spiritual paths

Core issues of Catholic identity were fundamentally challenged; the rules changed. We'll take a look at these changes next.

## The Altar Rail Comes Down: The Priest Turns Around

For years, the priest faced the altar with his back to the people while he said Mass. A railing separated the people from the front of the church where the altar was located. No one other than the priest or the servers was allowed near the altar except in rare times during particular ceremonies.

To the average Catholic, the changes in church ceremony after Vatican II were nothing less than shocking. The altar was moved forward. The priest now faced the people during Mass. The altar railing that separated him from the people came down. Members of the congregation walked up to the altar and read the scripture at Mass. The

### For Heaven's Sake!

Don't look at going to Mass as a chore. Indeed, you shouldn't go to Mass to get something out of it, but to put something into it—yourself! Mass becomes most meaningful when you approach it not as a duty, but as an invitation to come together and celebrate God's presence in the world.

### S'ter Says

A **parish council** is an elected group of church members whose job it is to plan and secure the resources for the mission of the parish.

Mass was no longer said in Latin, and during the service, members of the congregation turned to one another with a handshake. Even the priest left the altar to walk up and down the aisle and greet members of the crowd by name.

Like the culture around it, the church reflected the atmosphere of informality that characterized the 1960s. Worshippers wore jeans to church, and sometimes folk music played in the background. In some churches, you might have seen a bareheaded young woman and her longhaired boyfriend carrying the communion bread and wine up to the altar to be consecrated. Perhaps most striking of all, the priest handed the bread of communion to church members rather than placing it on their tongues. In the past, only the priest, whose hands had been consecrated, was allowed to touch the communion host.

In addition to these very public changes, Vatican II also fundamentally altered the organizational structure and authority of the church. It began to move away from a highly centralized power structure into which it had evolved over the years to a broader power base. Prior to Vatican II, a "father-knows-best" attitude prevailed throughout the church. All decisions were made on the highest level by the pope and handed down to the bishops, who handed them down to the priests. In the parish, the priest made the decisions and handed them down to the people. Now, in the post-Vatican II church, laity were invited to participate in church governance through *parish councils*.

Councils were also established to work with the bishop at the level of the diocese. These councils were composed of both priests and lay members of the church. In a similar fashion, at the highest level of the church in Rome, the bishops worked in a more collaborative relationship with the pope than had ever existed in the history of the church. Although many people still tend to think that the pope holds all authority in the Catholic Church, in reality Vatican II changed all that.

## The Rosary Gives Way to the Bible

Another crucial change for Catholics after Vatican II involved the role of scripture. Prior to Vatican II, the church did not emphasize it. In fact, Catholics were cautioned against private interpretation of the Bible and instead were directed toward the Catechism, a book of Catholic teachings. Over the years, this lack of emphasis had translated into an unofficial, but very definite, lack of Biblical familiarity among Catholics. They found they had to bow to the expertise of the Protestants when it came to quoting chapter and verse. After Vatican II, Catholic education began to focus on scripture rather than on memorizing the Catechism.

In addition to the changes in the Mass, popular devotions changed dramatically after Vatican II. Prior to 1960, Catholics might celebrate the month of May by marching through the streets of their town in a rosary procession; after 1960, Catholics were more likely to gather in the church for the Liturgy of the Word, commonly called a *Bible Vigil*.

Today, many people choose to share their faith in small gatherings in homes during which they read from the scripture, a tradition that departs radically from what had always been the "Catholic way." One result of Vatican II was to promote the concept of God's presence in the sacred word of the scripture as well as in the sacraments, where the emphasis had been placed prior to the council.

**S'ter Says**

A **Bible Vigil** is a post-Vatican II liturgical ceremony in which the Bible is prominently displayed on the church altar and the service consists of reading and reflection on biblical texts.

## Church as Listener

Perhaps the most revolutionary concept to come out of Vatican II identified the church as a listener. Its new relationship to the culture demanded that it pay attention to the times—a direct reversal of what had been centuries of church antagonism toward cultural changes. The pre-Vatican II church's position was to inform culture, not to learn from it. The new direction was to listen and learn.

The world of science was one of the arenas upon which this age-old conflict clashed most dramatically. People lived in two worlds that did not connect: the world of matter (science) and the world of spirit (religion). The rift between faith and science was wide and deep. Remember that it was the Catholic Church that placed astronomer Galileo, one of the greatest scientists in history, under house arrest back in the 1600s.

In the spirit of Vatican II, the church issued a long overdue apology to Galileo, recognizing him posthumously as a great scientist and removing their sanctions against him. Although this apology may seem totally ridiculous to the present-day reader, it represented a complete change in church policy. Popes, like kings and queens and many other political and religious leaders, traditionally did not—and still do not—apologize. To do so, showed a complete change of protocol. This expression alone represented one of the most remarkable and revolutionary changes of identity that resulted from Vatican II.

### Epiphanies

Galileo (1564–1642), Italian mathematician, physicist, and astronomer, was one of the first men to emphasize scientific observation rather than philosophical speculation to learn how the natural world works. He invented many instruments and was able to apply mathematical laws to determine that the Earth moves around the Sun rather than the reverse, which was the popular belief of Europeans and the church of his day. He was brought before the church authorities in 1633, where he was forced to take back his teachings and was put under permanent "house arrest." As he left the court, it is said he murmured, "and yet it moves," referring to the Earth's revolution around the Sun.

## Science and Faith Reach a Compromise

One of the ways the church has begun to reflect its new role as listener is by paying attention to some of the visionaries in its ranks. Pierre Teilhard de Chardin, who lived from 1881 to 1955, was a visionary who bridged the gap between the two worlds of science and religion in his writings and teachings in modern time. He was a paleontologist and a French Jesuit theologian.

Chardin's writings ended the mind/body duality for both the secular world and the church. His positive vision helped to set aside conflicts between religion and science and inspired the spiritual journeys of many men and women in search of a world view that is beyond the conflicts of dualism.

Chardin told of his two loves, one for the world of matter known by science and the other for the world of spirit revealed by faith. He said that at one time they were like two stars that divided his allegiance. Through his love and devotion to both science and religion, he eventually reconciled the two, seeing matter and spirit as indivisible and evolving together.

## From the Sanctuary to Selma

Change and surprise characterized the voice of the church's visionaries in the 1960s. In opening the church's windows, the Vatican Council gave the green light to active involvement in the world's culture. The world the church stepped into was one in massive turmoil over almost every social issue: race relations, international relations, and sexual relations. Every hot topic was being examined from the Catholic perspective.

Suddenly, priests were joining protest marches and advocating for social and political change from their pulpits, activities almost unheard of in the United States before the 1960s. This radical confrontation with the real world was often shocking to the image many Catholics had held of their clergy. But Catholics had to learn to overcome their shock during the six o'clock news on television, where they not only saw young people dragged off and arrested by police, but also their beloved nuns, priests, and bishops.

Although Catholics always had a strong presence in charitable work through building institutions to care for the poor, aged, and orphans, they began to look below the surface to examine the very structures of the society. There was a shift in focus from charity to justice. Rather than simply helping the poor, Catholics began to push their leaders to look at the causes of poverty.

**For Heaven's Sake!**

Pay attention to what's important. The words of Amos, the Old Testament prophet, spoke loudly to the social activists of the 1960s: "Take away from me the noise of your songs; to the melody of your harps I will not listen. But let justice roll down like waters, and righteousness like an ever-flowing steam." (Amos 5:23–24)

Indeed, after Vatican II, a profound change came in the way that Catholics practiced the faith. Social justice became a core focus—to be a Catholic was to be involved with the issues of the world and to seek justice. In the United States of the 1970s and 1980s, church leaders talked, wrote, and preached about peace, justice, racism, poverty, nuclear war, and ecology. In Latin America, clergy seeking justice for their people risked torture and death to challenge what they considered to be unjust authorities. Previously, the voice of the church restricted itself to spiritual matters or church rules, but Catholics in great numbers overcame the dualism of faith in God and the desire for change in the world after Vatican II.

# Ecumenism: Catholics' Relationship to Other Christians

Ecumenism is a term that describes the oneness of all Christian believers. Prior to Vatican II, Catholics divided the world into two distinct categories: Catholics and non-Catholics. After Vatican II, in the spirit of John XXIII, they referred to other Christians as "separated brethren," a marked shift in the church's belief that it was the only true church. The Vatican Council declared that the term *church* included all Christians, not just those who practiced the Catholic faith.

Ecumenism has very practical consequences for average Catholics. In the past, the church placed major

**Your Guardian Angel**

Use inclusive language. Rather than saying someone is a non-Catholic, acknowledge his or her denomination by referring to the person as a *Methodist, Baptist,* or *Lutheran,* for example.

restrictions that discouraged marriage between Catholics and others. For example, if a Catholic married a Protestant, the service was often performed in the privacy of the priest's office rather than in the church. Very little public recognition was given to "mixed" marriages.

Today, not only can mixed marriages take place in the sanctuary, but often the priest also invites the partner's minister or rabbi to witness the ceremony. With the permission of the bishop, the marriage can take place before another Christian minister or rabbi. Today it would not be uncommon for the partner of a Catholic to participate in Catholic Church services and functions, including being a member of the parish council.

Many commissions and dialogues have been established to improve communication and bring about greater understanding between all Christians. Preachers from other Christian faiths have been invited to speak in Catholic churches. Cooperative ventures in social justice efforts such as "Room at the Inn," a program to house homeless people in the winter, bring many churches together to open their doors to each other as well as to the needy.

## Expanding Interfaith Relationships

Vatican II not only took a more open stance toward other Christians, it also reached out to mend relationships with other faiths, particularly the Jewish people. For example, the church removed prayers from the liturgy that implied Jewish culpability in the death of Jesus. For centuries past, these prayers and the attitudes they represented contributed to anti-Semitism on the part of the Catholic Church and many Catholics.

In addition, efforts have been made in the religious education curriculum to revise prejudicial stands toward the Jews and to teach about the Hebrew faith. This new attitude toward the Jewish faith has led church scholars to encourage a deeper respect for sacred Hebrew literature, referring to the Old Testament as the "Hebrew Scriptures" or "The First Testament." These writings are seen as important to the faith on their own, not just as an introduction to the "Christian Scripture" or New Testament.

A major effort of the church since Vatican II has been to reevaluate the Catholic Church's role in the Holocaust. Pope Pius XII has been criticized by many for failure to take a stand against Nazi Germany's persecution of the Jews. Pope John Paul II has spoken out on this matter, offering an apology to the Jewish people for the church's conduct. Clearly much more investigation and explanation is necessary before any moves toward reparation can be meaningful.

### Saints Preserve Us

**St. Maximilian Kolbe, August 14**

St. Maximilian was a Franciscan priest from Poland who was imprisoned during the Nazi invasion and sent to the Auschwitz death camp. In a reprisal against the escape of some prisoners, ten people were condemned to die. Maximilian took the place of a young husband and father chosen for death, offering himself instead. Many believe that Kolbe's canonization is, in part, an attempt of the church to give its members an example of a correct attitude toward the Jewish people.

In addition to attempts to repair relations with the Jewish people, the church has reached out to Muslims, meeting with Muslim leaders and delegations in Rome and around the world. The pope has spoken to large gatherings of Muslims in Morocco, Indonesia, Mali, and elsewhere. Formal dialogues have been held from time to time with Islamic organizations to promote good relations between the Christian world and the Islamic world.

Within Catholic monastic life, the hand of friendship has been extended to members of Buddhism, Hinduism, Confucianism, Taoism, and Shinto. Buddhist and Catholic monks have joined together in practices and studies of the mystical life. Thomas Merton, a twentieth-century popular Catholic mystic, met with Buddhists to talk about the mystical life and social justice issues during the Vietnam War before he died in Thailand in 1968.

## We Throw Open Heaven's Gate: Religious Liberty

Vatican II issued "The Declaration on Religious Liberty." In this important paper, the council declared that all people have the right to religious freedom. This means that all men and women should be free from coercion regarding religious choices. No one can be forced to act against personal convictions in choice of religion and practices.

This document held particular importance to U.S. Catholics, because the United States was the first western country to be constitutionally founded on religious freedom. During his campaign for president, John F. Kennedy made it clear that Catholics championed this separation.

"The Declaration on Religious Liberty" also had a profound effect on Catholic missionary activity. No longer was it acceptable to disregard the beliefs of others. As a result, mission efforts have been much more concerned with sharing beliefs rather than imposing the Catholic faith.

# Conscience Reigns Supreme

Catholic teaching has always taught that you must obey your conscience. Vatican II strengthened that stand. Prior to Vatican II, Catholics generally would seek and follow the advice of their priest in moral matters. Since Vatican II, they have been urged to search their own hearts and minds to come to their own informed moral decisions.

**For Heaven's Sake!**

Take responsibility for yourself and your actions. The post–Vatican II Catholic Church emphasizes personal responsibility for moral decisions, which means that you cannot simply follow directions. You must seek instruction, pray and meditate, and make your own moral choices.

Here is an example of the way the changes might be seen in the life of everyday Catholics. Theresa (let's call her) was a Catholic mother during the 1960s. She and her husband had been practicing the rhythm method, the only means of birth control condoned by the Catholic Church. They have three "rhythm" babies: the youngest is six weeks old, and the oldest is five. Theresa and her husband do not feel they can bring any more babies into their family, and a life of celibacy together does not seem like a good idea to either of them.

This devout Catholic couple decided to practice birth control, even though they knew they were on dangerous theological grounds. One Saturday afternoon, Theresa brought her moral dilemma to the confessional. Laying the situation out to her confessor, she found that her decision had already been made. Rather than confess birth control as a sin, she informed him of her choice to use it. Surprisingly, the priest sympathized with her. He understood the difficulty of the choices Theresa had to make and encouraged her to pray, search her heart, and only then to make a moral decision about what she believed was God's will for her in this situation. The priest would not have offered such advice before Vatican II. Before Vatican II, it would have been very difficult to find a priest who would offer such advice.

# A Painful Side Effect of Vatican II: Loss of Tradition

Although Vatican II brought positive changes to the lives of Catholics, many of the faithful felt a deep loss as traditional and beloved beliefs and practices were altered or dropped altogether in an effort to update the church. In addition, the church lost some of its uniqueness. Once so clearly defined by their difference from other faiths, and characterized by separation from the world, many Catholics were left with a vague sense of the church being "less Catholic" than it used to be.

# Mea Culpa, Mea Culpa, Mea Maxima Culpa

*Mea culpa, mea culpa, mea maxima culpa* is Latin for "I am sorry, I am sorry, I am heartily sorry." It was a line from a prayer said at the beginning of the Mass, but it also spoke to the sentiment of many Catholics who regretted the loss of their Latin prayers. Until Vatican II, all Catholics heard the Mass in this ancient language. Thus, it was possible to attend Mass in any Catholic Church in the world and hear the prayers said in exactly the same way. In the pre-Vatican II days, uniformity was the rule, and diversity and individuality were discouraged.

### Epiphanies

Prior to Vatican II, all the courses in the seminary were taught in Latin, which was the church's way of assuring that the teachings would remain the same. Although that's all changed, Latin remains the language of the Vatican for official business and teachings. For the most part it is gone for the everyday Catholic, and with it went favorite prayers, hymns, and the beloved Gregorian chants of yesterday. As the music changed, many traditions went with it.

Because church music was written and performed in Latin, when the language of the Mass was changed to the vernacular, meaning the language of the country, the music changed, too. Music had been a central gathering point for many in the church, and as the choir was de-emphasized and the congregation was urged to sing, many felt a painful loss of their religious identity.

For example, before Vatican II, choir practice was a very special ritual. One woman recalls going to choir practice every Wednesday evening and Saturday afternoon for as long as she could remember. The whole week revolved around Sunday morning. "We arrived at 9:30 in the morning to prepare for the 11 o'clock service," she reminisces. "We didn't finish until at least 1:00 in the afternoon. Afterward we went to lunch together. There were other events, too—potluck suppers, parties, and the annual choir picnic. Life-long friendships were formed—it was all about the music and about the religion."

Then suddenly everything changed with Vatican II, "They came in and took our sheet music and carted it away, stacks and stacks of Gregorian chant. We had spent years collecting it, and it was all destroyed in a day. The choir was replaced by a fellow with a guitar in the front of the church who tried to lead us in songs not only that no one knew, but songs many of us believed did not belong in church."

Until this point, the Catholic Mass relied heavily on the Gregorian chant and classical music in addition to hymns and psalms sung in Latin. Their loss after Vatican II was deeply felt by many Catholics. Churches are now following what they believe the council recommended by making a sincere attempt to update the songbooks and having congregational singing.

# Fasting and Fish Rules Relaxed

One of the more derogatory insults flung at Catholics was the nickname "mackerel-snappers." This moniker derived from the fact that Catholics were forbidden to eat meat on Friday to honor the day Christ died—a rule most Catholics held as absolute to their identity.

### Your Guardian Angel

Make Friday your fish day. Every Catholic over the age of 50 knows at least 10 recipes for tuna casserole. Here is a favorite one: Mix one large can drained tuna fish with one can cream of mushroom soup, add two cups cooked macaroni or rice, and top with crushed potato chips. Bake for 20 minutes in a moderate oven. Deeeeeelicious!

Another pre-Vatican II dietary rule involved the fasting requirements for Lent and in preparation for holy days. Basically, a Catholic could not have more than one complete meal on the specified days. In a similar way, Catholics observed a complete fast from all food and water from midnight until they received Communion the next morning. There were many sad stories of the little boy or girl who made a mistake on First Communion Day and took a drink of water from the fountain as his or her classmates gathered in the school for the procession over to the church. Doing so meant he or she couldn't receive communion with the class, which was not only embarrassing but meant that he or she couldn't share in the joy of the celebration of the day. Often, nuns would tie off all the drinking fountains with white rags to avoid such mishaps.

Today, such dietary restrictions have been relaxed so that Friday meat abstinence is urged only during Lent (the 40-day period of preparation for Easter) and fasting before communion can be limited to one hour before reception. Some wonder if this relaxation does not take the "Holy" out of "Holy Communion," make Catholics forgetful of the Lord, and diminish the celebration of Easter.

## Shifting Prayers and Practices

Several practices once considered an integral part of the Catholic faith and ritual either have been eliminated or their importance has been diminished. Let's take a look at some of the practices that once characterized a Catholic:

➤ **Spiritual bouquets.** A spiritual bouquet is the name for a gift of prayers that one might pledge to say as a present for another person. They could include 10 Hail Marys, 10 Our Fathers, 15 Glory Bes, 1 Rosary, 5 Masses, and 5 Communions. The one offering the bouquet writes down the prayers that will be said and signs the piece of paper as a promise.

➤ **Scapulars.** These brown and white pieces of cloth worn around the neck looked like oversized postage stamps connected by two strings. Representing a monk's robe, the scapular is meant to remind the person who wears it that he or she has been called to a life of prayer.

➤ **Ransoming pagan babies.** This was the common term for a practice that introduced children to the missionary activities of the church. Children were encouraged to save nickels, dimes, and quarters until they had $5. With this amount, they could select the name of a child in Asia or Africa whom the missionaries would baptize in exchange for the donation.

➤ **May Day.** On a spring day in May near the end of the school year, everyone gathered for the May Day ceremony. The boys wore white pants, shirts, and white ties. The girls dressed in beautiful white dresses with veils. One girl would be selected to climb the ladder and place a crown of flowers on a statue of Mary while the entire congregation sang, "Oh, Mary we crown you with blossoms, today. Queen of the Angels, Queen of the May ..."

These ceremonies, practiced faithfully for decades, gave Catholics a clear image of what it meant to belong to a particular tribe of people—to be Catholic. With the passing of time, many of these practices have been dropped from the Catholic portfolio, and for many people, the loss of these ceremonies has resulted in the blurring of their image of what it means to be Catholic.

Attendance at Mass has dropped and, as the definitions about sin have been softened, people no longer line up outside the confessional on Saturday afternoon, as was once the weekend ritual. Catholicism lost its absolutism, and for many it also lost its certainty.

## Mary Loses Center Stage

Prior to Vatican II, people often asked Catholics why they worshipped Mary. The answer was that Catholics didn't worship her, they honored her. The reason someone might have asked this question was the extremely high profile she had in Catholic life. Devotions to her often rivaled all other services. Every Saturday Mass was dedicated to her. Many of the major feasts in the church calendar are devoted to her. Typically the first girl in a Catholic family was named Mary.

*Here is a spiritual bouquet a child might have given to her mother.*

*(Designed by authors)*

**A Spiritual Bouquet**

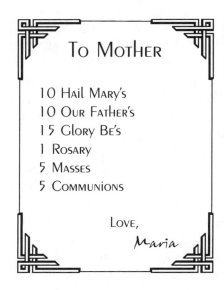

To Mother

10 Hail Mary's
10 Our Father's
15 Glory Be's
1 Rosary
5 Masses
5 Communions

Love,
Maria

### Epiphanies

There's something about Mary: Catholic scholars, theologians, and Church leaders might dim Mary's light a few watts, but soon it begins to glow even brighter in the hearts of the people. Hundreds of thousands flock to sights wherever she is purported to appear, and devotions to her continue as an important part of Catholic prayer life. Paying attention to what people are saying about Mary might be a way for the church to know what people are saying about God. For many, she is God's feminine face.

The prayer most closely associated with Mary is the Rosary, and it has long been the favorite prayer for many Catholics. Often people opted to pray the Rosary during Mass rather than read along in their prayer book. You can find out more about this very Catholic and very popular devotion in Chapter 14, "Catholic Prayers and Music: Tangible Poetry."

At Vatican II, the church attempted to de-emphasize Mary, putting her in her place, so to speak. With the focus on the Mass as the primary Catholic devotion, Catholics were discouraged from praying the Rosary during Mass. Devotions to her were greatly reduced, because the new liturgy emphasized Christ and the scriptures.

## The Saints Suffer

Devotion to the saints has long been a favorite Catholic practice. There is a saint for every day of the year, and a saint is designated as the patron of almost everything from countries to careers, to conditions. At Vatican II, the church attempted to clean up its roster of saints, determining which ones had a historical basis and which ones were simply part of the folk legends of the people. In the process, they removed many saints from the records. In doing this, church leaders discovered that the people were not willing to let the saints go.

Regardless of whether there was a historical basis for these saints, the virtues represented in the stories about them were important to the people. They had become part of the fabric of church mythology, and the church leaders could not unravel it. St. Christopher, a beloved character in Catholic mythology and popular with non-Catholics, too, was one of the saints that was declared to be no longer part of the official directory. However, devotion to him has continued. Today, as always, people keep St. Christopher medals in their cars and feel protection under his care.

## Dress Code: Defrocking the Clerics

With the changes of Vatican II came changes in the relationship between the clergy and the people they served. This change was most obviously apparent in the way the clergy and other religious members dressed. Before Vatican II, priests wore black suits with the Roman collar as we described earlier. They seldom appeared in public without their formal attire. Even more distinctive was the elaborate dress of the nuns.

After Vatican II, dress codes were relaxed. Many nuns moved out of the convents into other living arrangements; some even took secular jobs. There has been a mixed response to these changes. Catholics liked the fact that their religious leaders could be so easily identified and that the greater community showed them respect. Many people feel the change in dress code resulted in a general lack of regard for the church and its leaders. Others feel that the old style of dress set religious leaders apart too much and emphasized separation of the religious leaders from the people they were to serve.

## Numbers Tell the Story

Numbers told the story of the changing face of the church. In the pre-Vatican II days, a large parish typically would have four or five priests. Today, very few parishes have more than one in residence. Often the parishes are much larger. There has been a big exodus of priests, nuns, and brothers from the church ministry since the 1960s, and the numbers of people entering religious life has dropped. This downsizing of clerical ministers is seen both as a sign of the times and a result of Vatican II's strict adherence to celibacy. Many persons had expected a change in this regulation.

*Sister Mary Catherine, CSJ (Congregation of St. Joseph), in the traditional pre-Vatican II habit of her order.*

*(Author photo)*

*Here Sister Mary Catherine appears in a post-Vatican II style of dress.*

*(Author photo)*

The reduction in religious vocations is a great challenge the church faces in the post-Vatican II time. Many feel that the shortage will eventually cause the church to rethink its stand on celibacy and on the ordination of women. In addition, a major focus of the council was toward giving more responsibility to the people. The reduction in church staff has certainly resulted in more participation by the lay members of the church. We'll look in detail at some of the ways this is happening in Chapter 20, "The Church: Moving from Steeple to People."

We've just taken a quick look at the church both before and after Vatican II. Now we're going to go back in time to the beginnings of the religion and see how it developed. We'll look at its roots, the Bible, Jesus, and the beginning of his followers' journey.

### The Least You Need to Know

➤ Vatican II was an important turning point for Catholics.

➤ The church focused the religion less on institutional structure and more on the people.

➤ Better relations between Catholics and Protestants, Catholics and Jews, and Catholics and the rest of the world were fostered.

➤ In updating the church, some traditions that were important to many Catholics were lost.

➤ The church continues to change as a result of Vatican II.

# Part 2

# Putting the "Ism" in Catholicism: Becoming Catholic, Becoming Different

*Tevia in* Fiddler on the Roof *sings about a very important word, "tradition." Like it was for their Jewish forbears, tradition is a key word for Catholics. One of the differences between Catholics and Protestants is the feeling toward tradition. The Catholic Church insists that to understand God's revelation we must equally consult scripture and tradition. For many Protestants, the focus must be on scripture alone.*

*So to get into Catholicism, it is necessary to get into its tradition. This tradition, as you will see, is deep and broad, going both to the center of the earth as well as to its four corners. Tradition is what each successive group of Catholics found from the previous generation regarding vital issues such as who is God, how do we know him, what does he want from us? These issues are the core of religion and are as alive and elusive today as they were yesterday. The story of this religion called Catholicism is the story of this progressive development called tradition. That's what you'll learn about in Part 2.*

# Chapter 6

# "It's Elementary, My Dear Watson"

## In This Chapter

➤ The roots of Catholicism are in the earth

➤ Catholicism draws its identity from the Jewish scripture

➤ Greek learning gives Catholicism a heady start

➤ Catholics gain power and might from the Roman tradition

➤ The Celts pave the way for a rich mythology

In this chapter, you'll see how the Catholic religion came upon the scene within the context of human history. We'll explore the experiences, images, stories, and gatherings that make up the ritual, creed, and code of the Catholic Church. You might be surprised to find the sources of its ritual in the earth, air, fire, and water ceremonies of ancient people. We'll look at the culture and religion of the Jews, Greeks, Romans, and Celtic people and see how they influenced the formation of the early church and how their influence is still present in the modern church.

The church's official birthday is Pentecost, the day the scriptures tell us the followers of Jesus went out into the community to tell of their experience with him. But the story has much deeper roots than that. The church is a composite of many quite ancient rituals that speak to the heart, mind, and actions of its members.

# Ritual: The Old Religion, Roots, and Renewal

One of the hallmarks of Catholics is their long tradition of ritual and ceremony. In order to understand the religion, it helps to understand how rituals work to transmit spiritual truths. We don't know exactly how that happens, but we do know that rituals work to reveal deep spiritual meanings to those who participate in them.

Earth is the first church. To get to the core of the Catholic religion, we're going to go on a very deep journey into the heart of our planet. The roots of this old tradition go to the very beginnings of the human story, back to birth, death, and regeneration. Ever since humans conceived of some power or spirit beyond themselves, they have enacted and reenacted elementary themes of life and death in what is called ritual. Ritual began as our way of reinforcing what we intuitively knew.

The term *Judeo-Christian* describes Catholics' connection to the Jewish religion and acknowledges our common history. Yet even further back than this tradition is a culture developed by the people who lived in the Fertile Crescent, an ancient region made up of what is today the Middle East, Turkey, and Greece. The people of this culture, sometimes called *pagans,* had well-developed societies, raised children, built towns, made pottery, worked with metal, said prayers, and enjoyed productive, artistic lives. Some were monotheistic, believing in one God, and others polytheistic, believing that God takes many forms. Although their cultures died away more than 1,100 years before Catholicism, vestiges of them remain in the rituals we practice today.

### For Heaven's Sake!

Watch your language! The word pagan can be a derogatory term. If you're talking about someone who believes in more than one god, you many be better off using the word polytheistic, if that is what you mean.

Pagan is a word that was originally used as a derogatory term to describe one who lived in the country rather than the city. Another word for pagan would have been country bumpkin. The meaning was further shortened to describe anyone who is not a Christian, Moslem, or a Jew. The term pagan often is applied to ancient peoples, especially the Greeks and Romans. Heathen originally described those who lived on the heath. It is now applied to the people regarded as worshipping false gods. In light of modern scholarship, both terms are considered culturally insensitive.

## *Elementally Speaking*

To revisit these people and explore their faith is vital to the understanding of Catholicism because, fundamentally, all religion is about understanding who we are and our connection to the Creator, as well as understanding the way humans have interacted in the world throughout history. The word *religion* comes from the Latin *religare,* which means "to bind back, to bind together." Understanding religion, then, means connecting to the past and learning the story of the communities of people on earth who came before us. Their simpler, peaceful societies are an important contribution to the human story. We can't go forward until we go backward and connect their stories with our own.

For many thousands of years, it was believed that all physical matter was composed of four elements: earth, air, fire, and water. These elements symbolized God's real presence in creation. The seasons and cycles of nature translated to our own human spiritual process. Our creativity was connected to the Creator and reflected in the earth's abundance. Crops planted in the earth would be nourished by the sun and rain and would produce food. Winter was like a death: inevitable and a part of life. Nature shut down and regenerated itself again in spring. To die was to be reborn. Ceremonies celebrating the seasons of the year were deeply rooted in the human psyche; they affirmed that life would continue.

## A Visit to Antiquity

Imagine you're a member of a tribe living thousands of years ago. Summer is ending. The days grow shorter. A distinct chill fills the morning air. The vines no longer produce their fruits. You're concerned about the food supply. (Remember that this is before the age of microwaves and corner grocery stores. When the food was gone, it was gone!) If the winter is as long and cold as it was the previous year, will there be enough food? Will the old people and the children stay warm enough; will they survive winter? Winter connects us to thoughts of death and also to renewal.

Today, as well as in ancient times, ritual and rites explore these themes. In the past, drummers gathered in a circle outside the cave and beat their drums in rhythms that matched the human heartbeat to make the spirit strong for winter. Then dancers circled the fire, echoing the beat and pounding the experience of hope renewed, moving it up through the legs into the body and into their hearts.

Hope is strengthened through the rhythms of *ritual* and enactment of *ceremony*. In Baptism, for example we light the candle, which is our ritual fire. We are immersed in water, and through it we are born into the new life of the spirit just as God once gave us physical life through our mother. We are connected in a sacramental way to God's renewing spirit. We are reborn.

Within the Catholic Church, the rituals and ceremonies celebrate not the passing of seasons as they did in ancient times but rather the physical presence of Christ on

**S'ter Says**

**Religion** concerns what exists beyond our comprehension. It is different from philosophy in that it operates from faith or intuition rather than reason.

The words **ceremony** and **ritual** are often used to describe the same thing: a formal act or set of formal acts established by custom or authority as proper to a special occasion, such as a wedding or other formality. They describe the process by which we observe something that we want to honor as important or sacred.

earth. His availability to human beings, walking and talking with them in their everyday experiences, is a key belief for Catholics. They believe he showed us that God is, was, and will always be present to his people. We can realize his presence through all of creation. We can understand that we are loved and cared for in all ways. God is in the earth, providing food, shelter, and all the material things we need to sustain us.

Catholics connect to the earthly presence of God by enacting rituals. Through rituals, they're able to physically touch and be touched by God's presence. The Communion bread is made of the wheat that grows in the fields. The Communion ritual says: "I am here with you. This is my body. I will feed and nourish you. This is how I am intimate with you." This earthy ritual manifests the physicality of God.

Rituals are tribal events. They're acted out in a community. It is only when we find a connection to the symbols of hope with others that we become certain of their validity.

# "Yada, Yada, Yada"

As we stated earlier, Catholics share a common history with the Jews. In Hebrew, the word for faith is *yada,* which the Greeks translated as *gnoskin,* meaning "to know." For Judeo-Christians, *yada* (knowing) is something we do more with our hearts than with our minds. *Yada* comes from having earthy experiences, not by standing back from the world at an intellectual distance. Indeed, faith and knowing are action words that require a lot of living to achieve. A Catholic's faith is expressed through action in the world, and its roots stem from the Jewish tradition of *yada.*

**For Heaven's Sake!**

The "Old Testament" is old, but not out of date. It is called old in relationship to the "New Testament" that begins with the life of Christ. The stories continue to give us fresh meaning and insight, and are integral to the religious understanding of both Christians and Jews.

To strengthen and develop this faith, both Jews and Catholics look to scripture. The term *Bible* is commonly used to designate the sacred writings of the Christians, but it contains both the Jewish and the Christian scriptures. In fact, the word *Bible* comes from the Greek *ta biblia* meaning "the books," which describes its contents rather accurately. When the term was translated into Latin, the plural was dropped, making it the singular "The Book" we know today (Chapter 7, "The Bible," explores the Bible further).

### Epiphanies

The abbreviations B.C. (before Christ) and A.D. (*Anno Domini*, which means "in the year of our Lord") have been in existence a long time and are widely accepted by the entire world, but they are strictly Christian in origin. Many believe these abbreviations are insensitive to non-Christians. Sometime in this century, people began using the new terms B.C.E. (before the common era) and C.E. (common era). Jewish people, Moslems, Buddhists, Hindus, and many other religious groups agree that these new terms are more accurate for all people. We'll use them in this book.

To Catholics and Jews, scriptures are inspired, meaning that they have divine origin and provide guidance and comfort as well as the special sense of connection with the divine. Scriptures contain common themes, stories, and characters that give an identity to a religion and by which a religion can interpret the unfolding events of the day. These stories and characters provide a mirror in which people look to see who they are and where they came from as well as where they are headed.

## Paradise Lost, and Paradise Found

To gain a quick understanding of any culture in the world, note how it describes its own creation. A culture's creation story gives you the basics on what the people of that culture believe about God, the world, and themselves. The Judeo-Christian creation story begins in the Garden of Eden.

Genesis, the first book of the Jewish scripture, explains that God has been involved in a huge project called Creation. God created the earth, the sea, the sky, the animals, Adam (the first man), and Eve (the first woman). In this book, God places humans in a beautiful garden and cares for their needs. The humans walk and talk with God on a regular basis. Right from the beginning of the story, God is shown to be personal and caring.

### For Heaven's Sake!

Don't think the Genesis creation story is the only one available. There are over 20,000 known creation stories. Virtually every group of people has a story about how the world was created and how its culture came into being.

God puts only one stipulation on Adam and Eve. He tells them not to eat the fruit of a certain tree. A serpent, representing evil, enters the garden and tempts them to eat the forbidden fruit. As they eat the fruit, they immediately experience terrible consequences. They are cut off from the very close relationship they enjoyed with God, and they are, as the scripture says, "cast out of the garden." However, later in Genesis, God promises the people that he will not forget them.

The human journey depicted in Genesis begins in travail and loss, but also with promise of reunion. Christians believe that Jesus brings the long-sought-after reunion with God, the reunion God promised. Here's what the story of Genesis means to Catholics' understanding of their relationship to God and relationships among men and women on earth:

1. Creation has a master plan. It has meaning.

2. We are created in God's image, which means we are intelligent, compassionate, and creative.

3. There are sacred laws and rules that we must follow.

4. We have free choice, and our choices carry responsibility.

5. God is compassionate and will stay with us. He has a covenant relationship with the people.

The creation story in Genesis conveys both a sense of loss and of promise. This theme runs throughout Christianity. In Judaism, it is expressed as the covenant relationship between God and the people. Christians believe Jesus fulfills the covenant.

**S'ter Says**

A **covenant** is made of two separate agreements. Each party agrees to abide by certain rules of the covenant. If one party fails to keep the covenant, the other party is still obligated. This makes a covenant different than a contract because, in contracts, default can take place. Covenants have no default.

## The Covenant

The idea of the *covenant* is the central theme in the Hebrew scriptures of the Old Testament. In the covenant relationship between God and the Jewish people, God promises to stay faithful to his people, and the people promise their faithfulness to him. This theme of covenant is expressed in the following stories.

In the story of Noah (found in Genesis 9:9–11), God sends a flood to punish the people. Noah is saved because God judged him and his family to be just. When the flood is over, God places a rainbow in the sky as a symbol of his promise to the people, the animals, and the earth that he will never send another flood to destroy them:

> I will establish my covenant with you and with your descendants after you; and with every living creature that is with you, the birds, the cattle, and

every wild animal with you; all that came out of the ark, even the wild animals. I establish my covenant with you. Never again shall all living things be destroyed by the waters of the flood; never again shall there be a flood to destroy the earth." And God said, "This is the token of the covenant; I set it between me and you and every living creature that is with you, for all generations to come. I will set my rainbow in the clouds, and it shall be a token of the covenant between me and the earth." (Genesis 9:9–13)

In a later story, God tests Abraham by asking him to offer his son, Isaac, as a sacrifice. Abraham is grief-stricken but obeys God and prepares to kill his son. God stops him and forms a covenant, promising Abraham that because he has obeyed, he will become the father of a great nation and that the land of Canaan will be its permanent possession. (Genesis 22:1–19)

**Your Guardian Angel**

Here's how to find the text when reading the Bible. Let's take Genesis 9:9–13. The name Genesis refers to the book of the Bible in which the information is located. The first number is the chapter (9), which is followed by a colon, and the next two numbers (9–13) are the verses in that chapter.

## Moses Receives the Law

At Mount Sinai, God seals a special covenant with the entire people of Israel through Moses as he gives Moses the law. Catholics believe in the covenant relationship as it is presented in the Hebrew scriptures. Both Judaism and Catholicism are based on the understanding that God is constant and available and that we have a choice in entering into relationship with him. To be in this relationship means we have the responsibility to live in accordance to his laws.

Law is the second central theme of Jewish identity. The Ten Commandments are the core of Jewish law. God gave them to the people through one of their leaders, Moses. Jews do not experience the law as an external obligation, but as an expression of God's care. God gives his people the law as an act of love, as his side of the covenant. The people respond to it as their side of the covenant. It is through obeying the law (right action) that the Jewish people know of God's love.

The Jews were a wandering nomadic people who had no homeland. They carried the presence of God with them on a portable throne contained in an object called an ark. The ark housed the throne and the scriptures that contained the law, their covenant with God. Eventually when they established a homeland, the Ark of the Covenant was placed in the holiest part of the temple. The temple, then, became the place where Jews could be in physical contact with the sacred relationship that was signified by God's law.

### Epiphanies

The Ark of the Covenant resided in the most holy place in the Jewish temple. It was entered on one day only per year, the Day of Atonement (Yom Kippur). Access was restricted to one person, the high priest. The ark itself was a small box made of acacia wood, overlaid with gold. Two long bars, also made of the same wood overlaid with gold, carried it. It contained three sacred items of the Jewish religion: the two stone tablets of the law given to Moses, Aaron's rod that budded, and the golden pot of hidden manna. Catholics keep the Communion bread in a similarly sized box, which they call the tabernacle. The tabernacle occupies a place of honor near the altar.

The Hebrew Scriptures talk of "knowing the Lord." This means that God takes the initiative, and the people respond to this encounter as it happens in events, in relationships, and in creation. In other words, such knowledge is gained here and now, not in an otherworldly way. Knowledge of the Lord is knowledge of the law and demands obedience to God's will.

In following this tradition, a Catholic's knowledge of God is not a fixed possession but is an activity. Knowledge develops in the life of the Catholic as lasting obedience and reflection. Faith is not a defined set of beliefs; it is an ongoing relationship with God.

## A Summary of Jewish Influence

These important aspects of Catholic identity come from the Hebrew Scriptures:

➤ **Monotheism.** The belief in one all-knowing God is central to both Catholicism and Judaism. Unfortunately, monotheism carries with it an intolerance of other religions.

➤ **God's presence.** Judaism's central theme is the covenant between God and the people. Faith is a living response.

➤ **Free will.** Catholics and Jews believe that we are all personally responsible for our actions. Actions bear consequences.

➤ **Moral law.** The Old Testament forms the basis for Christian morality as it does for the Jewish people.

The key difference between Judaism and Catholicism is that Christians believe that Jesus came as the fulfillment of the Old Testament covenant Scriptures.

# Influences of the Greeks, Romans, and Indigenous Peoples

Although the influence of the Jewish faith is most easily recognized because Catholics and Jews share common sacred writings, two prominent cultural philosophies, the Greek and the Roman, also affected the formation of the early church. Less prominent, yet equally important, were the indigenous peoples of the Middle East and their understanding of mystery.

## *The Greeks Decapitate the Mind from the Body*

What is called the Golden Age of Greece had been in full glory, influencing Jerusalem and the surrounding areas, for at least 300 years before Christianity. The view of the world held by the ancient Greeks is paradoxical. On the one hand, they contributed much of what is considered Western civilization in the way of art, education, health, philosophy, and mathematics; Greek order and beauty as well as Greek love of thought are the foundation of our understanding of culture.

### Epiphanies

The Greeks ruled civilization between 332 and 141 B.C.E. Alexander the Great, a Macedonian general, conquered the Eastern world. The Golden Age of Greece refers to the establishment of the Greek language, culture, and religion throughout the East. Greeks founded or reestablished many cities through the area in the Greek style, for example, Alexandria and Antioch. Greeks believed in many gods and goddesses. In 167 B.C.E., they destroyed the temple in Jerusalem and installed their Greek gods. This sparked the Maccabean revolt by the Jews in 164 B.C.E.

On the other hand, the official religion of Greece was one based in power struggles and domination in which the god Zeus established and maintained his supremacy through acts of cruelty and barbarism. Greek philosophy was based on the belief that humans are ruthless, grasping, and self-centered. The Greeks had a very strict class system which required force to uphold—a force the Greeks believed was natural and right. The most influential thinker of the time was Plato. His perfect society was one in which the strong dominated the weak, and it became the model for Greek culture.

Plato was a Greek philosopher who lived 400 years before Christ. His thinking greatly influenced both the Greek and Roman world at that time and for the next 1,500 years. The church reflected Plato's teachings in its own way. Plato believed that the

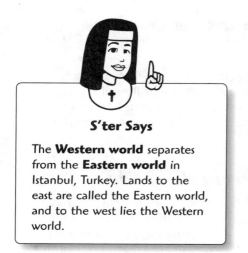

**S'ter Says**

The **Western world** separates from the **Eastern world** in Istanbul, Turkey. Lands to the east are called the Eastern world, and to the west lies the Western world.

human soul is eternal and that learning occurs when the soul remembers its former life. It then becomes one with the eternal perfect idea.

Plato believed God was the ideal form of Good and that the goal of humans was to become more like God. His ideal world was composed of incorruptible, perfect forms held as ideas. The physical world contrasted sharply and was considered inferior to his perfect world of ideas.

Plato's philosophy is dualistic in that it sharply divides reality into two separate parts: either mind or matter, rather both mind and matter. The shift in thinking from either/or to both that has occurred in more recent eras may seem like a small shift now, but it had major impact on the cultural development of the *Western world*.

This duality between the spiritual world and the physical world began to infiltrate the church right from the beginning. As Christianity moved out of the Jewish world into the Greek world, it met the dualistic mind. According to Plato's philosophy, to progress toward accomplishing union with God, we must move away from the imperfection of the material world of the physical body into the more perfect world of the mind. This philosophy put Christians at war with the physical body. Rather than being sacred in itself, the body was considered an impediment to the spiritual nature.

## Roman Power and Might

Although the Greeks certainly left a philosophical mark on the development of Western civilization, Rome ruled the world by the time of Christ. This was the world in which the church developed. "All roads lead to Rome" was a saying of the time. Roman roads flowed both ways. As people and goods flowed into Rome from elsewhere, Roman ideas and Roman soldiers traveled outward, influencing all areas of the known world. When you think about it, Catholicism spread largely because of the work of Roman road builders.

The Romans borrowed much from Greek culture. In addition, they developed technology, architecture, administration, trade, and law. This combination established the foundations of Western civilization. However, some of the destructive elements of Roman rule were found in its militaristic mentality. The Romans developed a competitive, patriarchal culture in which the greatest value was placed upon accomplishment in battle, physical strength, and fearlessness. In addition, self-denial and service to the state were ways to achieve excellence in this society.

The warrior aspect of the Roman world influenced the culture at the time of the early church in three main ways. First, Rome ruled by its undisputed power and might. What it decreed, became law. Second, Rome was able to back up its laws with the authority of its military. Finally, Rome had a hierarchical ranking system upon which all militaries are formed.

In its first 100 years, the new church struggled for survival in the midst of Roman chaos. As we shall see in Chapter 21, "Roman Establishment," when Catholicism became the religion in the Roman Empire, the church modeled itself on Greek ideas and the Roman sense of law.

The Church adapted a hierarchical and patriarchal ranking system for its clergy, placing them above the people they served. The top of the hierarchy was the Bishop of Rome, as Rome was the center of all things. Roman influences brought strength and unity to the newly developing church, and created problems as well.

Two major concepts that were woven into the Church in its early years are patriarchy and hierarchy. Patriarchy is a society led by older men having authority over members. Hierarchy describes a ranking system where a group of persons or things are arranged in order of rank, grade or class, and thus are accorded privilege.

Problems inherited from the patriarchal and hierarchical paradigm are the social, religious, and ecological forms of domination it created. This worldview supports and promotes the strong conquering the weak, the rich exploiting the poor, males ruling over females and children, and human society dominating the earth. It found racial expression in the dominance of light-skinned people over dark-skinned.

In the hierarchical worldview, each order has sovereignty over those below it. Power flows from the top down, exclusively. It can be compared to a communal worldview using a circle. The circle represents the Divine and contains all the other groups. The eight pieces of the pie represent each of the kingdoms: mineral, plant, animal, child, woman, man, saints, and angels. The circle worldview is relational, all the groups meet in the center. It is based in equality and shared power.

The hierarchical worldview is less relational as each individual kingdom only touches the one next to it. The early church formed in communities that are represented by the communal paradigm. As the church became increasingly influenced by Roman politics, its institution developed according to the hierarchical form.

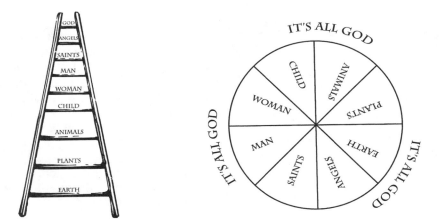

*The hierarchical and communal worldviews.*

(Bob O'Gorman and Mary Faulkner)

# Indigenous Peoples of Western Europe

Anyone who has family roots in central and western Europe probably shares a common heritage. Tribal people living on the edge of the Roman world existed more than 3,000 years ago across most of Europe. They were constantly being taken into the empire as it expanded into their lands. Many were captured and served as slaves, joining the households of their captors. Although the tribes were in no way unified, they shared similar beliefs, languages, and practices.

Each tribe was distinct from the others and had its own community identity and its own gods, laws, and customs. Unlike the Romans and the Greeks, these people had an integrated worldview. They did not separate religion from the activities of daily life, but they instead celebrated God's mystical presence in the natural world. The concept of the presence of God in daily life was a reality to them, because their gods and goddesses lived with them in nature.

What the indigenous people contributed to the early formation of the Catholic Church was a mystical understanding of the world in which logic and order did not always prevail. This understanding is the basis of a faith structure that believes in God's presence through his son, Jesus Christ. Such a belief defies science and cannot be thoroughly substantiated by history. In many ways, the Catholic Church, although it has a highly developed theological base, remains what is called a mystery religion. What is meant by that is that Catholics fully accept that many of their doctrines cannot be understood or accepted other than by faith.

# Cultural Influences

The influence of other traditions and cultures on the development of the early Catholic Church is outlined in the following chart.

| Cultural Influences | Time Span | Contributions |
|---|---|---|
| Judaism | 1800 B.C.E.–70 C.E. | Love of the law, patriarchal structure, monotheism, God present to his people, a rich written tradition in the Hebrew Scripture |
| Greek | 332 B.C.E.–141 C.E. | Love of thinking, dualism, hierarchical structure, a better world awaits us elsewhere, authority outside of self, a loss of intuitive knowing |
| Roman | 63 B.C.E.–600 C.E. | Authority, militaristic enforcement of the rules, hierarchical structure, ability to reach many people through Roman expansion |

| Cultural Influences | Time Span | Contributions |
|---|---|---|
| Indigenous tribes | 3000 B.C.E.–300 C.E. | Love and loyalty to leaders; mystery, myth, and symbol; real presence of God in the world; community; intuitive knowing |

Now that you understand the major points that surrounded the beginning of the Catholic Church, you're ready to see just how it developed into a major world religion. But first let's take a look at the source for Catholics' story of their religion: the Bible.

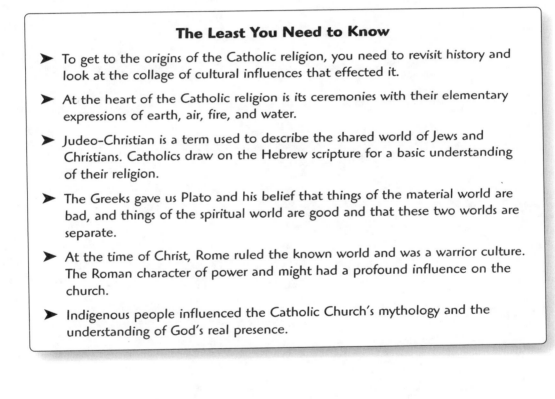

### The Least You Need to Know

➤ To get to the origins of the Catholic religion, you need to revisit history and look at the collage of cultural influences that effected it.

➤ At the heart of the Catholic religion is its ceremonies with their elementary expressions of earth, air, fire, and water.

➤ Judeo-Christian is a term used to describe the shared world of Jews and Christians. Catholics draw on the Hebrew scripture for a basic understanding of their religion.

➤ The Greeks gave us Plato and his belief that things of the material world are bad, and things of the spiritual world are good and that these two worlds are separate.

➤ At the time of Christ, Rome ruled the known world and was a warrior culture. The Roman character of power and might had a profound influence on the church.

➤ Indigenous people influenced the Catholic Church's mythology and the understanding of God's real presence.

# Chapter 7

# The Bible

---

### In This Chapter

➤ The Jewish people and Christians share a common scripture base

➤ The Old Testament had at least four different writers

➤ Four different communities wrote the Gospels

➤ Some books are sacred, and some are not

---

The last chapter explained how the stories of the Old Testament created the basis for Catholics' understanding of their relationship to God. This chapter provides a glimpse of how the Bible works as the storehouse of sacred information for the church. Who wrote the sacred texts? What were their reasons for writing them? How did the church decide on what would be included as sacred texts? To find out the answers to these questions, read on!

## Sacred Scriptures

The *Bible* is the sacred book or scriptures of Jews and Christians. The Bible as we know it today is divided into two parts. The first part, the Hebrew scriptures or the Old Testament, is the written record of the Jewish people from Abraham (1800 B.C.E.) until Maccabees (168 B.C.E.). The second part of the Christian Bible is the New Testament, which contains the life and work of Jesus, as well as the faith experience of the early Christians until about 100 C.E.

### S'ter Says

The word **Bible** is derived through Latin from the Greek *biblia,* or "books," the diminutive form of *byblos,* the word for "papyrus" or "paper," which was exported from the ancient Phoenician port city of Biblos.

### Your Guardian Angel

A good way to approach the Bible is to see it as a faith history. The stories teach how to handle life's experiences. The events in the Bible are the recorded wisdom of those who have gone before. Through these stories, experiences are kept alive, and important moments are preserved.

The word *testament* means agreement and refers to the belief that God, the creator of life, has initiated a personal relationship with his creatures. The Old Testament is the Christian name for the agreement God made with the Hebrew people that they would be his special people in whom he would reveal his love. Christians believe that in Jesus, God has revealed himself in a new way. They believe Jesus is both human (completely accessible to everyone) and divine (fully acting as God). They believe that what Jesus teaches about God and his care for humanity is a new testament. Catholics believe the Bible is the "word of God," inspired by the Holy Spirit and written by humans. They consider both testaments as one Bible, not two.

Like all good stories, the Bible has a plot. The basic plot revolves around God's love for the people and his willingness to be with them. It begins in Genesis with God speaking, "Let there be light." It ends in the book of Revelation with a prayer, "Come Lord Jesus!" In between, there is a constant dialogue between God and the people, rich stories, and an amazing cast of characters.

## The Old Testament

The Old Testament is an essential part of sacred scripture for Catholics, and they believe the books that comprise it are divinely inspired. The Old Testament is more than a book of history or culture. It is a book of religion: Israel's witness to its encounter with God and its faithful response to him. As the faith journey of the Jewish people, the Old Testament is a sacred history to both Jews and Christians. They turn to these stories for guidance in life's events. Ultimately, the stories disclose the meaning of human life. The 46 books of the Old Testament contain a wealth of teaching on God, as well as wisdom about the affairs of human life. They are a treasure house of prayers.

The Old Testament was formed gradually; its books were composed over many centuries. The *Pentateuch* is the first five books of the Old Testament: Genesis, Exodus, Leviticus, Numbers, and Deuteronomy. The Hebrew name for these five books is *Torah.* Torah is a difficult word to capture in translation, but a close meaning is law, and a better one might be "teaching." It contains the divine guidance given by God for the historical pilgrimage of the Jewish people. The teachings stand for all time. Most of all, Torah is an expression of God's care. It is summed up in the phrase: "I will be your God, and you will be my people." As such, then, the law of God is the Jews' expression of care and response.

Jewish, Protestant, and Catholic scholars agree that the books known as the Pentateuch are a composite of several sources. Nearly 200 years of study have determined four main literary strands, which are identified as follows:

> **S'ter Says**
>
> **Pentateuch** is a word based on a Greek term referring to "the book of the five scrolls (the *pentateuchos biblos*)," also known as the **Torah.** Moses commanded that the Torah be placed in the Ark of the Covenant. The book of Joshua and the Torah were placed in the ark, and these sacred books were kept there during the wilderness journey.

> A Judaean source, using the divine name Yahweh and written about 950 B.C.E.

> A North Israelite source that favors the use of the divine name Elohim and was written about 850 B.C.E.

> A source reflecting the style and theology of the period of Josiah's reform about 650 B.C.E. and later

> A source from the time of the Babylonian Exile, 550 B.C.E.

These different strands, each having a different perspective on the stories, were woven together in a final form that emerged in about 400 B.C.E. (For more information on the themes and stories referenced here, we suggest consulting a more detailed resource. See Appendix B, "Recommended Readings.") The Old Testament ends in what some have described as an incomplete drama. According to the beliefs of many Jewish people, it leads to the Talmud (the authoritative writings of Jewish tradition) and a continued wait for the messiah. According to the Christians, the story leads to Jesus Christ who came not to destroy, but to fulfill the law.

## The New Testament

The New Testament is the story of God's son Jesus Christ, his teachings, the story of his death and resurrection, and the church's first 100 years of life. Like the Old Testament, the New Testament also developed gradually. As Christian communities began to spread to other parts of the Roman Empire, specifically the lands around the Mediterranean basin, the followers of Jesus took with them their memories of their time with him. They had been firsthand witnesses to the events, and they taught others about Jesus' life and works from their experiences. However, they wrote none of it down. As the first witnesses were dying, it became apparent that someone had to record the information.

The first written material consisted of the letters written by Paul to the various faith communities; the early Christians circulated these letters. Paul was a convert to the new religion. He was the first missionary, founding churches all over the Mediterranean. He wrote letters to these communities offering guidance. These letters were written about 52 C.E. to 64 C.E. and are the earliest works of the New Testament. His letters, called *epistles*, offer valuable and practical instructions to the new church for living out Christ's teachings.

### Epiphanies

Paul's dramatic epiphany began on the road to Damascus where he was enroute to suppress a group of Jesus' followers. Before his conversion, Paul was called Saul and was a Roman soldier. He was struck by a light from heaven and knocked to the ground. Jesus spoke to him telling him: "I am Jesus, whom you are persecuting." Saul was blinded for three days until Ananias was sent by God to heal him. Ananias was told that "This man is my chosen instrument to carry my name before the Gentiles and their kings and before the people of Israel." (Acts 9:15) The scales fell from Paul's eyes, and he became one of the first missionaries of the church. He is known as the Apostle to the Gentiles.

Next came the Gospels, which are the books of Matthew, Mark, Luke, and John. The Gospels form the heart of the New Testament. Gospel is a word meaning "good news," and the Gospels of the Bible contain important stories of Jesus' life and teaching. Between the years 70 C.E. and 100 C.E., the community acknowledged four Gospels to be the most authentic because they appeared to be written by those who were most intimately connected with the apostles. Scholars believe they were developed in four major communities of the Christian world. Mark was written in Rome; Matthew in Jerusalem; Luke in Antioch; and John in Ephesus.

The communities that produced the New Testament material operated as writers and editors, and they were inspired in this regard. The roles of the writers (evangelists) were understood to be the following:

1. **Selectors.** From the many things Jesus did, they chose what they wanted to include and emphasize.

2. **Arrangers.** They organized the material in blocks, often by themes rather than chronologically.

3. **Shapers.** They adapted their sources and told the stories in ways that would emphasize what they wanted to stress.

4. **Theologians.** They reflected on the meaning and significance of the events in light of their belief in God and in Jesus.

### Saints Preserve Us

**St. Mark, April 25, Patron of Notaries**

St. Mark wrote his Gospel in Rome before the year 70. He wrote to the Gentiles in the Greek language. The story goes that the Romans asked Mark to write down the teachings of St. Peter. This story seems to be confirmed by Peter's prominence in this Gospel. Thus, this Gospel becomes the record of the life of Jesus as seen through the eyes of Peter.

Matthew, Mark, and Luke constitute the *Synoptic Gospels*. That means they are looking at the same events and describing them in similar ways. Scholars generally agree that all four gospels were written in Greek and drew on the stories that were being told about Jesus and his life.

John's Gospel reports several incidents not mentioned in the other stories. Likewise, some of the events mentioned in the Synoptic Gospels do not appear in John. He gives a different order to the events and gives different dates for the Last Supper and Crucifixion. It is generally believed that John's material was written after the Synoptic Gospels. He may or may not have been aware of them when he wrote.

### S'ter Says

**Synoptic** means seeing with one lens. Matthew, Mark, and Luke all give a common view of Jesus, and they are called the Synoptic Gospels. John has a different perspective.

All the Gospels differ from one another in terms of author, time of writing, audience, and purpose. Although each Gospel is a separate and unique portrait of Jesus, no one Gospel tells us everything we need to know about him. To gain a fuller understanding of Jesus, we must consider all four Gospels together.

Around 70 C.E., a companion of the apostle Peter named Mark, sometimes referred to as John Mark, probably wrote the Gospel attributed to Mark. It is the earliest Gospel. It's called "the Gospel of action" because Jesus is always on the move. It emphasizes the humanity and suffering of Jesus and portrays him as the unrecognized messiah. It was directed toward Gentile members of the church living in Rome.

95

**For Heaven's Sake!**

Don't make the mistake of thinking that the four evangelists—Matthew, Mark, Luke, and John— wrote all their own material. The Gospels were a composite of writings gathered by their respective communities.

A Gentile doctor around 85 C.E. possibly wrote Luke. This Gospel stresses the central role of the Holy Spirit in Jesus' life. It shows Jesus' compassion, mercy, and concern for sinners in the miracle stories. It is the first part of a two-part work; part two is the Acts of the Apostles (the story of the beginning of the church). It appears to have been written for Gentile Christians and perhaps for well-to-do ones, at that. Its message seems to be about the universality of Christianity. It shows women and poor people in important roles.

Matthew, written around 90 C.E. for Jews who were converting to Christianity, emphasizes Jesus as the fulfillment of promises made by God in the Hebrew scriptures. It demonstrates Jesus' role as a teacher and preacher and talks about the responsibilities of Jesus' followers.

John was probably written by followers of this beloved disciple of Jesus and was written around 95 C.E. It reflects theological sophistication and is considered to be more poetic and more spiritual in nature than the other accounts. It presents Jesus as "the Word of God" and highlights God's presence as flesh and blood with us—his incarnation. It urges the reader toward faith, emphasizing that faith comes from God and is most present when the believer is without visible evidence of God. John creates poetic and memorable images of Jesus such as the vine and the good shepherd.

**S'ter Says**

**Canon,** from the Greek *kanon,* means "a reed, a straight rod or bar, a measuring stick, or something serving to determine, rule, or measure." The word is used to designate those writings that came to be accepted as authentic Biblical texts.

# The Canon: How Are We Sure What Texts Are Sacred?

The canon of the Bible refers to the definitive list of the books that are considered to be divine revelation and are included in the text. Slightly different books were selected for the Catholic canon than for the Protestant canon. Catholics include 46 books in the Old Testament, and Protestants have 39. Both groups accept 27 books for the New Testament, for a total of 73 and 66 books, respectively.

How did the disciples' writings come together to form the New Testament canon, the collection of books that the church acknowledges as genuine and inspired Holy Scripture? The leaders, guided by the authority of the Spirit, determined which books God inspired. The actual canonization process took a long time. There were many questionable gospels and epistles circulating. Careful, prayerful, and deliberate examination proved which books were genuine and which were false. Pope Damasus at the Council of Rome in 382 listed the books of today's canon. At that time, the canon was closed, and no more books were entered. Here's what it includes:

### The Old Testament

➤ **The Pentateuch.** Genesis, Exodus, Leviticus, Numbers, and Deuteronomy

➤ **The historical books.** Joshua, Judges, Ruth, 1 and 2 Samuel, 1 and 2 Kings, 1 and 2 Chronicles, Ezra, Nehemiah, Tobit, Judith, Esther, and 1 and 2 Maccabees

➤ **The wisdom books.** Job, Psalms, Proverbs, Ecclesiastes, the Song of Songs, the Wisdom of Solomon, and Sirach (also called Ecclesiasticus)

➤ **The prophets.** Isaiah, Jeremiah, Lamentations, Baruch, Ezekiel, Daniel, Hosea, Joel, Amos, Obadiah, Jonah, Micah, Nahum, Habakkuk, Zephaniah, Haggai, Zachariah, and Malachi

**The New Testament** (in parentheses: total number of chapters/total number of verses for each book)

➤ **The Gospels** according to Matthew (28/1,071), Mark (16/678), Luke (24/1,151), and John (21/878)

➤ **The Acts of the Apostles** (28/1,008)

➤ **Thirteen letters attributed to Paul,** written to particular communities and individuals in the following cities: to the Romans (16/433), 1 (16/437) and 2 (13/257) Corinthians, Galatians (6/149), Ephesians (6/155), Philippians (4/104), Colossians (4/95), and 1 (5/89) and 2 (3/47) Thessalonians

➤ **Letters to individual Christian leaders** (the first three are called the Pastoral Letters): 1 (6/113) and 2 (4/83) Timothy, Titus (3/46), and Philemon (1/25)

➤ **One biblical sermon,** for which neither the author nor the audience is explicitly mentioned: Hebrews (13/303)

➤ **Seven epistles** that are attributed to early apostles and written to more general audiences: the Letter of James (5/108), Peter 1 (5/105) and 2 (3/61), John 1 (5/105), 2 (1/13), and 3 (1/14)

➤ **The Letter of Jude** (1/25)

➤ **The Apocalypse** in the Book of Revelation (22/404)

---

**For Heaven's Sake**

Follow the rules! The Bible says "God descended to the top of Mount Sinai and summoned Moses to come to the top of the mountain." (Exodus 19:20) There, God gave the Ten Commandments as well as other laws to help the people in their relationships to one another and to God. They form the basis of much of the Church teaching.

## Catholic Beliefs Regarding the Bible

Catholics hold these beliefs regarding the Bible:

- ➤ The Bible contains both the Hebrew Scriptures and the Christian Scriptures as one book.
- ➤ The sacred Scriptures are the inspired word of God. God is the author because he inspired their human authors.
- ➤ The Catholic Church accepts and venerates as inspired the 46 books of the Old Testament and the 27 books of the New Testament.
- ➤ The four Gospels occupy a central place in the Bible because Jesus Christ is their focus.
- ➤ The unity of the two testaments reveals the whole of God's plan.

There are no copies of the original Scriptures. The early manuscripts were written on scrolls and later copied by monks. When Latin became the commonly used language, the manuscripts were translated into Latin from Greek texts.

Since Vatican II, new translations of the Bible are available for Catholics, and Bible study is encouraged. New research continues to add to the body of knowledge around these sacred texts. Today, Bibles are composed by the collaboration of Jewish, Catholic, and Protestant scholars. Rather than a means of separation, the Bible has become an interfaith event.

## What Place Does the Bible Hold for Catholics?

Catholics constantly find nourishment and strength in the scriptures. The four Gospels hold a unique place in the church and are read each time that the Mass is offered.

The Catholic Church understands that in sacred scripture, God speaks in a human way. To interpret scripture correctly, you must listen for what the human authors wanted to say and what God wanted to reveal through their words. To do this you must know something about the culture, writing style, and times in which it was written.

The church distinguishes between two interpretations of scripture: literary and spiritual. The literary (or scholarly) meaning is discovered by following the rules of sound interpretation. The spiritual meaning comes through understanding the allegorical, moral, and symbolic levels of the scriptural stories.

The scriptures are understood to have parallel (allegorical) meanings: thus the crossing of the Red Sea could be a sign of Christ's victory and also of Christian baptism. They are also understood in the moral sense by leading us toward right action. Finally, the symbolic level reveals an ultimate spiritual or mystical meaning.

The Catholic Church teaches that interpreting scripture is ultimately up to the judgment of the church. It believes that it is the task of scripture scholars to work toward a better understanding and explanation of the meaning of sacred Scripture.

Now that you have a fairly basic understanding of the Bible as the faith source for Catholics, let's move on and meet the one from whom Catholicism truly emerged: Jesus.

### The Least You Need to Know

➤ The Old and New Testaments work together to create the Bible.

➤ The Bible was written over a long period of time and has many authors; it was inspired by the Holy Spirit and written by human hands.

➤ The four Gospels work together to give a complete picture of Jesus' life and work.

➤ At a certain point in time, the church decided which books were authentic and which were not and closed the canon.

➤ Catholics do not believe in simply a literal interpretation of the Bible.

# Chapter 8

# Birth and Spirit of a New Religion

As established and powerful as the Catholic Church may seem today, it had a rocky start, and its history is a long and fascinating one with lots of ups and downs. (You'll learn more about it in Part 6, "The Church's History.") This chapter focuses on Jesus and shows you how his message became a religion, how this religion became organized, and how it survived persecution. We will take you to the point where it became the established religion of and the key force in Western civilization.

## How We Know What We Know About Jesus

As you read in Chapter 7, "The Bible," followers of Jesus compiled the historical references to Jesus and his teachings, but these references weren't formally written down until a generation or two after his death. These written accounts were interpretations of the experiences his followers had of him and of his teachings.

### Your Guardian Angel

For many years, it was the custom to capitalize all pronouns that refer to Jesus: He, Him, His. One of the major developments of Vatican II was to emphasize the human side of Jesus. As a result, religious writers now generally use lowercase pronouns when referring to Jesus. The reasoning behind this is to recognize Jesus' likeness to us.

### For Heaven's Sake!

Don't judge a book by its cover. There was a saying in Jerusalem at the time of Jesus, "Can anything good come out of Galilee?" Jesus was more than something good; he was the son of God, and he was from Galilee.

Very few facts are known about the true history of Jesus. We know that someone like him lived and preached in Galilee, a region in northern Israel, and in Jerusalem. Someone like him was crucified in Jerusalem, probably on a combination of charges of blasphemy against the Jewish religious leaders and treason against the Roman authorities. The rest of what is known of him comes to us through the stories that his followers told about him and what they believed the stories to mean.

## The Wellspring of Galilee

Who was Jesus? Jesus was a Jewish preacher and teacher who lived and taught in Galilee. But "Jesus Christ" is more of a description than a name. Jesus is a Latin version of the Greek *Iesous,* itself a form of a Hebrew name, *Y'shua.* Christ is not a name, but a title. It comes from the Greek word, *Christos,* which in Hebrew means "the anointed one," translated from the Hebrew word *messiah.* Messiah is a term used to describe a figure of great importance chosen or "anointed" by God. As Jesus' name already shows, he lived in the Jewish, Greek, and Roman worlds.

Unlike Jerusalem, Galilee was not a particularly important cultural or religious center for the Jews. In fact, Jews who lived so far away from the temple in Jerusalem were thought to be ignorant and lax in religious matters. In the society of the time, the Gentiles scorned Jews, and even the Jews of Jerusalem scorned a Galilean Jew like Jesus.

Yet, in its own way, Galilee was a natural geographic region to spawn a new religion. It was a natural crossing place for international travel routes, and people of many nations gathered there: Phoenicians, Syrians, Arabs, Greeks, Asians, as well as Jews. These international contacts meant that ideas flowed in from the four corners of the known world. Its distance from Jerusalem, where the Jewish law and teachings prevailed, gave it a freedom of thought that would not have been available nearer the temple. Its people were relatively unschooled in Jewish law, but were ruled by common sense and wisdom. The people practiced a Jewish faith that was simpler and more spontaneous than the more conservative faith of the Jerusalem intelligentsia, and these qualities greatly influenced Jesus' teachings.

## Jesus the Jew

Jesus himself was a bit of a character. Growing up having contact with diverse people and cultures, he then invited diversity into his inner circle. He broke class and cultural rules, bringing fishermen, tax collectors, and women into his ranks.

But make no mistake: Jesus was born, lived, and died a Jew. His community, the Jews, related to God in two ways: in observing the law and in visiting the temple. Jesus and his followers came out of this intense experience of Judaism's personal and faithful relationship with God.

What did the people find so interesting about Jesus and his teachings? Jesus claimed to have a special experience of God, which he said he could share with everyone. This new level of relationship was captured in the very intimate way he addressed God as *Abba* ("my dear papa"). His relationship with God was simple and direct, and most important, it was available to all. The followers of Jesus saw themselves as the ones who shared this special intimacy or presence of God just as Jesus did.

The love of God that Jesus experienced was so compelling that he spent his whole life on earth bringing it to others in what he called the "reign of God." First, his preaching addressed the evils of his society: poverty, hunger, illness, and injustice. Second, he demonstrated a willingness to be with the people. He lived and walked among them. He didn't seem to require anything of them and spoke to them of how much they were loved by God. People began to take notice, and he acquired a band of loyal followers.

# The Key Stories of the Christians

All religions have their great stories. Chapter 6, "'It's Elementary, My Dear Watson,'" outlined several stories that were important to the Jews: Adam and Eve and the creation story, Abraham and the covenant, and Moses and the law. Christians, too, have their stories that reveal something special and deep in the recorded historical events. Christians have three great stories of Jesus: his birth, his death and resurrection, and his abiding presence in the community that lives after him.

## Jesus' Birthday: Christmas

The story goes that Jesus was born in Bethlehem of simple parents named Mary and Joseph, who were a young couple from Galilee. This story makes it clear right from its start that something very important was happening. The night Jesus was born, angels burst into song. Shepherds heard them and came to the place where the baby lay. They bowed, knowing instinctively that they were in the presence of a "great one." News of his birth traveled far and wide. Kings and wise men from distant lands saw a star in the Eastern sky, and they came in search of him.

Jesus' father, Joseph, made a living with his hands as a carpenter. We assume that Jesus grew up working in his father's shop. Jesus did not receive a formal education.

However, when he visited the temple in Jerusalem at the age of 12, the story says that he impressed the Jewish scholars with his knowledge and understanding of Jewish law. We don't hear much more about him until he began his public life of preaching at the age of 30. Most of the events of his public life took place in and around Galilee and on the road to Jerusalem. His life ended at the age of 33.

## His Mission, Death, and Resurrection

From the beginning of his public life, Jesus astonished all who came into contact with him. To the leaders of the Jews, he was an uneducated upstart, a hayseed from the boondocks of Galilee. Yet he astounded others with his knowledge and wisdom. His attitude of welcoming those people whom society had rejected challenged the convictions of the Jewish leaders of the time. The Jews had endured much and survived as a culture and religion by making sure they remained pure and true to the law. Jesus invited everyone into a relationship with God and opened his teachings to all who wanted them. He had a message of liberation, and he lived it in his attitude, which was friendly, unassuming, and caring.

### Epiphanies

Christmas takes its name from the central act of Catholic worship, the Mass. Christmas means "Christ's Mass," a ritual that celebrates his birth as a human. Most languages, except English, use a word signifying nativity or birthday of Christ to designate the feast of Christmas: in Latin, *Dies Natalis;* in Italian, *Il Natale;* and in French, *Noel.* Wherever you are and whatever language you speak, what is being celebrated is the birth of Christ. The way this event is commemorated and renewed is the Mass. Legend says that Christ was born moments past midnight on December 25, and Catholics celebrate this occasion by the tradition of midnight Mass.

The stories tell that he worked *miracles.* His first miracle occurred at a wedding feast in Cana where he turned jugs of water into wine to prevent the embarrassment of his host, who was running out of wine for the guests. His followers, some of them fishermen, tell that he had power to calm the sea, walk on water, and know where fisherman should place their nets in order to catch the most fish. It was reported that he turned a small amount of fish and bread into enough food to feed 5,000 people who had gathered to hear him speak. He cured others from physical illness, even bringing them back from the dead. After three years of preaching and teaching in Galilee, Jesus went from the outskirts of the Jewish world to Jerusalem.

Jerusalem was the symbol of established power for the Jews. Everything about it had religious significance. It was the holy city, the site of the temple, and the reference point of Jewish identity and belonging. It was also elitist and the center of the powers that oppressed and excluded many of its people. Jesus took his message, which attacked the very concept of elitism, to Jerusalem to confront the leaders of the establishment. With his simple philosophy and nonconformist actions, he forced their hand, and they played it. The authorities had him arrested, charging him with political sedition because he challenged the Romans' power, and religious blasphemy because he claimed he was the son of God. When he said this, he claimed that he had a special relationship with God—and that we all have this relationship, too. We are all sons and daughters of God.

### S'ter Says

A **miracle** is an event that breaks through the laws of nature. Miracles are extraordinary happenings that provide a glimpse of God at work.

### Epiphanies

Crucifixion was a method of capital punishment practiced by the Greeks and Romans in ancient times. It was used frequently in putting down Jewish opposition to the Roman conquest of Israel. The Romans used wooden beams crossed like a T. Typically the one to be executed was scourged (whipped) and required to carry the cross to the site of the execution. The prisoner was either nailed or tied to the cross. Death came by asphyxiation. Crucifixion was abolished when the Roman Empire became Catholic.

Jesus' trial was swift, and he was sentenced to die by a common method of Roman execution called crucifixion. Most of his followers abandoned him at the hour of his death; only a handful remained with him. After his death, his body was hidden in a cave. Three days later, when some women in his close circle came to anoint his body for burial, they found an empty tomb. An angel appeared to them and told them the Jesus had risen. During the next six weeks, there were a series of sightings of him, and then he was seen ascending into heaven. That was the end of the historical Jesus.

## Pentecost: The Birthday of the Church

Fifty days after Jesus' death, his followers gathered together in the room in which they used to meet with him for meals. Jesus had told them to wait there because he would send his spirit to be with them.

A sudden storm began to rattle the shutters on the windows, and it grew dark. The room began to glow. Tongues of fire appeared over each of their heads. The people in the room said they experienced an inspiration to go and proclaim all the things they had seen and heard. They reported feeling especially strong. Jerusalem was filled with thousands who were gathered there for religious ceremonies. To their amazement, they could understand the apostles, each in his own language.

### Epiphanies

Pentecost celebrates the descent of the Holy Spirit on the early church. *Penta* comes from the Greek word for 50 and refers to the fact that this event occurred on the fiftieth day after the Resurrection. In addition to the courage and ability to teach that the disciples received, it is also said that they received the gifts of the Spirit based on Isaiah 11:2: wisdom, understanding, knowledge, fortitude, counsel, piety, and fear of the Lord. The Spirit that descended is the same Spirit by which Jesus lived, the Spirit he promised to send after his death.

In a very bold action, Jesus' followers decided to tell the world their stories of him. Given that he was so recently put to death, telling these stories was a pretty risky thing to do. They began by saying that Jesus had risen from the dead and had walked among them and that he was the messiah, the son of God. The story says that 3,000 people were baptized as a conversion to Jesus' teaching. Jesus' followers were encouraged by this response and decided to gather together and actively pursue bringing Jesus' vision into being. As you shall soon see, although the followers had undergone a change, the society in which they began to preach had not.

Jesus Christ's followers came to believe he was both a human man and the divine son of God. They believed he fulfilled a promise God made to the Jewish people. They believed he was the messiah sent to help them and to fulfill the promise of the law. The followers believed he fulfilled the law in his teachings, which emphasized mercy and forgiveness.

Jesus' popular ministry, which challenged the accepted social and religious rules of the day, embraced sinners and social outcasts. His rather simple and straightforward message promoted love, tolerance, and belief in God. His core message seemed to be: "All people, especially the poor and rejected, are invited to come into the kingdom of my Father." This message, which was spiritual in nature and political in its effects, began to worry both the Jewish leaders and the Roman authorities.

In addition, Jesus' nontraditional teachings about equality revealed new insights into the understanding of God and what it meant to be a human. Almost all societies appear to have a way of accepting some people and rejecting others, thereby defining who will be the "in" group and who will be the "out" group. Most groups of people have classifications that determine who is a success and who is a failure, what it means to be good or bad, normal and abnormal. Jesus challenged many of the cultural assumptions of his day. His core message was one of unity. He taught that all are one in the Father.

# Was Jesus the First Catholic?

The big question you might be asking about Catholicism is: Was it really founded by Jesus? Like all big questions, there is no simple answer to this one. We can find clues by looking at what his followers said about these early years.

### Saints Preserve Us

**St. Mary Magdalene, July 22, Patron of Prostitutes**

St. Mary Magdalene was a close friend of Jesus from the town of Magdala in Galilee. She has often been confused with the woman who washed Jesus' feet and Mary the sister of Martha. She was devoted to Jesus during his public life, and was present at the foot of the cross when he died. It was she who anointed him for burial and to her that he first appeared as the resurrected Lord. He then gave her the command to go and tell the others. She has been called the "Apostle to the Apostles." Her feast day is July 22, and she is the patron of prostitutes, although there is no biblical references to her being one. Stories confusing Mary Magdalene with prostitution began in the fourth century, as her story became confused with the stories of other women.

On the surface, Jesus' ministry seemed to be a failure. He did not liberate the people from Roman oppression. Many of the people who had been part of his following lost interest and continued living their lives in very much the same way as they did before they knew him. A handful, however, were inspired to continue his work because they realized his teaching about the kingdom meant building the kingdom within and restoring human dignity. Jesus preached to the down and out, telling them they were God's sons and daughters. His followers banded together in small groups in order to keep his work and his memory alive. Nearly 2,000 years later, the work continues.

## The Core Beliefs

Here are Jesus' main ideas:

➤ The law of the Old Testament is based in forgiveness and love.

➤ The kingdom of God is within and accessible to the individual.

➤ Everyone can have a personal relationship with God.

➤ Social class, education, and economics have little to do with God's love.

Jesus' core message was and continues to be that God is available to everyone. Jesus' followers believed that the real presence of God they had experienced in Jesus continued after he was physically gone.

## The Calling

Jesus' followers did not immediately formalize a church. They lived in communities and met mostly in homes. They were simply called disciples at this time. Only later would they be called *Christians*. Their mission was to bring the "reign of God" to others the way that Jesus had brought it to them. Early writings use these terms in describing the followers: a household, a family, God's assembly, a new creation, and the body of Christ.

**S'ter Says**

It was in Damascus that the followers of Jesus were first called **Christians,** and it was used as a derogatory term. Christians didn't adapt the name until the next century.

You met Paul in the last chapter. An early convert and a leading missionary, Paul spread the teaching of Jesus throughout the Mediterranean world. He established communities from Syria to Turkey, Greece, and Rome. Paul's most lasting influence has been felt through his writings to the communities, which, as we have noted, were the earliest and most extensive writings in the New Testament.

The spiritual tasks the followers dedicated themselves to were celebrating, teaching, and serving:

➤ **Celebration.** Jesus celebrated his relationship with the Father. He did this as he gathered with the common people, sharing meals and enjoying camaraderie. His followers remembered how special these times were, and they wanted this memory to be a part of their communities.

➤ **Teaching.** Jesus taught who God is and how good and loving he is. Perhaps his teaching is best captured by the prayer he taught his followers: the "Our Father," which is also known as the Lord's Prayer:

> Our Father, who art in heaven,
> hallowed be thy name;
> thy kingdom come,
> thy will be done,
> on earth as it is in heaven.
> Give us this day our daily bread,
> and forgive us our trespasses,
> as we forgive those who trespass against us;
> and lead us not into temptation,
> but deliver us from evil. Amen.

Jesus declared that God was intimate and accessible to all. His followers gathered the memories of his teachings and passed them on.

➤ **Serving.** Jesus served the people, caring for their physical and spiritual needs. He healed the sick, cured the deaf and blind, and fed the hungry. His followers wanted to carry on these important ministries.

### Your Guardian Angel

Catholics end the Lord's prayer with the line "deliver us from evil." They don't say, "For Thine is the kingdom, the power and the glory for ever," as is the Protestant custom. So if you're attending a Catholic service, don't get confused by this.

At first, Jesus' followers believed that he would come back to take them to the Father if they just managed to hold on for a few years. During prayer services, there was a part of the ritual where one person would leave the congregation to look up in the clouds to see if he was coming. When the person reported that Jesus was not coming, the service would continue. Eventually, they came to understand that he was not coming back in the form they thought he would, but that he was with them in spirit always.

We can answer our opening question about whether Jesus founded the Catholic Church by saying there was no institutionalized Catholic Church at the time of Jesus or for many years after. The early followers of Jesus were considered to be members of a sect of Judaism. They said they had a new experience of God's presence unlike any before. Knowing Jesus was so powerful that they banded together to keep his presence alive. As they realized he would not return in their lifetime, they began to build an institution to hold his memory.

# Catholics Separate from the Jews

For many years, the Jewish people had offered resistance to the growing oppression of the Romans and had suffered much at their hands. In the year 70 C.E., the Romans crushed a Jewish rebellion, which resulted in the destruction of much of Jerusalem, including the temple.

During the next few years, Jewish leaders met to reorganize. Some of this reorganization included expelling sects of Judaism they identified as heretical. When the Jews tightened their ranks, Jesus' followers were closed out of the circle, which encouraged them to emerge with an identity and authority separate from Judaism. Outcasts already, the followers of Christ further split from the Jewish religion as a result of this series of events. From this time forward, the religions were separate.

## *The Martyrs*

In the beginning, few people converted to the new religion. Many came from the non-Jewish world. The new religion appealed largely to the urban poor, women, noncitizens, social outcasts, and slaves. The message was that they did not need money or education to belong to the kingdom. The idea that no man or woman could be a slave in God's world was appealing. They liked the idea of Jesus being a common man, a martyr with a message. They liked his promises of a better tomorrow and refuge from pain and suffering. The new, available God had infinitely more appeal than the distant gods of Greek and Roman mythology who gave the people no real guidance for morality. These early converts formed communities, giving whatever resources they had in exchange for security. The communities provided housing, food, and cared for the elderly and widows.

Roman authorities viewed the spread of Christianity as a threat to the state. More and more, the lines between the emperors and the gods they worshiped blurred. Roman leaders had begun to perceive themselves as divine and required homage to be paid them. Christians were becoming separatists, and more and more often and in greater numbers they refused to burn incense before the emperor's statue. Increasingly, Christians became the targets of mockery and violence.

Technically, Christianity was an outlawed religion, although the authorities didn't always enforce the law against it. However, whenever acts of civil disruption against the Romans erupted, regardless of who was

**S'ster Says**

**Gladiators** were slaves (including Christians) and prisoners of the Romans who were trained for the sport of hand-to-hand combat, as well as fighting wild beasts. The result of this combat was often death. **Martyrs** are people who are killed because of their religious beliefs. The church considers martyrdom to be the highest form of witness to the faith; therefore, martyrs go straight to heaven and become saints.

behind them, Christians were blamed, and punishment was severe. Christians were sometimes put into the arenas with *gladiators* or wild animals, which usually resulted in their martyrdom. Christians also suffered other forms of execution (crucifixion, for example). On and off, the early church endured 300 years of persecution.

Often Christians were offered a chance to recant, which meant they had to offer incense to the Roman gods. If they didn't, they were killed. Many opted to recant; however, many more chose death and became *martyrs*. They became the saints of the early church.

**For Heaven's Sake!**

Don't think that the candles on the altar are just for decoration! The church lights candles at every Mass, and it is the custom that a relic of the saints (a fragment of their bones) be contained in the altar as a reminder of the early martyrs.

The Greeks and Romans did not believe in burial and instead cremated their dead. Jews and Christians were allowed to bury their dead, but they had to do so outside of the city limits. Catacombs were built as cemeteries of the early Christians. They were extensive subterranean vaults and tunnels around Rome and other cities. Besides serving as places of burial, the catacombs became hiding places for Catholics fleeing persecution. Later catacombs were honored as shrines to the saints and martyrs.

Martyrdom for one's religious beliefs became an early part of Catholicism's identity. St. Stephen is believed to be the first martyr. Several of the 12 disciples closest to Christ were also put to death for their faith. The stories of the bravery of the early Christians nourished the young religion. Strangely, it became the source of many more conversions because people were curiously attracted to this new religion for which so many would willingly die.

## Designing the Structures

The next task that faced the developing church was to design a structure that would hold them together. The goals of the church founders were to carry on the work and keep the teachings consistent. Local communities gathered with other communities in the region under the guidance of leaders that they called *bishops*. The lines of authority and offices of leadership they established continue even today. The followers believed that Jesus had selected Peter to lead them. He went to Rome, where the church eventually established its center. His position as the bishop of Rome was later given the title pope. Catholics claim a direct line of succession of their leader, the pope, back to Peter.

Although the Roman Empire was still the controlling force as Catholicism started, its decline as a world power had begun. Many forces contributed to its decline: increased invasions by warring tribes, the outrageous cost of maintaining the military, and the growing decadence of the aristocrats. As taxes continued to increase alarmingly, more people grew disenchanted with the state and turned instead to religion. The church's more austere lifestyle and moral code was attractive by contrast, and the social services it offered were attractive as well. Christian communities offered care for widows and orphans, health care, and care for the elderly. As Rome declined, the church grew.

### Saints Preserve Us

**St. Stephen, December 26, Patron of Stonemasons**

St. Stephen, a disciple of Christ, was the first martyr. He was described as "full of grace and fortitude," and the effect of his work was great among the people. He was accused of blasphemy against Moses and against God and was brought before the authorities who condemned him to death by stoning. Kneeling down before his murderers, he cried out with a loud voice saying, "Lord do not lay this sin against them." He was stoned to death in 35 C.E. His feast day is December 26, and he is the patron of stonemasons.

## The Desert Fathers and Mothers

During these early years of the church's growth, a movement called the Desert Fathers and Mothers developed in the desert near Jerusalem. Rejecting everyday life with its many earthy and tedious concerns and distractions, and wanting to follow their new-found and deeply felt faith, many of the members of the new church established communities in the desert where they meditated and prayed.

### S'ter Says

**Bishop** is from the Greek word *episcopos* and means "overseer." A bishop is in charge of the church in a local area.

Anthony, the man who began this movement, lived in 251 C.E. and was the son of Christian parents. As a young man, the word of Christ inspired him to give away all of his possessions to the poor and go to the desert. He lived the life of a hermit for many years, devoting himself to prayer and meditation. He began to attract hundreds of followers whom he guided in their spiritual life.

With this movement, an important tradition of monasticism and the contemplative life began within the church. This tradition would grow and develop over the next centuries to become a strong core of Catholic life. Many of the early Christian thinkers who lived in these communities helped define and clarify church teachings. These writings are still a part of Catholic life. Their observations and writings were crucial to establishing the spirituality of the church.

The next chapter examines how the present-day church keeps the message of Jesus alive and how it keeps his spirit present through ceremonies, rituals, and celebrations.

### Epiphanies

One of the most famous of the early Christian writers is St. Jerome, who became a biblical scholar. He was educated in Rome and spoke both Greek and Hebrew. He worked with the scriptures to create as accurate a text as possible based on the original languages in which they were written. His Latin version of the Bible would be used for more than 1,000 years. He was named a "doctor of the church." Doctor is a title awarded by the church to someone who is found to be wise, holy, and learned and whose work can be counted on as a sound church teaching.

### The Least You Need to Know

➤ Jesus invited all to participate in "the reign of God."

➤ The followers of Jesus formed the church as a way of keeping his presence alive and bringing the reign of God to the people.

➤ The church began as a persecuted community.

➤ The contemplative tradition is integral to the foundation of the church.

# Part 3

# The Sensuous Side of Catholicism: How Catholics Experience God

*Catholics believe God is present in all things. Sacraments awaken sacramental memory, the presence of God deep within us. They mark significant events in the spiritual life, celebrating and connecting the one receiving the sacrament to God's presence in life's events: birthing, nourishing, sustaining, and bonding the community of his followers. Their purpose is to develop sacramental awareness by sharpening the ability to sense the presence of God everyday.*

*God's revelation is an inspiration, the spirit of God becoming available to humans. Jesus is the sacrament of God; the church is the sacrament of Jesus; and Mary is the people's sacrament. We'll learn all about these sacraments in the following chapter.*

# Chapter 9

# Tasting, Touching, Smelling God

---

**In This Chapter**

➤ How the senses are God's gateway

➤ How Catholics use their whole brain

➤ How Catholics differ from Protestants

➤ What is Catholic imagination?

---

The spiritual side of Catholicism does not begin with the rational mind. The faith of the Catholic is not something to be proven. It does not even ask, never mind answer, the question *why*.

Faith is an experience of religion. Through faith, Catholics open up to the transcendent. Rational explanations of faith follow, but never quite completely capture, the experience. Experiences continue to occur in the "real world," but rational explanations are often insufficient. Indeed, experiences are dynamic, and explanations are static.

The Catholic religion involves feeling, thinking, and being. It is first of all an experience. Then it becomes a thought (or a teaching or belief), and finally Catholicism becomes a response or action. Catholic ritual stimulates the imagination through the senses. Senses connect us to our feelings. The stimulation from imagination and feeling leads to spiritual insight. Insight is the voice of God. This chapter discusses this process.

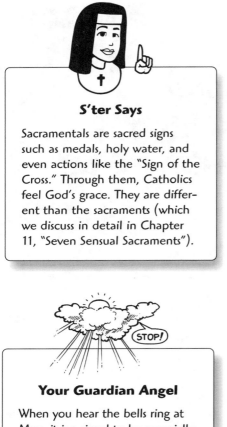

### S'ter Says

Sacramentals are sacred signs such as medals, holy water, and even actions like the "Sign of the Cross." Through them, Catholics feel God's grace. They are different than the sacraments (which we discuss in detail in Chapter 11, "Seven Sensual Sacraments").

### Your Guardian Angel

When you hear the bells ring at Mass, it is a signal to be especially attentive to a sacred moment. Bells are used to get your attention.

# A Full-Bodied Experience

How does an awareness of God come to Catholics? For most, it arrives through the senses, through touch, taste, smell, sight, and sound. The senses are God's gateway to the human mind and imagination. For this reason, Catholics emphasize ritual more than learning. If the imagination is not excited, the intellectual and philosophical underpinnings are meaningless. The bells, beads, and candles used in Catholic rituals are not just decorations; they are essential to spirituality and to effective Catholicism.

One of the strengths of the Catholic tradition is that Catholics are a people convinced that everyone is able to sense God. They can touch God, feel him, taste him, bring him inside themselves through the scent of incense, and see him in the colors of the vestment. Upon entering church, they dip their fingers in water. Incense at Mass fills the nostrils. The priest wears vestments of various colors: purple at Advent and Lent, white at funeral masses celebrating the Resurrection, Easter, and Christmastime, and green on all other Sundays. These vibrant colors touch the eyes. Catholics call these things—holy water, incense, rosaries, and vestments—*sacramentals* or little sacraments.

# The Bell: Call to Worship

The Catholic church fills with the sound of bells carried by the air. Bells call the faithful to worship. They get our attention. Bells awaken hearing and tune the ears for what God has to say. The ringing of bells has always marked Catholic experiences of worship. The church bells ring in the neighborhood to announce Mass. As the priest enters the sanctuary, another bell rings to signal his arrival; the congregation stands in reception. Altar servers ring bells to invite a sacred response at the moment the priest consecrates the bread and wine. Bells remind Catholics to pause and reflect on the great mysteries of God's presence.

In the early morning hours, as day breaks, the church bells ring the Angelus, a special prayer offered three times a day. The bells ring this prayer again at noon to mark midday and at six in the evening to signal the close of the day.

*The Angelus:*

> The angel of the Lord declared unto Mary.
> And she conceived of the Holy Spirit.
> Hail Mary.
> "Behold the handmaid of the Lord."
> "Be it done unto me according to your word."
> Hail Mary.
> And the word was made flesh.
> And dwelt among us.
> Hail Mary.
> Pray for us, holy mother of God.
> That we may become worthy of the promises of Christ.
> Let us pray:
> Lord, pour forth we beseech thee,
> thy grace unto our hearts
> that we, to whom the incarnation of Christ thy son
> was made known by the message of the angel,
> may be brought, by his passion and cross,
> to the glory of his resurrection
> through the same Christ our Lord. Amen.

The Angelus ends with a two- or three-minute full ringing of the bells.

In his painting entitled *The Angelus,* Jean Françis Millet depicts peasants pausing in the field and reflecting on the great mysteries of salvation and redemption (see the following figure). In the foreground, a man and woman stand praying in response to the ringing of the bells of the distant church. In the work, Millet portrays the peasant as one close to God. The abundant dirt is a reference to creation. He has blended the figures into a tone almost equal to that of the ground.

You'll also hear a bell tolled once every few seconds as a beloved parishioner is carried into the church for the last time. As the hearse pulls away, the bell tolls again. Bells carry the voice of God.

**For Heaven's Sake!**

Don't get caught without your rosary when you go to a Catholic wake. It's the custom to have a Rosary service the night before the funeral.

## Books and Beads: Touching the Word of God

When Catholics touch their rosaries, they touch their God. Beyond the specific prayers associated with the beads, the beads themselves transmit a spiritual meaning through touch.

119

*Jean François Millet,* The Angelus.

*(Courtesy Alinari/Art Resource, New York)*

Late one evening in his bed, an 82-year-old, lifelong Catholic suffered a sudden loss of breath and was unable to speak. His son arrived just as the paramedics responded to his wife's frantic 911 call. As his son accompanied him to the ambulance, his father expressed a great frustration, wanting the son to get him something but being unable to speak. Although his words were unintelligible, the son knew that his father expected him to understand what he wanted. Both of them became more and more agitated. Finally, when they got to the hospital and the father received enough oxygen to speak, he unleashed his great frustration by blurting out: "Get me my rosary, God damn it!"

The father wanted that rosary in his hand. He was a Catholic to the bone. Throughout his life he had partaken of the sacraments, said his Rosary, dipped his fingers in holy water each time he entered the church, and fervently walked to the altar to receive communion. Through his faithful practices God had become present to him. When he reached a moment of crisis, he wanted to reach out for God and he turned to what he knew and trusted: the Rosary. For Catholics, sacramentals make God present.

## Candle: The Fire of Change

Another important ingredient in Catholic ceremony is fire, which is why candles are a requirement for any Catholic Mass. On a weekday morning, there may be only two small candles burning, but on a big feast day, there might be as many as 12. The first thing Catholics see when they enter a church is the sanctuary lamp burning on the altar. A sanctuary lamp is a solemn tradition in the Catholic Church. Its eternal flame signals the sacramental presence of Jesus in the tabernacle, as shown in the following figure.

### Epiphanies

All of the candles used on the altar have to be at least 51 percent beeswax to represent purity and must be blessed by the priest in a ceremony. Candles for the church are solemnly blessed on February 2, known as Candlemas Day. Candlemas Day is also the feast of the Presentation of Jesus in the Temple 40 days after his birth, following the Jewish tradition. On this feast, candles are blessed and carried in procession with appropriate prayers and ceremonies.

Before leaving the church, most Catholics will probably place a few coins in a metal stand that holds 20 to 40 small candles, shown in the picture. They might then light a candle and say a prayer for a special intention or for a loved one. The candle burns for several hours as a reminder of the prayers being offered. It also tells God, "If I could stay longer, I would, but I have to go now, so I'll leave this little candle burning in my stead."

During the Easter vigil, the most dramatic moment occurs outdoors as the priest announces Christ has arisen while simultaneously lighting the Easter candle from a bonfire called the "new fire." The Easter candle is carried into a completely dark church, and the flame is passed candle by candle to all who have come to witness the risen Christ. In no time, the church is ablaze with new light.

Fire accompanies Catholics at the beginning of their church life and at the end. Throughout the year, baptismal candles are lit from the Easter candle. When a person dies, a vigil light, similar to the sanctuary lamp, is left burning beside the casket.

*Sanctuary lamp signaling the sacramental presence of Jesus in the tabernacle. Cathedral of the Incarnation, Nashville, Tennessee.*

*(Courtesy of H. L. [Dean] Caskey)*

*A stand of vigil light candles. Christ the King Catholic Church, Nashville, Tennessee.*

*(Courtesy of H. L. [Dean] Caskey)*

# The Left Brain/Right Brain of Catholics

One of the popular theories about how the human brain works postulates that we register experience in the right hemisphere while logical thinking takes place in the left hemisphere of the brain. From the beginning of Catholicism until the middle of the twentieth century, the religion has been very "right-brained." That is, it has been filled with ritual and ceremonies heavily packed with colors, sounds, smells, and movement. These rituals grew from Catholicism's tribal roots in central and northern Europe.

### Epiphanies

A priest lights the new fire with flint and steel before the celebration of the Easter Vigil Mass. This dramatic ceremony takes place after sundown on Holy Saturday. Everyone gathers outside the darkened church, and the fire is lit and blessed. From this fire, the Easter candle, representing the risen Christ, is carried into the church and from it the candles of all the faithful are lit, lighting up the church.

In addition to their tradition of ritual, however, Catholics are also known to be pretty "left-brained" as well, and they remain at the forefront of religious scholarship. There is no better an example of a product of the left brain of Catholicism than Thomas Aquinas and his rational treatise on the nature of God called the *Summa Theologiae*. Catholics base much of their theology on his employment of Greek philosophy.

### Your Guardian Angel

If you're looking for proof of the existence of God, consult the writings of Thomas Aquinas. His five proofs of God have fascinated believers and nonbelievers for centuries.

The *Summa Theologiae* is the premier work of Catholic theology. All major Catholic universities and seminaries teach it and theologians and philosophers of religion of all denominations study it. Of St. Thomas's many works, these five volumes present a systematic treatment of several hundred important theological questions, ranging from God, the Trinity, and the nature of Christ, to the nature and psychology of the human person and the nature and mission of the church.

Down through the ages, there are stories of people attracted to the thinking aspect of the Catholic brain, people who reasoned their way to God. An equal number of people were attracted to the feeling aspect of Catholicism; these people were poets and artists who embraced the mystery. Today's Catholicism enjoys a new synthesis of body and mind and intellect and sensuality when it comes to perceiving God.

A Catholic often lives a dual life: attending a church filled with exotic colors, overwhelming pageantry, and powerful incense while living in the workaday world of the mind. One of the major challenges Catholics face in contemporary cultures like the United States is how exclusively left-brained they are forced to become in modern society.

## The Sensate Stuff: Opening the Catholic Spirit

Imagine a Catholic boy when he has his first opportunity to serve the Christmas midnight Mass. He is 10 years old, in third grade. This is his first time staying up so late. His younger brother and sister are both at home in bed. He feels excited as he goes out in the chilly night air. The church is one block away, so he walks there alone. He has had a bath and is wearing a new, clean white shirt, black pants, and shined shoes. He has put a dash of cologne on. This night is special. He is about to engage in a ritual that will move him from the world of childhood toward the adult world.

As the boy approaches the church, cars are already packed in the lot. When he enters the sacristy, the anteroom to the sanctuary, he finds a bustling crowd of people: several servers, all older. Three priests are vesting and several people from the choir are putting on their choir robes. Flowers, freshly starched and ironed altar linens, and extra collection baskets brush by him carried by other helpers. The organ is playing carols.

**For Heaven's Sake!**

Don't be late for midnight Mass! Christmas brings many to church who are not regular attendees, so the church is usually crowded. If you don't want to stand for this long ceremony, plan on getting there at least a half an hour ahead of time.

The group is lined up to go out into the church. The priest calls the young lad up to the front of the procession and hands him the statue of the baby Jesus, wrapped in a white cloth. The door opens, and he leads the large group out into the church as the choir behind him begins to sing "Silent Night." This is a time for him to take in all the experiences he is seeing, hearing, smelling, and touching. Catholic experiences are being stored in his brain's memory. What is happening all around him becomes part of his psyche, experiences by which he will measure, for the rest of his life, what it means to be Catholic.

During events like these, something important has happened to you. You may not be able to put words to it yet, but the pomp and ceremony tells you something of significance has occurred. What's happened is a shift to a deeper state of consciousness. Ritual, ceremony, and routine stimulate your senses.

Catholics' relationship to God is physical, and they use the senses in their rituals to connect to sacred memories. For example, you might have good memories associated with your grandmother and the smell of apple pie baking in her kitchen. Now when you smell apple pie, you are connected to the emotions and feelings of love and safety you felt in her kitchen. Your whole body feels it. Through the smell of the apple pie, you have made the physical connection to her. Connections to loved ones can come from things you see that remind you of them, things you hear, or even through taste. It is through the senses that we make the connections—the connection is physical. Catholics connect to the sacred through the sense experiences of their rituals. Through them, they feel a physical connection to their God.

# God Whispers in the Ear

Ritual changes our consciousness and puts our brain in a dream-like state. This dream state is an important part of Catholic religious experience because God speaks to us through dreams. The Bible records several instances in which people heard God in their dreams. The challenge today, as always, is to know how to hear the voice of God. Catholic ritual is attuned to this dream communication.

Notable dream communication in the Bible includes the Genesis story of Joseph, Jacob's son, who dreamed that he would rule over his brothers (Genesis 37:5). The book of Matthew tells of the important dream of another Joseph that warns him of Herod's plot to kill all male babies after the birth of Jesus (Matthew 2:13). The Bible is full of important dreams.

**Your Guardian Angel**

Dreams can be an important part of your spiritual life. Throughout religious history, God has spoken to people through their dreams. Today people often share their dreams with a spiritual counselor for insight.

Following ritual, a deepening and a quieting takes place. Inner awareness increases. In this quiet space within, we can hear the voice of God. It comes as an insight, an inspiration, a desire, a "knowing." For example, in such a time, you might suddenly think a-bout a phone call you need to make to a sick friend. This thought is how God might direct you to perform a simple activity.

# Follow Your Conscience

The ultimate purpose of religion for Catholics is love. Catholics believe God's will calls them to respond to the world and the inhabitants of the world with love. Catholicism by nature is relational.

Making a decision is not simply a rational act for Catholics. It has an emotional impact as well. When the feeling side of the brain is left out of decisions, empathy (love of others) and instinct (God's voice within) are lost. If you cannot feel your inborn sense of right and wrong, your conscience is impaired.

Catholics do have codes of behavior, such as the Ten Commandments and the teachings of the church, to inform them. But the key to conscience is to match intuitive knowing with what we have learned, which is why the church has always said the bottom line in making a moral decision is "to follow your conscience." In order to do this, you have to be able to access the part of the mind where feelings reside. Again, Catholicism's high degree of ritual and ceremony makes this access easier.

### Saints Preserve Us

**St. Peter, June 29, Patron of Fishermen and Watchmakers**

St. Peter, the patron saint of fishermen and watchmakers, was a fisherman of Galilee named Simon who gave up his family and possessions to follow Christ. Christ changed his name to Peter, which means "rock," and made him the "rock" on which his church was to be built. Catholics recognize him as the first pope of the new church. Peter was known for his humanness: his anger, his imperfect faith, his impetuosity. When Jesus was arrested and the soldiers asked Peter if he knew him, he denied it three times. Under Nero's reign in the year 67, he was crucified with his head downward, at his request, because he said he was not worthy to die as did his Divine Master.

### S'ter Says

**Transcendence** describes the belief that God exists at a higher plane, such as heaven. God is beyond humans' ability to perceive. **Immanance** describes the belief that God exists throughout all of creation and that humans can experience God's presence on earth.

# Now You See Him, Now You Don't: How God Is Present

Every religion has to wrestle with just how present God is to his creatures. The classical terms used to talk about this issue are *transcendence* and *immanance*. Transcendence refers to how far away God is from his creation. Immanance refers to how close God is to his creation. All the classical religions have basic positions on this issue. Christianity goes further than any religion with its insistence on Jesus as both human and divine. Within Christianity itself, Protestants, the name that describes other denominations within Christianity, and Catholics can be characterized by their different emphasis on God's closeness to creation. Part 6, "The Church's History," contains an extensive explanation of the differences between Catholics and Protestants.

# Protestants Worship from the Neck Up/Catholics Do It from the Neck Down

Do Catholics have a particular kind of religious sensibility? That is, is there a particular way Catholics access God that contrasts to the way or ways of other religions?

This question is not asking which way is better, only whether there are different and distinctive ways of relating to God. Specifically, do Catholics have a different style of Christianity than Protestants do?

Generally speaking, you could say that Catholicism is more right-brained than Protestantism is. This right-brainedness shows up in some very concrete ways. If you walk into most Protestant churches and look at the center of attention you will notice a cross. In a Catholic church, your eyes will focus on the crucifix, as shown in this picture. A cross is a crucifix without Christ's body. The difference is the Catholic sacramental character. The Catholic experience of God is first a sensual connection to him as close, actually within creation. Second is his transcendent or heavenly nature. When you contemplate the cross, you think about the crucifixion. As you contemplate a crucifix, you feel the crucifixion by your emotional reaction.

*The Cathedral of the Incarnation, Nashville, Tennessee.*

*(Courtesy of H. L. [Dean] Caskey)*

Perhaps the best example of the vitality of Catholic imagery is the Catholic veneration of Mary, which may well be the place where Protestants and Catholics differ most. Through Mary, Catholics experience the female face of God. She is a mother, loving, relational, and most of all, flesh and blood. So when you enter a Catholic church and see Jesus hanging on the cross, you have a powerful sensual stimulus, a feeling that brings a reaction. This is Mary's child, our brother. This is a real person, not just an idea of God. For Catholics, the world is a sign (a sacrament) of God. God is in the world and is accessible to us through it. Protestants are concerned about idolatry, superstition, and magic, a real fear of identifying God too closely with nature. Thus, they emphasize God's otherness or difference from the world.

## The Hound of Heaven

Another difference between Protestants and Catholics is captured in what is called in theology the "Protestant Principle." This refers to the Protestant insistence that when you talk about God you first say what God is not. Protestant writings emphasize how God is different from objects, events, experiences, and persons in the natural world. The "Catholic Principle," however, is one of analogy. When Catholics talk about God, they are more likely to do it by saying how God is like objects, events, experiences, and persons in the natural world. A famous poem for Catholics is Francis Thompson's "The Hound of Heaven." In this poem, the author declares without any qualification: God is the hound of heaven chasing you down the paths of life until you are his. Protestantism originated in the age of the printing press, and it tends to use words and concepts as the first language describing God; image is the first language of Catholics.

### Epiphanies

The magical term *hocus-pocus* comes from the most sacred moment in Catholic ritual: the consecration of the bread as the body of Christ by speaking the words "This is my Body," which in Latin is *Hoc est Enim Corpus Meum.*

## God's Constant Comment: Catholics' Cup of Tea

Catholic sacraments, ritual, and ceremony build what is called a Catholic imagination. Religious imagination is the quality of viewing the events of your life through a religious or spiritual lens. A well-developed religious imagination is a way of perceiving and thinking about the world as God's realm.

How do we know someone? We know him through our senses. We see him, hear him, smell him, and touch him. We feel what it is like to be near him. Senses are physical evidence that something is present, and senses are how the Catholic knows God. Catholics activate the senses through ritual and ceremony and create a dialogue with God that happens at the physical level. They feel God's presence; therefore, God is present. In other words, the more a Catholic's senses are awakened, the more contact she has with God, and that contact equals spirituality. Spirituality, for Catholics, is about developing increasing awareness.

We have taken a look at how Catholics use ritual to feel God's presence and next we will see how Jesus is the ultimate sense experience of God.

---

## The Least You Need to Know

➤ Catholics use their senses to connect to God.

➤ Ritual is particularly important in the Catholic religion.

➤ Ritual connects Catholics to an inner voice and calls them to a moral response.

➤ Catholics emphasize God's presence in creation.

➤ Catholics use analogy to talk about God.

# Chapter 10

# Jesus: The Original Sacrament

> ## In This Chapter
>
> ➤ The mysterious and untouchable God
>
> ➤ The available and touchable Jesus
>
> ➤ The explanation of sacraments
>
> ➤ The church as a presence of Jesus
>
> ➤ The presence of God in all things

A song in the early 1960s titled "What's It All About, Alfie?" could be the motto for all of us as we struggle to know life's meaning. We wonder how much we really know about the people and events in our lives. We constantly strive to know what is real only to find out there is more than we thought. We conclude everything has a greater dimension than what we can imagine. Why can't we take it all in? Why can't we know what it's all about? The answer is because we can only know through what we taste, touch, hear, smell, and see. We can get in touch with "what it's all about" only through our senses, and the senses take in the surface, not the inner hidden dimension. Creation has two dimensions: the visible and the hidden.

The Catholic Church began with a new experience of God that came through sensual contact with the man called Jesus. He brought a different experience of God, an extremely intimate one. He talked to him like a parent and called him *Abba,* meaning papa. He taught that we could be intimate with God, too.

The early Catholic community understood Jesus as the flesh-and-blood connection with a mysterious, elusive God. Jesus' surface dimension of flesh and blood revealed

### S'ter Says

A **sacrament** has three parts: an oath or promise, a mark or symbol, and a mystery. Sacrament originally meant mystery, a sense of something hidden. Later, in Roman times, it was translated as the word for the oath a soldier took when entering the military. He was marked or branded with the symbol of the person he was to serve.

the inner and hidden dimensions of God's presence. For Catholics, Jesus is "the sacrament of God." A sacrament is Catholics' connection to the hidden dimension of creation. Jesus is the sacrament of God, and the church defines itself as the sacrament of Jesus. We focus on this idea in this chapter.

# Just What Is a Sacrament?

The Catholic Church uses the word *sacrament* in many ways, which can cause some confusion to those unfamiliar with the religion. For instance, the church refers to Jesus as the "sacrament of God," and it calls the church "the sacrament of Jesus." It specifies seven rituals as sacraments, the principal one of which is holy communion. The church often refers to holy communion as "the sacrament." Finally, the church describes things such as rosaries, statues, holy water, candles, and incense as sacramentals or little sacraments.

## Getting from Here to There

In a sacrament, three elements are present. Specific words are said, promises are made, and a mark or symbol such as water, oil, bread, or wine is used. The third part, the symbol, is the mystery of the sacrament, the sense of the hidden dimension and its unknowable quality. Sacraments function at the symbolic level. The word *symbol* comes from the Greek noun *symbolon,* which means "pulling together." Symbols bridge the gulf between the concrete experience and the meaning, which goes beyond the experience. In a sacrament, the mark or symbol makes a physical connection between the person and the spiritual meaning of the event.

As symbols, sacraments are mediators connecting the visible to the invisible and the exterior to the interior dimensions of reality. Jesus is the mediator who connects human beings to God. The church is the body that mediates or connects us to Jesus. The sacraments are the way these connections are made in the church.

## Jesus, God's Sensible Side

Before Jesus, God was untouchable. His name could not be spoken. The Hebrews refrained from saying the name of God. They referred to God as Yahweh, literally, "I am who am," which is not a name but a description. Catholics understand Jesus as the one who came in flesh and blood to close the gap between heaven and earth. His physical presence confirmed God's physical connection to the people. Jesus is the word of God, existing in human form. Through his birth, Jesus became God's gift of himself. Jesus is the touchable reminder of God's constant presence in the world and is God's very real connection to the human story.

Catholics believe that Jesus put a whole new spin on God. He did this through his actions and his teachings. He changed the social boundaries, and thus altered the way people lived together. He invited women into his close circle. He hung out with the "wrong crowd": the poor, the uneducated; and others who more traditional religious leaders did not consider qualified to understand religious matters. He taught his followers that the presence of God is within each person. His message was that God is not separate from his creation and that his creatures should not be separate from each other.

### Your Guardian Angel

Get out and help others. To be a Catholic is to reach out to others who are in need. A Catholic cannot ignore or refuse this mission and stay true to the teachings of Jesus.

Catholics believe not just that Jesus was a historical figure, but that his message about God lives on. Catholics believe that the connection Jesus made between God and the people lives in the church's sacraments and rituals, and through them, God is made more present and touchable.

## The Church, Jesus' Sensible Side

When the resurrected Jesus appeared to his followers after his death, he appeared in a transformed state, a spirit, yet apparent to them. They could see him, hear him, and even touch him. After he did this, he imparted his Holy Spirit to be in the hearts and minds of the community he had gathered. This community of followers became the church. Catholics believe that the church (the followers of Jesus) became the "body" that would now contain his spirit. They call themselves the new body of Christ. When the church gathers, especially to share the ritual meal of bread and wine as they once did with Jesus, the spirit of God is present.

### Epiphanies

The Holy Grail is the cup from which Christ drank with his disciples at the Last Supper. It passed into possession of Joseph of Arimathea, and he gathered the precious blood of Jesus when his body was taken from the cross. Romantic legend says that it came to England, and it was the task of the knights of King Arthur to find it.

# Wonder Bread

A central Bible story for the church is Jesus' last meal with his friends in Jerusalem the night before he died. In an upper room, where they had gathered to celebrate the Passover, he took bread, blessed it, broke it, shared it with them, and said, "This is my body." He did the same with a cup of wine. Since that day, Catholics have continually repeated this action with the belief that God becomes real through the ritual eating and drinking of bread and wine. For Catholics, this body of Jesus is literally his true body and blood under the appearance of bread and wine.

In Jesus' culture, a shared meal was a sign of a community's true intimacy. It was based in peace, trust, and nurturing. During the Last Supper, Jesus connected God's gift of nourishment, in the form of bread and wine, with his own body and blood. In light of his death that soon followed, he speaks of himself as a sacrifice. The Latin word for sacrifice is "to make holy." He is bringing to a closure his time on earth. He is allowing his followers to continue to share in the intimacy they have had together and the intimacy with God that he has brought to them. He does this by instructing them to continue the ritual meal in his memory. As he breaks the bread, so his body will be broken. As the wine is poured out, his blood will be spilled. As he connected his physical suffering to the touchable elements of bread and wine, he created a sacrament.

**Your Guardian Angel**

At a Catholic Mass, communion is offered as both bread and wine. However, it is not necessary to partake of the wine in order to experience the full sacrament of the Eucharist.

## The Church as Sacrament

The experience of the Last Supper was so powerful for the apostles that it etched itself into their memory. The repeating of the ritual further inscribed it. Each time the ritual is enacted, the memory of it is experienced again. As the ritual continues over the years, it makes God present for future generations.

The ritual sharing of bread and wine is called the sacrament of the Eucharist. It celebrates the intimacy between the church and Christ and the communion within the church, as well. The Last Supper became the ritual the disciples did together at meals after the resurrection following Jesus' request: "Do this in remembrance of me." The Catholic Church becomes a sacrament as it continues to enact this ritual.

# The Kingdom of God Is Within

We are spiritual beings in human form. We are spiritual along with all the rest of God's creation. Religion is not about becoming more spiritual, but rather it is about becoming more aware of your spiritual nature. Jesus made this point the central teaching of his Gospel when he said, "The kingdom of God is within." The mission, should we choose to accept it, is to become more aware of human's divine nature and to lovingly embrace the human form in which it is expressed. This is called sacramental awareness.

As a person becomes increasingly aware of the sacredness of all creation, her or his imagined separation between the self and God disappears. One is acutely aware of the interconnectedness of all life and the hidden presence of God in all things. The church would say that a person with this awareness becomes a living sacrament.

For Catholics, the major point of Jesus Christ's incarnation was not to see him as different from them, but to recognize his likeness in themselves and others. As the God who took human form to be with the people, he shows them that they have a divine nature, too. Going against the dualism of the time in which he lived and even of our time today, Jesus demonstrates that the sacred and the worldly are not separate and that God exists in all life forms.

## Ignatius Loyola's Spiritual Exercises: A Journey into Sensual Imagination

Spiritual exercise has a long history in church tradition. It refers to a disciplined and systematic approach to spiritual development. It was found in the desert traditions, the monasteries, and the cloistered life of the Middle Ages. Such practice is a vital part of Catholic life today.

The key phrase for the spiritual exercises of St. Ignatius of Loyola is "allowing the creator to deal with the creature." St. Ignatius set the traditional form of these exercises in 1556, and they are more popular than ever with modern Catholics and others.

The participants in these spiritual exercises attend a retreat center away from their homes and observe silence for four weeks, sometimes less. The intention of these retreats is to break "inordinate attachments" so that decisions will be clear and unencumbered. Under the leadership of a *spiritual director*, participants are led through meditations and encouraged to "play" with God and Jesus through their imagination. The leader takes the participants on an inner journey of imagination by using Biblical stories.

**S'ter Says**

A **spiritual director** is person trained to work with people spiritually, much like a psychologist works with someone emotionally. Spiritual directors work with individuals and with groups of people in retreats. There is additional training for those who lead the spiritual exercises of St. Ignatius Loyola.

If you were looking for an answer to a question in your life, for instance, you would take this question with you into a spiritual journey and ask Jesus for advice. In your meditation, you might walk with Jesus on the road to Emmaus. The leader would ask you questions like: What does the countryside look like to you? What is the temperature there? What does the road feel like to your feet? What are you wearing? What colors do you see? Who, besides Jesus, is there with you? What does it feel like to be there with Jesus?

## Saints Preserve Us

### St. Ignatius of Loyola, July 31, Patron of Retreats

St. Ignatius of Loyola, patron saint of retreats, was born in 1491 in Spain. After having painful surgery performed on his legs, he began reading devotional books. In a radical transformation, he dedicated himself to Christ. A depression drove him inward where he began to develop his spiritual awareness. He formulated his process into the spiritual exercises that bear his name and are still practiced today. He founded the Jesuit order, and his feast day is July 31.

As the senses are engaged by the questions, your imagination is activated, and you go deeper into your inner world. You are directed to imagine asking Jesus for his advice on the situation you are struggling with and to imagine Jesus' response. Through this process, you are able to encounter the divine spirit within you and receive deep spiritual insight.

St. Ignatius believed that God speaks to us through our imagination. The leader, acting as a guide, does not give advice, but helps direct people into their inner worlds, where the spirit of God resides and the answers can be found.

In this chapter, we have looked at how God is present to Catholics through Jesus, whom the church calls the "sacrament of God." In the next chapter, we will get into the specific occasions in the life of Catholics when they experience God in a very special way. The church has designated these occasions as sacraments.

## The Least You Need to Know

➤ Jesus came to connect creation more fully with the Creator.

➤ Sacraments are symbols that connect the visible and invisible dimensions.

➤ The church understands itself as a sacrament.

➤ Jesus' presence in the world reminds us of the sacredness of all life.

# Chapter 11

# Seven Sensual Sacraments

The seven sacraments form the framework of Catholic life. Catholic children learn them like the days of the week. Sacraments mark key transitions in life, bringing spiritual meaning and power to the individual. The life of the Catholic community is lived through the sacraments; they bind Catholics together.

As we discussed in Chapter 10, "Jesus: The Original Sacrament," sacraments are at the heart of the Catholic religion. They are physical as well as spiritual. Each sacrament has specific form: it uses certain words, is accompanied by a prescribed action, and involves the symbolic application of an element. (Sacraments use the physical elements of fire, water, oil, bread, and wine to effect spiritual meaning.) Catholics celebrate seven significant spiritual events that are divided into three groups.

The first group of sacraments is the sacraments of initiation:

➤ Baptism
➤ Confirmation
➤ Holy Eucharist

The second group is called sacraments of state of life:

➤ Marriage

➤ Holy Orders

The third group is called sacraments of healing:

➤ Reconciliation

➤ Anointing of the Sick

This chapter examines these sacraments and explains what roles they play in Catholic life and faith.

# Baptism: More Than Just Water on the Head

Along with confirmation and Eucharist, baptism is one of the three sacraments of initiation, and it starts a Catholic on the faith journey. Baptism is a naming ceremony. A Catholic tradition is to name the child after one of the saints. Baptism also introduces Catholics to the community with whom they will live and grow spiritually. With the sacrament of baptism, the Catholic community commits to be the baptized person's guide and companion on the journey.

**S'ter Says**

The **baptismal font** is a large container of water often made of marble and placed at the entrance of the church. At it, the priest or deacon pours the water that is used in the baptism of the candidate entering the church. In some churches there is a pool of water for immersion.

## *Water on the Head*

At an infant baptism, you will see a young couple presenting their new baby at the *baptismal font,* along with several family members, members of the parish, and the priest. After addressing a greeting to the people, the priest turns to the infant and signs her with the cross in what Catholics call the imprint of Christ. The priest reads a text of scripture proclaiming the word of God. He anoints the child's forehead, lips, throat, and chest with holy oil as a protection from spiritual harm.

The priest then blesses the baptismal water. The climatic moment comes when he pours the water over the child's head. He does this in three distinct gestures while saying the words, "Mary (the child's name), I baptize you in the name of the Father, and of the Son, and of the Holy Spirit." Next the priest takes perfumed oil to anoint the child as a sign of the enlightenment of the Holy Spirit.

The godparents hold the child's special candle, lit from the Easter candle on the main altar of the church. Godparents are friends or relatives of the one to be baptized.

They are chosen to sponsor the new candidate as he or she enters the church. In the case of infant baptism, they speak for the child. They profess the faith for the child by responding to a litany of beliefs and reciting the prayer of Jesus, the Our Father. With a solemn blessing, the priest concludes the ritual and congratulates the parents.

*Baptismal font and pool. Here you see a baptismal font in the foreground. Behind it is a shallow pool for immersion. Notice the Easter candle. Cathedral of the Incarnation, Nashville, Tennessee.*

*(Courtesy of H. L. [Dean] Caskey)*

An important element in the sacrament of baptism is water: the priest either pours water over the forehead of the person, or the person is immersed in a pool. Water signifies the medium of birth, the sea that God breathes over and from which all life arises, and it is seawater that surrounds the child in the mother's womb. God brings forth living things from the sea in creation.

The anointing with sweet-smelling oil signifies the wisdom that comes from being part of the community that professes Jesus as Lord.

## Who Can Baptize?

Although a priest or deacon usually performs baptism ceremonies at the church, anyone can baptize in an emergency situation. Any person (Catholic or not) can pour the water and say the words. The only requirement is to follow the wishes of the person you are baptizing. The church recognizes the baptism of Christians from other denominations as valid and would not rebaptize such a convert. Virtually all Christian religions baptize in a very similar way.

### Saints Preserve Us

**St. John the Baptist, June 24, Patron of Blacksmiths**

St. John the Baptist's feast day is one of the oldest feasts in the church. He was the son of Zechariah and Elizabeth, a cousin of the Blessed Virgin Mary. An angel announced that many would rejoice in his birth. John began his mission on the banks of the river Jordan, preparing the way and announcing the coming of the Redeemer. On the eve of St. John's day, "St. John's fires" were lighted on the hills and mountains in many countries. The tradition continues today. John, the patron saint of blacksmiths, was beheaded. His death occurred about a year before the death of Jesus.

### Your Guardian Angel

When you attend a baptism, know that you are there to offer your support in developing the child's spiritual growth. This could mean your presence at meaningful times in the child's life, sending a card on the anniversary of the baptism, and being available to the child for guidance.

The church teaches that children who die before baptism are in God's loving care. Previously it taught that babies who died before being baptized went to "Limbo." This was a "happy resting place," but not heaven. Now the church is much clearer on how baptism of infants is a baptism based on the intention of the parents.

## How Do You Assist at a Baptism?

If you're invited to a baptism but are unfamiliar with Catholic ritual, accept the invitation and let yourself be dazzled by all the ceremony. You'll see the child dressed in white, the name bestowed, the candle lit, promises made, and the child anointed with oil. This is a sensuous ceremony. Pay more attention to the actions than what is being said, and you will more fully experience this ritual. Thirty years ago, this ceremony was conducted in Latin and hardly anyone present except the priest followed the words. The event was understood by the symbols more than by words.

## The Origins of Baptism

The prototype of this rite of initiation occurred when John the Baptist baptized Jesus in the waters of the river Jordan. According to the Bible, the heavens opened, and those who were present saw the spirit of God descending like a dove upon Jesus. A voice from the heavens announced, "This is my beloved son with whom I am well pleased." (Matthew 3:16–17) This event teaches two important points: first, the Holy Spirit is present at baptism; and second, baptism recognizes the person being baptized as a child of God.

St. Paul understood baptism as a drowning or a death and rebirth as a new being. Catholics believe that baptism washes away all sins.

### Epiphanies

Catholics recognize three types of baptism. The most common is baptism by water. The Catholic Church also recognizes baptism by blood and baptism by desire. Baptism by blood would occur if a person were martyred for their faith without having been officially baptized. Similarly, baptism by desire happens if someone dies during the instruction process before the ceremony takes place, or if the person has a desire to be baptized but has not had an opportunity.

In the first centuries of the church, adult baptism was the common form of the rite. Joining a new community that wasn't Roman, Greek, or Jewish meant a radical change in one's life. As the religion became part of the Roman Empire, both the numbers of people who were becoming Christian and the way whole pagan tribes converted caused a decline in emphasis on instruction. In a few generations, infant baptism became the norm.

Faith continues to grow after baptism. Catholics who attend Mass at Easter renew their baptismal promises.

# Confirmation: It's No Longer a Slap on the Face

A typical memory of growing up Catholic several decades ago is being 12 years old and standing before the bishop, trembling with fear and awaiting the slap on the face that went with confirmation. Although the slap was merely a token touch, it signified that the person was now an adult facing life's challenges. Taking the slap was the sign that the young Catholic was ready and willing to stand up to the spiritual challenges he or she would face in life.

Although the ritual slap on the face is no longer part of the sacrament, confirmation increases and deepens the process begun at baptism and brings spiritual strength. Because many Catholics received baptism as infants, confirmation is the time when they make a conscious choice to accept the faith of the Catholic Church. In addition to furthering the commitment, confirmation strengthens the bond between the individual and the community. During confirmation, a person is awakened to the presence of the Holy Spirit and is further united with Christ.

**Your Guardian Angel**

If you're invited to a confirmation celebration, it is customary to give the guest of honor a small gift. (May we suggest a copy of *The Complete Idiot's Guide to Understanding Catholicism?*)

## Oil and Words

The rite of confirmation takes place as the candidate makes a conscious choice to accept his or her faith. It gives the candidate the ability to be Christ's presence and to bring this presence to others. The confirmation rite confirms that the spirit of God is awakened and lives within the candidate.

The candidate must be of age to understand what he or she is committing to. In order to be confirmed, candidates must have studied the religion and developed a sense of belonging to the church and to the community. Often candidates will display this sense of belonging by taking part in a service project, such as working for a community agency such as Habitat for Humanity or Meals on Wheels. In addition, the candidate chooses a sponsor to help prepare him or her, as well as to provide lifelong guidance. Often, one of the baptismal godparents plays this role.

The confirmation ceremony is almost as mystical and solemn as the sacrament of Baptism. There are two essentials of the ceremony:

1. The renewal of baptismal promises
2. The profession of faith by the candidates

The ones to be confirmed stand in front of the congregation, and the bishop, who usually administers the sacrament, extends his hands over the group and says a prayer. Since the time of the apostles, the extending of the bishop's hands over the group has signified awakening of the Holy Spirit.

Each of those being confirmed chooses a name that will be added to his or her baptismal name. The bishop says the new name as he anoints the forehead of each candidate with chrism (holy oil), followed by a laying on of hands, saying the words, "Be sealed with the gift of the Holy Spirit." The oil the bishop uses represents abundance and joy. Being sealed with oil means to be marked as belonging to Christ. It signifies the one receiving the seal is committing to align his or her will to the will of God. The very name *Christian* means anointed, and this is why the confirmation rite is essentially an oil rite rather than a water rite like baptism. To conclude the rite, the bishop offers the sign of peace, which is a handshake, affirming union with the community.

## The Seven Gifts

Catholics believe that confirmation awakens certain spiritual attributes called the seven gifts of the Holy Spirit:

➤ Wisdom

➤ Understanding

➤ Right judgment

➤ Courage

➤ Knowledge

➤ Reverence

➤ Fear (awe) of the Lord

**Your Guardian Angel**

Don't be fearful when you hear the phrase "fear of the Lord!" This gift of the Holy Spirit refers to the Old Testament idea of trembling in awe or wonder in the presence of God. Thus, its deep meaning is reverence for God, not being fearful of God.

Confirmation strengthens the will and aligns it with the will of God. It calls the person to "right" action and gives him or her the means to discern what is proper action. Catholics believe that all members are called to share in the priesthood of Christ in that they will be called to publicly and officially profess and mediate the faith of the Catholic Church at times in their lives. Confirmation is the sacrament that opens this "priestly" function.

**Epiphanies**

Confirmation corresponds to the appearance of the Holy Spirit to the apostles on Pentecost. In the first centuries, when baptism was generally administered to adults, confirmation accompanied it. This is still the case when an adult is brought into the church today. Eventually, as the practice of infant baptism grew, the time between the two sacraments lengthened to include the age of discernment, and it became the tradition of the bishop to administer it.

# Eucharist: It's More Than Just a Bite of Bread

The Catholic Church uses the term Eucharist in two ways: to describe the celebration of the Mass and to define the sacrament of the Eucharist, also called Holy Communion. In this section, we are going to talk about it as the sacrament.

**143**

### S'ter Says

**Eucharistic ministers** are un-ordained parishioners chosen by the parish to assist the priest in the distribution of the elements (bread and wine) at communion time during the Mass. Prior to Vatican II, no one but an or-dained person could touch the host (the consecrated bread and wine).

Holy Communion is a ritual enactment of the Last Supper, during which Christ promised his ongoing presence to his disciples. During their last meal to-gether, he blessed bread and wine saying, "This is my body. This is my blood. Do this in memory of me." The priest repeats these same words as he consecrates the bread and wine.

Typically, Catholics receive the sacrament of the Eucharist for the first time at about the age of seven at the rite called the First Holy Communion. The ritual then becomes central to Catholic spiritual life. Unlike the first two sacraments, Baptism and Confirmation, which are received only once, Catholics receive the Eucharist at every Mass.

If you were to go to a First Communion celebration, in some churches you would see little girls in white dresses, shoulder length veils, white stockings, and white shoes. The boys would be wearing white suits, white shirts, and white ties. They might enter the church in a procession, sitting in the first several pews in front. This exciting time in the Catholic child's life is like being invited to sit at the grown-ups' table at Thanksgiving or Christmas. The children are being included in one of the most central rites of the Catholic Church, Communion. A child's First Communion celebration is often held on Mother's Day.

Holy Communion is offered at every Mass. Specially prepared bread and real wine are used. After the priest speaks the words of consecration, the bread and wine, now trans-formed into the body and blood of Christ, are given to the people. Along with the priest, *Eucharistic ministers* assist in the distribution of the sacrament. Catholics come forward and are offered both the Communion bread and wine. It is customary to return to your place and kneel, and then meditate or offer prayers of thanksgiving until the rite is com-pleted. For the sick and homebound, the priest or other Eucharistic minister will bring Communion to the home or hospital where a prayer is said and thanksgiving is shared.

## Eucharist: A Catholic's Thanksgiving

Eucharist is a term that means thanksgiving. It described the Hebrew practice of giv-ing thanks during a meal for God's creation, redemption, and sanctification. In addi-tion, for Catholics, Eucharist is a symbol of God's nurturing care. Jesus offers life to the people in the form of bread and wine. Catholics believe in the presence of Jesus Christ in the form of the bread and wine, which is consumed during the sacrament of the Eucharist. For them, it is the way Christ remains present and accessible to his church.

Preparation for First Communion centers on teachings about Jesus' Last Supper. Because the new communicant will also be receiving the sacrament of Reconciliation (confession) before Communion, preparation for the First Communion includes instruction about confession, too. (Shortly we will be discussing confession in detail.) This is the time in a child's life when he or she will begin to assume moral responsibility.

Catholics are encouraged to receive communion every time they attend the Mass, but they must receive it at least once a year. It is reserved for people who are in full relationship with the Catholic Church. Usually, if you are a guest at a Catholic Mass, you do not partake of the Eucharist.

## Food for the Road

United with Christ in the Eucharist, the congregation is united with each other, becoming one body. Because it is both physical and spiritual food, communion serves as a reminder of the practice of charity toward others less fortunate, teaching compassion for the poor.

**For Heaven's Sake!**

Don't eat breakfast just before you go to Mass! Out of respect for the sacrament, Catholics refrain from eating or drinking anything but water for an hour before receiving Communion. Before Vatican II, Catholics were not supposed to eat or drink from midnight until they received the Eucharist.

## Menagé à Trois: It's More Than Just Two in a Marriage

In a Catholic marriage, three parties are involved: the husband, the wife, and Jesus Christ. Not only is marriage a lasting relationship between partners, it is also a loving covenant, based on the covenant relationship between God and his people. Thoughtful preparation and prayer precede the marriage vows, and for Catholics, marriage is for life, with very few exceptions.

## I Do! I Do!

A Catholic marriage usually takes place during a special "Nuptial Mass." Often, you will find liturgy books in the seats that will help you follow the service. The wedding party enters the church in a ceremonial way, taking places in the front of the church near the altar. The celebration of the Mass begins, and the exchange of vows begins. Prayers and scripture readings for the service have been selected in advance by the couple.

The exchange of consent between the spouses is the indispensable element of the sacrament of Marriage. Consent consists of the vocal statement by which the parties mutually agree to give themselves to each other: "I take you to be my wife." "I take you to be my husband." This consent is fulfilled in the two becoming one flesh. The priest or deacon receives the consent of the spouses in the name of the church and

**Your Guardian Angel**

Check your Sunday bulletin for Wedding Banns! Catholic parishes announce the forthcoming weddings of their parishioners in what are called the "Wedding Banns." These are usually published in the Sunday bulletin.

**For Heaven's Sake!**

Look before you leap! Marriage is a lifelong partnership commitment, based in love, for the well-being of the spouses and for the purpose of having and nurturing children. It is absolutely dependent on the free consent of the couple.

gives the blessing of the church. The Best Man and Maid of Honor represent the connection of this marriage to the church community.

A covenant, like a marriage, is more than a civil agreement; it is also religious in nature, and religious covenants cannot be broken. Catholics believe that God enters into the covenant relationship with the couple, which means they will be given the spiritual support and insight to maintain the marriage as long as they keep the covenant. In other words, God gives the couple a spiritual guarantee to stay present to them and to help them grow individually and together over their lifetimes.

## A Covenant Relationship

A Catholic marriage is a covenant relationship with God. The couple partners with God in creation; this means one of the prime intentions of marriage is to have children. The marriage bond is a spiritual partnership agreement, established by God himself. It requires the free consent of the couple, which is sealed by God. Unlike the other six sacraments, the bride and groom are the primary ministers of the rite, and the priest or deacon is a witness of the church. In other words, the couple does the marrying. A Catholic bride and groom entering into a sacramental marriage proclaim their love for one another as Christ loves the church.

Catholic marriage involves a wholeness of experience. The body, mind, and soul of the couple come together as one. It is a joining of the spirit and will with feeling and passion.

## Forever Is a Long Time

A Catholic marriage cannot be dissolved. Because consent is key, there is a mandatory preparation for marriage known as the Pre-Cana sessions. These group sessions, typically six in number, include prayers and possibly a retreat weekend in which the religious and spiritual aspects of the marriage relationship are addressed. The sessions are practical as well. They include communication skills, finances, and lectures about human sexuality and health issues. Although the parish priest coordinates these sessions, parish laypersons facilitate them.

In the case of mixed marriages, where one party is Catholic and the other is not, further instruction and preparation is required. The purpose is to find helpful ways in which the couple can fully express their love and faith so that unity can be established.

Divorce is the civil dissolution of a marriage. The church does not recognize divorce between two baptized people of any denomination. It recognizes separation: in cases where it is impossible for a couple to live in harmony, the church permits a physical separation. However, the man and woman involved are never free to contract a new union.

Again, the key element in the sacrament is consent. If for any reason it can be shown that this consent was given under constraint, the marriage would not be valid. Should the parties contest the validity of consent, the church could declare that the marriage is null, which means the marriage was never valid. The process of annulment is lengthy. It is handled in a church court.

## Marriage: The Two Ends

From the beginning, the core of the church was the "domestic church." That is to say that the church was largely made up of believers who were part of a household. Generally, people did not convert to the new religion as individuals, but did so as whole families. Vatican Council II restated the expression "the domestic church" and applied it to the Catholic family. It is in the family that the faith is first taught to children, and marriage represents the first school of Christian life.

### Saints Preserve Us

**St. Elizabeth of Portugal, July 4, Patron of Marital Problems**

St. Elizabeth of Portugal (1271–1336) is invoked against marital problems because she had a reputation around town for interceding as peacemaker in many marriages. After the death of her husband, Elizabeth joined a convent of the Sisters of St. Claire, which she had founded.

From the time of Augustine up until Vatican II, church teachings specifically stated: "the primary end of marriage is the procreation and nurture of children; its secondary end has to do with sexual satisfaction." Vatican II again restated both of these principles and added a new dimension to the teaching by stating there was to be no hierarchy of the goals implied. This means having children and sexual enjoyment together constitute the primary intention of marriage.

# Holy Orders: It's More Than Just Oil on the Fingers

Holy Orders is a sacrament by which a man commits his entire life to serve the faith community and in so doing becomes a symbol of God's presence. With this commitment, the church grants him the responsibility and power to offer Mass, forgive sins, give blessings, administer other sacraments, and attend to the spiritual life of the people he serves.

Vatican II stated that all Catholics share in the priesthood of God. At the same time, it recognized that ordained persons must meet certain obligations of service of a higher degree than those who are not ordained. Two primary responsibilities are interwoven in the history of ordination. First, the priest takes care of the spiritual needs of the people. Second, he cares for the institutional church, meaning its rules and regulations.

Although Holy Orders is a "one-time only" sacrament, it is received in levels as three separate ordinations, from deacon to priest to bishop:

➤ **Deacons** are assistants to the bishop and usually work in charities in parishes they are assigned. They perform a number of sacramental ministries, especially marriage and baptism.

➤ **Priests** celebrate the Eucharist. They are appointed as the pastors of parishes.

➤ **Bishops** celebrate the sacrament of ordination and appoint priests and deacons to parishes. They are in charge of the parishes that make up a diocese.

In the early centuries, there were only bishops. These leaders carried out both the day-to-day pastoral ministry to the faithful as well as any institutional responsibilities. The bishops were assisted by two groups, a council of advisors (presbyters, later called priests) and assistants in the liturgy and works of charity (deacons). Eventually, the presbyters did more and more of the hands-on leadership, and the bishops confined themselves increasingly to administration. The Church recognized Holy Orders as a sacrament in the 1100s. Since Vatican II, the Catholic Church has clarified that this sacrament covers all three levels: bishops, priesthood, and the diaconate.

## The Ceremony

Bishops are the only ministers of the sacrament of ordination. Catholics trace *ordination* in an unbroken line back to the apostles. This line is called *apostolic succession*. Three bishops are required at the ordination of a new bishop. One officiates, and the other two are witnesses.

### Epiphanies

There are two types of deacons. Prior to Vatican II, ordination as a deacon was only a stepping stone on the way to priesthood. A man would be ordained deacon about six months before he was to be ordained priest. Today that step continues for those going on to priesthood; however, the church has restored the "permanent diaconate" of the early church as an order of leadership and service in its own right. Presently, the church requires that only men can be ordained deacons. They can be married; although should their spouse die, they may not remarry. They must be 35 years of age or older.

The ritual of Holy Orders for all three levels follows essentially the same form. A bishop administers them during a special Mass whose readings are focused on ministerial leadership. It's performed on Sunday in a cathedral in the diocese with as many of the faithful taking part as is possible.

The rites begin with a presentation of the candidates and the calling forth of those who will be ordained. There is "instruction" by the bishop, who tells them what is expected of them as they receive this office. He then asks a series of questions to examine the adequacy of the person seeking ordination. The questioning is symbolic, because the preparation for this sacrament has been extensive. A litany of the saints is recited, followed by the bishop laying his hands on those to be ordained. This is the visible sign of this sacrament.

Those being ordained as bishop are anointed with holy oil, given the book of the Gospels, a ring, a special hat (called a miter), and a staff (called a crosier). Priests are presented with a paten, which is a gold plate on which the communion bread is placed during the Mass, and a chalice, which is the container for the communion wine. Their fingers are anointed with holy oil because they will be handling the consecrated host. Deacons receive a book of the Gospels.

## A Few Good Men

The common phrase describing a man's decision to enter the priesthood is *vocation;* the word is from the Latin and means calling, which signifies that God is the one who calls. The first quality of the priest is his openness and ability to listen to God's will or "call." Because priesthood is a service to the church, its demands are high. It requires special qualities in the character of the one being called, including holiness, closeness to God, and selflessness.

**Your Guardian Angel**

If you or someone you love feels "a calling" to enter the priesthood, you should first speak to a priest about it; he will give you further information on how to proceed.

Celibacy is mandatory for priests and bishops. Being celibate means you cannot get married or have sexual relations. Celibacy was instituted gradually over the first millennium. There is an exception to this rule in the Eastern Rite for priests. In addition, married clergy from other denominations who seek Catholic ordination can be accepted as married priests and remain married. Deacons also can be married.

Ordination is considered for life, so there is a long process of discernment before one is admitted into the final stages of the process. The process of making a decision is mutual: personal willingness and assessment of fitness by church officials. It can take as long as four or five years of seminary training after college. A seminary is a graduate school that has two purposes: one is academic training, and the other is spiritual formation of the candidate. Not only must a man demonstrate his intellectual ability, but he must also show his spirituality and willingness to serve.

The church restricts ordination to men, although women also feel the call to public service in the church just as men do. A woman can take many different routes toward church service or ministry. Traditionally women have joined religious orders and through them have served as teachers and health care workers. Because this process is not ordination, we will discuss it in Chapter 20, "The Church: Moving from Steeple to People."

# Penance: It's More Than Just a Kick in the Pants

Many Catholics can remember weekly Saturday afternoon trips to the church for the act of confession. Imagine a summer day in 1955. You and your friends are in the heat of a ball game as your mother's voice rings out across the field reminding you that it was time for confession. You splash water over your head, run a comb through your hair, and set out. As you open the huge front door of the church, the cool air combines with the darkness inside, bringing you quickly into a sense of quiet—perhaps a troubling quiet. The task you now face is to kneel down and recall the events during the last week in which you sinned against God or otherwise failed to do his will. You enter the confessional box and say, "Bless me father, for I have sinned …" You whisper your sins and conclude with the Act of Contrition. You receive the gentle admonitions of the parish priest, along with your penance, several prayers: Hail Marys, Our Fathers, and Glory Bes. The priest releases you, guilt-free, to go back to your ball game and "sin no more!"

An Act of Contrition is a Catholic prayer said at the time of confession, at the time of death as well as an evening prayer. Here is an Act of Contrition prayer:

O my God,
I am heartily sorry for having offended thee,
and I detest all my sins because of thy just punishments,
but most of all because they offend thee, my God,
who art all-good and deserving of all my love.
I firmly resolve,
with the help of thy grace,
to sin no more and to avoid the near occasions of sin.

For years, Catholics observed this weekly rite of examining their conscience, sorting out greater and lesser sins, and entering the confessional box to anonymously whisper them to the priest who sat on the other side of a tiny screen door. Today most Catholics do not observe the weekly rite of confession. However, this sacrament remains an important part of church practice. This section looks at the practice today.

## Confession Is Good for the Soul

Reconciliation was once called "confession" or "penance." There are two parts to the sacrament: the confessing of your sins and forgiveness by the priest in Christ's name. The person going to confession does the following:

➤ Tells his or her *sins* to the priest

➤ Expresses true sorrow

➤ Makes a firm commitment to change his or her behavior

➤ Prays the act of contrition

➤ Performs the penance given

In turn, the priest does the following:

➤ Extends the forgiveness of Christ through the church

➤ Determines the reparation or penance

> **S'ter Says**
>
> **Sin** is a thought or an action that is contrary to the will of God. If left unchecked, it creates a pattern of problematic behaviors. The sacrament of reconciliation helps uncover the pattern and correct it.

Mortal sin is a consistent and pervasive action and fundamental negative disposition to God's will. Mortal sin carries serious consequences. Venial sins concern lesser offenses and carry lesser consequences. Reconciliation means "to go with again;" it heals the brokeness of sin. The concepts of sin and forgiveness will be discussed in greater detail in Chapter 19, "The Teachings of the Church: More Than Just the Party Line."

# Examination of Conscience

The examination of conscience, during which a person reviews his or her sins before confessing to the priest, has several levels. At one level, one goes through the commandments, making a mental list of his or her failures or sins. In a more comprehensive approach, one goes to a deeper level, asking questions such as the following:

➤ How could I have responded (in a given situation) in a more loving way?

➤ What habit or tendency do I have that needs to be changed?

➤ Where have I contributed to problems in my world?

➤ Where am I having problems in my spiritual life?

➤ Where do I need healing?

Examining their consciences in this way helps Catholics become aware of their need for God's grace by identifying thought patterns or behaviors that limit spiritual growth.

**Your Guardian Angel**

Give face-to-face confession a try. Many people who have experienced it have said that it made the act of confession more personable and less fearful. They described it as being like baring your soul to a good friend.

# The Little Black Box

Even to Catholics, the rite of confession seems mysterious and strange. It begins with a greeting by the priest, followed by the confessor uttering, "Bless me father for I have sinned. It has been (how long) since my last confession." Then the person tells his or her sins and the priest asks questions to help the person clarify the sins.

After the person reveals his or her sins, the priest then asks whether the person, also known as the penitent, is sorry. The penitent says the Act of Contrition. The priest gives a penance, says, "Your sins are forgiven. Go now and sin no more," and gives his blessing. To be forgiven by God, the penitent must perform the penance and make a firm commitment to change.

In the past, it was common to receive this sacrament in the confessional box, as shown in the illustration of a traditional confessional. The priest sat in the middle of three stalls. There was a small, screened sliding door on each side, opening to the other stalls. When the penitent on the right was confessing, the other door was closed so that others could not hear. There were no lights, conversation was whispered, and there was a sense of anonymity.

Today, Catholics have the option of face-to-face confession in a reconciliation room. In this style, a person sits down with the priest and confesses in a more conversational and interactive manner.

In addition to private confession, parishes hold communal penance services to emphasize the corporate nature of sin. The emphasis in communal services is to make clear the social consequences of all sin. In such a service, there are biblical readings and reflections about the correct Catholic response to social issues. Such a service concludes with the opportunity for individuals to go to confession privately.

*A traditional confessional. Christ the King Catholic Church, Nashville, Tennessee.*

*(Courtesy of H. L. [Dean] Caskey)*

## The Sacramental Seal

Reconciliation celebrates forgiveness and the healing action of Christ. Through it, sinners are reconciled with God and with their community. Reconciliation develops introspection and moral responsibility. The Catholic Church teaches that an individual is responsible for their actions from the age of discernment, which is some time between the ages of 7 to 12, as the child develops a sense of right and wrong. From this age onward, Catholics must receive the sacrament of Eucharist and reconciliation, if necessary, at least once a year. The church teaches that all sins are forgivable. The priest is bound under a severe penalty to keep absolute secrecy regarding what he hears in the confessional. This rule has no exception and is called the *sacramental seal.*

### For Heaven's Sake!

Remember, you won't be forgiven if you aren't really sorry, if you don't do your penance, and if you don't have an honest intention to make a really big effort not to do it again!

## Guilt: The Gift You Leave Behind

The sacrament of reconciliation recognizes that sins create a block between a Catholic and God. The effect of reconciliation is to restore the person to God's intimate friendship. It is usually followed by a sense of peace and serenity, a strengthening of the spirit, and joy. Forgiveness absolves guilt. The penitent goes forward, unencumbered by the past, and participates more fully in Catholic life.

*A contemporary confessional with the option of face-to-face confession, shown by the two chairs or traditional confession with the screen. The Cathedral of the Incarnation, Nashville, Tennessee.*

*(Courtesy of H. L. [Dean] Caskey)*

**Epiphanies**

If you think saying a few Hail Marys is a difficult price to pay for sin, consider that in the early days sin often resulted in excommunication from the community. Forgiveness depended on penance done in public, which included wearing a sack cloth and ashes, followed by absolution by the bishop. Around the year 700, penance took the form of private confession.

Sin damages relationships within the community. No sin is entirely private—it affects others. It's not just the penitent who is affected by the sacrament, but also the sense of community and trust within the church.

# Anointing of the Sick: More Than a Simple Good-Bye

Before Vatican II, this sacrament of anointing the sick was commonly referred to as "the Last Rites." Many a story has been told of a Catholic waking up from a deep sleep during a serious illness only to find a priest administering the Last Rites.

Because the Last Rites was the spiritual equivalent of calling 911, or worse, such a sight told the follower that he might not recover! You can imagine the effect this might have had. Even today, chaplains report that when they go to visit a sick Catholic, they are often greeted by, "You don't need to visit me today; I'm feeling just fine!"

The Last Rites was a popularized name for the three sacraments given to a person in danger of death, those seriously ill, or the frail and elderly. The Last Rites comprise the three sacraments of Reconciliation, Holy Eucharist, and the Anointing of the Sick. The old name for this sacrament was *Extreme Unction*. It was generally administered only at the point of death. The new name, Anointing of the Sick, makes it clear that this sacrament is about healing.

The old rules tended to reserve this sacrament for Catholics who were at the point of death, and it would be administered only once. Under the reformed rite, use has grown to include it as a healing aid for those who are seriously ill, and the elderly and frail. It can now be received more than one time. It offers God's healing to those with serious physical illness and those in need of inner healing. Nowadays, it might be offered to Catholics who are victims of substance addiction and emotional or mental illnesses. Catholics also can receive anointing before undergoing serious surgery.

The priest lays hands on the sick and prays silently over them. He anoints theforehead with blessed oil (oil blessed by the bishop on Holy Thursday). He says, "Through this holy anointing may the Lord in his love and mercy help you with the grace of the Holy Spirit." He then anoints the hands of the sick person saying, "May the lord who frees you from sin save you and raise you up." The practice can be preceded by reconciliation and followed by Holy Eucharist.

**S'ter Says**

**Extreme Unction** was one of the former names of this sacrament of anointing of the sick. Extreme refers to the condition of those who are departing, and unction means oil. Receiving the Eucharist is part of the Last Rites. The sacrament of the Eucharist is called Viaticum when a dying person receives it. Viaticum is a Latin word meaning "on the way with you."

The sacrament honors both the physical and spiritual healing presence of Christ. It holds both strengthening and curative powers and brings wholeness and well-being to those who receive it. This sacrament brings the following gifts:

➤ Cures in the form of strengthening, peace, and courage to overcome the difficulties that go with serious illness or the frailty of old age

➤ The gift of finding spiritual meaning for health and physical struggles

➤ Preparation and fortification for the final journey

➤ Forgiveness of sins

Just as the sacraments of initiation (Baptism and Confirmation) begin the Catholic journey with anointing, this last sacrament points to the end of life's journey by strengthening through anointing.

## *Transformation for the Community*

Before the reform of this sacrament at Vatican II, Extreme Unction was a very private affair between the priest and the dying person. Today, however, with a greater awareness of the effect of illness and death on the family and the community, friends and family are invited to be a part of this rite.

During the first 800 years of Catholicism, Catholics brought blessed oils home with them from Mass to anoint sick family members. Until Vatican II, anointing was restricted to the ministry of the priest and was kept for "deathbed situations." This restriction did not properly take into effect the physical as well as spiritual healing available through the sacrament. It has become quite common on given Sundays throughout the year to make anointing ceremonies part of the Mass. At these ceremonies, people in need of special healing come forward for anointing. The membership of the church witnesses, prays, and supports the person's healing.

In such a setting, an intense transformation can take place when a large group of people pray for those who are sick. The event opens the participants to shifts of consciousness, resulting in a deeper sense of community and awareness of one's personal journey.

As you might imagine, the seven sacraments are essential to the life of devout Catholics. In the next chapter, we'll tell you about Mary, who has been called "the people's sacrament."

---

### The Least You Need to Know

➤ Sacraments mark events in the lives of Catholics.

➤ Sacraments give spiritual and physical support in the life journey.

➤ Catholics practice seven sacraments honoring events from birth until death.

➤ Sacraments use specific elements and prescribed procedures that draw on both biblical and natural tradition.

➤ Sacraments transmit meaning, give grace, and give spiritual order to the Catholic's life. They are the presence of the Risen Christ in the church.

# Chapter 12

# Who Is Mary?

> **In This Chapter**
>
> ➤ How a simple Jewish girl became the mother of God
>
> ➤ How the stories of many cultures meet in Mary
>
> ➤ How Mary functions as mediator and co-redeemer
>
> ➤ How Mary continues to appear to the people all over the world
>
> ➤ How people pray to Mary

It would be impossible to imagine Catholicism without Mary. Her place in the church is unrivaled. Just as Jesus is the sacrament of God, and the church is the sacrament of Jesus, Mary is the people's sacrament. From the earliest years to present time, she has been celebrated in prayer, music, song, processions, devotions, and special Masses worldwide. The most famous cathedrals and basilicas in the world were built to honor her. Small roadside shrines where pilgrims hold vigils for her dot the countryside. All of this is testimony to the love that the people hold for her. Mary is the people's ambassador at large. She is deeply and tightly woven into the Catholic fabric. This chapter will explain the importance of Mary to the Catholic faith.

## Do Catholics Worship Mary?

There are two central questions for most people regarding Mary and her place in the Catholic Church: First, who is Mary? And second, do Catholics worship her? Let's begin with the second question.

No, Catholics do not worship Mary. They are devoted to her, they venerate her, and they honor her as the mother of Jesus, but they do not worship her. Catholics worship only God in the three persons of the Trinity: the Father, Son, and Holy Spirit. Mary is revered because of her relationship with God through Jesus. Over time, she has been called the mother of Christ, the mother of God, the new Eve, virgin mother, mediator, co-redeemer, queen of heaven, and mother of the church. She has many titles, fills many roles, and is a powerful character in a Catholic's spiritual life, but Catholics do not consider her divine, and so she is not worshipped like God. The question then arises: If Catholics do not worship Mary, what is her position in the church?

# Mary, the People's Choice

Just who is Mary? Much has been written about her, yet this question continues to perplex theologians and scholars today as it has for many centuries. It is perhaps easier for the common folk to comprehend her mystery than it is for the experts. For it is to the common people that Mary appears and speaks, and they intuitively understand her. Images, shrines, prayers, poetry, and great churches all over the world are built in her honor. Each year, thousands of pilgrimages are made to the places where she has appeared. Many who make these journeys claim that miracles take place there. Mary's connection to the folk is often a problem to the analytical, intellectual Catholic, but she cannot be explained away.

### Epiphanies

Information about Mary is drawn from many New Testament passages, specifically in the infancy stories of Jesus, which are the first two chapters of Matthew and Luke. John tells us about Mary in the story of the miracle of Cana and in Jesus' words from the cross (John 19:25–27). Matthew, Mark, and Luke report stories and remarks by Jesus about Mary. She is mentioned in events immediately before Pentecost. Finally, John records the mysterious picture presented in the book of Revelation of a woman clothed with the sun.

# *Mediator and Co-Redeemer*

*Mediator* is a Latin word that means "one who goes between." In Christianity, Jesus is the mediator between humanity and God; Jesus is the redeemer. He came to redeem the human race from the effects of Adam and Eve's sin, disobedience to God's direction not to eat the fruit of a particular tree in the Garden of Eden. Because of their sin, the gates of heaven were closed, breaking the relationship between God and his people. Catholics, like all Christians, believe that all humanity shares in the consequences of the disobedience of Adam and Eve in the Garden of Eden.

➤ She cooperated with God by knowingly and willingly saying yes to God's request to give birth to Jesus Christ.

➤ Mary birthed Jesus, thereby bringing redemptive grace to the people.

➤ As a mother witnessing her son's death, she actively shared in Jesus' redeeming sacrifice.

The church has used the title mediator for Mary for many hundreds of years when referring to her role as the one who cooperated with God in bringing Christ into the world. It has been applied to her in the East since the fifth century and in the West since the ninth. Her role in *redemption* is the subject of debate, however. The key question surrounding the issue is: Did what Mary endure in bringing Jesus into the world and being a part of his suffering, death, and resurrection constitute her as mediator and *co-redeemer* with her divine son?

Mary's very special recognition in the church as the mother of God has always earned her a prominent place in Catholic spiritual life. The title co-redeemer takes her position a step further. In recent times, a commission has been established to examine her status in this regard. No papal decision has as yet been declared, although the pope's writing refers to her as mediator many times.

> **S'ter Says**
>
> **Mediator** also refers to Mary, like Jesus, as "one who goes between" God and humans to speak for humans. **Co-redeemer** is a title celebrating Mary's part in the redemption. The term **redemption** describes the act that was accomplished by Jesus' life, death, and resurrection that bridged the gap between God and humanity caused by the sin of Adam and Eve.

## Mary, the Mysterious Woman

Mary, a woman who is called the mother of God, is intricately connected to Catholic history. Nothing was written about her until 30 years after Christ's death. It is perhaps because of the very sketchiness and brevity of biblical references that Mary has grown in the hearts and minds of the people. She is a mystery and, as such, leaves much to the imagination.

Every period of history contains images of Mary, and through these images, we can see reflections of religious faith. Yet nowhere does there seem to be a complete picture: not in Scripture, not in theology, and not in popular writings. To understand Mary and the position she occupies in the Catholic Church, it is helpful to look at all these sources as well as the beliefs that existed in the pre-Christian cultures of North Africa, Greece, Rome, and Turkey. It helps to see the influence these beliefs had on the way Mary's role in the church was understood and defined.

### Epiphanies

The rise of Mary's popularity and the understanding of her roles in the Catholic Church are intricately connected to the cultures in which her legend grew. The gods and god-desses of ancient Greece and Rome were powerful archetypes in the minds of the people up through the first and second centuries. From the very beginning of Catholicism, their characteristics were assimilated into Mary's story.

For example, images of Mary suspended in the heavens on the orb of a crescent moon with her head surrounded by a circle of stars, were popular artistic expressions. These images are based on ancient beliefs and understandings. In the classical world, the moon is the archetypal female symbol. In these artistic representations, Mary, filled by the sun's light, held it in her essence until morning, where she released it to the morning sky, symbolizing her giving birth to the sun.

### S'ter Says

In ancient times, **virginity** described a state of independence or autonomy. It referred to a woman who made her own decisions. When used to describe Mary, it means she said yes to God of her own free will, acting independent of any influence or coercion.

## *Virgin and Mother: Not a Problem*

The title of Virgin Mother originated in the East in the early New Testament years. Although today it seems a contradiction to speak of a mother being a virgin, this title for Mary was applied from a pre-Christian culture. In the pre-Christian world, a virgin birth often signaled a man's divinity. In other words, gods were born of virgins, and this event happened on a fairly regular basis within pagan religions. Virgin birth is a key to understanding Jesus' birth as the son of God because it signaled to people that the child was conceived by divine origin rather than earthly and resonated with the stories from other religions. Virgin birth told the people a miracle was taking place.

In the ancient world, the term *virginity* was associated with autonomy and did not have physical or moral connotations. It signified freedom of choice. Even later in history, Elizabeth I, the Virgin Queen of England, was not a virgin in the modern use of the term, but instead was a woman of power who could not be subjected or possessed. Virginity was a mental and emotional quality. Mary's virginal state represented her complete autonomy as she said "yes" to God's request, making the Incarnation (the birth of God in Jesus Christ) possible. In this understanding of the term, Mary's ongoing state of virginity was not a stretch of the imagination for the culture in which her stories developed.

## *"Now and at the Hour of Our Death …"*

Two other important roles that Mary plays for Catholics are as mother and as Queen of Heaven. She was given the title "Queen of Heaven" to show her power over death. Catholics believe she defied death to be taken up into heaven body and soul because her body did not deteriorate in the grave as a human body would, but instead was preserved. This belief has been defined as the "assumption of Mary into heaven." Catholics believe Mary rules over death as the queen of heaven.

*Michelangelo's* Pieta.

*(Courtesy Alinari/Art Resource, New York)*

### Epiphanies

The idea of Mary as the one who presided over death arose in part out of the Hellenistic mythology of Artemis (later called Diana by the Romans). The goddess Artemis presided over birth, nurturing the new mother and child and administering to the mother the sacred herb, artemesia, to help dispel the pains of childbirth. Artemis ruled over death as well. She was the one who was present at the end of the life journey, assuring safe passage to the other world.

Mary is the "mother of mercy, sweetness, and hope." Mary's role as mediator with her son Jesus gives strength to the living, but her greatest function is in the Catholic understanding of death and redemption. According to Catholics, because Mary is human and has the closet connection to Christ, Jesus cannot refuse her requests. Mary is the merciful one, the one who will not judge, but will simply love. In the last phrase of the Hail Mary, the plea, "pray for us sinners now, and at the hour of our death," expresses the popular belief in Mary's mercy and her particular association with death and heaven. Catholics turn to her to plead their case before God's justice. Mary gives God his human face in heaven as she did on earth. Mary has a way of touching God's heart. Through her, he becomes tangible as the "God of mercy."

### For Heaven's Sake!

You don't have to be devoted to Mary to be a good Catholic, and don't think that Catholics worship Mary! They worship only God. Many Catholics have love and respect for Mary because she is the mother of Jesus and made it possible for him to be born into the human race.

## Mary's Incomplete History

Again, who is Mary? The New Testament contains little information about her origins, family, birth, or even how she met Joseph. Joseph was a carpenter who was engaged to Mary. When he discovered she was pregnant, he was concerned for her reputation lest she be treated as an adulteress. An angel appeared to him and told him the child was conceived by God. He married her and became her protector. Was Joseph an older man? He isn't mentioned after Jesus' infancy, and thus we don't know what happened to him. Was Joseph with Mary at the wedding feast of Cana?

How old was Mary at the time of the Annunciation, when the angel came to her and asked her to be the mother of God's son? Did the Annunciation take place in the usual interval between engagement and marriage? How could a simple Jewish girl like Mary be as familiar with Hebrew Scripture as it appears she is in Luke 1:46–55 (in which Mary repeats the words of the prophet Isaiah as says: "My soul magnifies the Lord")? Did Jesus have brothers and sisters? We are left with many questions.

Mary's parents, Anne and Joachim, were old, possibly past the normal age of childbearing. Mary's name has been said to be derived from the Hebrew word meaning myrrh and from the word for "bearer of light." St. Jerome called her *Stella Maris,* meaning a "drop from the sea." This name later evolved into one of the many titles she bears, "star of the sea." Other sources connect the name Mary with Marah, the place of bitter water in the Exodus story. In this interpretation, her name would mean stubborn and even rebellious. It seems that even her name is a mystery.

# Council of Ephesus

Despite how little is told about her in the scriptures, Mary's legends continued to grow, especially around the city of Ephesus in Turkey, where the mother goddess was particularly popular. Pre-Christian legend says Artemis, a representation of the Great Mother, lived in the Arcadian forests, near Ephesus. Later Christian stories place Mary in the same area, living out her old age in Ephesus. It was also in Ephesus that Paul encountered the crowds cheering, "Great is Artemis of Ephesus," as he attempted to preach.

### Epiphanies

The scripture says that Mary, her sister, Mary Magdalene, and John, the "beloved disciple," were the only ones to remain at the foot of the cross. Jesus told John and his mother to take care of one another. It is believed that Mary went to Ephesus with John after Jesus' death and resurrection to live out her life. There is a shrine in Ephesus at the place that is believed to be her home. Many people visit there every year and light candles to honor her.

The Council of Ephesus took place in the year 431 C.E. in Turkey. The Church called it to settle the controversy around Mary and clarify church beliefs regarding Jesus' dual nature. The essential question was: Did Christ have two natures, one human and one divine? Or did he have a single nature that was both human and divine.

This issue raises a very important question about Mary. Was she the mother of God or simply the mother of Jesus? If Mary were called only the mother of Jesus, separate from being the mother of God, it would separate Jesus' nature into two different natures: one human and the other divine. This issue was a difficult dilemma for the church because it wanted to preserve its belief in Jesus' nature as being both human and divine.

The council decided on the doctrine that Jesus had one nature and was both true God and true man. It designated Mary as the mother of God, which elevated her to a central place in redemption. No longer was she simply a helper in God's plan, but her willingness to cooperate made human redemption possible.

**Saints Preserve Us**

**St. Gabriel, September 29, Patron of Communications Workers**

St. Gabriel, the archangel, was the angel who appeared to Zachariah to announce the birth of St. John the Baptist. He also announced to Mary that she would bear a son who would be conceived of the Holy Spirit. The name Gabriel means "man of God" or "God has shown himself mighty." The feast day for St. Gabriel is September 29, and he is the patron of communications workers.

**For Heaven's Sake!**

The Catholic Church forbids anyone to ascribe any "divine" attributes to Mary. Although she is considered holy, it is by the grace of God, and she is still fully human. She possesses no characteristics beyond those of other women.

## Theotokos: Mother of God

Mary was given her official church title, *Theotokos*, mother of God, which gave authentication to the growing popularity of liturgy, hymns, prayers, and stories coming out of the Eastern world. After this decision, theology and beliefs about Mary increased. It was believed that Mary was taken up body and soul by God to reign in heaven. This event is known as her Assumption. The church declared this belief to be true, and it has become an essential belief or church doctrine.

Mary evoked deep feelings in the people. The cultural flowering of the Middle Ages helped people fall in love with images of her, and then proclaim her reign as queen of heaven. What was central to the art of the East a few hundred years earlier became much of the focus of Western art. The Madonna and her divine child captured the cultural imagination. Mary became mother of humanity. Writers and thinkers of the time, including Thomas Aquinas, built the intellectual and theological framework that allowed her to be celebrated in the church. And celebrated she was—art, statuary, painting, stained glass, and architecture depicted her and helped to create a huge community devoted to her. Mary is what is missing for many, the feminine face of God.

# Apparitions: Here, There, and Everywhere

The Catholic Church defines an apparition as the appearance of a being in a supernatural state who would normally be beyond the human senses. Generally speaking, then, an *apparition* is the appearance of someone who has died. Apparitions of Jesus, Mary, the angels, and saints are a part of Catholic culture. There have been numerous visions or appearances of Mary around the world. Some of the most celebrated are her appearances at Lourdes, France; Fatima, Portugal; and Guadalupe, Mexico.

After an extensive investigation, the church can designate an apparition as authentic. When an apparition is declared authentic, this declaration does not bind Catholics to believe in the appearance. Instead, it means the church does not believe its members will be harmed by such a belief. Such

**Your Guardian Angel**

You don't have to go to Lourdes or Fatima to receive healing from Mary. A Rosary, a few prayers, or even a simple request given in any form will be heard. Think of her as a spiritual mother. As is often the case with mothers, Mary is very good at interpreting one's needs and is quick to send a blessing.

declarations of authenticity do not constitute an article of faith. *Articles of faith* are teachings Catholics have to believe and are found in the church's creeds. They include foundational beliefs such as the Trinity, Immaculate Conception, and Incarnation. After an article of faith has been declared, it becomes part of the unifying faith statement of the church. Apparitions are considered sources of grace and are understood as helpful to the worship of God.

## Lourdes: Healing Waters

Lourdes is a town in the southwest of France where Mary appeared to Bernadette Soubirous several times between February 11 and March 25, 1858. During this time, Bernadette reported seeing 18 different appearances of a very beautiful lady. The lady directed Bernadette to uncover a flow of water and to drink of it and to bathe in it. She said it would have healing effects. The lady then asked Bernadette to have a church built nearby. On her final appearance, she told Bernadette, "I am the Immaculate Conception." Four years earlier, the doctrine of the Immaculate Conception, which refers to Mary's conception in her mother's womb free from original sin, was declared an article of faith by the pope.

### Epiphanies

By the time of the last apparition of Mary at Lourdes, 25,000 people had gathered to witness the miracles. The lady was visible only to Bernadette. After rigorous examination by the church authorities, and based on Bernadette's simple and straightforward testimony, the apparitions were judged authentic. Five million pilgrims travel to Lourdes each year near the Pyrénées Mountains to experience and possibly receive healing from sickness and disease. A medical bureau on site at Lourdes is open to qualified medical personnel regardless of their religious creed. An international jury composed of experts in medical science and church law reviews the findings of the bureau.

## Fatima: World Peace

Fatima is a small town in the middle of Portugal where, in 1915, three young children had a vision of a veiled figure. Three times in the next year, they saw an angel who told them he was the angel of Peace. The angel urged them to pray to the hearts of Jesus and Mary. Following the angel's appearance, the children began to see the lady.

The Lady appeared standing on a cloud in an evergreen tree near a small cove. During her visits with the children, she talked intimately with them. On the sixth and final visit, she identified herself as the lady of the rosary. She emphasized the importance of praying the rosary daily as a devotion to the Immaculate Heart of Mary in order to bring about world peace. "If people do not turn to prayer," she said, "more war will break out." She asked for Russia to be consecrated to her Immaculate Heart. Four months after her warning, the Russian Revolution began. Many popes have honored the shrine at Fatima.

At Fatima, Mary promised a sign to show the authenticity of what she was saying. Despite efforts by local authorities to discredit the children, word continued to spread, and on October 13, in front of a crowd of 50,000 people, she made the sun dance in the sky. It left its orbit and appeared to many in the crowd to plunge to earth.

## Our Lady of Guadalupe: Patron of the Americas

The Lady of Guadalupe appeared in Mexico City in 1531 to an Indian peasant, Juan Diego. Her image was imprinted on his cloak and hangs in the Basilica built in her honor. She has been named the patron of the Americas. Scientists from MIT have examined the image on the cloak and verified an interesting phenomenon that is part of the miracle. The reflections of the people who were present when the apparition first appeared can still be seen in her eyes. The cloth, made of a woven grass, remains in remarkable condition. Experts have noted that a similar cloth would have normally disintegrated by now. The Guadalupe shrine is a popular pilgrimage for people from all over the world. Her story can be found in Chapter 23, "The Birth of the Church in the New Land."

## Feasts and Devotions to Mary

There are 16 feasts of the Blessed Virgin throughout the liturgical year. In addition to these feast days, the months of May and October are dedicated to Mary and are the focus of many devotions. This section looks at seven of her major feasts.

## Immaculate Conception of Mary: December 8, and Mary's Birthday: September 8

Many people mistakenly believe the term *Immaculate Conception* refers to Mary's sinless conception of Jesus, but it actually honors Mary's unique position of being conceived without original sin. It shows that she existed from her conception as prominent in God's redemption plan. God arranged sinlessness as a tribute to her and to prepare for the arrival of the savior through her. The Feast of the Immaculate Conception became a holy day of obligation in 1854. Catholics in Spain celebrate this day by decorating houses with flowers and flags and burning candles in the windows the night before the feast.

**For Heaven's Sake!**

Images of God come in many colors. Of course, there is no adequate representation of God. However, in Western culture, God, Jesus, Mary, and the disciples are usually depicted as Caucasian. Coming from the Middle East, Jesus would likely have dark skin. Although religious images are helpful to give us a feeling of connection, they can also limit our understanding.

**For Heaven's Sake!**

Don't forget to go to Mass! Holy days of obligation, like Sundays, are days on which Catholics must attend Mass. There are six holy days of obligation in the United States, and three of them are feasts of Mary.

Mary's birthday falls nine months later. This day honors Mary as God's gift to the people. Traditional feasts, which existed previous to this date and are now associated with the nativity of Mary, include thanksgiving celebrations, the beginning of Indian summer, and fall planting season. Harvest blessings are given in many Catholic Churches.

# The Annunciation: March 25, and the Visitation: May 31

Near the vernal equinox, the Annunciation marks the celebration of the conception of Jesus in Mary's womb. It occurs nine months before the feast of Christmas, the birth of Christ.

In medieval Europe, pageants and processions marked the celebration of the Annunciation. A child, dressed as an angel and representing Mary, was suspended on a rope in midair. As the angel descended, mothers dropped candy in the pews for the children. The children believed that Gabriel had brought these goodies from heaven. In Russia, large wheaten wafers were blessed and distributed after the Mass. The people saved pieces of these wafers to be buried in the fields to assure a good crop, signifying the connection between Mary's fertility and the fertility of the earth.

The feast of the Visitation celebrates Mary's visit to Elizabeth immediately after the Annunciation where the baby in Elizabeth's womb, John the Baptist, stirred in recognition of the messiah in Mary's womb.

**Your Guardian Angel**

Many of the church's feast days follow the ancient pre-Christian calendar of festivals and correspond to the seasons of the year. Christmas, the birth of the son of God, is near the winter solstice when the sun returns. Easter is near the spring equinox when new life abounds. In fact, Easter is still determined by the full moon following the spring equinox.

## Mary, Mother of God: January 1

"Mary, Mother of God" is a feast first instituted in Jerusalem as early as the middle of the fourth century. It was called the Presentation of the Child Jesus in the Temple and was celebrated on January 1, which followed the custom in Jewish law of presenting the baby in the temple on the eighth day following birth. The feast focused on the obedience of Mary and Jesus to Mosaic law. At one time, this feast was moved to February 2 and coincided with the pagan feast of lights. This feast day is also called the Solemnity of Mary.

## The Assumption: August 15

The Assumption marks one of the oldest feasts of Mary and is an important date in the liturgical year. It celebrates Mary's body and soul being taken up into heaven and her coronation as Queen of Heaven. Liturgical processions began as early as 701 C.E. In some European cities, Mary's journey to heaven is symbolized by carrying her statue through town. Huge candles are taken to churches and lighted in a procession called candelieri.

The Blessing of the Herbs is a medieval tradition on the Assumption, and it was called "Lady's Herb Day." Blessings were given to the herbs to enhance their healing properties. First grapes were offered to her, and blessing of the fishing boats occurred on this day. In England and Ireland, an ancient tradition is to perform ritual bathing on this day to preserve good health. Catholics in the United States celebrate it on August 15.

**For Heaven's Sake!**

Catholic teaching does not state that Mary ascended into heaven. That would constitute a divine power. She was taken up into heaven by God's power in an act called the Assumption of Mary into Heaven.

## Our Lady of Guadalupe, Mother of the Americas: December 12

Our Lady of Guadalupe is the patron saint of the Americas and is key to understanding the Catholicism of the New World. On December 12, Mary is remembered as patroness of the Americas. She is the mother of all the people and, because she was once poor, has particular favor for them. On this day, her appearance to Juan Diego near Mexico City in 1531 is honored.

Mary, as the universal mother symbol, is a reminder of the common relationship of all people. She offers her son, Jesus, to break through the old structures and categories of caste, class, religion, race, and gender by constantly reminding us that we are all children of the same God. More of her story is found in Chapter 23.

## May Altars

In a Catholic schoolroom during the month of May, you might still find a May altar. A few years ago, it would have been a sure thing to find one. May altars were built in classrooms and in the homes of Catholics as part of the May devotions to Mary. May altars featured a statue or picture of Mary prominently displayed, often against a cloth backdrop, and surrounded by fresh flowers. It was the duty of the students to keep fresh flowers for Mary all month. In addition, a candle was kept burning in front of her. Another popular May devotion from the past was the May crowning ceremony, in which a statue of Mary was crowned with flowers.

Mary is one of the figures that Catholics are best known for. In this chapter, you have had a chance to learn a lot about her and the devotions that honor her. Part 4, "Imagination and Prayer," describes other favorite Catholic devotions, sacramentals, and prayers. So if you have ever wondered what holy water, statues, mysticism, chanting, and a lot of other Catholic stuff is about, here is your chance to find out.

### The Least You Need to Know

➤ The stories of Mary were drawn from the rich cultural heritage of many sources.

➤ Mary holds a unique place in salvation and devotion.

➤ Mary is revered as the mother of God.

➤ Our Lady of Guadalupe is the patroness of the Americas and brings with her a model for unity and peace.

# Part 4

# Imagination and Prayer

*The imagination is a storehouse of all the sights, sounds, smells, sensations, and emotions we've experienced throughout our life. This sensory data is stored in a part of the brain called the imagination. Imagination forms the lens through which we view life, and it forms our perspective on life.*

*In this part, we will look at Catholic imagination in terms of the words Catholics use, their music, and their everyday practices and rituals. Then we will focus on the central place where Catholic imagination and prayer are communally enacted: the Mass.*

# Chapter 13

# Feeding the Imagination

## In This Chapter

➤ Learn the difference between the cross and the crucifix

➤ Find out why Catholics use statues, holy cards, and other Catholic stuff

➤ Recognize some of the gestures that identify a Catholic

➤ Understand how the liturgical calendar keeps sacred time for Catholics

As we've discussed, Catholics relate to Jesus and God through the senses and through the imagination. Indeed, the Catholic imagination is filled with images that allow Catholics to understand the world from a spiritual perspective and respond to the world in prayer. In this chapter, we'll explore the use of sacramentals—"little" sacraments that help develop the *Catholic imagination* and make everyday life more spiritual. Sacramentals relate us to the immanence of God, his touchability, as well as to his transcendent, otherworldly nature.

## Sacramentals: Little Sacraments

If you walk into a Catholic Church, you will see a crucifix, a cross with the image of Jesus on it. You might also notice lots of color, texture, smells, and shades of light in the church. You will find colorful stained glass windows that typically depict scenes from the life of Christ, angels, saints, or some modern art. In the church itself, you will find three or four shrines, in addition to the central or main altar, with statues or icons of St. Joseph, Mary, or others.

*Stained glass window in a church, depicting the Annunciation. Christ the King Catholic Church, Nashville, Tennessee.*

*(Courtesy of H. L. [Dean] Caskey)*

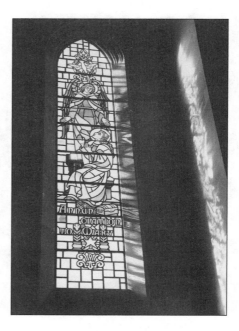

Like pictures of admired ancestors, holy pictures and statues connect us to the memories we hold of those being pictured. They connect us to what that person was all about, particularly the values they espoused. Almost everyone has a favorite object that belonged to a grandparent, parent, a relative, or friend and that he or she holds sacred. When you see such an object or use it, you remember the stories that go with it.

For instance, you might have dishes or silverware that belonged to your mother. As you set the table, you remember the influence she had in your life and the values she represented. As you do so, her spirit comes alive for you. It is as if she could reach through time and space and be there with you again. The dishes are functioning in a sacramental way by connecting you to the things about the person you hold sacred.

The difference between official sacramentals and personal ones is that the church's sacramentals relate to God and to the saints rather than to anyone's personal family archives. They connect the faithful to the life and times of Jesus.

## Why Do Catholics Have Jesus on the Cross?

Probably the most widely used sacramental for Catholics is the crucifix. For Catholics, the crucifix is a sacramental because it connects them to the story of Jesus and the values he taught. Although most other Christian religions do not use the term sacramental, all use the symbol of the cross, but the cross you will see in the Protestant world differs from the Catholic crucifix. A crucifix is a *cross* upon which the body of the crucified Christ is shown.

Catholics prefer the crucifix to the plain cross because it helps them feel more connected to Jesus as human. For many non-Catholics, the image of Jesus' crucified body seems harsh. But for Catholics, the image of Jesus on the cross makes the story of his life, death, and resurrection come alive. Many Catholics also feel that the cross without Christ tends to become an idea rather than a real-life event that happened to a human man who was also the son of God.

The history of the cross and the crucifix is a long one. Constantine, Roman emperor of the early 300s, dreamt of a cross and was told in the dream that "in this sign you will conquer." Constantine put the sign of the cross on all his shields, and then won the battle by which he became emperor of Rome. He then liberated the church, making Christianity a legal religion in the empire.

### S'ter Says

A **cross** is made of two planks of timber, one placed across the other, like the picture shown in this section. It was the instrument of execution in Roman times, and Jesus was put to death on a cross.

Since then, the cross has been the universal symbol for Catholicism. There are some 400 varieties of crosses in use. Sometime in the Middle Ages, the body of Jesus was affixed to the cross, and the image became known as a crucifix. The crucifix has been one of the most easily recognized symbols of the Catholic religion. Catholics display the crucifix prominently on the altar of the church, in their homes, and sometimes on pendants around the neck.

*Crucifix prominently displayed over the altar. Christ the King Catholic Church, Nashville, Tennessee.*

*(Courtesy of H. L. [Dean] Caskey)*

*Four different styles
of crosses.*

*(Bob O'Gorman
and Mary Faulkner)*

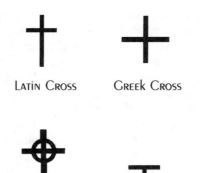

LATIN CROSS   GREEK CROSS

CELTIC CROSS   TAU CROSS

### Your Guardian Angel

Consider marking a special occasion with a holy card. You can remember a baptism, a first communion, a wedding, or a funeral with a personalized printed holy card.

## Catholic Stuff: Statues and Holy Cards

Statues are everywhere in the Catholic world: in church, in the home, out on the yard, and even mounted on the dashboard of the car. On the side altars of Catholic churches, you'll see statues dedicated to saints: Mary, Joseph, the patron saint of the parish, St. Michael the archangel, St. Anthony, and St. Teresa are particularly popular. A favorite statue in many churches is the infant of Prague. It is a statue of the Christ child represented as an infant king. The custom is to adorn the statue with elaborate robes.

Church statues range in size from 1 or 2 feet tall to 10 or 15 feet. They can be very modern pieces of art or traditional representations that have not changed since the Middle Ages. Since Vatican II, the presence of statues in Catholic churches has been deemphasized; however, for the most part, it remains a tradition the people won't give up.

Another favorite sacramental is a holy card. In the past, students at a Catholic school would receive a holy card as a prize for getting the top grade in a quiz. Holy cards are about the size of a playing card. On one side is a picture of a saint; on the other side is a prayer. A holy card illustrates events in the life of Jesus, Mary, angels, or saints. Beautiful in their presentation, holy cards are like gold-edged Catholic baseball cards; young people collected them as such, sometimes using them as bookmarks in prayer books or trading them during church (until they got caught).

Perhaps the most common use of holy cards today is at the funeral parlor. As you sign the visitors' book, you will be offered a holy card with a picture on one side and a psalm or other prayer on the back with the name and dates of the deceased. These cards can be saved in your prayer book or at home in the family bible as a reminder to pray for the deceased.

Another group of sacramentals include medals, which are small, coin-like objects with an image of Christ, Mary, or a saint imprinted on them and worn on a chain around the neck. Like other objects, medals must be blessed in order to be considered holy objects. Medals make good gifts for religious occasions or holidays. Often the patron saint of the person is selected. The purpose of wearing a medal is to invoke the aid and protection of the saint whose image is on it.

### Saints Preserve Us

**St. Christopher, July 25, Patron of Travelers**

St. Christopher is one of the most popular saints, and St. Christopher medals are among the most common sacramentals. Legend has it that Christopher was a giant of a man who made his living carrying people across a raging stream on his shoulders. One day his passenger was a small child who grew so heavy that Christopher feared they would drown. The child then revealed that he was Christ and that the heaviness was caused by the weight of the world he was carrying on his shoulders—hence his name, Christopher, which means Christ-bearer. Christopher is the patron saint of motorists and travelers and is invoked during storms. St. Christopher medals are typically affixed to the sun visor or dashboard of the car.

## Advent Wreaths: O Come, O Come, Emanuel!

Advent wreaths are sacramentals that appear in Catholic life both at home and in church during Advent, the four-week period before Christmas. An Advent wreath is a green pine wreath with four candles placed at equal distances around the circle. Three of the candles are purple, and the fourth is pink. The four candles represent the four centuries people waited for the birth of Christ.

In church each week, the priest lights a candle and says special prayers preparing Catholics for the coming of Jesus. On the third week, he lights the pink candle. Its purpose is to uplift the spirit during the long, dark four weeks before Christmas. On the fourth week, all four candles are burning and your heart knows Christmas will soon arrive.

*An advent wreath. Christ the King Catholic Church, Nashville, Tennessee.*

*(Courtesy of H. L. [Dean] Caskey)*

**Your Guardian Angel**

Try keeping an Advent calendar! Another practice to prepare for Christmas is to use an Advent calendar, which has a special scripture reading for each day of Advent. You can get one at your Catholic bookstore or make one yourself.

A large wreath is used in church; sometimes wreaths are suspended from the ceiling in the front of the altar. At home, Catholics place a wreath on the table where it is used as family devotion. It is customary for a parent to perform the blessing of the wreath before it is used. Before dinner, a member of the family lights a candle and says a prayer. Advent wreaths teach the spiritual meaning of the season and give children eager for Christmas something to do as they wait for the big day.

## Sacramental Gestures

From the swirling Sufi dancers of the Islamic religion to the more staid Congregationalists of New England, all religions, including Catholicism, have certain gestures or movements they use in worship. Almost everyone who visits a Catholic Church and attends Mass comes away amazed at how much standing, kneeling, and sitting goes on. This section describes some of the gestures and movements that define Catholics.

### The Sign of the Cross

One of the most obvious gestures that identify Catholics is the sign of the cross. Indeed, one of the first things Catholic parents teach their children is how to bless themselves. It would be rare indeed to watch a basketball game without seeing someone using this gesture before shooting a basket.

The sign of the cross is made using the fingers of the opened right hand:

➤ You touch your forehead as you say, "In the name of the Father"

➤ You touch your heart as you say, "and the Son"

➤ You touch your left shoulder as you say, "and the Holy"

➤ You touch your right shoulder as you say, "Spirit"

➤ You bring your hands together as you say, "Amen."

Most prayers begin and end with the sign of the cross. The priest also uses this gesture as he gives his blessing to the people. The sign of the cross expresses one of the basic truths of the faith: the existence of the Father, Son, and Holy Spirit as Trinity.

## Blessings for Everything!

We bless God for what he has done for us. In return God we receive God's blessing. Catholics receive blessings from the priest, and the priest also blesses objects. What gets blessed? Name an object or being—boats, cars, bicycles, horses, dogs, cats, crops, fields, gardens—and there is probably a blessing for it and a special story to go with it. There's hardly anything that can't or doesn't get blessed.

Many parishes invite members to bring pets to church to be blessed on October 4, the feast of St. Francis. Stories of St. Francis's love of nature and all animals have captured the hearts and imaginations of people of all religious faiths. In farming communities, priests bless fields, tractors, and other equipment; in fishing communities, the boats are blessed; and in all communities, cars and homes are blessed.

Blessings are not just a Catholic practice. Probably most religions ask the divine to pay special attention in some way. Blessings acknowledge people's dependence on God and confirm their belief that God concerns himself with their daily activities. Blessings connect Catholics more closely to God's *omnipresence*.

**Your Guardian Angel**

Don't forget your blessings! Bless your food before you eat by making the sign of the cross over it.

**S'ter Says**

**Omnipresence** means all-present. It means that God is everywhere.

When a priest gives a blessing, he uses holy water, which is water that has been blessed and set aside for sacred use. He might sprinkle the person or object and will most likely make the sign of the cross on the head of the individual being blessed. If he is blessing an object or a crowd of people, he will make the gesture of a cross in the air with his hand. He says something like, "May God bless you and keep you safe in the name of the Father, the Son, and the Holy Spirit. Amen."

The priest blesses all sacred objects before they are used sacramentally. The act of blessing reserves the object for use as a spiritual tool. From then on, those who use it must treat it with respect. Blessings change consciousness about the object; they change the understanding of it and the treatment of it. Crosses, beads, medals, and other Catholic stuff are just plain objects until a priest blesses them.

## Hands, Knees, Heads, and Hats

Another sacred gesture involves the tradition of folding the hands together with fingers pointed upward as the common position for prayer. This hand position symbolizes that the one praying is focused on God. Some say the practice led to the shape of church steeples. Of course, prayer is acceptable in any posture at any time.

As an earlier chapter described, Catholics genuflect before the altar to show respect for the presence of God. They usually do this just before taking their seats in church. They may also genuflect at any time when passing in front of the altar.

Kneeling is another Catholic practice, leading many visitors to remark on the ups and downs of a Catholic service. It's also customary to bow the head or even tip your hat when passing a church. The head is often bowed at the name of Jesus.

**For Heaven's Sake!**

Treat all sacramentals with respect when you're no longer using them. There is, for example, a protocol for retiring palm leaves. They are burned for distribution as ashes on Ash Wednesday.

# Sacred Elements: Earth, Air, Fire, and Water

As we discussed earlier, many of the Catholic rituals are rooted in the elements of air, earth, fire, and water. The elements connect Catholics to their physical world and remind them that God is present here and now, in the everyday world. The sacramental use of elements sanctifies Catholics' relationship with the earth, with one another, and with the Creator.

## Palm Leaves and Ashes

Palm branches are sacramentals used once a year on Palm Sunday, the Sunday before Easter. On that day, Jesus rode triumphantly into Jerusalem, and the crowd waved palm leaves and placed them in his path as a sign of honor. In like manner, the church distributes palms to be held during the reading of that Gospel story on Palm Sunday. Catholics traditionally braid the leaves and place them behind a holy picture or a crucifix in the home.

Ash Wednesday signals the beginning of Lent, which is the six-week period before Easter. The Ash Wednesday service starts with Mass, and attendance at this event is greater than any other day during the year. People come to participate in one of the favorite practices in the church: having their foreheads anointed with ashes.

Priests prepare the ashes by burning last year's palm leaves for this ceremony. At some point, either before or after Mass, the people come up to the front of the church. The priest dips his thumb into a small glass vial that contains the ashes and rubs a cross on each person's forehead as he gives the biblical reminder, "Remember that you are dust, and unto dust you shall return." (Genesis 3:19)

Garry Wills, a Catholic writer, talks about the very earthiness of this ceremony and describes it as a time when the Catholic comes face to face with death: "Certain feelings are not communicable. One cannot explain to others, or even to one's self, how burnt stuff rubbed on the forehead could be balm for the mind. The squeak of ash crumbled into ash marks the body down for death, yet makes this promise of the grave somehow comforting." During the day, activities slowly brush away the ashes, but perhaps a small cinder is left as a reminder of the ceremony.

## Holy Water!

As a Catholic opens the doors of the church, he or she instinctively reaches out with the right hand to dip his or her fingers into the holy water font, which hangs on the wall just inside the door. The Catholic then blesses himself or herself with the holy water by making the sign of the cross. Holy water is water that has been blessed in a special ceremony as part of the Easter Vigil rituals and is used throughout the year.

The signing of the cross with water is a renewal of a Catholic's baptism. During the sacrament of Baptism, the priest pours water over the forehead and makes the sign of the cross. Blessing yourself with holy water upon entering the church is a cleansing rite. It symbolically washes the outside world away and shows that you are entering sacred space.

**Your Guardian Angel**

Check your holy water supply. It is a Catholic custom to keep a bottle of holy water in the home. It can be used for blessing at the time of sickness and to protect the home against danger.

## Holy Oil!

Holy oil is blessed and set aside for use in administering several of the seven sacraments. Traditionally, oil is used as a healing balm, as a cleansing agent, and as a strengthener. In the church, it is used in Baptism, Confirmation, Holy Orders, and the Sacrament of the Sick.

The use of oil for anointing has become more common in the church now than it used to be, because healing ceremonies have become more popular. In many parishes, one Sunday a month is set aside for the faithful to come to receive prayers and anointing to help with physical or emotional healing. The parish also may hold a special ceremony of consecration for someone who is about to volunteer for a year or so of mission service. That person would be blessed and anointed with oil.

## *Superstition?*

As we've said, Catholics believe that God is present in all things and is accessible in all of nature. Catholics' use of sacramentals often raises the question of superstition and idolatry. In response, Catholics answer that there is a need for the tactile in religious imagination. Sacramentals are a way of acknowledging God's presence in all things. It brings the very elusive and ethereal spiritual aspect of God into a form that humans can grasp. Sacramentals raise the awareness of Catholics to the fact that God is everywhere by putting that idea into concrete form.

# The Liturgical Calendar: Sacred Time

If you are visiting relatives in Ireland and you are issued an invitation to a dinner, make sure you ask if the time specified is "Irish time." If the answer is yes, you would be wise not to be rushed by the movement of the hands on your watch. In their leisure, the Irish have a different meaning for time than they do during the workday. Every culture has different ways of experiencing time, and Catholics do too with regard to their sacred time.

### Your Guardian Angel

Get a liturgical calendar to hang next to your regular calendar. The liturgical calendar connects you to the spiritual seasons of the year. Liturgical calendars indicate the scripture passages for each Sunday and are available from your Catholic bookstore.

## *The Sacred Wheel of Time*

The church follows time according to the birth and resurrection of Jesus by what it calls the liturgical calendar. This calendar establishes the pattern for the feasts and seasons that occur each year. It cycles around two major celebrations in the life of Christ: his birth at Christmas and his resurrection at Easter.

➤ **Advent** begins the liturgical year with the first Sunday of Advent and goes to December 24.

➤ **Christmas** begins with the vigil of Christmas on December 24 and goes through the Sunday after January 6, the feast of *Epiphany*.

➤ **Ordinary time** begins after the Sunday following January 6 and continues through the day before Ash Wednesday.

➤ **Lent** begins on Ash Wednesday and lasts until the Holy Thursday Mass of the Lord's Supper.

➤ **The Easter *Triduum*** begins with the Mass of the Lord's Supper on Holy Thursday and lasts until Easter Sunday.

➤ **Easter season** begins on Holy Thursday and lasts for 50 days until Pentecost. Easter is celebrated on the Sunday following the first full moon after March 21, the spring equinox. This system of determining Easter's date comes from the way the Jews calculated the feast of Passover.

➤ **Ordinary time** continues the day after Pentecost and ends the day before Advent. Ordinary time refers to times between major seasons of Christmas and Easter.

**S'ter Says**

**Epiphany** is defined as a sudden intuitive perception or insight into the essential meaning of something. It marks the feast when the kings or wise men visited the Christ child in Bethlehem. It is celebrated on January 6. **Triduum** is most often used when referring to the Easter Triduum that includes the three days prior to Easter Sunday: Holy Thursday, Good Friday, and Holy Saturday.

In addition to the Sunday cycle shown here, there are two other cycles of feasts on the church calendar. The second cycle is composed of the saints' days, one for every day of the year. The third cycle is made up of Mary's feasts. This cycle is "unofficial," but popular. It consists of the months of May and October, which are devoted to special celebrations of Mary. Additionally, there are more than 15 feasts through out the year celebrating her, beginning with the Immaculate Conception on December 8 through the Assumption on August 15.

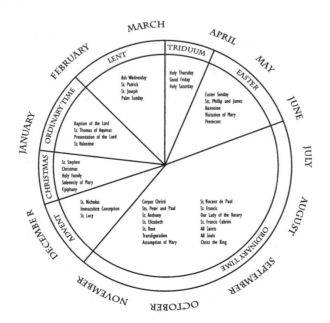

*The liturgical calendar of church feasts shown on a wheel of the year.*

*(Bob O'Gorman and Mary Faulkner)*

## Celebrating the Seasons

Catholics celebrate each of these seasons by reading the Bible texts appropriate to the feasts. Generally, there is a reading from the Old Testament, an Epistle, and a Gospel at each Mass. The readings revolve on a three-year rotation. The Gospels are drawn from Mark, Matthew, and Luke respectively. The color of the priest's vestments and the color of the various church decorations are changed according to the liturgical season. Naturally, the music of the Mass also changes with the season.

You've learned a lot about the sacred objects and practices of Catholics. In the next chapter, you'll find out about favorite Catholic prayers and sacred music.

### The Least You Need to Know

➤ Sacramentals are reminders of the sacredness of the everyday world.

➤ Catholics have the image of the crucified Christ on their cross as a reminder that he isn't just an idea, but the son of God made man.

➤ The church uses candles, holy water, ashes, and holy oil as sacramentals to ground spirituality in the physical world.

➤ Sacramentals are just objects until they are blessed, which is when they become sacred.

➤ The rituals of the church follow a rhythm according to the liturgical calendar.

# Chapter 14

# Catholic Prayers and Music: Tangible Poetry

---

## In This Chapter

➤ How Catholics pray

➤ What a rosary is

➤ The church's mystical tradition

➤ Gregorian chant, the heart of the church's music tradition

---

Prayer lifts our minds and hearts out of our everyday problems and opens the soul to receive God. Prayer is not simply an event, nor is it only words or actions. It is all of those things and more. As we become mindful of God's presence in us and in all things, our whole life becomes a prayer. Prayer opens us to our deepest level of being: our soul.

Prayer is like poetry offered to God. It becomes tangible when it is connected to certain objects such as the rosary or to sacred music, such as Gregorian chant. Fingers touch beads while the mind evokes images of the mysteries of Christ's life. The sounds of psalms chanted awaken the ear. The mind quiets, contemplates, and is touched by God. There are many forms for prayer. In this chapter, we'll look at three of them.

# Personal Prayer

Since the beginning of time, people have experienced a hunger, a deep instinctual need, to make sense out of life. This sensation creates the idea that there is something with which we long to make contact. This recognition is a prayer in itself. You could begin to define prayer as the attentiveness to this primal urge.

Personal prayer represents an intimate, one-on-one relationship with God. It forms the foundation of spirituality. Although the church has many formal community rituals and celebrations, the Mass being the most central of these, Catholics are urged to develop their personal prayer life.

The standard Catholic definition of prayer identifies four kinds of prayer:

➤ **Petition** is by far the most common type. Petition asks God for assistance in life's needs; it seeks God's intervention.

➤ **Gratitude** thanks God for blessings and gifts, both the asked for and the unexpected.

➤ **Adoration** expresses devotion, love, and recognition of a Catholic's absolute dependence on God.

➤ **Reparation** asks forgiveness, recognizes one's faults, and expresses sorrow.

The methods of personal prayer include the following:

➤ **Recitation,** such as the Rosary, litanies, the Way of the Cross, and other memorized prayers

➤ **Spiritual reading,** including passages from the Bible, particularly the Psalms

➤ **Recollection,** which is defined as taking a few moments throughout the day for a quick recall of God's presence in oneself and others

➤ **Contemplation,** including quiet time spent in inner reflection

➤ **Journaling,** or writing favorite passages and recording your interpretations and reflections on them

One way of praying is not better than another, and there is no one right way of praying. Traditional Catholic prayers include different types of prayers and different ways of praying. Prayer is personal and intimate. How one prays is not the point; that one prays at all is the more important concern!

# The Rosary

Of all the Catholic prayers, the Rosary is perhaps the most popular devotion. The word *rosary* means "garland of roses." The rose is one of the flowers used to symbolize the Virgin Mary, and the prayer of the Rosary is very closely associated with her. A story says that Mary has revealed to several people that each time they say a "Hail Mary," they are giving her a beautiful rose. When you say a Rosary, it becomes a garland of roses.

The rosary itself is a string of beads that Catholics use to count the group of prayers known as the Rosary. The beads can be made out of wood, glass, gems, or even a knotted string. They range from very simple to very elegant in appearance. Rosaries are simply attractive objects until the priest blesses them. At that time, they become sacred and should be treated with respect.

If you were to ask what sacramental practice most represents Catholicism, the answer would probably be the rosary. A Catholic image familiar to most people of any faith is that of Catholics kneeling in church, their lips moving in silent prayer as beads slip through their fingers. Another is of nuns in traditional dress with large rosaries at their waist and looped down their side, nearly touching the floor; huge crosses are tucked neatly in their belt, six-shooter style. Rosaries often hang from the rearview mirror of Catholics' cars. You will know that the person is a Catholic at the end of his life because the rosary beads will be wrapped around his hands as he lies in his coffin; he will be buried with them.

### For Heaven's Sake!

Treat your rosary with respect. Don't wear a rosary as a piece of jewelry or use it as a decorative object. While they are attractive, remember that they have been blessed for use in prayer.

As a ritual, the rosary involves two elements: mental prayer and vocal prayer. The mental prayer consists of a meditation on the mysteries of the life and death of Jesus Christ and his mother Mary. The vocal prayer consists of saying the prescribed prayers shown in the following section. Together these elements create a focused meditation, which helps to quiet the mind.

### Epiphanies

Meditation has existed as a prayer form since the dawn of history. Early forms of the rosary (although not known by that name) can be traced to India, where people still use it in worship. It spread through Hinduism to Buddhism and later to Islam. Wooden or tasseled amber worry beads soothe frazzled nerves as they are worked with the fingers. The tourist can find these beaded prayer forms in markets and shops.

## Origins of the Rosary

It is commonly believed that St. Dominic (1170–1221), the founder of the Dominican order, received a vision of Mary in which she instructed him to encourage people to pray the Rosary to her as a means of invoking her aid. The Rosary was part of the monastic spiritual practices for centuries before Dominic. Prior to that, the custom of counting repeated prayers by using a string of beads, knots, or even pebbles in a bowl was in common use among the Moslems, the Buddhists, and other non-Christian religions.

Christian monks used beads to count the 150 psalms they chanted in Latin as part of their prayer life. Because some of the monks, as well as most of the common people, couldn't read Latin, they improvised a substitute for the 150 psalms. They began using beads to count 150 Our Fathers, divided into groups of 50. In time, Hail Marys were added to the prayer form. At that time, the Rosary was called Our Lady's Psalter, marking the 150 Hail Marys that corresponded to 150 psalms.

### Epiphanies

How did St. Dominic get the credit for starting the rosary? It seems that during the years 1470 to 1475 a zealous Dominican preacher, Alan de Rupe, preached all over Europe and told the story of Mary's appearance to Dominic and how she gave him the Rosary. De Rupe was a born exaggerator, or perhaps he realized the value of a good story as a preaching device. His claims were taken as truth. Regardless of whether the story of St. Dominic and the Rosary is true, it has become part of the legend of the Rosary and has linked inextricably the Dominicans with this favorite tradition.

## How to Say the Rosary

Of the many versions of the Rosary, the most popular is the Dominican one. In its complete form, the Rosary consists of saying 15 decades. *Decades* are groups of 10 beads on which a prayer is said. The common rosary has only five decades. The following illustration shows a picture of the rosary.

As we said earlier, the Rosary uses repetition and meditation—it is a spiritual practice. Here is how it is said:

1. While holding the crucifix, make the sign of the cross and then recite the Apostles' Creed.

2. Recite the Our Father prayer on the first large bead.

3. On each of the three small beads, recite a Hail Mary asking for an increase of faith, hope, and charity.

4. Recite the Glory Be to the Father before the Our Father on the next large bead.

5. Recall the first Rosary mystery and recite the Our Father on the next large bead.

6. On each of the adjacent 10 small beads, recite a Hail Mary while reflecting on the mystery. This completes a decade.

7. Each succeeding decade is prayed in a similar manner by recalling the appropriate mystery, reciting the Our Father, saying 10 Hail Marys and one Glory Be, and reflecting on the next mystery.

8. When the Rosary is completed, it is traditionally concluded with the prayer, "Hail Holy Queen."

**Your Guardian Angel**

Don't think you have to always say formal prayers. Your conversation with God is personal. Feel free to say what you need to say the way you need to say it.

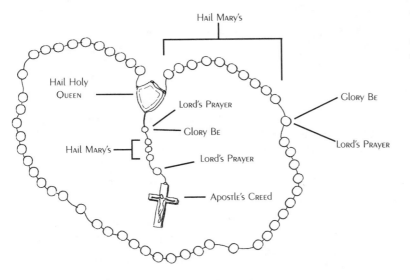

*The Rosary.*

*(Bob O'Gorman and Mary Faulkner)*

# The Prayers of the Rosary

The following prayers make up the Rosary. Note that Catholics often refer to The Lord's Prayer as the Our Father; it's just one of those Catholic things.

➤ **The Our Father.** Our Father, who art in heaven, hallowed be thy name. Thy kingdom come; thy will be done on earth as it is in heaven. Give us this day our daily bread; and forgive us our trespasses as we forgive those who trespass against us; and lead us not into temptation, but deliver us from evil. Amen.

➤ **The Hail Mary.** Hail Mary full of grace, the Lord is with thee. Blessed art thou among women, and blessed is the fruit of thy womb, Jesus. Holy Mary, mother of God, pray for us sinners now and at the hour of our death. Amen.

➤ **Glory Be to the Father.** Glory be to the Father, to the Son, and to the Holy Spirit. As it was in the beginning, is now and ever shall be, world without end. Amen.

➤ **The Apostles' Creed.** I believe in God, the Father almighty, Creator of heaven and earth. And in Jesus Christ, his only son, our Lord; who was conceived by the Holy Spirit, born of the Virgin Mary, suffered under Pontius Pilate, was crucified, died, and was buried. He descended into hell; the third day he rose again from the dead; he ascended into heaven, sits at the right hand of God, the Father almighty; from thence he shall come to judge the living and the dead. I believe in the Holy Spirit, the holy Catholic Church, the communion of saints, the forgiveness of sins, the resurrection of the body, and life everlasting. Amen.

➤ **The Hail! Holy Queen.** Hail! Holy queen, mother of mercy, our life, our sweetness, and our hope. To you we cry, poor banished children of Eve. To you do we send up our sighs, mourning and weeping in this valley of tears. Turn then, O most gracious advocate, your eyes of mercy toward us, and after this our exile, show unto us the blessed fruit of your womb, Jesus. O clement! O loving! O sweet Virgin Mary! Pray for us, O holy mother of God, that we may be made worthy of the promises of Christ. Amen.

## The Fifteen Mysteries of the Rosary

You will often hear the word *mystery* used in the Catholic religion. It describes important beliefs about God, Jesus, and Mary that are part of the religion but cannot be substantiated outside of religious belief. Another way of saying it is that they are important expressions of the faith of the people. The 15 (in head) mysteries of the Rosary are in three groups of five and represent joyful events, sorrowful events, and glorious events in the life of Jesus and Mary.

**S'ter Says**

**Mysteries** are beliefs of the religion that are taken on faith. They are events in the life of Christ that are vital to the spiritual life of Jesus' followers.

As stated earlier, the Rosary is a spiritual practice. It uses prayer and meditation. The repetition of the prayers quiets the mind and prepares it for contemplation on the events in the life of Christ. The beads soothe busy or nervous fingers, giving them something to do. Here are the stories or events upon which Catholics meditate or contemplate while saying the Rosary; they are the common stories of the religion.

**Joyful Mysteries**

1. The Annunciation
2. The Visitation
3. The Nativity
4. The Presentation
5. The Finding of the Child Jesus in the Temple

### Sorrowful Mysteries

1. The Agony in the Garden
2. The Scourging at the Pillar
3. The Crowning of Thorns
4. The Carrying of the Cross
5. The Crucifixion

### The Glorious Mysteries

1. The Resurrection
2. The Ascension
3. The Descent of the Holy Spirit
4. The Assumption of Mary
5. The Coronation of the Blessed Virgin Mary

## When Is the Rosary Said?

The Rosary is both an individual prayer and a group devotion. The church encourages families to use the Rosary as a family devotional practice during May and October, as well as throughout the year. May and October are months dedicated to Mary, and daily devotions using the Rosary are held in many parishes.

Besides praying the Rosary, the beads themselves have become a favorite devotional item. Catholics often carry them in their purse or pocket, keep them by the bedside, or hang them on sacred pictures. A priest blesses the rosaries in a ritual by which they become sacramental rather than simply secular beads. Many Catholics place special importance on rosaries that have been blessed by their bishop or the pope.

**Your Guardian Angel**

Any portion of the Rosary is a complete prayer! If you have time only for a single decade or even a single bead, it is still a prayer.

Praying the Rosary became a national enthusiasm after the appearance of Our Lady of Fatima. As you may remember from Chapter 12, "Who Is Mary?" Fatima instructed people to pray the Rosary for the conversion of Russia from communism and Catholics took up the cause. During May, Rosary processions were held in many cities. They involved tens of thousands of people who gathered and walked throughout the downtown area reciting the Rosary and singing hymns. Radio stations all over the country broadcast the Rosary in the early evening and families were encouraged to use this time for family prayer. Today, the Catholic Church broadcasts the rosary on radio, television, and the Internet.

# Monasteries, Mysticism, and Contemplative Prayer

*Contemplative prayer* is the practice of a church tradition called *mysticism*. Mysticism and contemplative prayer developed as part of the prayer life in the monasteries. Of course, contemplation, mysticism, and even monasteries exist in other traditions as well.

In the Catholic Church, contemplative practice began back in the early years when many new believers went out into the desert to get away from the world and all its complication (not to mention persecution) in order to pray and meditate without interruption. It has existed in every age of the Catholic Church: St. Augustine in the 400s, St. Hildegarde of Bingen in the Middle Ages, the English mystic of the 1500s Julian of Norwich, a little later, Teresa of Ávila and St. John of the Cross, and in modern times, Thomas Merton. The mystic tradition of contemplation is still alive today in monasteries all over the world.

Monastic life lived in convents was one of the arenas in the church where women were provided equal opportunity. It was their first chance for an active role in the church and society since the early years of the church under the leadership of Jesus, where women were full participants in the inner circle. Convents became centers for learning, prayer, and good works.

**S'ter Says**

**Contemplative prayer** is a form of prayer developed in the monasteries. **Mysticism** describes the process of being contemplative. You are contemplative when you meditate and go within yourself to a quiet place where it is possible to experience God. **Monasticism** is the tradition of taking yourself away from the mainstream of society for the purpose of developing your spiritual practice.

## Monasticism: The Great Getaway

The basic idea of *monasticism* is seclusion or withdrawal from the world or society. The object is to achieve life whose ideal is different from the dominant culture. Monastics separate from the world in order to preserve ethical beliefs that are being threatened by the culture. Monasticism is found in every religious system that has attained a high degree of ethical development and is often organized around self-denial, commitment to specific prayers, fasting, and hard work, and even self-denial. Underlying its practices is a deep commitment to preserving a set of ideals.

Monasticism had its beginnings in the early years of the church. Christians felt the need to make a strong commitment to each other and to create a safe structure in which to operate. They took *vows* concerning life together. The life of the early monastic was often one of extreme deprivation and hardship. In the 500s, monasticism came under the influence of St. Benedict, and the emphasis on self-denial was tempered.

# Liturgy of the Hours

All over the world, people of all religious traditions are praying 24 hours a day, 7 days a week, all year round. This human phenomenon represents the acknowledgment of the sacred relationship between God and creation. The form these prayers take in the Catholic Church is called the Liturgy of the Hours.

The Liturgy of the Hours acknowledges the inherent powers of nature contained in times of the day and seasons of the year. The oldest documents of civilization describe sacred times of sunrise, noon, sunset, and night as times when prayers were offered and hymns were sung. The Jews adapted these practices from their neighbors, using the book of Psalms as the source of their daily prayers. Early Catholics followed the ancient tradition as a way of living the Biblical command to "pray constantly." Great events in Christianity follow the maps of ancient sacred times: morning is the time of Resurrection, midmorning is the time of Pentecost, noon is the time of the Crucifixion, mid-afternoon is the death of Christ, and evening is the Last Supper.

**S'ter Says**

**Vows** are the promises made when one goes into a religious order. They are like wedding vows. The principal three are poverty (giving up private ownership to the community), chastity (giving up the right to marry and have intimate sexual relationships in order to devote themselves to the church), and obedience (submitting to the authority of superiors for assignments).

This liturgy, along with the daily celebration of Mass, is part of the official prayers of the church, which means that the church says them everyday. Ordained leaders in the church are expected to say the Liturgy of the Hours daily. In monasteries and convents this prayer is chanted in community according to its designated hours.

The Liturgy of the Hours is composed of hymns, psalms, scripture, and prayers. The seven traditional Hours and their spiritual character follow:

➤ **Vigils** is the time of watching in the night. This prayer is celebrated at the midnight hour as one is enveloped in darkness in the silence of prayer and meditation while awaiting the coming of morning.

➤ **Lauds** is the prayer at daybreak; thanking God for the first light, as at the beginning of creation, and for the light of Christ's resurrection. New beginnings, awakened innocence, joy, and optimism are expressed in the prayers.

➤ **Terce** (Latin for third hour) is said at midmorning; the prayers call for strength as work begins and the day waxes strong. This hour is a reminder of Pentecost and the coming of the Holy Spirit, who strengthened the apostles.

➤ **Sext** (sixth hour) is prayed at noon when the sun burns directly overhead. One has become weary, and mindfulness of God is all but impossible. The prayer is a call for perseverance; a reminder that Christ's crucifixion began at this hour.

➤ **Nones** (ninth hour) is prayed at midafternoon and calls for more perseverance and strength to continue as one exceeds his or her prime and must keep going. The sun is descending. By acknowledging this hour of Christ's death, one touches finitude.

➤ **Vespers** is celebrated at day's end. The evening light bathes the world in gold, transfiguring it. One sees beyond the struggles of the day. This is the hour of wisdom, and rest in thanksgiving after the work of the day.

➤ **Compline** is from the Latin meaning "complete." It is the last prayer before retiring for the night. It foreshadows life's end and leads back to the darkness of night and the darkness of God's mystery. This prayer is a gentle daily exercise in the art of dying.

## Mysticism: The Feminine Force in the Church

Mysticism literally means mystery and can be understood as the practice of meditation. It has been called the highest form of prayer. In the meditative state, the mystic has an experience of God. The practice of mysticism achieves a state of consciousness that takes the practitioner beyond the level of ordinary religious experience to a deep place within the self, where God is experienced intuitively. Mystics talk of exquisite sensations of burning desire for God. They report being consumed by his love in ways that are incomprehensible and are beyond words. A mystical experience is beyond reason, argumentation, or concern with proofs of God's existence. Through such an encounter, the mystic comes to know God's nature. Two women who had a great influence in mysticism and in convent life were St. Catherine and St. Teresa.

## A Woman out of her Place

If Catherine of Siena (1347–1380) were alive today, she would be described as a woman with an attitude! This spunky, spontaneous, fly-in-the-face of convention young woman told kings how to behave, rebuked cardinals, and chastised the pope—and lived to tell about it! Catherine had many mystical experiences she wrote about.

Catherine's writing took another form as well. She often wrote letters that she used for "counseling," and she did not seem to be shy about her mission. She wrote to Pope Gregory XI, who was caught up in a religious/political skirmish. She basically told him to let it go, to "… be not a timorous child, but manly," and to get back to work. She wrote to another pope telling him he needed to control his temper. Her letters provide a window into the history and culture of the period. They are valued in particular because they show that her activity extended far beyond the normal boundaries for women of her time and position in the church and society.

Catherine's greatest gift may well be the gift of common sense she brought to the church. She is known for the spiritual insight she provided into the caring nature of ministry. The keynote to Catherine's teaching is self-knowledge. Although she didn't learn to write until almost the end of her life, her writings earned her the title of doctor of the church. She died at the young age of 33 and was declared a saint only 81 years later.

### Epiphanies

As a child, Catherine of Siena dreamed of dressing up like a man so that she could be accepted as a Dominican friar. From her earliest years, she knew she had a calling to religious life. She was born into a world that limited women in many ways, and although her parents opposed her vocation, they must have known their willful child would succeed in her goal. At 16, she entered the convent of the Sisters of St. Dominic. Her religious life centered on her numerous visions and ecstasies, and later she began writing.

## Teresa of Ávila

Teresa of Ávila (1515–1582) was considered outrageously attractive, possessing a beauty matched only by her irascible spirit. Born to a wealthy Spanish family, she was at home in many worlds. She sang, danced, played a tambourine, was a shrewd businesswoman, cooked, was a Zen master, and had an admirable knowledge of what ails and what heals the human body and spirit. She was a sixteenth-century Spanish nun who inspired a school of spirituality that is still followed today.

Teresa may have been the first to espouse the "Let go and let God!" principle. Although she was an educated and intelligent woman and believed in reason and learning, she urged those she taught to lay reason aside and surrender the intellect to a higher power. She wrote about "knowing ourselves" and the great spirit of freedom we get by quieting the thinking self and joining with God. She was described as a warrior spirit with a fiery temperament. She was awarded the title of doctor of the church.

### For Heaven's Sake!

Don't worry! Be happy! Teresa of Ávila said, "Let go, and let God! Surrender the intellect to a higher power." Teresa felt strongly that we should learn to "get out of our heads," meaning that we should slow down our minds and learn how to experience God's love by feeling it, not just thinking or talking about it.

A major contribution of mysticism is the spiritual literature it produced and the deeper understanding it offered of the nurturing and loving nature of God. Like the Hebrew Song of Songs, mystical

**195**

writings were sensuous, poetic, and filled with profound understandings of Christ's nature and ways to relate to him. Teresa's meditations brought a new understanding of God's relationship to us. She spoke of God seeking our friendship and needing our companionship. A great legacy is found in her writings, reflections, prayers, and poetry. In them, she dealt with the everyday human conditions of love and intimacy, friendship and family, dreams and nightmares, suffering, prayer, and the mystery of God. Her style has been characterized as lavish, elegant, extravagant, and flamboyant. In that regard, it matched her life and reflected her zest and enthusiasm.

### Saints Preserve Us

**John of the Cross, December 14, Patron Saint of Mystics**

A contemporary of Teresa of Ávila, John of the Cross lived from 1542 to 1591. He was a Catholic mystic, poet, and member of the Carmelite religious order. St. John suffered from depression and despair and wrote his greatest poetry during this time. His major work is "The Dark Night of the Soul," which describes his profound insight into how his depression and despair were lifted through his contemplative practice. "The Dark Night of the Soul" has become the modern metaphor for despair and the subsequent inner journey to healing that happens through meditation. St. John is a good reminder that the saints struggled with many of the same human conditions that are part of our journey, too. He is the patron saint of mystics, but he would also be a good patron saint for those suffering from depression.

## Mysticism Today

Contemplation has been said to quiet the mind, still the body, and open the heart to God. It engages the whole self in the meditative process and moves the practitioner beyond thoughts, emotions, or words, into a state of true being. In this sacred space, practitioners are able to hear and feel God's presence within.

In present times, responding to an apparent deep hunger for spirituality, Catholics are having a renewed interest in contemplative prayer, and now this practice is no longer restricted to the monasteries. A contemporary contemplative practice is called *centering prayer* and comes from the tradition of John of the Cross. It awakens people to the presence of God within and builds contemplative attitudes of listening and receptivity. This practice is a synthesis of the wisdom of Zen (Buddhism) and Hindu traditions of meditation with the contemplative tradition of Catholicism.

This type of prayer often follows four steps:

1. Reading of sacred scripture

2. Reflecting on the scripture

3. Focusing on a key image

4. Resting in contemplation

Meditation is the practice of teaching the mind to stay pleasantly focused in the present moment. Many approaches to meditation can be grouped broadly as contemplative and mindful meditation. Contemplative meditation focuses on a single point (often the breath) and stills the mind. Mindful meditation opens the mind to observe the flow of thoughts, feelings, and sensations passing through one's awareness without thinking about them. Regardless of the type practiced, meditation's benefits to the whole self (body and spirit) are great. The body gains a deeper state of relaxation than that produced by sleep. Meditation increases awareness, intelligence, and creativity. Virtually all physiological systems are positively influenced by meditation. As a result, meditation is being taught in hospitals all over the country.

In the past 15 years many books on Catholic contemplative practices have been published. Our bibliography in the appendix cites many of these works. Catholic organizations for contemplative and centering prayer have developed across the country and throughout the world. Retreats and classes devoted to contemplative prayer are now widely available.

# Sacred Music

Music is worship; it is prayer. It is an essential element to Catholic worship. Music used in worship services is called liturgical music. During Vatican II, when the church reviewed its music along with other practices, it stressed music's importance in the worship service and identified the necessity of it as an integral part of the Mass. The council promoted full participation of the faithful in the Mass, especially by way of its music. Vatican II represented a major shift from music that was in Latin and performed by choirs to a new music in English that is sung by the people.

### Your Guardian Angel

When planning your church celebrations (marriages, anniversaries, and funerals), choose music that sounds right for you and fits with the liturgical calendar. Talk with your priest if you have any questions.

## How Sacred Music Functions

In order for music to attain its liturgical purposes (to provide the listeners with spiritual sustenance), these qualities should be considered:

➤ **Aesthetic**, to connect the holy to the beautiful

➤ **Diversionary**, to eliminate boredom during tedious times during the Mass

➤ **Emotional**, to express hope and joy when words alone cannot do it

➤ **Enjoyable**, so that it is pleasurable to hear and perform

➤ **Involving**, so that it unites and draws people together into deeper participation in the Mass

➤ **Mood-setting**, to make the worship capable of addressing a wide range of human emotion

➤ **Revelatory**, so that it explores and reveals the religious experience

➤ **Text-enhancing**, to underscore the sacredness of certain texts

In most parishes, the choir director and the pastor work together to select music that matches the liturgical calendar and captures the meaning of the feasts.

## Gregorian Chant

Once a definitive Catholic sound, Gregorian chant almost dropped out of use in the Catholic Church after Vatican II. Today, it's enjoying a resurgence of popularity throughout the culture. New understanding of its effects on the listener have found that its melodies quiet the mind, soothe the nerves, open the heart, and prepare one for worship. Several recordings of it have become best-sellers.

**Your Guardian Angel**

Chill out with chant! People believe that Gregorian chant assists in unifying body, soul, and spirit. It works its spiritual wonders both on the singers and the listeners. Chant creates a relaxed state in which the mind is stilled, the emotions are quieted, and the soul experiences a sense of peace.

Named for Pope Gregory, Gregorian chant was compiled and arranged in the sixth century and was derived from chants sung in ancient Jerusalem. Many more chants were composed in later centuries. Gregorian chant was sung both in the cathedrals and in the monasteries, and credit for its survival is given to the Benedictine monks in northwest France, who began restoring the texts in the latter half of the nineteenth century.

Gregorian chant is also called plainsong or plainchant, which describes it quite well. It is a plain, monophonic, vocal music printed in square notes on a four-line staff. There is no chromatic scale or chromatic progression, and usually there is no modulation from one mode to another in the same melody. The melodies conform to the voice's natural range. Gregorian chant uses no defined rhythm. It functions as an extension of speech, as compared to metrical or rhythmic or polyphonic music

(Greek for "many voiced"), in which two or more strands sound simultaneously. Notes are generally equal in time length in Gregorian chant, but the speed of singing is a matter of style preference.

Although Gregorian chant provides the foundation for Western music, it was designed for prayer and has a strong spiritual component. Key to its importance as a worship device is its close association with the psalms. Chant was designed as a means of singing them.

### Saints Preserve Us

**St. Cecelia, November 22, Patron of Musicians**

St. Cecelia lived in Rome during the second century. She had made a vow of virginity to God; however, her parents forced her to marry. Her husband was not a Catholic, although he converted soon after their marriage. Cecelia reported hearing music from God all during her wedding. Both she and her husband were martyred. Church choirs have always remembered her name, and she is one of the saints mentioned in the prayers of the Mass. She is the patron of all musicians and of church music. Organ builders, composers, and poets all claim her as their patron as well.

In the Bible, Paul identifies three types of text sung during the early period of the church (Ephesians 5:18):

➤ Psalms

➤ Canticles, poems from the Bible

➤ Hymns, the earliest of which deal with the identity of Christ and the meaning of his life and death

## Gregorian Chant Today

At the beginning of the twentieth century, the pope made a statement to the effect that Gregorian chant, and the polyphonic music that came from it, was the supreme model of liturgical music. After Vatican II, Gregorian chant almost disappeared, replaced by popular music and a renewed liturgy. It is important to note, however, that chant and liturgy developed together in an organic process. Chant is filled with the spirit of centuries of religious feeling and thought. Polyphonic music that developed

**199**

**For Heaven's Sake!**

Don't throw the music out with the bath water! In its attempt to modernize, some mistakes may have been made. For centuries, people used chant as a form of prayer. Its simplicity allows the chanter to concentrate on the meaning of the psalm being sung rather than having to pay attention to complicated melodies.

out of Gregorian chant carries with it a similar spiritual content. The standoff between traditional and popular music may be near an end as the church begins to consider its music history as a valuable theological tradition. Hopefully a synthesis can be accomplished that would offer the best of both worlds.

Chant has many more effects than meets the ear. Beyond its theological application lies another surprising benefit of Gregorian chant. It seems as though it has a positive effect on physiology and emotions as well. A story circulating in the world of church music tells that back in the 1960s, a French physician was summoned to a Benedictine monastery in the south of France to investigate a strange set of circumstances. The usually happy and productive monks had become despondent. In the wake of Vatican II, several hours a day of chanting had been suddenly eliminated from the daily routine. Following a hunch, the doctor told the abbot he would like to put the men back on their regular routine. The effect was dramatic.

Within six months, they had become vigorous and happy again. They needed less sleep, and their monkish productivity increased. Gregorian chant lowers blood pressure, elevates the mood, and soothes the nerves. It seems it has something to offer the twenty-first century after all.

We've looked at some favorite Catholic prayers and practices and touched on Gregorian chant. In the next chapter, you'll learn about some of the opportunities for spiritual growth in the Catholic Church.

## The Least You Need to Know

➤ Prayer is one's personal relationship to God. It cannot be captured in any one prayer or contained in any one form.

➤ The Rosary is a popular Catholic prayer. Praying the Rosary is a spiritual practice that contains both contemplation and spoken prayer.

➤ Contemplation is a mystical practice that takes practitioners to their deepest center to experience their relationship with God.

➤ Gregorian chant has a long history in the church. Its use of monotone unifies the body, mind, and spirit.

# Chapter 15

# For Catholics Prayer Is More Than Just Words

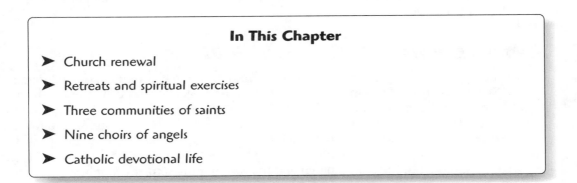

## In This Chapter

➤ Church renewal

➤ Retreats and spiritual exercises

➤ Three communities of saints

➤ Nine choirs of angels

➤ Catholic devotional life

Catholicism is a communal religion; being Catholic means being a member of a tribe. To understand the Catholic religion, you have to understand that prayer and other practices are more than just rituals. They are the ways in which Catholics sustain and develop community. Religious imagination guides relationships with others. At the base of all religious and spiritual practices is the goal of love: loving God, loving self, and loving others. In this chapter, we'll look at these relationships as an extension of Catholic prayer life.

# Church Movements and Retreats: What's Happening!

Religious movements within the Catholic Church have a long and interesting history, and renewal is a key concept throughout, underscoring a characterization of the

Catholic Church as *semper reformanda*, "always reforming." The Catholic Church has always been a church in process. These movements are usually the inspiration of a charismatic person, most likely a priest or a nun with a strong sense of what needs to happen in a given time. In the past, these movements have often taken the form of new religious orders, groups of priests, monks, or nuns who live a particular lifestyle and attend to a certain aspect of Catholic life.

Today, lay people are becoming involved in creating and sustaining such movements. Movements are inspired by the needs of the community, generally emerging in a country or area of a country and spreading worldwide. They are encouraged by the Vatican as well as by local bishops who appoint a director for the movement in his diocese. The benefits include the revitalization of parish life through the strengthening of community. The way to locate retreats and spiritual movements is through the local parish, diocesan newspaper, or a phone call to the local diocese. The diocese will have a schedule of which parishes are participating in the various programs and other information.

This section describes some of the popular movements currently happening within the United States.

## Renew: Community Circles of Faith

Renew is the name of a popular movement for the twenty-first century, originating in a New Jersey diocese and spreading across the country. Small faith communities are at the heart of the movement: People meet in small groups in homes once a week to read the Sunday scriptures, to share their experiences in light of these scriptures, and to discern ways in which they can apply their faith during the week. The relationships that develop in these groups strengthen the individual, who in turn reaches out to the larger parish and then to the larger church and the surrounding secular community. The program is multigenerational, and special attention is given to keeping the groups small and the commitment manageable with today's schedules.

As an international movement, Renew is proving to be very successful. Participants in the first season numbered over 400,000 in English-speaking communities and 35,000 in Spanish-speaking communities in the United States alone. The intention of this movement is most clearly stated this way: a process that can help a parish grow from being a committee to being a community.

The Prayer for Renew captures the spirit of the movement:

> Gracious God,
> We are your people embraced by your love.
> We thank you for your presence with us throughout all time.
> As we celebrate the 2,000 years since the birth of Jesus … create us anew.
> Liberate us from that which keeps us from you.
> Enable us to re-create our world and restore justice.

Heal us from every form of sin and violence.
Transform us to live your word more profoundly.
Reconcile us so enemies become friends.
Awaken us to the sacred; nurture our relationships;
Enliven our parishes; strengthen our families.
Fill us with joy to celebrate the fullness of life.
Empower us to be a community of love growing in your likeness.
We ask this in Jesus' name. Amen.

## Cursillo: Centering on Christ

Cursillo literally means "little course." It is a program of spiritual renewal that originated in Spain about 50 years ago and came to the United States almost 30 years ago. This movement developed in order to teach about the need for Christ in one's life. International in scope, Cursillo exists in countries all over the world. The point of this movement is to help Catholics network with one another for prayer, spiritual reading, and discussion. Participants in Cursillo attend a structured program of three courses. Each course takes three days. After completing the coursework, participants continue to meet weekly in small groups. The courses and the groups are designed to form attitudes and behavior in the members that will support them as they transform their everyday environment.

## Marriage Encounter: Heart to Heart

Marriage Encounter is a marriage-enrichment program originating in Spain in the early 1960s. The movement spread from Spain to Latin America and then, in 1966, to the United States. The goal of Marriage Encounter is to deepen the marriage bond and to encourage open communication from the heart. The program is not designed as marriage therapy; its purpose is to work with solid marriages to make them more spiritual.

Couples in the Marriage Encounter program go on a retreat weekend to work at deepening their relationship through reflection and structured dialogue with each other and with other couples. A priest and a presiding couple lead the retreat. The methods of the encounter include shared stories by other couples, journal writing, and writing letters to each other in which the husband and wife share their deepest feelings.

## Retreats: Holy "R" and "R"

Like all relationships, a person's relationship with God must be nurtured. To help nurture this all-important relationship, Catholics have a tradition of going on spiritual retreats. They take a few days away from work and family and spend time at a retreat center. Almost one million people attend more than 600 retreat centers in the United States and Canada alone each year.

### For Heaven's Sake!

Shhhhhhhhh! Most retreats are silent retreats, which means participants observe silence throughout the retreat or during parts of it.

Retreat centers are often comfortable but no-frills hotel-like buildings and are usually under the direction of a religious order. Each order structures its retreat a little differently, but daily Mass is the rule at most retreats, along with a series of talks by a retreat master on religious themes or on the mysteries of the life of Christ and their relevance to life today.

In addition, one-on-one conferences with a spiritual director are available. Spiritual direction is a process of counseling the spirit. A spiritual director is a church professional, usually a priest or a nun who has studied the spiritual life and been trained in spiritual counseling. Often they have this ministry as their sole occupation. Others may be teachers or pastors who do spiritual direction as an avocation. The relationship with a spiritual director is a therapeutic relationship similar to the one you would have with a trained counselor; however, the focus is on attending to the religious or spiritual rather than psychological needs of a person. You might take an issue that involves your prayer life to a spiritual director, or you might ask how to make your work and home life more meaningful.

Spiritual reading and journaling are encouraged during retreats. Participants are urged to treat themselves well by getting lots of sleep in comfortable beds and eating good food. Retreats are often set in beautiful places in nature, where walks in the woods or along the shore are encouraged.

### Your Guardian Angel

You don't have to be Catholic to enjoy a retreat. Many people of all faiths enjoy this tradition. Spiritual directors are trained to work with individuals of all beliefs, assisting them in discovering personal truths and learning to live their lives according to the things they value.

## Spiritual Exercises: Toning up the Soul

The spiritual exercises of Ignatius of Loyola have been in constant use for 450 years. They represent a heavy-duty form of retreat. Currently more people are using them than at any time in history. It is estimated that the exercises as written by Ignatius have been reprinted at least once a month since their conception in the 1500s, a frequency that increases yearly. Once only fully trained Jesuits directed people through the 30-day process. Today, the church trains both lay and clergy men and women as leaders.

A Spanish priest who founded the Jesuit order, Ignatius wrote the exercises before becoming a priest, and many believe they are inspired writing. Contemplative in nature, they express the foundational belief that all comes from God, all moves under God's direction and care, and all returns to God in and through his son, Jesus Christ. They stress action as an expression of gratitude. The exercises emphasize service to others because it is through service that we find God. The process teaches contemplation and builds spiritual awareness of God's presence within. In modern times, we are challenged to find God in the events of the world. We live in an age of rapidly developing technology, where limits and boundaries continue to be breached almost quicker than we can adapt to them. Many people search for meaning beyond the mere consumption of goods. It seems the numbers of people drawn to these spiritual exercises are finding them surprisingly relevant for today, because they work to change the way we see the world.

**For Heaven's Sake!**

The spiritual exercises are not a spiritual escape! They involve learning how to live more spiritually in the world. They teach how to be contemplative while being active.

Although earthly relationships are attended to through church movements and special retreats, there is another area of relationship that exists in the Catholic world that reaches beyond the temporal realm. The Catholic community extends beyond life on earth and sees all its members past and present as functioning in a united community. The purpose of this community is to help one another along the "path to glory."

# Sacred Relationships: Communion of Saints

The term *communion of saints* links three aspects of the church: those who are pilgrims on the earthly journey, the deceased who are in heaven, and the dead who await entrance into heaven. In linking the church members in this way, the Catholic community moves beyond the boundaries of linear time of past, present, and future. It operates from a more spiritual concept of time, which is the eternal now. Through this concept of communion, the present-day Catholic feels connected to Christ's life and the lives of others who have come before and has a sense of the future church, including those yet to be born.

**S'ter Says**

**Communion of saints** is a phrase from the Apostles' Creed that describes the church as a Catholic family that includes those who are on the earthly journey and those who have left the earth.

The communion of saints is a way of placing us all in one family. When you consider your family heritage, you think of all your ancestors. Many people make a study of their family tree, identifying the members of their family far back into history. The events of their lives become part of the family legend, affecting how present family members understand themselves and their place in the world. The communion of saints is a way of understanding Catholics as a family.

## The Church Marching

The church on earth is called the *church militant*. This term describes the living members of the church in their spiritual struggle to lead good lives. In the broadest sense of the term it includes all beings striving to lead spiritual lives. In the past, the emphasis was on a Catholic community to the exclusion of other Christians and non-Christians. Since Vatican II, the image has become much more inclusive. The council stated that the Holy Spirit is believed to be at work wherever people labor to make life more human and that the Spirit's gifts can be found outside the visible boundaries of the Catholic Church. The emphasis of Vatican II is toward uniting all God's people.

## When the Saints Go Marching In!

The *church triumphant* refers to saints, who are deceased members of the faithful who have gone to their heavenly reward. Catholics honor saints as wise ancestors and petition them for spiritual assistance. Saints serve as models of the virtues Catholics hope to attain, but Catholics do not worship them. An extensive roster of saints exists, and they watch over almost every earthly task or event.

To grow up Catholic meant reading about the lives of the saints. Each school day began with a student writing the name of the saint whose feast day it was on the blackboard. The saint's story was read, and it was often followed by a discussion on the virtues and bravery exhibited by the saint. In much the same way a public school child would write about Abraham Lincoln or Betsy Ross, Catholic school kids would give reports about their heroes and heroines.

It takes a special type of person to become a saint and a special process, too. It is called *canonization*. Before someone can be declared a saint or canonized, proof of their good works must be documented. Their history along with biographical data, any writings or stories about the person, and at least one miracle are thoroughly investigated. First they are awarded the status of beatification, and following further investigation the holy person may elevated to sainthood by the pope.

Traditionally, Catholics have had a highly developed sense of connection to their "glorified brothers and sisters." It has been a Catholic tradition to name children after saints, and a saint is chosen at the time of confirmation, as mentioned in the discussion of confirmation in Chapter 11, "Seven Sensual Sacraments." In addition, Catholics might develop a relationship with the patron saint who watches over their lives or has a particular quality they seek to develop within themselves. Catholics develop this relationship through practices such as reading about the saint, celebrating their feast day as a sort of second birthday, and having a statue, medal, or holy card of the saint.

### Saints Preserve Us

**St. Jude, October 28**

**St. Rita, May 22**

If you are up against something in your life that seems impossible, here are two saints that offer you spiritual support. They don't guarantee you will "get what you want," but they will help give you the strength to deal with difficult times. The first is St. Jude, who was a relative of Jesus and preached the gospel message throughout the Middle East. He was martyred in Armenia. The other is St. Rita, who lost her husband and her two children, and dedicated her life to Christ. She became ill and suffered much for the rest of her life, dying in 1457, never losing faith. St. Jude's feast day is October 28 and St. Rita's is May 22.

## "Oh, Yes, I Want to Be in Their Number ..."

The *church suffering,* or the "poor souls in purgatory," refers to the state of the soul of a departed brethren who may have died with some unfinished spiritual business. Purgatory was once thought to be an actual place, but it is now commonly believed to be a condition of purification necessary before being admitted to the glory and happiness of heaven. It is a state of passive suffering, which means that the suffering stems from being delayed in seeing God and enjoying the heavenly reward. Catholics believe that, just like the relationship between the living and the glorified exists, a relationship exists with the departed in purgatory, too. All Souls' Day is a time in the church calendar dedicated to prayers for the dead to speed them on their way. Rituals, prayers, and good works are offered for the dead all through the year.

### Your Guardian Angel

When choosing your child's name, consider consulting a book on the lives of the saints. Saints represent values. You might choose a name of a saint or a biblical character whose story has meaning to you.

Psalm 130 is a traditional prayer to be said for the dead:

> Out of the depths I cry to you, O Lord.
> Lord, hear my voice!
> Let your ears be attentive to the voice of my supplications!
> If you, O Lord, should mark iniquities, Lord, who could stand?
> But there is forgiveness with you, so that you may be revered.
> I wait for the Lord, my soul waits, and in his word I hope;
> my soul waits for the Lord more than those who watch for the morning, more than those who watch for the morning.
> O Israel, hope in the Lord!
> For with the Lord there is steadfast love, and with him is great power to redeem.
> It is he who will redeem Israel from all its iniquities.

## Angels: God's Winged Army

Angels are beings created higher than humans. The word *angel* comes from the Greek *aggelos,* which is a translation of the Hebrew *malakh,* meaning messenger. This word describes their job rather than their being. They praise God, they reveal God's will to earthly beings, and they generally do God's bidding. They are also present in Islam and other traditions.

The Catholic Church teaches that angels are spiritual beings with intelligence and will. They have been present since creation. The scriptures tell of angels in both the Old and New Testaments. For instance, in Genesis 3:24 angels with fiery swords guarded the gates of paradise. One timely dispatched angel stopped Abraham from slaying his son Isaac. An angel of mercy saved Daniel in the lion's den. In the New Testament, the Archangel Gabriel was sent to ask Mary's cooperation in the Incarnation of Jesus. Hosts of heavenly angels heralded the birth of Jesus. In the book of Matthew, Jesus describes 12 legions of them awaiting his command. Angels are important in the book of Revelation because they announce the Second Coming of Christ and the Last Judgment.

Christianity developed the tradition of choirs of angels serving in the heavenly ranks. Sometime in the fifth century, the following hierarchy of angelic beings was established:

➤ Seraphim

➤ Cherubim

➤ Thrones

➤ Dominions

➤ Virtues

➤ Powers

➤ Principalities

➤ Archangels

➤ Angels

The first three types of angelic beings are dedicated to the contemplation of God. The next three govern the universe. The last three are God's messengers. Only three angels are mentioned by name in the Bible: Michael whose name means "like God," Gabriel, whose name means "God announces," and Raphael, meaning "God heals." Catholic tradition, based on the Bible passage Matthew 18:10, holds that guardian angels guide and protect us.

Here is a prayer Catholics teach their children about angels. It is often one of the first prayers they learn and is said at bedtime.

> Angel of God,
> My guardian dear,
> To whom God's love commits me here.
> Ever this day be at my side,
> To light, to guard, to rule, and guide.
> Amen

Angels remain a popular subject of religious art. Early renderings show them as men; later artists depicted them as having wings. The tradition of picturing angels as cherubs creates a limited understanding of their apparent place in creation. The communion of saints and angels provide an understanding of what it means to be in a relationship and on a common path. Common images are developed, and common language is formed. The bonds of community once established are then strengthened through shared ritual experiences. The following sections describe some of the more popular rituals of Catholic worship.

# Church Devotions

Devotions are prayers and rituals that express reverence to God. The church holds many communal devotions throughout the year. It is part of a tradition called Catholic piety. Many of the devotions honor or recall an aspect of Christ's life, Mary's life, a particular saint, or a doctrine of faith. Some are seasonal, but they are not strictly part of the liturgical calendar of the church and are optional. Although these devotions have been greatly de-emphasized since Vatican II, they remain an important part of Catholic life.

## Novenas

*Novena* means nine. Novenas are devotional prayers repeated for nine days or one day a week for nine weeks. The novena is based on the fact that the apostles prayed for

### S'ter Says

**Novena** is a Latin word, *novem*, meaning nine. In the Catholic religion, a novena is a devotion repeated nine successive times.

nine days before the Holy Spirit came to them on Pentecost. Novenas are usually directed to a specific religious figure for special intentions. They most likely include Mass and special prayers.

Catholics offer novenas for a variety of intentions. Here is a novena to St. Peregrine, the saint for those afflicted with cancer. Catholics say this prayer along with daily attendance at Mass for nine consecutive days:

> O glorious wonder-worker, St. Peregrine, you answered the divine call with a ready spirit. You left all the comforts of a life of ease and all the empty honors of the world to dedicate yourself to God in the order of his most holy mother. You labored zealously for the salvation of people, meriting the title of apostle. In union with Jesus crucified, you endured the most painful sufferings with such patience that you were healed miraculously. With a touch of the divine hand, your incurable leg wound disappeared. Deliver us from the infirmities that often afflict our bodies.

### Saints Preserve Us

**St. Peregrine Laziosi, May 1, Patron Against Cancer**

St. Peregrine Laziosi (1260–1345) was born in Italy of well-to-do parents and was active as a youth in the anti-papal party, *Romagna*. After an encounter with St. Phillip, he was inspired to profoundly change his life. He joined a religious order where he was subsequently ordained. He became famous for his preaching, his austerities, his holiness, and as a confessor after experiencing a miraculous cure. An advanced cancer on his foot was miraculously healed after he had a vision. He was made a saint in 1726 and is the patron who may be invoked against cancer.

Nine First Fridays is a novena devotion consisting of attending Mass and Holy Communion on the first Friday of the month for nine consecutive months. It includes the recitation of certain prayers and is done in honor of the Sacred Heart of Jesus.

## Stations of the Cross

On the walls of almost all Catholic churches you will see a series of pictures or plaques, such as the one shown here, representing 14 events of the passion and death of Christ. Early Christians traced the steps of Jesus' walk to the cross, and pilgrims visiting the Holy Land today do so as well. The Stations of the Cross is a prayer service held in the tradition of pilgrimage and consists of meditation on the suffering, death, and burial of Jesus.

The Stations of the Cross are commonly part of the parish Lenten devotions. The priest leads a procession, accompanied by two or more altar servers carrying a cross and lighted candles throughout the church and stopping at each of the stations. The people say prayers and sing hymns as they travel through Jesus' journey, from his condemnation through the crucifixion to the last station where Jesus is laid in the tomb. Stations of the Cross can be a private devotion or a communal prayer form.

Although the church has many devotions and practices, the center of Catholic spiritual life is the Mass. Many visitors find the ritual fascinating and puzzling at the same time. Perhaps after reading the next chapter, you will gain a deeper understanding of this most central Catholic prayer.

---

### The Least You Need to Know

➤ Community is at the heart of the church.

➤ The church is always renewing itself.

➤ Retreats and movements are ways in which church renewal happens.

➤ The boundaries of the church's community extend past time and space.

➤ Devotional rituals reinforce the bonds of community.

# Chapter 16

---

# The Mass: The Catholics' Big Dinner Party

## In This Chapter

➤ What is a Catholic Mass?

➤ The two parts of the Mass and its seven activities

➤ What Catholics understand Holy Communion to be

➤ How to participate in the Mass

You've probably switched on the evening news only to be greeted by the image of the Pope celebrating a Mass with 10,000 people in attendance. Other times the media reveals glimpses of the Catholic faith in practice is at a Catholic celebrity wedding or during a funeral when pallbearers carry a notable person's casket through the doors of a Catholic Church after a funeral mass.

More than any other practice, the Mass marks Catholicism. Why is this so? Just what is the Mass? What happens during it? What do you do if you attend it? The answers to these and other questions are what this chapter is all about.

## Celebrating a Sacrifice: What Is the Mass?

Catholics can use one of three terms to describe their central ritual: Mass, Eucharist, and Holy Communion. All three terms mean the same thing and can be used interchangeably.

An old saying that is especially appropriate in seeing how important the Mass is to Catholics is: "What we act out is what we believe, and what we believe we act out." This is a great rule of thumb for examining any of our principles: personal, family, business, or political. What the church acts out most is the Mass. Mass is not only offered and attended by Catholics on Sunday, but it is offered everyday. There is no hour of any day on this planet when a Catholic Mass is not being offered!

The Mass has two parts and a series of seven activities:

**Part I: Liturgy of the Word: Instruction**

➤ Gathering

➤ Proclaiming

➤ Explaining

➤ Praying

**Part II: The Liturgy of the Eucharist: Breaking Bread**

➤ Offering

➤ Consecrating

➤ Communion

**Your Guardian Angel**

If you are a person of another faith and are attending the Catholic Mass, it is acceptable to sit throughout the service. Or you can sit, stand, and kneel along with the other folks.

The two parts of the Mass are reflected in the New Testament story of the two disciples on the road to Emmaus the day of Jesus' resurrection (Luke 24:13–35). In the first part of the story, Jesus walks with them, but they do not recognize him. He quotes the Jewish scriptures that talk about the coming of the messiah. They still don't recognize him. Then he sits down to dinner with them, and he blesses and breaks bread. They now recognize him. The two acts of the story are the quoting of scripture and the breaking of the bread. It's easiest to look at the Mass as divided into these two major parts. Let's begin with the first activity in the first part: the gathering.

## The Guests Arrive

The first activity of gathering perhaps best identifies the Mass with the real meaning of the church. After Jesus' resurrection, his followers gathered together for the purpose of keeping his work alive. The gatherings of the early communities grew, and thus the church was constituted. Gathering remains the primary function of the church. If Catholics quit gathering, the entire Catholic Church would cease to exist.

At the beginning of the Mass, the congregation stands. The gathering begins by acknowledging God's greatness and the need for his help with a Greek prayer called the *Kyrie:*

> Lord have mercy.
> Christ have mercy.
> Lord have mercy.

Other gathering prayers of praise include the *Gloria,* which can be spoken or sung. It begins with the words, as recorded in scripture, that the angels used to announce the birth of Jesus: "Glory to God in the highest!"

The priest then recites a prayer. The prayers and scripture readings follow the cycle of the liturgical calendar. That is, the themes change depending on the season and historical events in the calendar. The liturgical calendar appears in Chapter 13, "Feeding the Imagination."

## Proclaiming the Word of God

After the priest's prayer, the congregation sits. At this point, a layperson known as a lector reads an Old Testament passage (or a passage from the Acts of the Apostles or the Book of Revelation). Lectors are members of the congregation who have been formally commissioned to read the readings in their parish.

Next, the congregation either sings or recites one of the psalms. Usually a lector or cantor recites or sings a verse, to which the people respond with a verse from the psalm.

The second reading follows with a passage from one of the New Testament letters. At this point, the congregation stands and sings the *Gospel*
Acclamation, a great "Alleluia!" The alleluia is to welcome the word of God in the Gospel. Finally, the priest or deacon reads a Gospel passage from the New Testament.

**S'ter Says**

The word **gospel** means "good news" and refers to the good news that Christ has come. The Gospel is taken from the writings of Matthew, Mark, Luke, and John.

## A Word to the Wise

At the conclusion of the Gospel, the people sit to listen to the priest's homily. This is the talk in which he reflects on the various readings and their application to everyday life. Generally this talk lasts about 10 to 15 minutes on a Sunday. During the weekday Mass, the homily, if one is given, is no more than five minutes.

Following the homily, the congregation has a short time to reflect quietly on what the priest has said. Then the people stand to recite the Nicene Creed together. The Nicene Creed is the formulation of Catholic faith or belief statements:

➤ We believe in one God, the Father almighty, maker of heaven and earth, of all that is seen and unseen.

➤ We believe in one Lord Jesus Christ, the only son of God, eternally begotten of the Father, God from God, light from light, true God from true God, begotten not made, one in being with the Father. Through him all things were made. For us men and for our salvation, he came down from heaven: by the power of the Holy Spirit, he was born of the Virgin Mary and became man. For our sake, he was crucified under Pontius Pilate, he suffered, died, and was buried. On the third day, he rose again in fulfillment of the scriptures. He ascended into heaven and is seated at the right hand of the Father. He will come again in glory to judge the living and the dead, and his kingdom will have no end.

➤ We believe in the Holy Spirit, the Lord, the giver of life, who proceeds from the Father and the Son. With the Father and Son, he is worshiped and glorified. He has spoken through the prophets.

➤ We believe in one holy, catholic, and apostolic church. We acknowledge one baptism for the forgiveness of sins. We look for the resurrection of the dead and the life of the world to come. Amen.

### Epiphanies

In a recent homily on the passage "Blessed are they who hunger for justice ..." from the Sermon on the Mount, a priest suggested to the people of his parish that the Sermon on the Mount is a challenge to them to transform their world to Gospel values. He told stories about a visit some of the parishioners made to a parish in a poorer section of town during the past week. By doing so, he illustrated for the entire congregation that it was possible to begin to transform the world by putting up sheet rock, cleaning up the park, and helping kids learn to read, and explained how meaningful and spiritual such activities were at their heart.

## The Prayers Go out over the Land

Following the Nicene Creed, the people pray for the needs of the world in the prayers of the faithful. A lector will usually read a short intercession to which the people respond: "Lord, hear our prayer." These prayers usually pray for the pope and the church, the leaders of the nation, for those in difficulty, for the sick and infirm (especially those from the parish, who will be named), and for the dead. The congregation then sits down for the offering.

### Epiphanies

The two common creeds Catholics pray are the Nicene and Apostles'. The Nicene was formulated at the church's first council in 325 C.E. As a council-formulated creed it is a "technical" document. As early as the first century there is evidence of a creed that was the statement of the beliefs of the Apostles—The Apostles Creed. The Apostles Creed is a user-friendly version (for example it begins with "I believe" rather than "We believe"). Over the years the church has allowed the substitution of this creed for the Nicene Creed, for example at baptism and in masses for children.

## There's No Free Lunch!

At this point, the congregation prepares to move into the second part of the Mass: the liturgy of the Eucharist. Members (quite often children or a family) take the gifts up to the priest at the altar: the bread, which will become the body of Christ, and the wine, which will become his blood.

### For Heaven's Sake!

Use your envelopes. Most parishes ask parishioners to pledge a certain amount of money for the year and to use printed envelopes for the collection basket. It is easier on the parish bookkeeper and on you at tax time.

At this time, the collection is taken. The people are invited to give an offering that supports the operation of the church. The priest receives these gifts and says a blessing over them, offering them to God "as the work and fruit of our hands." Often the choir sings a hymn or a musician plays music.

The priest prays that God will "cleanse him of all iniquity" and symbolically washes his fingers that will touch the bread. The people pray that God will accept the gifts "for the praise and glory of his name, for our good, and the good of all his church."

## Blessing the Bread

The priest recites a short prayer of praise to God while the congregation kneels. The altar server rings the altar bells three times as the people sing the *Sanctus:*

> Holy, Holy, Holy Lord,
> God of power and might,
> Heaven and Earth are full of your glory

Hosanna in the highest!
Blessed is he who comes in the name of the Lord
Hosanna in the highest!

The priest begins to pray the great prayer of thanksgiving and supplication to God called the Eucharistic prayer. This prayer is the most important prayer of the Mass. There are several Eucharistic prayers to choose from. The one that follows draws upon the liturgical traditions and imagery of the ancient church.

**Priest:** "Lord, you are holy indeed, the fountain of all holiness. Let your spirit come upon these gifts (bread and wine) to make them holy so that they may become the body and blood of our Lord Jesus Christ. Before he was given up to death, a death he freely accepted, he took bread and gave you thanks. He broke the bread, gave it to his disciples, and said, 'Take this all of you, and eat it. This is my body, which will be given up for you.' When supper was ended, he took the cup, and again he gave thanks and praise, gave the cup to his disciples, and said, 'Take this, all of you, and drink from it. This is the cup of my blood, the blood of the new and everlasting covenant. It will be shed for you and for all so that sins may be forgiven. Do this in memory of me.' Let us proclaim the mystery of faith."

**All:** "Dying you destroyed our death, rising you restored our life, Lord Jesus, come in glory."

**Priest:** "In memory of his death and resurrection, we offer you, Father, this life-giving bread, this saving cup. We thank you for counting us worthy to stand in your presence and serve you. May all of us who share in the body and blood of Christ be brought together in unity by the Holy Spirit. Lord, remember your church throughout the world; make us grow in love together with our pope and our bishop and all the clergy. Remember our brothers and sisters who have gone to their rest in the hope of rising again: bring them and all the departed into the light of your presence. Have mercy on us all; make us worthy to share eternal life with Mary, the virgin mother of God, with the apostles and with all the saints who have done your will throughout the ages. May we praise you in union with them and give you glory though your son, Jesus Christ. Through him, with him, in him, in the unity of the Holy Spirit, all glory and honor is yours, almighty Father, forever and ever."

### For Heaven's Sake!

Hush! It's a tradition to observe silence inside a Catholic Church. If you need to talk, be sure to whisper.

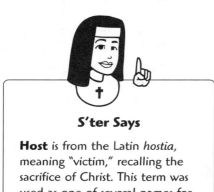

### S'ter Says

**Host** is from the Latin *hostia,* meaning "victim," recalling the sacrifice of Christ. This term was used as one of several names for the Eucharistic bread in the Middle Ages.

## Breaking the Bread

The people then stand to say the Lord's Prayer together and to share the "kiss of peace" with each
other (usually a handshake or a nod of the head).
The priest then breaks the host, symbolic of the
breaking of Jesus' body on the cross, while the people pray the *Agnus Dei:* "Lamb of God, who takes
away the sins of the world, have mercy on us."

In an act of reverence, the priest then invites the
people to acknowledge their unworthiness in the
prayer: "Lord, I am not worthy to receive you, but
only say the word, and I shall be healed." The
priest then eats and drinks the consecrated bread
and wine that have now sacramentally become the
body and blood of Christ before proceeding to distribute the sacrament to the people.
Those who are to receive the Eucharist walk up to the altar. Upon returning to their
seats, they kneel in prayer and meditation. After some time, the congregation stands.

**Your Guardian Angel**

Don't be shy about expressing
peace with those around you,
even if you don't know them.
Don't worry, you don't have to
kiss them, a handshake will do.

At the end of the Mass, the priest blesses the people and dismisses them with the
commission: "Mass is ended! Go in peace to love and serve the Lord!" He sends them
out into the world to take Christ and make him known to whomever they meet. During the blessing, the people make the sign of the cross. The priest then exits the
church while people sing a final hymn.

# It's More the Food Than the Talk: The Liturgy of the Eucharist

We are now going to look at the second part of the Mass, the liturgy of the Eucharist,
in closer detail. During this part of the Mass, the bread and wine are turned into the
body and blood of Christ and offered to God.

The main difference between a Protestant worship service and a Catholic Mass is the
liturgy of the Eucharist. Not that Protestant churches don't serve communion—many
do—but the Catholic sacramental imagination makes the difference. For Catholics,
the Eucharist is the primary act of the service; it's more important than the sermon!
They believe in the consecrated bread and wine in sacramental terms as the body,
blood, soul, and divinity of Jesus. Indeed, the Eucharist, which is another name for
the Mass, has two meanings: a memorial supper of Jesus' own celebration of the Last
Supper and a memorial of his sacrifice on the cross. Let's take a look at each of these
meanings in more detail.

# Is It Real, or Is It "Memorex"?

The memorial supper occurs when Catholics gather and re-enact the Last Supper. Jesus told his followers to bless the bread and wine and think of him every time they got together for supper. He would be right there with them. Remembering departed loved ones allows them to continue to exist because our bond with them continues. We are still in communion with them; they are still real. Memory is not static; it is dynamic. Each time we recall the people, we connect to them through the events of our relationship with them. Each time we do this, our memories of them are reinterpreted. We now understand them in light of the new experience of our life. The memories take on new and deeper meaning each time they are brought forward. This is how we grow in wisdom.

---

### Saints Preserve Us

**Sts. Cosmas and Damian, September 26, Patrons of Druggists**

St. Cosmas and St. Damian were brothers and were skilled in the science of medicine. They were filled with the spirit of Christian charity and never took money for their services. They were held in high esteem and greatly loved by the people of their town. When the persecutions broke out about the year 283, they were arrested because of their prominence. After undergoing various torments, they were finally beheaded.

---

Catholics use the term *re-enact* when they talk about their celebration of the Eucharist. Jesus told his disciples to remember him by the events he performed at the Last Supper. Each time Catholics repeat these events, their relationship with Jesus comes alive through the memories that are being evoked.

Another way to understand the importance of this ritual is to explore how Jewish people remember events. Jews keep memories through story and ritual. The Passover was one of the primary events in the Jewish story. It refers to the deliverance of the Jews from Egyptian slavery. The Jews celebrate it with a ritual supper. This was the same Passover supper Jesus celebrated with his disciples as the Last Supper, the night before his death. Catholics believe Jesus declared that the sacrifice of his life would now achieve for all the deliverance of the Passover. In declaring this, he fused the memory of these events, the Passover and the Last Supper ritual.

## The Meaning of Sacrifice

Why do Catholics call the Mass a sacrifice? The word is from Latin *sacrum* meaning holy and *facere* meaning "to make." Sacrifice literally means to make something holy. Catholics use the word *sacrifice* when they talk about the Mass, because they are bringing the gift of themselves to God at the altar. The word "altar" comes from the Latin *adolere*, which means "to burn up." An altar is a raised structure on which sacrifices are made. By remembering Jesus on the cross who turned over his will to God, Catholics surrender themselves to the will of God during this act of communion.

The reason Catholics surrender to the will of God is so God can transform them just as he did with Jesus in the Resurrection. *Eucharist* means thanksgiving. The Mass is the Catholic expression of thanksgiving to God for the Resurrection.

### Epiphanies

Each age has attempted to use language to express belief in the real presence of Jesus. **Transubstantiation** is a term from the Middle Ages. This term was used to describe the belief that the priest's blessing during the Mass changes the substance of the bread and wine. It expressed the difference between the appearance of the bread and its actual "substance," now believed to be Jesus' body and blood. But this language is incomplete today. More important than the substance of Jesus is his reality as a force or presence in the Catholic spiritual life. The church uses the term transubstantiation as one way to talk about the action of the Eucharist, but it is by no means the complete way.

# Here's the Church, and Here's the Steeple, Open the Doors, and See All the People!

Catholics worship in a building called a church. Walking into a church, you'll see a long aisle with benches on both sides that leads to the sanctuary where the altar stands. The church has two basic spaces: the pews or the rows of benches with kneelers in which the people worship, and the sanctuary where the priest, altar servers, and readers perform their respective tasks. The sanctuary and the pews face each other.

## Sacred Spaces

A pew may be long enough to comfortably sit 10 or more people. Each row of pews will have a *kneeler*, a cushioned board of wood hinged on both ends and attached to

**For Heaven's Sake!**

Make sure that the kneeler in the pew behind you *is* in the down position when you go to kneel. If not, your foot will probably push it down, creating a great racket.

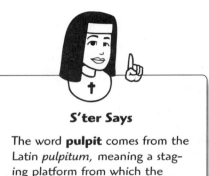

**S'ter Says**

The word **pulpit** comes from the Latin *pulpitum,* meaning a staging platform from which the priest proclaims the Gospel reading of the Mass and preaches the homily.

the bottom of the pew. When it is time to kneel, you put it down so it rests on the floor. When you need to move in and out of the pew, you raise it on its hinge so that the aisle is clear.

The sanctuary is a large space with several key pieces of furniture. The most important piece is the altar. The *altar* is a large table or slab of marble that is waist high. The surface of this table is smooth and polished. Five Greek crosses are engraved on its surface, one at each of the four corners, about 6 inches from both edges, and one in the center. The altar typically is 10 to 15 feet long and about 5 feet wide. It's covered with layers of cloth and will have candles burning during the liturgy of the Eucharist. Sometimes the candles are not on the altar but are placed around it. The altar is the symbol of Christ.

Perhaps the second most important piece of furniture is the *pulpit,* the stand from which the priest reads the Gospel and delivers the homily. The two parts of the Catholic Mass are celebrated around these two pieces of furniture.

Either on a shelf behind the altar or on a side altar, you will find a little marble or metal box called a *tabernacle.* It is covered with a cloth, and the door is locked with a key. The Eucharist, bread that has been consecrated at Mass, is kept there in reserve. It might be taken to a sick member of the congregation during the week. The sanctuary lamp sits near the tabernacle and is always lit. The lamp is a sign to Catholics that God is present in the form of the consecrated bread in the tabernacle. As mentioned before, there is always a crucifix visible near the altar. Additionally, the Easter candle is prominently displayed. There is more discussion of sanctuary furnishings in Chapter 11, "Seven Sensual Sacraments."

## *Putting on Your Glad Rags*

Those who participate at the altar during the Mass wear special ceremonial clothes. The priest's clothes are the most elaborate and unusual. Various colors of vestments are used as determined by the liturgical calendar and the seasons of the year. White signifies innocence and is used on the feasts of Jesus, of the Blessed Virgin, and of some saints. Red signifies love and is used on the feasts of the Holy Ghost and of martyrs. Green signifies hope and is generally used on Sundays during ordinary time. Violet signifies penance and is used during Lent and Advent. Gold is often used instead of white on great feasts.

*The Sanctuary. Christ the King Catholic Church, Nashville, Tennessee.*

*(Courtesy of H. L. [Dean] Caskey)*

Altar servers also wear special clothes, either a white gown, like the priest, or a black one called a cassock with a white type of blouse over it called a surplice. Generally the lectors, Eucharistic ministers, and ushers do not wear special uniforms.

## Who's Who at a Catholic Mass

The people participate in the Mass, and the priest presides, leading the congregation in offering worship to God. His words begin and end the Mass. He leads the prayers, reads the Gospel, and preaches the homily. He leads the praying of the liturgy of the Eucharist and says the words of consecration.

The priest may be assisted in several of these roles by a deacon, a man ordained to an office in the church just below the rank of a priest. Additionally, there are altar servers. Altar servers are boys and girls of grade school through college age who assist by carrying items used in the service, such as the book containing the prayers and scriptures. They may also ring the bells during parts of the Mass. There are also readers called lectors who read the Old Testament and Epistles. They also read the

**Your Guardian Angel**

Being a lector at Mass can be a rewarding experience. The parish offers workshops to train lectors in public speaking and instruct them in the meaning of the Biblical texts. Don't be afraid to volunteer!

prayers right after the homily. In addition, there are men and women who distribute the communion bread and wine. Altar servers, lectors, and ministers of the Eucharist are prepared for their jobs by special instruction. Serving outside the sanctuary are choir members and ushers. The ushers greet and seat people and take up the collection. Ushers are also prepared to handle emergencies should a person require assistance.

The key ministers in the whole service are the people. Since Vatican II, the people are seen as participants in the Mass, not just observers. They make up the body of the assembled church offering the Mass to God. The Vatican II document on the liturgy calls their role at the Mass "priestly."

## Guess Who's Coming to Dinner: Is It Just for Catholics?

All are welcome at a Catholic celebration of the Mass. If you're not Catholic and you attend a Mass, you should feel free to sit during the service or join in all the gestures and prayers if you are comfortable doing that. Typically, there will be a booklet available to help you follow the Mass.

However, you should forgive Catholics for what appears to be a lack of hospitality when it comes to communion. Catholics have always restricted communion to those who profess a belief that this bread is the real presence of Jesus. Catholic communion is just that, a sign of Catholic unity. Visitors to Catholic parishes often wonder why they may not join in receiving communion because other churches don't have such restrictions. The Eucharist symbolizes union with God and Catholics' union with one another. When persons from another Christian denomination become Catholic, they are said to be received into full communion. They are not rebaptized, but their participation in receiving communion becomes the high point of their transition into membership.

As a regular practice, Catholics do not share communion at non-Catholic churches. Exceptions exist, but they are rare. While theologians and Catholic Church officials debate the possibilities for full communion, ordinary folks find themselves separated by this difference in beliefs. The more unity Christians find among themselves, the closer all Christian churches will come to resolving differences and more closely modeling Jesus' words at the Last Supper: "that they may all be one." (John 17:21)

During communion, non-Catholic Christians are encouraged to pray for unity with the Lord Jesus and with one another, and non-Christians are encouraged to offer their prayers for the peace and the unity of the human family.

## "O Sacrament Host Holy, O Sacrament Divine"

In the early times of the church, Catholics would take the Eucharist bread home from Mass to serve to those who were unable to attend. As the church progressed through the Middle Ages, more emphasis was given to the role of the priest in presiding over the Eucharist than to the people participating in it. As a result, people became separated from the Mass. The emphasis was on the divine nature of Jesus in the Eucharist, and the people saw themselves as unworthy to receive it.

### Epiphanies

Forty Hours devotion is a Eucharistic observance consisting of meditation and prayers to the Blessed Sacrament. The consecrated host is displayed on the altar and the faithful meditate, taking turns over the 40-hour period so that the Blessed Sacrament is never left unattended. For many years, Forty Hours devotion was offered yearly at the parish church. Simpler, shorter devotions have replaced it for the most part.

As a consequence of this emphasis, devotions to the Eucharist outside the Mass have developed over the years. The Eucharist outside the Mass is called the Blessed Sacrament. Benediction, meditation before the Blessed Sacrament, processions of the Blessed Sacrament, and Forty Hours devotions are some of them. Benediction, a highly ceremonial celebration in which the priest wears beautiful robes, consists of prayers and song. Incense is used as part of this service.

## Benediction: Memories of a Schoolgirl

In the past, all parochial schoolchildren attended all the church services, which meant they were excused from classes to go to them, which most students felt was a good trade! Benediction, a ritual rich in splendor and ceremony, usually left an indelible mark on the memory. A Catholic who grew up in Minneapolis remembers how October could produce anything from a balmy late summer day to a howling winter wind. The day she recalls was one of the windy winter ones, with rain. The children in her school were excused at 11:00 A.M. to walk the half-block to the Church where Benediction of the Blessed Sacrament would be held as part of the Forty Hours devotion at the parish church.

The air inside felt warm against the outside. It had that peculiar smell of beeswax, linen, hand-rubbed, waxed wood, and wet wool. "We wore wool coats, hats, mittens, and scarves back then, and any moisture produced a smell not unlike damp sheep." Walking in hushed silence into the church, the children were reminded by the sister to genuflect on both knees as the Blessed Sacrament was exposed on the altar. She conveyed this message by grabbing the student at the head of the line by the scruff of his neck and dropping him to his knees as an example. "We all followed suit, almost in unison." Catholic children instinctually behaved as a unit. They had been rehearsed by years of hands clapping, crisply signaling devotional movements.

On this particular day, each grade spent thirty minutes in silent meditation before Benediction. They took their places, kneeling three to a pew. "Moments into the meditation, I broke a sweat. The furnace roared against the October chill, and it was as if the very fires of hell burned beneath the building. Twenty minutes into the meditation, I began to go in and out of consciousness. Each time, catching myself, I straightened my back and continued to gaze into the sunburst of ornate gold—the *monstrance,* in the center of which was Our Lord Jesus Christ, the Blessed Sacrament, in the form of a round white wafer." Leaning back against the seat was an insult to the Creator who had given the children good, strong backs.

**S'ter Says**

A **monstrance** is an ornate golden vessel containing the Blessed Sacrament pressed between two pieces of clear glass. It sits on the altar for Eucharistic devotions.

Thirty minutes into the meditation, the girl's best friend caught her attention and made a face, setting off a volley of barely contained, uncontrollable laughter. It took the form of snorting and intense physical shaking until they had the whole front row rocking. The sister flew up the aisle and dug a steel finger into her shoulder. "Shock and pain won, I hit the floor—out cold. A wet rag was applied to my head, and as I came around, I heard the organ playing and the *O Salutaris Hostia* being sung. Several classmates assisted me outside, sat me on the front steps, and propped open the door. The heat rushed out, carrying with it the acrid smell of incense. It mixed with the fall air, fixing the moment and the smell of it forever in my memory. I leaned back against the church as the cool mist gently washed my face."

This story from the past is the kind of thing of which Catholic identity is made. Today's practices, while different, continue to be rituals that the next generation will recall as important markers in growing up Catholic.

In this chapter, you learned about the Mass, the central Catholic ritual, which is the heart of being Catholic. In the next chapter, we'll look at a more public side of Catholic identity and the effect it has had on the formation of art, architecture, music, literature, and film.

---

### The Least You Need to Know

➤ The Mass is the central worship service for Catholics.

➤ Central to the Mass is the consecration and distribution of Holy Communion.

➤ Catholics believe that the real presence of Jesus is sacramentally contained in Holy Communion.

➤ Although the priest presides, the people are the ones who offer the Mass.

# Part 5

# Catholic Identity: What Makes a Catholic?

*We've looked at Catholics' Biblical roots. We've looked at their sacramental life and practices such as incense, bells, and holy water. We've sampled their rich prayer life. Now in Part 5, we'll look at how they think and where they meet. Is there a particular way Catholics engage the world? When you consider the broad population base of Catholicism, what does it mean to identify Catholics as a tribe? Is there a process in which Catholic culture and thinking is formed? How does the church maintain unity and diversity? Do Catholics all believe the same things? Do they all think alike?*

*In this part, we'll look at Catholic beliefs, examining some of the more controversial issues. We'll look at power within the church: Who has it, and who does not. We begin, however, by looking at Catholics as a community.*

# Chapter 17

# It's a Tribe

## In This Chapter

➤ The communal nature of Catholics

➤ The parish: where the tribe meets

➤ The parochial school: discipleship and citizenship

➤ The church's social face

➤ Getting in and getting out of the tribe

Catholicism has a distinctive cultural and ethnic mark that is more than the sum of its rules and beliefs. In this chapter, we'll look at where this ethos finds form, which is in the parish and the Catholic school that so often is an integral part of the parish. We'll look at the role Catholic schools play in forming Catholics as citizens.

A particular social sensibility is developed in the parish environment. It calls the faithful to the Biblical mandate to work for the transformation of all people, to bring forward the "reign of God." After looking at where Catholic identity is formed and where it is lived out, we'll end this chapter by looking at the process by which new people are initiated into the tribe.

## Where the Tribe Meets

Catholic priest and sociologist Andrew Greeley describes the ideal form of a Catholic parish as an "organic community." He means that a Catholic parish will be successful to the extent that it can make the sacramental moments of the peoples' lives central to the life of the tribe. It is successful when it is able to connect the Gospel message to the lives of the people and link its members with the world beyond the parish.

The parish is the neighborhood. The tradition was that Catholics attended the church in the neighborhood in which they lived. Although less true today, in the past, the lines of parish distinction were as clearly drawn as those of voting districts.

Greeley believes that the church should recognize the importance of establishing a religious base inside a local community. Especially now as the technological age advances, people need a sense of belonging to a community. The parish church can bring that sense of belonging. Church for Catholics is not in Rome nor is it at the level of the diocese, but it does exist down the block, on the corner. It's where you were baptized and where your older sister was married and where your grandparents' funerals were held. It is woven into your family history.

For many, Catholic churches also included Catholic schools. Approximately one third of all Catholic churches in the United States still have a Catholic school connected to them, and nearly half had one just 30 years ago. The school continues to be an important dimension of the organic sense of Catholic parish life. When the same beliefs and values are reinforced, a strong unifying statement is made through church, home, and school. The school is a forum to work specifically with the faith basis of peace and justice for the young people.

### For Heaven's Sake!

Support your parish! Your parish is your spiritual home base. It is where your records are kept such as your baptism, holy communion, and marriage papers. You are expected to be active in your parish and help in its support, even if you attend Mass somewhere else.

## Parish: Center for Belonging

Historically, Catholics were often not accepted into the larger community and thus gained their sense of belonging by gathering in their parish churches. Although times have changed, the need for belonging remains a strong human desire. Various organizations for men, women, and youth provide face-to-face connections with others who have similar interests, backgrounds, or spiritual goals. Such organizations include the Christian Family Movement, Marriage Encounter groups, The Knights of Columbus, the Legion of Mary, programs for divorced and separated Catholics, Great Books clubs, Scripture study groups, Girl Scouts and Boy Scouts, the choir, various ministries to the sick and bereaved, and gatherings for seniors, to name just a few.

Play and recreation are at the heart of community and remain integral to spiritual and religious experience. You might call it "sacred play." Indeed, many churches have a gymnasium for basketball and volleyball, as well as an auditorium ready for dances and other social events, such as variety shows or a haunted house at Halloween. Many parishes sponsor golf or bowling leagues, card clubs, and quilting clubs. They offer ball fields, playgrounds, and grounds for church picnics.

Positive social bonding is a religious and spiritual event. Social life in the parish allows Catholics to experience God as the unifying force in human relationships.

## Parish: Center for Prayer and Sacraments

At the heart of the parish is the church where Catholics gather for the Mass. The varieties of celebrations of Mass reflect the different character of parishes. In Los Angeles, Mass is celebrated each Sunday in over 50 different languages. Many Catholics still hold on to the Latin Mass, and a few parishes still offer it.

Music takes on the unique character of the parish. Depending on the preferences of the congregation and the church leadership, a parish might offer anything from folk music to Gregorian chant. Certain parishes might even offer a rock Mass performed by the youth choir. Music helps to set the mood and environment, which is a key focus in today's church. Some parishes even offer choreographed lighting and sound. In addition, banners, sometimes made by the children or youth groups, decorate the church and mark the seasons.

The church is where the parish celebrates its sacramental life through baptisms, weddings, and funerals. People also come to the church for public and private devotions. Throughout the week, people make a *visit* to the church for private prayer. On weeknights, novenas, benedictions, and seasonal devotions, such as the Way of the Cross during Lent, are held. All of these ceremonies and rituals work to create a sacramental identity that is communally shared.

**Your Guardian Angel**

If you'd like to experience the Catholic Mass as it was celebrated before Vatican II, call the local diocese and ask which parishes may offer one. The parishes that offer such Masses are called Tridentine. The prayers are in Latin.

**S'ter Says**

A **visit** is the Catholic custom of stopping in to the church for a few minutes during the day to say a quick prayer. A visit is also a good time to light a vigil candle for a special intention.

# Parish: Launching Pad to the World

Ideally in the Catholic scheme of things, the parish contributes to the political and cultural life of its city and the world. It does this by organizing and focusing the power of the people. One way to accomplish these tasks is through committees at the parish level that educate members on issues and organize them to affect political policies on issues as diverse as taxes, medical practices, wages, or capital punishment.

### Your Guardian Angel

Send your kids to Catholic schools if you want to promote their social awareness. According to sociological studies, Catholics educated in Catholic schools are substantially more likely to be in favor of racial integration and tolerant of members of other denominations than are public school Catholics.

Another way to affect social policy is through the parochial school. In parochial schools, children are educated to be better Catholics and better citizens. The school brings religious significance to skills and talents; learning is associated with bringing Catholic principles into being. In a way, Catholic students learn their ABCs and 123s in order to make a better world—which in Catholic terms means bringing about the reign of God.

One man remembers how the very architecture of his Catholic grade school was influential in transmitting Catholic identity. The grades closest to the church building where the children were baptized were the primary grades kindergarten through three, then came the middle grades four through six, and finally grades seven and eight were located at a distance from the church. The fellow felt this arrangement was a statement about life beginning in the security of the womb of the church, moving through school, and then out into the world.

Growing up Catholic had a rhythm to it. Each age group had its own playground, and this series of playgrounds was important in terms of status and self-understanding. Different aspects of Catholic life were sampled at different grades: Second grade was first communion time while fourth grade funneled boys into either football or academics. Fifth grade was altar boy time, a time when young men were placed under the guidance of the priest. Being trained one-on-one as a Mass server meant being away from the tutelage of the nuns. In school, the nuns reigned supreme.

By seventh and eighth grades, students were being prepared for the Catholic high school, and those who showed a particular interest in religion or church were encouraged to take up a vocation, as a life of service in the church as a priest or nun. Students would begin to wear the insignia of the Catholic high school. In these grades, identification as a Catholic moved from the parish to the high school.

Of course, growing up Catholic today has a rhythm to it as well; it's just a different beat. Chapter 25, "Face to Face in the Third Millennium: The Church Looks to the Future," describes today's young Catholics.

# Catholics' Social Face

The true measure of Catholic identity is how Catholics live their lives in the world. Jesus talked about bringing about the reign of God. The reign of God was not simply an idea to be expressed; it was an action to be taken. Jesus healed the sick, cared for sinners, and challenged the injustices in his society. His followers took on this mission from the start. The book in which the early doings of the church were recorded is called the Acts of the Apostles.

Transformation of the structures of society is an ongoing response to the Gospel message and happens when organized movements confront injustice in all areas of society and culture: labor, human rights, the military, private corporations, and the government. From its earliest days to the present, the church has taken on massive activities to bring about love and to effect justice. This work goes on at two levels: one is caring for people, and the second is seeking justice in the transformation of the structures of society.

The Church has expressed care for people in three primary ways:

➤ Health care for the community

➤ Education for the society

➤ Welfare for all those in need

Let's take a look at each of these concerns.

## *Catholic Health Care: More Than Chicken Soup for the Soul*

From its earliest years in the United States, the Catholic Church has been vitally involved in health care. Currently, Catholic health care institutions serve almost 80 million patients a year. Catholic hospitals constitute over 10 percent of all hospitals in the country and receive about 15 percent of all hospital admissions.

Both lay and religious men and women respond to the vocation of healing the sick and comforting the afflicted. Catholic hospitals employ almost 750,000 people, which is about 15 percent of all hospital employees in the country; their total payroll is in excess of 20 billion dollars.

**For Heaven's Sake!**

You can't be a good Catholic and pass the buck. Catholicism is a religion of action in the world. Being a good Catholic requires hard work; you are expected to be involved in your church and in the community.

In a recent address to the Catholic Hospital Association of Wisconsin, Archbishop Weakland of Milwaukee reminded Catholics of the following:

"There is no doubt that Jesus was eager to heal physically those who were in any way infirmed. He did not make the distinctions that we would make today between physical illness, diabolical influences on people, psychological phenomena, and the need for spiritual healing. His approach was holistic in the best sense of the term. He saw all such wounds as hindering people from being the full entity that God would want them to be …. When he talks of salvation, it goes beyond but does not exclude these more physical and more measurably visible healings."

Most of the church's health care institutions are banded together in the Catholic Health Association (CHA), the largest single group of not-for-profit health care providers. The CHA is organized to advance the health care ministry through advocacy, education, research, and development. It supports and strengthens health ministries in the United States and speaks out with one voice to address health issues.

## Catholic Colleges: Rocking the Cradle of Thought

In the United States, more than 200 Catholic institutions of higher education educate two thirds of a million students. About 5 percent of these places are research universities, 10 percent are two-year colleges, and the remaining 85 percent are four-year universities and colleges, equally divided between liberal arts and more comprehensive institutions.

### Saints Preserve Us

**St. Vincent de Paul, September 27, Patron of Charitable Organizations and Prisoners**

St. Vincent de Paul was a spiritual advisor to a wealthy woman in France. He became aware of the plight of the peasants and began his missionary work to them. He founded many orphanages and hospitals, the Congregation of the Missions (the Vincentians), and the Daughters of Charity. It was said that his way with wealthy women greatly enhanced the success of his work. He died in 1660. He is the patron saint of charitable organizations and prisoners, and his feast day is September 27. The charity that bears his name, the St. Vincent de Paul Society, was founded in Paris in 1833. It operates all over the world today.

Since the 1960s, both with Vatican II's openness to the world and the lessening of religious and ethnic identities in the culture at large, much has changed in these schools. Higher education in secular schools is no longer seen as a danger to the faith; in fact, many Catholic parents see it as desirable.

For the most part, Catholic colleges were founded by religious orders, such as the Jesuits, Dominicans, Franciscans, and Benedictines. As federal funding has required Catholic institutions to meet the test of independent control, most schools have moved to independent boards of trust that aren't controlled by the church hierarchy. The religious orders have become sponsors, not owners. The faculty is diversified. Not only are there very few of the members of the sponsoring religious orders teaching, but the replacement faculty are not required to be Catholic.

These schools now must decide how to be distinctive Catholic institutions. Will these Catholic schools go the route of many of the other religious schools, such as Harvard, Yale, and Northwestern, for example, all of which were once church schools? Will they simply become a historical memory of the church?

There are two reasons to believe that Catholic colleges and universities will retain their Catholic identities. For the most part, these institutions cannot successfully raise funds without making the case for their Catholic character and identity, which means that Catholics still want Catholic institutions of higher education to exist.

The other reason in favor of Catholic higher education is the pope's directive in the encyclical, *Ex Corde Ecclesiae,* which means "From the Heart of the Church." In this letter to Catholic higher education administrators all over the world, the pope declared that the primary role of the Catholic university is to bridge faith and culture. This directive calls for the schools to develop highly credentialed faculties in the arts, the social sciences, and the natural sciences, in addition to the disciplines of theology and philosophy.

**Your Guardian Angel**

Remember, there are many Catholic flavors to choose from! In large cities, you might find many Catholic universities, each run by a different religious order. While they have many similarities, each order has a different history and approach to its educational mission. If you are interested in a Catholic college, don't be afraid to shop around.

**Your Guardian Angel**

You can get a full education at a Catholic college. The primary goal of Catholic universities as most recently defined by Pope John Paul II is to mediate faith and culture. They do this by developing cultural understanding through the arts, social sciences, and natural sciences, partnered with theology and philosophy.

## Catholic Charities: More Than Just a Handout

Catholic Charities is the largest private network of social service organizations in the United States. It works to support families, reduce poverty, and build communities. Catholic Charities provides emergency and social services ranging from shelters and soup kitchens to day care centers, summer camps, centers for seniors, and refugee resettlement offices for more than 10 million people. Its annual budget exceeds two billion dollars.

### Epiphanies

Catholic Charities began in 1727 when Ursuline nuns began taking in orphans. In 1809, Sister Elizabeth Seaton opened an orphanage and free school. In the nineteenth century, ethnic parishes provided neighborhood services to their people and religious orders established child care and homes for the aging. By 1900, more than 800 Catholic institutions provided care to needy people, including dependent children, prisoners, the aged, and the sick. Today, the Catholic Charities network in the United States consists of more than 1,400 agencies.

## Dorothy Day and the Catholic Worker Movement

Dorothy M. Day, who lived from 1897 to 1980, was an icon of the Catholic social faith in this century. A journalist, she converted to Catholicism, and her belief centered on a philosophy that stressed the value and dignity of each individual person. She founded an organization she called "The Catholic Worker" in which she attempted to make this ideal available to all who desired it.

The Catholic Worker was a Catholic presence that announced a concern for the poor and oppressed. In 1933, Day sold *The Catholic Worker* newspaper in New York's Union Square for a penny a copy. It has been in constant production since that time and is still sold at a penny a copy! See the reprint of the paper's masthead in the illustration printed here. Embracing voluntary poverty, Day worked tirelessly, establishing both houses for the immediate relief of those in need and farming communes where each person worked to his ability and received according to his need. She modeled her organizations on early Christian communities. Day and her movement were a call to U.S. Catholics to reconnect to the church history of caring for others.

*Masthead from* The Catholic Worker *newspaper.*

*(Designed by Ada Bethune, courtesy of* The Catholic Worker*)*

Perhaps Day is best known for her proclamation of Catholic pacifism as the ideal response to war. Nonviolence was integral to her position, and her efforts at pacifism encouraged Catholics to change the social order by performing direct, albeit nonviolent, actions on behalf of peace and social justice. The pacifism of Dorothy Day and The Catholic Worker were at the heart of the American Catholic peace movement during the Vietnam War. The Catholic Worker movement spawned additional Catholic movements such as The Catholic Peace Fellowship and Pax Christi, U.S.A.

Dorothy Day reflected the Catholic's personal obligation of looking after the needs of fellow human beings as focused in the works of mercy. The works of mercy are seven charitable acts encouraged by the church:

➤ Feed the hungry

➤ Give drink to the thirsty

➤ Clothe the naked

➤ Visit the imprisoned

➤ Give shelter to the homeless

➤ Visit the sick

➤ Bury the dead

## Hungering and Thirsting After Justice

Still alive and very well today, the Catholic Worker has served as a prototype to many movements for social transformation in the church. Here are a few that might be of interest to you:

➤ **The Eighth Day Center.** In Chicago, various religious orders band together at this center to document major economic and political issues on a national as well as global scale, and similar centers exist all over the world. As international organizations, these centers are able to network broadly, quickly passing on information that will be used to bring about policy changes and create legislation in worldwide governments.

➤ **Volunteer groups.** One of the church's best-kept secrets is that more than 300 Catholic organizations, such as the Jesuit Volunteer Corps, recruit college graduates for a year or two of service. Volunteers take their services into the

### Your Guardian Angel

The works of mercy are practical ways to take your spirituality into the world. For example, when following the principle of giving drink to the thirsty, you might work on a project that is bringing water to a remote village in another country. You might also work at the local level by cleaning up the river in your own hometown. What this principle is saying is that everyone deserves clean water.

### For Heaven's Sake!

Put your money where your values are! If you are lucky enough to have money to invest, you must be a good steward and choose a company to invest in that reflects your values. Remember, spirituality has practical applications.

community in the form of education in inner-city schools, job training, and finding housing for the homeless. At the same time, the volunteers live a community life of prayer and poverty, transforming their understanding of what it means to be in the world. More than 100,000 Catholics are involved in this work.

➤ **The Jesuit Center of Concern.** A policy think tank in Washington, D.C., the Jesuit Center researches the social implications of proposed legislation and thus provides a voice for justice in policymaking.

➤ **The Wall Street Group.** Similar to the Eighth Day Center, Catholic religious orders have formed a Wall Street group that monitors the investments of their orders. They use their power as shareholders to call for corporate responsibility in the companies they have invested in.

## Getting In and Out of the Tribe

The majority of Catholics are born into the religion. Roughly 80 percent die Catholic as well. But there's another way of getting in and getting out: People can choose to join and leave as adults.

For those who were not born and baptized Catholic, the church has designed a comprehensive process of initiation into the tribe. As we've seen, Catholicism is more of a culture than an organization, which means that the word *initiation* is more accurate than the word *join*. There is a period of time in which the initiate gets to know the tribe and the tribal ways. The process is called the Rite of Christian Initiation and includes socialization, instruction, and ritual celebration that lasts a minimum of a year.

Entering the church is acknowledging the relationship God has with people. Do you remember our discussion of *covenant,* an Old Testament term that describes the nature of God's relationship to his creation? In this relationship, God claimed his people and told them he would never leave them.

Sometimes, people may find that their relationship with the church does not fulfill their covenant relationship with God, and they may choose to leave. In rare cases and for the most serious of reasons, the church may find it necessary to sanction the actions of one of its members. This would happen when the member's action threatens the unity of the church's teachings and beliefs.

## Joining Catholicism, Not a Quick Study

The Rite of Christian Initiation of Adults, commonly referred to as *RCIA,* is the process designed for adults to enter the Catholic Church. It's designed as a time of instruction and bonding with the community, culminating in receiving the sacraments of initiation and full membership in the church. You may remember from the earlier discussion of sacraments that this process sometimes includes baptism, as well as confirmation, and the Eucharist, celebrated at the end of the process.

The RCIA came out of Vatican II, yet it reaches back in time to the early Christian communities for its model. The early communities emphasized bonding and a time for questions, instruction, and faith sharing, as well as preparation to receive the sacraments and admission into the church, usually at the Easter vigil. This very old tradition outlines the process for today.

Just as the early church began with a time of getting to know one another, RCIA does, too. It begins with a year-long effort to welcome the stranger and to create a caring, cohesive community of believers. The individual determines how long the bonding needs to last.

For those who choose to move forward in the process, a period of inquiry begins, during which they meet with others from the parish. Everyone shares stories, asks questions, and learns about the basic beliefs of the Catholic faith. Someone from the parish acts as a sponsor and walks the journey with his or her candidate, the one seeking to join the church.

### S'ter Says

**RCIA** stands for the Rite of Christian Initiation of Adults. This year-long process of entrance into the Catholic Church begins with a time of making friends in the community, asking questions, and learning about the faith. When the person seeking entrance feels ready, there is a ceremony in which that person becomes a member of the church.

### S'ter says

**Catechumen** is a term used to describe a person who is seeking entrance into the church. It was a term used in the early church.

When the candidate feels ready and when the sponsor and the community confirm his readiness, he is enrolled as a *catechumen,* the title used to describe those seeking instruction. During this more formalized period of learning, candidates usually participate in Sunday Mass, leaving after the homily (sermon) to attend their faith-sharing groups. At the appropriate time, generally the beginning of Lent, those who are ready to move ahead with the process will enter the final stages of preparation. The willingness of the candidate, the advice of the sponsor, and the acceptance of the community determine the candidate's readiness.

Ideally, the Easter vigil is the time during which the candidates will receive the sacraments of initiation and be welcomed into full membership in the church. After this, the *neophytes*, the new members, enter a period of reflection on their experiences of receiving the sacraments. They are then assimilated into the parish.

### Epiphanies

The Rite of Christian Initiation of Adults was designed for receiving unbaptized people into the church. However, the church has adapted it for people baptized in other denominations who seek membership in the Catholic Church. It is also available for Catholics who may not have been confirmed and would like to deepen their understanding of their faith. During the Easter vigil, these people would not be baptized again, but they would receive confirmation and the Eucharist. It has also been tailored for children, usually children of the adult candidates. In the case of children, they must be of an age to understand the process and give consent.

The success of the RCIA depends on the parish community's participation. Without a genuine spirit of welcome, the process is vulnerable to becoming nothing more than a time of instruction. The caring of the community gives the rite vitality and life. This participation offers a challenge to some parishes, especially large congregations where members tend to be alienated from the sense of community themselves. The benefits of the program are twofold: the catechumen is provided a community experience, and the community is drawn together to offer one.

Here is a summary of the process:

➤ **Time of welcoming.** During this time, the candidate gets to know the community and experience the Gospel values it offers.

➤ **Acceptance as a candidate.** During a liturgical ritual of acceptance, the candidate expresses desire, and the community responds. This ritual is the entrance into a more structured process of instruction and faith sharing.

➤ **A time of development in the Catholic faith.** After the rite of acceptance comes this time of nurturing and growth in faith.

➤ **Election.** This formal, liturgical rite is usually celebrated on the first Sunday of Lent. The candidates express their desire to join the church, and the parish ratifies their readiness to receive the sacraments of initiation.

➤ **Celebration of sacraments of initiation.** Usually held as part of the Easter vigil, the elect are initiated through baptism, confirmation, and the Eucharist.

➤ **The honeymoon.** After their baptism, confirmation, and reception of the Eucharist, the newly initiated reflect on their experience of receiving the sacraments, and they are integrated into the community.

## Excommunication

*Excommunication* is a penalty that the church uses to exclude a Catholic from full participation in the church. Church authority imposes this penalty only for the gravest of reasons. Excommunication does not expel a person from the church, but it does restrict that person's rights within the community.

**S'ter Says**

**Excommunication** is an ecclesiastical censure depriving a person of the rights of church membership and excluding that person from full fellowship in the community.

Excommunication is not a moral condemnation of a person; it is the church's firm response to an action that jeopardizes the integrity of the church. The ultimate goal of this action is to safeguard the community as well as encourage repentance and reconciliation. Excommunication is the strongest censure the church can make, and at the same time, it extends the spirit of forgiveness. Excommunication is like a big "time out." As parents don't throw one of the kids out of the family, excommunication does not throw you out of the church. It does, however, firmly enforce the boundaries.

The history of excommunication goes back to the beginning of the church. References to it are found in the First Council of Nicaea in 325. Although the church has received a lot of publicity regarding notorious excommunications in the past, such as those involving Galileo, Martin Luther, and King Henry the VIII, excommunication is not invoked frequently.

Excommunication is more likely to be used to control church leaders than ordinary parishioners. Examples of behavior that might warrant excommunication include consecration of a bishop without papal mandate; a priest breaking the seal of confession (a priest is bond to confidentiality regarding a person's confession); profaning the Eucharist; or using physical force against the pope. Excommunicated people are

### Your Guardian Angel

Excommunication does not have to be forever! It's a big deal and is used only in very serious situations. However, unlike a military court martial, it can be repealed. If the offense was a public one, it requires a public apology. If it was a private matter, it can be resolved with your confessor.

### For Heaven's Sake!

Don't forget your Easter duty! To be a Catholic in good standing requires that you receive communion at least once a year, preferably during the season of Easter. In spite of what you've heard, Catholicism does not have a lot of requirements to stay in the tribe, but this is one of them.

not allowed to administer or receive the sacraments, and they may not function in any church office.

The church is hesitant about using excommunication, and officials consider a number of factors before resorting to it. Excommunication can be private, just between the person and his or her confessor. In public situations, the court conducts the excommunication process in a church court. As in a civil court, mitigating circumstances such as culpability (full awareness of one's actions) may be cited.

Excommunication is lifted when the prescribed penance has been performed. If the matter was private, it is handled between the person and his or her confessor. If it was a public situation, the penance or admission of guilt and apology must be delivered publicly; the lifting of the punishment is also done publicly.

## Maintaining Status: How Catholic Do You Have to Be?

As you may remember, we noted that 20 percent of Catholics leave the religion, and that the second largest "denomination" in the United States consists of former Catholics. These statistics pose an interesting question: Just what do people mean when they say they are Catholic? Because of Catholicism's tribal nature and cultural identity, it's character tends to stay with even the people who leave the religion. It is rather like being a German American, Mexican American, Asian American, or African American: you tend to keep your cultural connection to your tribe as a reference point.

From the perspective of the church, you are Catholic unless excommunicated. From the perspective of the individual, you are Catholic as long as you still practice or in some way identify yourself as such. Practice means going by the six precepts of the church that we listed in Chapter 4, "The Vatican: The Church That's a Country."

It is not unusual to hear people refer to themselves as Catholics when they have not attended church for 20 years or more. What about them is still Catholic? Most of the time, these people have maintained the Catholicism's sacramental and communal way of encountering God, the world, and others—their "Catholic wiring." They carry the church within them.

For some people, this lingering connection can be problematic. Their encounter with Catholicism has been so wounding that they have to "recover" from it. They spend a lifetime trying to exorcise it. Others leave the church because they feel it's not Catholic enough. Good or bad, the religion's tribal nature means its members carry it around in their bones.

## Broken Relationships

As we have seen, the Catholic Church leaves a deep imprint on its members. If this imprint has been negative, it poses a considerable problem. Unfortunately, a number of people's experience with the religion has been damaging, so much so that the term "recovering Catholic" has worked its way into the common language.

When an institution such as a large company, a government, or a church has enormous power in the lives of people, the potential for an abuse of this power exists. The church members who are most vulnerable to this abuse of power are the children. Many Catholics remember nuns and priests with dread and fear because these members of the church physically, emotionally, or sometimes sexually abused them. Betrayal by the very ones you're supposed to be able to trust leaves deep wounds.

**Your Guardian Angel**

If you have been the victim of abuse by someone in a leadership position in the church, there is help available to you. Talk to someone you trust, someone who can help you get the spiritual healing you need. Many counselors are now trained in recognizing and treating religious abuse.

## A Call for Reconciliation

The church has too often turned its back on the wounding of its members, ignoring them and even at times covering up for its leaders. Abuse is not to be tolerated, especially within the institutions that have the most influence in people's lives. At its core, most abuse is understood to be an abuse of power. With power must come a highly developed sense of responsibility. Leadership requires this degree of responsibility. As the power shifts in the church and as the people begin to take more control in their religious lives, the potential for this abuse reduces.

Reconciliation requires that the church educate itself on the nature of abuse and how to recognize when the potential for it exists in its ranks. Society in general is making strides in understanding the nature of power and the potential for corruption that goes with having power over others. We urge individuals who have been victims to seek counseling.

We've taken a look at the parish, some of the church's organizations, its outreach, and its tribal nature. Regardless of how the church identifies you—as a Catholic in "good standing" or a "backslider"—it is really your personal identity that is the important issue. How you choose to acknowledge or reject your alliance with the tribe differs with each individual. In the next chapter, we'll find out where Catholic teachings originate and how they become part of the traditions of the church.

## The Least You Need to Know

➤ Catholicism is more of a culture than an organization.

➤ Catholic education encourages students to take an active and informed role in society.

➤ Catholics have a strong presence in ministering to the sick and the needy.

➤ Catholics have a highly organized and effective network of people working for justice throughout the world.

➤ There is a comprehensive process of discernment to join the church.

# Chapter 18

# The Teaching Church: More Than Just a Slap with the Ruler

---

## In This Chapter

➤ The sources of Catholic teachings

➤ What is the Catechism?

➤ How Catholic teachings are formed

➤ Liberation theology from base communities

➤ Who controls the truth in the church?

---

One of the primary roles the church has taken on is that of guardian of the truth. It has an elaborate means to decipher the meaning of Jesus' teachings and to protect and maintain their unity. In other words, to be a Catholic is to subscribe to a particular set of beliefs. In this chapter, we'll talk about the church as teacher of the faith, examine the special book that lists the teachings of the church, and then explore the process called theology from which new discoveries about truth emerge.

## The Source of the Church's Teaching: Scripture and Tradition

The two primary sources of Catholic beliefs are the Bible and tradition. The Bible is a closed text, meaning nothing can be added or taken away from its content. On the other hand, tradition changes with time.

Periodically, new interpretations are made, new information is discovered, or new insight is gained that affects established beliefs. Thus Catholic tradition is informed by what is called "ongoing revelation." Catholics believe God continues to speak. Councils have been called throughout history to define a belief or to examine new information that will eventually produce new church teachings. Vatican II, which we discussed in Chapter 5, "The '60s: Seeds of Revolution," is a point in modern times where church teachings changed considerably.

## The Authority of Tradition

When exercising its teaching authority, church leaders first consider what the church has traditionally taught about the topic in question. Such a way of deciding truth is also used in the American judicial system: When judges make decisions about cases, they must consult existing rulings to see how previous judges have ruled in similar cases. This process is called establishing and following precedent.

### Epiphanies

In making decisions concerning their truths, the Catholic Church uses the authority of tradition. Very often, a question can be answered in doctrines that have already been defined. However, traditional teachings often need to be applied to new circumstances. For example, the church's traditional teachings concerning Adam and Eve and original sin have had to be explained in the light of modern science.

The process of interpreting traditional doctrines requires prayer, study, and dialogue. Church leaders take new facts and circumstances into account while remaining faithful to what God has already revealed. Often it takes decades or even centuries of prayer and discussion before the teaching authority is prepared to speak on a controversial matter. The tradition of the church is not static, but for some it seems to move at the pace of a glacier.

Tradition is summarized in three places: the Nicene Creed, the teachings of the councils as collected in the council documents, and the encyclicals, or letters of the popes. The *Catechism of the Catholic Church* organizes this material. We'll now take a look at the process the church uses to shape its beliefs from where they originate in the Bible to the new teachings that are informing and changing the church today.

## *Teachings from the Scripture*

At the base of all teaching lies experience. As we mentioned in Chapter 7, "The Bible," the church began because Jesus' disciples wanted to share a powerful new experience of the meaning of life with everyone they met. As the years passed, the various communities recorded their experiences in four Gospels, which marked the beginning of the teaching church.

Defining and recording these Gospels served two important functions. First, the Gospels attempted to put the memory of Jesus into a written form so that folks who did not know Jesus or his followers could read about the experiences and relate to them. Even at the time of Jesus, many stories, some true and some misrepresentations, were circulating about him and his teachings. The early church, made up of the followers of Jesus, chose what they felt were the authentic writings over those they considered to be less authentic stories. By doing so, they established the canon, and thus the church began to exercise its teaching authority over truth.

The Gospel stories relate these truths:

➤ God is revealed in Jesus, as one who loves us so intimately that we can call him "Papa (*Abba*)."

➤ The world is not the result of chance; it is the gift of the Father, and there is a purpose to life.

➤ Death, that which we fear most, is overcome in Jesus and is not the end.

Just as the church established a canon of the Bible texts it considered authentic, so it also began to list what beliefs it considered authentic, and it continually updates this list. When *beliefs* are declared authentic, they are called *dogmas*. The truths and beliefs of the early church were developed and written into what is called the Nicene Creed, which represents the church's foundational beliefs.

**S'ter Says**

**Catechism** is the book that contains the official teachings of the Catholic Church. You can buy the present *Catechism of the Catholic Church* from any bookstore. The word derives from *catechesis*, or *katechein*, which means "to teach by proclaiming," as the apostles did after Jesus.

**S'ter Says**

**Belief** describes a state of confidence in a person or idea. It is also a body of information held by a group to be true. **Dogma** is a word that is used to describe a formally stated official belief of the church concerning faith or morals.

## Teachings in the Creed

The first set of the church's dogmas is called the Nicene Creed, which was officially adopted at the church council in Nicaea in 325. The Nicene Creed is an essential part of the doctrine and liturgy of the church. In Chapter 16, "The Mass: The Catholics' Big Dinner Party," we presented the text of the Nicene Creed.

### Epiphanies

When church officials drew up the Nicene Creed, the chief enemy of the church was a false teaching called Arianism, which denied that Jesus was fully God. In the early 300s, Arius, an Egyptian from Alexandria, taught that God the Father created the Son and that the Son, with the Father, then proceeded to create the world. As you can see, this teaching makes the Son a created being, and therefore not really God. A council of bishops excommunicated Arius, but he continued in his teachings. Finally, the Emperor Constantine summoned a council of bishops in Nicaea, located across the straits from modern Istanbul, who repudiated Arius by a decided majority and produced the first draft of what is now called the Nicene Creed in 325.

These foundational beliefs are gathered in the Nicene Creed:

➤ God is almighty, the creator of heaven and earth.

➤ Jesus Christ is God's son; he was conceived by the Holy Spirit, was born of the Virgin Mary, was crucified, died, and was buried, and rose from the dead.

➤ The Holy Spirit is the third person of the Trinity and lives in the people, who are the body of Christ.

➤ The church is one; it's holy, catholic, and apostolic. Its sacraments are the way to participate in the life of Jesus.

➤ There will be a resurrection of our bodies for a life everlasting.

## Council Documents and Encyclicals (Letters of the Popes)

Since Nicaea, church councils have continued to shape the beliefs of Catholics. So far, the Catholic Church has convened 21 councils. The first one lasted 2 months and 12 days and included 318 bishops. As we discussed in Chapter 5, the most recent council was the twenty-first, the Second Vatican Council called Vatican II. More than 2,600 bishops from all over the world attended. It lasted from September 1962 to December 1965. The decrees from each of these councils, as well as all those in-between, form the body of teachings of the church and are preserved in what are called the Council Documents.

Additionally, the pope issues documents and writes letters called *encyclicals*. When a pope writes an encyclical, he writes to all the Catholic churches in the world. Pope John Paul II has written about a dozen of them. A recent example is called *On Human Work (Laborem Exercens)*. This encyclical serves as a frame for examining work as a major sociopolitical question of the day. Pope John Paul II wrote it on the ninetieth anniversary of a famous encyclical by Pope Leo XIII called *On the Condition of the Working Classes (Rerum Novarum)*, which was written as a study of social conditions in the late nineteenth century.

Encyclicals are instructions for Catholics. For instance, Pope Leo's emphasis on social justice for workers marked a significant change from the traditional church alignment with the aristocracy. On rare occasions, the pope will use the encyclical to declare certain dogmas, or required beliefs, of the faith. Church beliefs eventually find their way to the catechism. Let's take a look at it.

**S'ter Says**

**Encyclicals** are letters written by the pope to instruct the people. The pope can issue an encyclical on any subject he believes the church will benefit from. Encyclicals continue the tradition of Paul's letters to Christian communities back in the early days of the church.

**Your Guardian Angel**

Find it in the Catechism! You can check the Catechism for a clear answer to almost any question you might have on Catholic beliefs. Feel free to get a copy, even if you're just learning about the religion. The Catechism isn't difficult to read and is chock full of helpful information.

## The Catechism

Q. Who made us?
A. God made us.

Q. Who is God?
A. God is our Father in heaven.

Q. Why did God make us?
A. God made us to know him, to love him, and to serve him in this world and to be happy with him in the next.

When asked these questions, every Catholic over the age of 35 will automatically give the very same answers. They learned them by heart in the *Baltimore Catechism*, the definitive religious textbook for all Catholic children in the United States from the end of the last century until the Second Vatican Council in 1960.

The Catechism is a text that collects the fundamental Catholic truths. They are stated so clearly that most people can read them without need of further explanation. As is true for so much about the church, the Catechism has a long and interesting history. In ancient times and in the Middle Ages, the truths and the prayers of the faith were inscribed on tablets like the Ten Commandments and were displayed in the house or church where they could be easily seen so that everybody could understand their content.

Following the invention of the printing press sometime in the mid-1500s, what we know today as the Catechism was formulated. After the Council of Trent in 1566, *The Roman Catechism* was produced. It was a catalog of beliefs the church determined Catholics needed to know so as not to "fall into the errors of Protestantism."

**For Heaven's Sake!**

You don't have to read theology to be a good Catholic! Remember, Jesus didn't write any theology. He taught the people about God's love through his actions. He fed them, and he healed their illnesses. Through his attention, they were transformed. So if theology isn't your cup of tea, relax and read one of the many stories in the New Testament that tell of the works of Jesus.

At the First Vatican Council in 1869, *The Roman Catechism* was updated and reissued. It was translated into English in the United States in 1885 and became known as the *Baltimore Catechism*. One hundred years later, in 1985, the church began putting together a new Catechism. This was the first such major gathering of the teachings of the church since the 1500s! The whole church, giving input through their bishops, participated in its preparation. The pope officially approved it on June 25, 1992, in effect retiring the old *Baltimore Catechism*. The new book is called the *Catechism of the Catholic Church*.

The *Catechism of the Catholic Church* is divided into four parts:

➤ **The Nicene Creed.** What the Catholic Church believes.

➤ **The sacraments.** What the Catholic Church celebrates.

➤ **The commandments.** What the Catholic Church lives.

➤ **The Our Father.** What the Catholic Church prays.

The new Catechism is characterized by its invitational style. It is less dogmatic in its approach; it shows truth in a more complex way, with much less absolutism. It shows the evolving nature of belief. On the other hand, it avoids opinions, that is, teachings by Catholic religious scholars whose thoughts have not yet made it into official church teaching.

# Theology: Formulating New Beliefs

Writing the Nicene Creed and the creation of other church documents began with a process called *theology*, or talking about God. Theology is modeled on Greek philosophy, which means it uses concepts and abstract terms rather than stories or poetry, which Jews and other groups commonly used to pass on their teachings. Even as the church selected which stories were to be gospels, theology began. Theology is also called reflection or interpretation.

Theology began in the Bible with the writings of Paul. Because Paul did not know Jesus during Jesus' lifetime on Earth, his writings are "one time removed" from the experience: They are a reflection on direct experience. In the Epistles of the New Testament, Paul talks about God and explains the meanings found in the disciples' experience of Jesus. He was interpreting the events and giving them meaning, which is what theology is all about.

Theology began as an attempt to put the experience of Jesus into a language style that was understandable to the Greek and Roman mind. The Greek and Roman mind was formed in the structure of the classic scholars like Plato, Socrates, and Aristotle. Paul wrote of Jesus in a language that non-Jewish citizens of the Roman Empire would understand, not in Jewish stories and poetry as the Gospels do.

Starting with Paul, then, the church began to use a new style of teaching. It moved from story to philosophical statements, or dogmas, which is a process that continues today. New experiences meet old stories and make new beliefs. As you've learned in this chapter, these beliefs are formulated in church councils and in the tradition of letters begun by Paul.

**Your Guardian Angel**

Look beneath the surface for the meanings in the Bible. The teachings of Jesus changed people's lives, and they continue to have this power. He taught in parable form, meaning he told stories that had several meanings. People who have spiritual insight hear the deeper message.

## *Faith Meets Reason*

Although the process of theology began in the Bible at the time of Paul, the church didn't use the term until the eleventh century when Anselm, one of the early church writers, provided this famous definition of theology: "faith seeking understanding." This definition is particularly helpful because it recognizes that theology is a philosophical process that uses reasoning, yet it clearly acknowledges that theology is grounded in faith. Some articles of faith are not "reasonable," meaning that they cannot be proven or understood by logic.

**Saints Preserve Us**

**St. Anselm, Doctor of the Church, April 21**

In case you thought metaphysics was a New Age concept, you might be surprised to know St. Anselm, born in 1033, was considered to be a metaphysician. Metaphysics is the systematic investigation of the nature of ultimate reality. In contrast to physics, which tends to be concerned with more practical issues like building bridges or highways, it is concerned with otherworldliness and the nature of being. Anselm is best known for his systematic argument for the existence of God. He entered monastic life at the age of 27 and died in 1109. He has not been declared a patron of anything yet, although he is a doctor of the church. Maybe metaphysicians might want to adopt him!

Theology begins with people's experiences of faith and talks about them in terms of the meaning they have for life. Its purpose is not to prove or disprove the faith experience, but to help people understand and interpret it. Theology builds a logical discussion about an experience, drawing spiritual conclusions that help people practice their faith in everyday life. Just as any meaningful discussion must follow logical form in order to be understood by others, theology uses a precise framework to express its ideas. Theology works with scripture, church tradition, and faith experiences and reason to bring spiritual insight to a situation.

## Types of Theology—WWJD (What Would Jesus Do)?

Today, there are two basic types of Catholic theology: classical and contemporary. Classical theology begins its process with the truths of the Bible as interpreted by church teachings and applies these truths to daily life to provide a moral guide. This type of theology reigned supreme in the church until the twentieth century. Since that time, Catholic theology has followed a more contemporary approach.

A problem with philosophy and theology is the tendency of those espousing the ideas to build logical arguments on top of logical arguments on top of logical arguments until the conclusions are so far removed from everyone's life that the average person finds them difficult to connect with. Instead of beginning its reflections in church teachings that become abstract and distant from the experiences of the people, contemporary theology starts with the lives of the people.

After listening to the voices of the people who are asking questions and demanding answers of their faith for the realities of their human condition, contemporary theology then goes directly to the text of scripture where the experiences of the people today touch the experiences of the people of the Bible. This process opens church teachings to new insight. It's a bottom-to-top model. In this approach, the human struggle leads to the discovery of new meaning from the traditional understanding of scripture and church teachings. The scriptures come alive, making people more open to changing conditions rather than simply accepting them. The stories of Jesus are brought face to face with the stories of the people when they ask their questions: How would he have responded? What is he telling us to do?

**Your Guardian Angel**

Theologians write theologies on any of a number of subjects: the nature of God, Jesus Christ, the Trinity, sin, redemption, the nature of the church, politics, war, the economy, and ecology.

Catholic thinkers are constantly developing theology, and the subject matter for it is unlimited. Through theology, Catholics understand their faith better; however, theology is a human endeavor and is never a substitute for faith. There is a difference between theological reflections and what will become part of the faith of the church. Not every theology that is developed makes it to the level of church teaching. The pope and the bishops alone are responsible for making the decision about which theologies become official teachings.

## Feeding New Ideas into the System

We've mentioned the creation story of Adam and Eve a couple of times in the book. The creation story is a foundational belief of the church, and many other beliefs are built on it. One of these beliefs is the church's understanding of human nature. Then there is the doctrine of original sin. From this doctrine, Catholics understand human weakness. Sin calls for redemption, and redemption is God's grace in the form of forgiveness. Even church teachings that death is the consequence of original sin are built on the foundational story of creation. A whole system of beliefs sits on top of a foundational belief in the story of creation.

What happens to a whole system of beliefs when the foundational base is challenged? The Catholic Church excommunicated Galileo because of his challenge to foundational beliefs. Later, you'll see how a theologian was silenced in more recent times because of his teaching.

But then, how do new ideas make it into church beliefs? Right away, you can see that does not happen easily or overnight, but it does happen—and it did happen in this century with the concept of evolution.

### Epiphanies

As scientists working in the fields of geology, astronomy, and physics began to examine earth in light of recent discoveries, they began to develop new concepts of how the world and the solar system were formed. Following scientific procedure for building new arguments, they presented new theories. They began teaching the theories, and as enough people started to believe in the theories, new cultural beliefs were formed.

As the culture gradually shifted to understanding creation in geological time rather than Biblical time, theologians had to rethink the doctrine of creation. Did they have to throw out the Biblical story of creation? No. The stories remain important ways that truth about God has been passed through history to us in the present time. The old way was to think of science as different than religion. Yet scientific truth and Biblical truth are not inherently different; religion (from *religio,* meaning "to bind together") is the arena in which all areas of life come together.

### S'ter Says

**Myth** is a story that tells the beliefs of a group of people regarding their origins, history, and destiny. Myth is neither historically true nor false. Myths transmit truths that cannot be understood apart from the story. In other words, you must look below the surface of the mythological story to find the meaning of it.

## Stirring the Pot of Change

How can Biblical teaching be realigned in the light of new truths? One way is by rethinking how the Bible functions. Many have come to see that the Bible is transmitting important truth to the people at the level of poetry and *myth*. It is following the old Jewish way of teaching through the use of story. The Bible is the faith story of the people of God. As new discoveries are made, and new understandings develop, basic beliefs about life are reformulated. New experiences of the people affect how the old stories are heard, so the meanings of the stories change. This is how the Biblical text continues to have meaning today.

As we've stated earlier, a belief is a belief only when the people believe it. Church teaching changes as the people's beliefs change. Although the church is slow to change, so is human consciousness. Yet they both change.

Who are the people who help stir the pot of change? In the secular culture, they are called philosophers, and in the church, they are called theologians. They are the ones who make the creative connections between the people and the teaching and shape new thought and new church beliefs.

Theologians affect the church teachings in three ways:

➤ **As communicators.** Communication requires both listening and speaking. Contemporary theologians have their ears to the ground; they listen to the people and to the culture and are able to speak effectively about what they hear.

➤ **As connectors.** They connect the present-day people's truth to people's stories of yesterday by weaving the past to the present point in time.

➤ **As creative thinkers.** Because of their skills and training, theologians hold the "big picture." They are able to listen to the people, and they also have a broad knowledge of church teachings. They are the ones who can creatively connect the voice of the people (experience) with Biblical teaching (story) and weave it into church teaching (tradition).

## The Dynamic Triangle: The People, Theologians, and Bishops

Imagine a triangle connecting the theologians to the people and to the bishops. Let's make it a dynamic triangle, meaning that an exchange of energy in the form of ideas and power moves among the different points on the triangle generating creativity.

The movement begins with the experiences of the people. The theologians hear the people, and a dialogue begins between them. (Remember, theologians are the communicators; they have their ear to the ground, and they listen as well as talk.) New understandings about life and what it means to be human emerge. Theologians help formulate these understandings into ideas that can be presented to the bishops; the theologians act as spokespersons.

Bishops, whose job it is to be the guardians of church truth, act as moderators. They consider what the people are saying through the theologians and also what the church has taught in the past. If the bishops feel strongly that the new teaching is in error, they will not accept it into official church belief. If they see the truth of it, new beliefs are formed. Not every idea of the people, formulated by the theologians, will make it to the level of church teaching, and the people will not believe every belief stated by the bishops.

**Your Guardian Angel**

Not every idea in theology becomes a belief of the church. The theologians' job is to come up with new ideas; the bishops' job is to sort through them.

*The Dynamic Triangle of Belief.*

*(Bob O'Gorman and Mary Faulkner)*

**S'ter Says**

**Liberation theology** describes theologies that attempt to articulate the faith from the perspective of a group's experience of its struggle to overcome oppression. **Base communities** are groups of 10 to 20 people who gather together for scripture reading and discussion and use these discussions to make decisions about the conditions in their community. They also hold Communion services in the absence of a priest.

A new teaching goes out to the people, usually in the form of a letter from the bishops. The people choose to accept the belief or reject it. Keep in mind that the church acts as an advisor in matters of faith; it is ultimately up to the people to determine what is true for them.

The Holy Spirit exists in every relationship; it is the glue connecting all creation. Whenever people are communicating, the Holy Spirit is present and is influencing the dynamics, bringing new insight and divine wisdom. The Holy Spirit connects the segments of the belief triangle. Whenever there is communication, the potential for divine revelation is present.

# Bargains from the Border: Liberation Theology and Base Communities

Not too long ago in Latin America, a creative exchange in theology ignited and sent sparks flying through society and the whole church. This exchange resulted in two major additions to Catholic theology and church structure: *liberation theology* and the birth of a new kind of church known as *base communities*.

Since the time of the Spanish conquest in the 1500s, Latin America had modeled its art, politics, literature, architecture, and theology on European traditions. Scholars from Latin America traveled to Europe for their training and returned to their own land to teach others the European ways.

## The Mirror of Change

In the 1960s, the model for theology in Latin America radically changed. A crop of young seminarians studying in Europe at that time met French, Belgian, and German priests, who changed the rules of the game.

Imagine for a moment that you are a young man living in a small village. You have attended the mission church and school all your life. You have served at Mass, tended to the chores of the missions, and studied hard in addition to working in the fields and performing the endless chores necessary to help your family. Your hard work and arduous studies have finally paid off. You have been selected to attend the university and then experience the exquisite honor of going to Europe to read the works of the church's greatest theologians.

Your family and the entire village is proud because they have all worked to help you attain this great honor. They probably feel that they may never see you again, but they are rejoicing in the service you will be giving to God and the people and your opportunity to make something of yourself by escaping the poverty of the village and the limitations of village life. A hometown boy makes good!

### Saints Preserve Us

Born in 1917, Oscar Romero was archbishop of San Salvador, El Salvador and is remembered for his bold preaching on behalf of the rights of the peasants. Although he became the country's most respected and popular figure and was nominated for the Nobel Peace Prize, his decisive stand with the poor created a rift between him and the government. In 1980, a rightist death squad assassinated Archbishop Romero while he was preaching at Mass in the chapel of the cancer hospital where he lived. Many regarded his death as martyrdom. His cause has been introduced for canonization.

You have been prepared well by your teachers in Mexico City; you know what to expect, and you are looking forward to exploring not only the ancient and beautiful cities of Europe, but also the great classical texts of Augustine, Aquinas, Luther, and Calvin. As the first day finally arrives, you hurry to class along with the other young men from all over Latin America. You are yet unaware of the radically different situation that awaits you in the huge mahogany-paneled library of the university. Rather than being given the beautiful, leather-bound, gold-leafed books to read, you and your fellow students have been singled out for a different experience.

You are handed a mirror and are instructed to look into it. You begin your study of theology by looking at your own reality. The teachers want to show you the power of discovering God by looking at yourself. The teachers ask: "What do your experiences tell you of the nature of God?" You wonder, "What could this mean?" It is difficult: To look at your life is to face poverty, enslavement, domination, and inferiority. You are not proud to bring these harsh and shameful realities to the light of reflection. You fear looking into the mirror.

In contrast to the traditional theological training, these men in the 1960s received much more. They learned how to work with the people to help them transform their lives through theology. Their new teachers insisted that the authentic study of God needed to start with "the present realities." Reluctantly, the young men began to look into the mirrors they held. They saw their own faces and the faces of their people, the faces of enslavement and poverty. The process had begun. For hundreds of years, when the peasants complained about their condition, the church taught them that to be poor was to be more "Christ-like." They were told to accept their situation.

### Epiphanies

Base communities are very popular in Latin America, Africa, and Asia. They began in Brazil in 1956 as "Sunday services without a priest" and spread like a revolutionary wildfire throughout parts of Latin America throughout the 1970s and 1980s. These groups grew during the oppressive military regime when the priests and bishops were repressed and could not be in contact with the people. The communities carried on the work of the church. Today, Brazil has over 100,000 base communities. These communities are showing a new way of "being church," and this vision is finding a home in North America.

Now they were being taught that their needs and the needs of their people were important, to be denied no longer. The reign of God was here and now. The seminarians were encouraged to search the Gospels for the saving message of "good news." They found it in the liberating message of the Gospel. Jesus had worked to end the oppression of the people. The word of God, for these young men and for the people they represented, became the promise of God's liberating action. Liberation theology was born.

These scholars returned to Latin America and, unlike their predecessors, did not impose classical theological teachings on the people. Instead, as their teachers had done, they began to listen to what the people were saying and search for a response in the Gospel. Over and over again, the Gospel told of good news for the poor and promised liberation. As the people realized that God had not abandoned them, the message began to heal the deep spiritual wounds caused by the church and politics that they had lived with for many centuries.

Latin American theologians have contributed a substantial body of literature to church teachings known as liberation theology. It set the tone for similar theologies to emerge that begin from the experience of the people: black theology, woman's theology, Asian theology, as well ecological theology, a theology that deals with the liberation of Earth itself. These theologies have begun to ask questions and make demands on the church and the political structures to become more responsive to the needs of the people.

## Church in the 'Hood

Liberation theology takes place in small, face-to-face gatherings of neighbors, where people talk about their lives and tell their stories. These gatherings are called base communities. Characteristically, the stories told are those of political or economic oppression. For example, a factory avoided paying into a health care plan and thus deprived the workers of benefits when they needed them. Other examples are low wages that make feeding a family almost impossible or the lack of clean drinking water in the community. These everyday issues become the common story of the group.

The group then examines the scripture for God's identification with their plight. They find new meaning in what they read and may be inspired to organize and take action.

This is a new sense of church: A church that is small and face-to-face and a church that expresses salvation not in the future sense of heaven, but in the here and now of everyday life. This grassroots church challenges the long patriarchal tradition of Catholicism.

## Power, Power, Who's Got the Power?

There is major controversy regarding what gets taught as official church doctrine and what does not. This controversy goes all the way back to the beginning of church history, and issues of authority continue to be worked out in church politics today. Dogma is decided in church councils through a voting process. Theology informs the voters on the issues, but there are no guarantees on how it will go. On the other hand, bishops can silence theologians whose work they find to be too controversial or against church beliefs.

The Vatican maintains a watchdog office called the Congregation for the Doctrine of the Faith that constantly surveys the theologians and teachers and their published work. This office is the genetic remnant of the Inquisition, which we'll discuss later in Chapter 22, "Division, Debauchery, and Reform: The Church's Second Millennium."

Silencing is the term used to describe the process of disciplining teachers judged to be questionable. Silencing is a "time out" ordered by the bishop. Those receiving a silencing spend six months or a year in reflection until they come to an understanding that is agreeable with that of the bishop.

### Epiphanies

A present-day example of a theologian being silenced is the case of Matthew Fox. In 1987, Fox, a Dominican priest, headed up a popular program in spirituality and ecology called The Institute for Creation-Centered Spirituality. He had an unorthodox curriculum and faculty, and his writings were on the cutting edge of ecological spirituality. Fox was reprimanded by Rome and given the option of closing his program or being silenced for six months. He chose to be silenced rather than compromise the effectiveness of his program and his staff.

As is true in any political arena, viewpoints in the church tend to be polarized between liberals and conservatives. Control over what becomes church teaching follows these lines as well. The decisions about the meaning of faith are not always worked out in the church's offices and schools, however. The bottom line rests with the people. When all is said and done, a dogma or teaching of the church is not a belief of the people unless they believe it.

In this chapter, you have seen how the Catholic Church exercises its role as teacher and how this role has developed and changed over the years. The next chapter examines the teachings themselves.

## The Least You Need to Know

➤ Catholics draw their beliefs from both the Bible and tradition.

➤ The Nicene Creed contains the basic beliefs of Catholics.

➤ Beliefs are developed through a dynamic process among the people, theologians, and bishops.

➤ The Catechism summarizes the church's beliefs.

➤ The final decision about beliefs rests in the beliefs of the people.

# Chapter 19

# The Teachings of the Church: More Than Just the Party Line

---

**In This Chapter**

➤ Learn all about sin and forgiveness

➤ Find out about heaven and hell and who goes where

➤ Discover the relationship between sexuality and Catholicism

➤ Appreciate the "seamless garment of life"

---

It's been said that sinning is easier to do in Catholicism than any other religion because Catholics have so many beliefs, rules, and regulations. Questions about what constitutes a sin dominate discussions about Catholicism. For many years, the Catholic Church focused its teaching and preaching on sin. Every requirement or belief of the church was backed up by what consequences it carried. The issue of sinning is often the first thing people think of when they hear the word *Catholic*, and this attention to sin has been very self-destructive to the church.

Sex and sin became synonymous, and for some this connection is still true today. However, the good news is that for the most part, sin is not the major subject of the church's teachings today, and much has been done to repair the relationship between sexuality and spirituality. In this chapter, we'll look at definitions of sin and free will, afterlife, human sexuality, and important Catholic social teachings that guide the faithful in their interactions in the world.

## Sin After Vatican II

Post-Vatican II church morality takes a larger and more positive approach to sin than the Catholic Church did in the past. The church now focuses on helping its members

### For Heaven's Sake!

Don't think the church is getting soft on sin! Recent shifts in the church's understanding of sin and virtue may appear to some that the church is taking a soft line on sin. This is not the case. Instead, the church focuses on developing virtue as a first line of defense against sin rather than using fear of punishment as a deterrent.

### S'ter Says

**Moral** distinguishes between right and wrong. Morality requires that we act in accord with established standards of good behavior and in agreement with our consciences.

foster Biblical virtues by promoting loving, peaceful relationships and working together to bring the reign of God forward for more people to enjoy.

Moving away from the emphasis on sin and punishment follows a general pattern of rethinking beliefs and redefining sin. New beliefs emphasize people's basic goodness and build on it. Yet remnants of the old thinking still remain. Certainly not everyone in the church is living out the new definitions of spirituality and what it means to be a Catholic, but the direction has been established, and the trend is positive.

## Sin: Missing the Mark

Sin is a religious term. In the Old Testament, sin is understood as a break in the covenant relationship with God. It's the result of not following the will of God as we know it in our hearts. Although sin is often thought of as a violation against God, it is actually a violation against ourselves, our neighbors, and all creation. Most often, when the term *sin* appears in the New Testament, it is used in the phrase, "forgiveness of sin."

In the past, Catholics saw sin primarily as disobedience to God and to "lawful superiors." Obedience became inextricably bound up with the Catholic identity; obedience was a Catholic's dominant *moral* characteristic.

When preparing for confession, people commonly performed "an examination of conscience," which meant they evaluated their obedience to the laws of God and to the church. The church emphasized degrees of sin. In figuring out the numbers and types of sin, Catholics became preoccupied with law and measurement. Sin and guilt drove Catholics' moral attitude. To be moral was to avoid wrongdoing rather than promote "right doing," which limited Catholics' ability to live the fullness of the Gospel message: love of self, love of God, and love of neighbor.

The understanding of sin today is focused on the law of love and informed by the human sciences. Moral reflection is no longer centered on personal shortcomings but rather on the unconditional love of God. This change shifts moral reasoning from a reactive stance to a proactive one.

The new theology of sin teaches that sin is a limit, with the understanding that we are most God-like in our freedom. The new theology is based on the belief that God wants us to live creatively and be free to grow to our full potential. Sin, then, is whatever blocks our freedom to develop fully. Present teaching encourages Catholics to look at a wider context of social justice, because injustice limits the human spirit. If anyone is not free, no one is free. Catholics are encouraged to work for their own liberation and that of all others. Sin is that which violates human dignity and blocks freedom for others or ourselves.

## Categories of Sins: Specks and Logs

Traditionally, there were two different kinds of sin in the Catholic Church: mortal and venial. Mortal sins are more serious than venial sins. An analogy might be that a mortal sin corresponds to a felony, and a venial sin is like a misdemeanor. The Biblical references to the difference in the magnitude of sin come from two passages. Matthew 23:24 describes the difference between a gnat and a camel; Matthew 7:3 discusses the difference between a speck and a log.

Nowhere in the New Testament is there a list of mortal sins, nor is the punishment for them described. However, the church has decided that certain extreme behavior should be classified as mortal or deadly sin. Mortal refers to the death a sin brings to the soul. Mortal sin constitutes a serious rupture in a person's relationship to God and to the community. In order to restore this relationship, those who have committed a mortal sin go to confession and work with their confessor to heal the damages caused by their actions. Three things are necessary for a sin to be classified as mortal:

➤ It is a serious offense.

➤ The person must have full knowledge of the seriousness of it.

➤ It is committed with full consent of the will and with no coercion.

Venial sins are described as lesser offenses. They do not cause a rupture in the relationship with God like mortal sins do. They are the everyday transgressions we are all subject to. However, any sin, like an illness in its early stages, can lead to more serious consequences if left unchecked. Paying attention to venial sins helps people locate troublesome patterns within themselves.

Newer approaches to understanding sin should not lead to laxity, but instead to a deeper sensitivity to the human condition and the

**For Heaven's Sake!**

Big sins call for quick action! When you have transgressed your moral boundaries and know you're in serious spiritual trouble, get help quickly. Go to confession. When you are in sin, you have separated yourself from God and may be in spiritual jeopardy. God's forgiveness is guaranteed.

development of compassion. When the definition of sin is broadened to include all the ways in which we might be refusing God by limiting our engagement with life, it is not easy to draw up a list of sins as was once the practice. Although the commandments and the laws of the church are still part of the process of moral discernment (the process of identifying right and wrong), they in no way represent the whole picture.

### Your Guardian Angel

If you sin, look within! If you notice you're continually falling short of what you know to be right, you're in a potentially sinful pattern. At the end of the day, spend a few moments going over your day to see whether you are acting in accordance with your ideals.

### For Heaven's Sake!

Don't let guilt get you down. The church's teachings on sin have created a lot of guilt. Sin is known to be a human condition, yet forgiveness is always available. Forgiveness requires taking moral responsibility for your actions, and making the adjustments necessary to live in accord with what you know is right.

New ways of assessing your moral condition could include asking yourself if you did all you could in a situation to bring God's love forward. Your moral response is then rooted in love, justice, and peace. Your failure to take action then becomes a measure for sin. The pre-Vatican II approach to sin was to look at it as commission, meaning what people did; the post-Vatican II emphasis is on "omission," or what people have failed to do.

## Original Sin: One Day in Paradise

The concept of original sin helps to explain how evil can exist in a world created by a good God. Although there's no specific Biblical mention of original sin in either the Old or New Testaments, it has always been a central church teaching.

The name "original sin" did not enter into church teachings until the time of Augustine. He identified original sin as a basic yearning for self-gratification that turns people away from God. His views on original sin became part of the official church teachings in 418. During the Middle Ages, the interpretation shifted away from an emphasis on humans' corrupt nature to the break in the relationship with God that Adam caused by committing the first sin. Thomas Aquinas described original sin as a "weakened, disordered precondition." There has been little change in the theory of original sin up until present time.

In this pre-Vatican II teaching, it was understood that guilt also existed in all human beings. It existed prior to any wrongdoing on the part of the individual. Guilt was a condition of the soul that we inherited from our ancestors much as we inherit other physiological characteristics.

The doctrine of original sin is still a central dogma of the Catholic Church, and contemporary theologians struggle to keep its meaning relevant in the light of science and psychology. The underlying belief is that Christ's redemption, which is characterized by love and forgiveness, is at the very heart and soul of the divine plan. All humans are in need of the redemption he offers. The Biblical story of Adam, Eve, the snake, and the tree (pictured here) is not a literal description of a historical first sin, but it is a description of what it means to be human. It is not necessarily telling what happened at the beginning of human history, but rather is reminding us of what is happening all the time in the human struggle.

*Adam, Eve, and the Serpent.*

*(Alinari/Art Resource, New York)*

When viewed this way, the story of the fall tells us of the inevitable mix of good and evil contained in human existence. Our highest motives at best are mixed and ambiguous. Human frailty leaves us vulnerable to lapses in good judgment, and we can be fooled by circumstances. The ultimate human dilemma is to exist in the midst of a sinful world, yet strive for goodness. Part of the struggle is to overcome a lower nature that sometimes wants to pull us off course.

The modern interpretation of original sin recognizes basic human qualities and world conditions. Most important, it recognizes God's participation with us in our struggles. To be human is to be in need of God's grace. In other words, we need the gift of God's help to navigate our earthly existence. The doctrine of original sin can be said to illustrate the adage, "Where sin exists there also does grace abound."

## The Seven Deadly Symptoms

The church has determined that certain human emotions or concerns are the root of our problems. These emotions are called *capital sins.* The seven capital sins were immortalized in Chaucer's "The Parson's Tale" in *The Canterbury Tales* and in Dante's description of the terraces of purgatory in the *Divine Comedy.*

The seven capital sins are:

1. Pride
2. Envy
3. Anger
4. Sloth
5. Greed
6. Gluttony
7. Lust

### S'ter Says

**Capital sins** are the thoughts and behaviors that the church has determined to be dispositions toward sinning. These tendencies or weaknesses in the human character, if unchecked, may lead to sin.

These seven sins are said to be the wellsprings from which all sinful thoughts and behaviors flow. The term *capital* comes from the Latin word *caput,* meaning head, and refers to capital sins being the source or headwaters for sins. These sins have also been called the "seven deadly sins." Although they are called sins, these seven characteristics are not sins in and of themselves. Instead, they describe tendencies toward sinning or character weaknesses through which sin occurs.

## Good Guilt and Bad Shame

We conclude our discussion of sin with a look at good old-fashioned guilt and perhaps answer the question of whether Catholics have more than their fair share of it. Guilt is a subject for consideration both in the church and in the world of psychology. Guilt, within the context of religion, is an intuitive understanding of wrongdoing. It seems to be an inborn feeling that helps to guide us in our selection of what to do and what not to do. As such, it is a healthy and helpful quality.

Guilt needs to be distinguished from shame. Guilt is innate; shame is developed. Guilt corresponds to a genuine violation of a value. Shame is the result of

### For Heaven's Sake!

You can't sin in your mind or heart. People tend to regard feelings and emotions as having moral significance. Emotions and feelings are not sinful. Some Catholics confess anger and lust when they have not acted on these feelings. By themselves, the seven capital sins are human conditions that we all struggle with. It's acting on these feelings that is the sin.

childhood conditioning. If a child has been punished about his or her normal developmental processes (like bed-wetting or thumb sucking, for example) he or she may experience an inappropriate feeling of guilt that is better described as shame.

Shame is a problem at the spiritual and psychological level and is best addressed by both a minister and a psychologist. For example, many people who have suffered child abuse experience shame. When abuse occurs, a person is left with a broken relationship with God. Parents are our first understanding of what God is like. If parents fail to love and instead bring injury, the child's soul (psyche) experiences a loss of its natural connection to God. This loss results in severely damaged self-esteem, which progresses to despair and self-hate. Despair is a spiritual condition in which you believe you are beyond help.

**Your Guardian Angel**

Check your terms. Guilt is feeling bad about something you've done. Shame is feeling bad about yourself. There is a big difference!

When we are experiencing shame, we cannot operate fully and creatively, and even more damaging, we cannot experience forgiveness. Appropriate guilt, on the other hand, tells us we have done something wrong to ourselves or to another. After the wrong has been righted, we can experience forgiveness, and the guilt dissipates.

Confession is a healthy practice from both a spiritual and psychological perspective. Having someone to tell one's sin to and experiencing a formal process of forgiveness frees the participant of guilt. Absolution occurs after the person makes a confession, expresses sorrow, and makes clear the intent to change this behavior. The priest, allowing Christ to act through him, absolves the person of the sin and the guilt that goes with it. (We'll talk more about absolution in the next chapter.)

## Free Will, Judgment, and Afterlife

Free will describes the human ability to choose a course of action. Both common sense and church teaching agree that moral responsibility depends upon free will.

The nature and degree of free will are the subjects of much theological and philosophical debate. Studies of human personality and development have shown that a person's free will is subject to his or her conditioning. Some studies go so far as to claim that the ideal of free will is a complete illusion and that all actions are governed by external causes.

Catholic moral teaching functions much like civil law regarding free will. It teaches that free will can be greatly impeded by a variety of factors, such as fear, coercion,

### For Heaven's Sake!

If you've been to confession, have been forgiven, and have made reparation and still feel guilty, get help. You may be suffering from shame. Shame can be a destructive and crippling emotion that requires spiritual and psychological healing.

### S'ter Says

**Evil** describes morally bad or wrong choices. Synonyms of evil include wicked and depraved. Evil concerns conduct regarded as immoral.

ignorance, emotional disturbance, passion, and the use of drugs, for example. In this regard, free will exists as an ideal. The human condition imposes limits to this ideal.

The church teaches that consequences of our free will accompany us beyond death, that there is a direct relationship between moral action on earth and existence beyond death. It also assures us that God's judgement never exists separately from his mercy, meaning that God has the whole picture and knows both our heart and our struggles.

## Evil: Bad to the Bone

*Evil* does not exist as something in itself; it exists in the absence of good or the lack of wholeness. We, however, have free will and can choose not to fulfill God's will and not to fulfill our potential. Thus, evil is exercised in choices made in opposition to God's will.

These choices may be personal ones or those made by a community. When we talked about sin, we discussed personal moral choices that can result in evil. However, there are times when evil begins to have a life of its own, such as when a community, large corporation, or an entire society sustains it. Two horrendous examples of evil such as this are slavery and the Holocaust. In such cases, humans create a culture of evil, and free choice is severely restricted. The potential to do God's will is so greatly reduced that evil prevails temporarily. It is temporary because the church teaches that good is stronger than evil. Evil exists only in a temporal way, meaning that it is limited. Good has an eternal quality.

## The Devil Made Me Do It ... or Did He?

The Devil is often represented as a symbol of evil. Church teaching about devils maintains that they are spiritual creatures subject to God. Christ's death and resurrection overcame their power, the power of evil in the world. Humans can overcome evil by choosing Christ. The important theological point is that humans have free will.

### Epiphanies

The Devil is not mentioned all that often in the Old Testament. The snake in the Garden of Eden was not meant to symbolize the Devil. At a later time, Jewish and Christian writers applied the Devil to it. Originally, the snake came to awaken Eve's curiosity to the human journey. God curses the serpent in the Genesis account because of the Hebrew's disdain of paganism. The serpent is an important symbol in many pagan religions.

Scripture clearly teaches that good and evil are not equal. It would be dangerous and a misunderstanding of church teaching to say, "The Devil made me do it." The church is clear that the Devil is not the source of all evil. Human beings have free will, and they can choose to participate in evil or good.

## Demonic Possession/Exorcism: "Get Thee Behind Me, Satan"

Demons do not occupy a significant place in Catholic Church teachings. Many church teachers do not believe in demonic possession. However, most acknowledge that there is evil in the world beyond the personal power to create it. Evil has a depth beyond human control. Exactly how this plays out, no one really knows for sure. The belief in demonic possession defines it as occurring when the psychic power of a demon takes over the personality of a human so that the human no longer has free will.

### S'ter Says

The **Roman Ritual** is a liturgical book containing special rites and blessings commonly performed by priests. Since Vatican II, this book is now called the *Book of Blessings*.

Possession manifests itself in bizarre ways, including hysterical behavior, incoherent speech, and uncontrolled physical movements. The person can become self-destructive as well as destructive to others. There is brief mention of demonic possession in the Old Testament, and the New Testament tells of Jesus ministering to many who are possessed by demons. In the Gospel of Mark, Jesus exorcises a group of demons. He asks their names and casts them into the sea (Mark 5:1–20).

Exorcism is a rite performed to expel evil from a person or a place. It involves prayers and specific actions. Such liberating action is not different from the works of Jesus and the disciples. The Catholic Church proceeds carefully in cases of possession. It requires that the person undergo both physical and psychological examinations. When the church does perform an exorcism, it chooses a priest who is known for his holiness and strength of character and who has received special training. The rite of exorcism is found in the Catholic book of rituals, called the *Roman Ritual*.

## Death: The Last Good-Bye?

Catholic teaching on death is based in the resurrection and says that death is not the final state. Teachings from Vatican II state that God has created humans "for a blissful purpose beyond the reach of earthly misery."

The Greeks thought of the human soul as immortal. At death, the soul shed its body and was thus "freed" from the "prison of the flesh." Early Jewish belief portrayed death as a passage of the person from the land of the living to the dark and cheerless realm of the dead where there can be no happiness and no praise of God, known as *sheol* in Hebrew (Psalms 6:5; Isaiah 38:18). Christianity follows a later Jewish tradition that death is not the last word, but an invitation to a more perfect union with God.

A contemporary Catholic teacher, the late Cardinal Joseph L. Bernardin of Chicago, provided his insight on death. He was featured on the cover of *Newsweek* with the headline, "He taught us how to die." In the article, Bernardin told how his struggle with cancer moved him from a fear of death to seeing death as a friend.

### Your Guardian Angel

Don't be afraid of death. One of the promises of living the good life is everlasting life in Christ. Although no one knows exactly how that works, we can trust that it is a good thing! In Catholicism, death is not the end, but a passage to perpetual life.

## Hell: The Eternal Loss of God

The church believes God's purpose in creation is for humans to form a personal relationship of love with him. Furthermore, the church teaches that this relationship reaches its perfection in eternal life with God. Our free will allows us to cooperate or not to cooperate with God and to accept or refuse to enter into the loving relationship we are offered.

"Eternal damnation" is not attributed to an act of God, because in his merciful love, he can only desire our complete life with him. Hell is the pain produced by our choice of utterly and deliberately refusing to live in relationship with God, if such a choice is even possible. Hell is only a possibility because we take seriously the quality of free will God has created in us. It puts the punch into free will.

Speaking on the subject of hell, Pope John Paul II said not to consider it a place, but rather a state that the soul suffers when it denies itself access to God. Hell is the ultimate consequence of sin. To describe this reality, scripture uses symbolic language. The images of hell that appear in sacred scripture must be properly interpreted, according to the pope. They are used as an analogy to show the complete desperation and emptiness of life without God. Images of hell are a poetic warning. The pope's remarks are directed at correcting the improper use of Biblical images of hell that create anxiety and despair. Again, rather than a place, hell is a condition of the soul separated from God.

The pope went on to say that God has never revealed "whether or which human beings" are eternally damned. As stated earlier, damnation is the result of a serious sin and requires that the person absolutely knows what he or she is doing. The church does not say this has ever happened to anyone. A good illustration occurs in the New Testament when Jesus does not condemn those who have participated in his crucifixion. Rather he says, "Father, forgive them, for they do not know not what they are doing." (Luke 23:34)

### Epiphanies

The Bible often teaches with parables, stories, and metaphors, so the Biblical images of everlasting fire are poetic warnings of what it would be like to be without God. Biblical images of hell abound: Matthew calls it a fiery furnace where people will "weep and gnash their teeth." (Matthew 13:42, 25, 30, 41) Mark says it is like Gehenna with its unquenchable fire. Mark (9:43) and Luke (16:19–13) tell the story of the rich man that explains hell as a place of eternal suffering with no alleviation of pain. Finally, the Book of Revelation (20:13) speaks of the "pool of fire."

The popular images of hell that have dominated Catholic thinking, although rooted in the Bible, were amplified and popularized in literature and art. Over the years, the poetic level of these images was lost, meaning that people forgot that the Bible tells stories to teach lessons. The analogous images of hell began to be interpreted as a real place. The pope has taken a bold step toward modifying the destructive fire and brimstone images of hell that have often limited our understanding of our relationship to God.

## *Heaven: "Where the Elite All Meet!"*

Heaven is the word used to define the final fulfillment for which we were created. It describes the ideal relationship between creation and God. Heaven is revealed in Jesus' resurrection, which shows us God's plan for the future of the whole creation.

The Old Testament uses the term *heaven* in a variety of ways. It describes a vault in the sky as the dwelling place of God. Later, the physical heavens were seen to be symbols of divine triumph. Heaven is associated with both the first creation as described in Genesis and the future action of God, who would create a new heaven and a new earth in which the hopes of Israel would be brought to fulfillment.

**S'ter Says**

**Heaven** describes the ideal relationship possible between humans and God.

The New Testament explicitly associates heaven with Jesus Christ. The word of God comes from heaven to take flesh in Jesus. (John 3:13) After the resurrection, Jesus ascends to heaven to sit at the right hand of God. (Matthew 26:64; Mark 14:62; Luke 22:69; Acts 7:55) From heaven, Jesus reigns as Lord and Messiah, and from there he will appear again as the judge at the end of time.

Through revelation, Pope John Paul II says, we are taught that "heaven or happiness" is "neither an abstraction nor a physical place in the clouds, but a living personal relationship with the Holy Trinity." In attempting to describe ultimate realities, language always falls short, he reminds us. In so doing, he has shifted to the language of relationship from the abstractions of traditional theology. In the new interpretation, heaven is not a place of ideal real estate, but a description of the soul when it is in its completed form.

# Human Sexuality: "Male and Female He Created Them"

Human sexuality refers to the state of being sexual, being in the world either as a female or a male. It includes anatomy, behavioral characteristics, bonding, and reproduction. Sexuality is a fundamental aspect of personal identity. Our sexuality enters into all aspects of our life and all personal interactions with one another and all aspects of self-expression and activity. There are no asexual or nonsexual human beings.

The role of the church regarding sexuality is to help the faithful understand their sexuality and act in sexually responsible ways. Determining what sexual responsibility is is an ongoing process of assessment and discernment that church teachers have addressed from the earliest times. Increasingly in recent times, lay people have added their voices to these teachings.

Vatican II called for the renewal of church teaching in light of new knowledge from the physical and social sciences. In this section, we'll look at some of the issues in human sexuality that Catholics are struggling with today: birth control, homosexuality, and celibacy.

## Birth Control: The Church's Big Headache

Contraception refers to the ways in which men and women can prevent conception of a new life from occurring as a result of sexual intercourse. The church's moral assessment regarding contraception is determined from the values considered to be important to human sexual activity. One value of human sexual activity is propagation, or having children. Until the twentieth century, the church taught that having children took precedence over all other sexual values. All attempts to block sexual action from the intention to procreate were considered wrong. The church considers them to be against *natural law*.

Vatican II introduced important changes in the church's teachings on sexuality. The mutual self-giving that is possible through sexual intercourse became a key value. Church teachings began to recognize that sexual intercourse strengthens the unity between couples. Church teachings also recognized that married couples had both the right and duty to limit the size of their family to correspond to their situation.

Following Vatican II, Pope Paul VI gave a strict interpretation of these teachings in an encyclical called *Humanae Vitae* (Latin for "of human life"). The pope declared, "Each and every marriage act must remain open to the transmission of life." *Humanae Vitae* set the church spinning. There were questions from bishops, theologians, pastors, and congregations that still have not been answered.

Sociological data reveal that approximately 80 percent of practicing Catholics do not follow the church's official and authoritative teachings on birth control. Catholics report that their parish priests support them in the decisions they make in this matter. However, abstinence and the rhythm method are the only acceptable forms of birth control.

**Your Guardian Angel**

Think of your sexuality as part of your spirituality. God created human beings as male and female. Sexuality, then, is a gift of God. Sexuality and spirituality cannot be separated. Both are calls to intimacy, and therefore two sides of the same coin.

**S'ter Says**

**Natural law** is a term that describes the nature of creation. Natural law refers to proper human action by people living in accord with the natural world, which is the use of common sense.

# Homosexuality: Yes and No

For the most part, the church has taken the position of "love the sinner, hate the sin" toward homosexuality. According to church beliefs, to be a homosexual is not in itself sinful, but to practice homosexuality is considered immoral. The church bases its belief in scripture (Genesis 19 and 20:13, Romans 1:24–27, 1 Corinthians 6:9–10, and 1 Timothy 1:9–10) and moral tradition based on natural law reasoning. Natural law reasoning is a process the church uses to examine human acts according to the "nature of things."

Some teachers in the church have attempted to propose a Catholic approach to homosexuality. This approach would remain faithful to the traditional teaching about the two goals of sexuality (procreation and love) and at the same time be a genuine response to the nature of homosexuality. These people argue that because a change of orientation is out of the question (it is generally accepted that a person does not deliberately choose their sexual orientation), homosexuals should be given the same moral choices as heterosexuals: celibacy or permanent exclusive partnership. The church, however, has not altered its position at this time. Although it mandates understanding and compassion toward homosexuals, it holds a firm line against them acting on their sexual inclinations.

### For Heaven's Sake!

The rhythm method may not be the most effective means of family planning. In fact, it has been called Vatican roulette! If you are going to use it, work with your health care professional to find out how it works. It depends on naturally occurring times of infertility in the woman's cycle and restricts intercourse to these times. Therefore, the church teaches it does not go against the processes of nature.

# Celibacy: Giving It Up for God

Celibacy is sexual abstinence. Sexual abstinence is defined as refraining from sexual intercourse or any other use of the sexual faculties. Celibacy describes a temporary choice married people make for spiritual purposes, the state of unmarried persons, or the permanent choice made by those taking religious vows (priests, nuns, and monks).

Celibacy of the clergy in the Western church grew more out of custom than law. It began in the 300s, continued to be shaped through time, and was reaffirmed in the 1500s at the Council of Trent when the lives of virginity and celibacy were declared superior to the married state. It is recognized that rules regarding celibacy are church laws, not divine laws. They can be changed if the church ever decides to change them.

### Epiphanies

St. Paul, writing in the early years of the church, urged his congregations to consider celibacy. Scholars now tell us the reason for Paul's teaching was the church's belief at that time that the end of the world was coming soon. Therefore, it was not the time to bring new life into the world. Additionally, for Paul, celibacy provided him unrestricted opportunity to be of service to the church.

The rules for celibacy have been questioned in the light of Vatican II. Arguments in favor of celibacy center on its pastoral effectiveness and its relevance for spiritual development. Arguments against celibacy include the following:

➤ Celibacy is based on church tradition, not divine law, and church laws are subject to change.

➤ Greater understanding of human psychology has led to questions regarding the impact of celibacy on the human development of the clergy.

➤ Many non-European cultures view celibacy negatively.

Several situations assure a continued debate regarding celibacy. One is the declining number of priests in active ministry. Another is the exemption from celibacy for married clergy who enter the church after having been ordained in other churches. A third is that in various parts of the world, especially in Africa and Latin America, celibacy is not observed.

## The Seamless Garment

Cardinal Joseph L. Bernardin of Chicago called for the use of a consistent ethic of human life. This ethic would be applied to the issues of abortion, capital punishment, modern warfare, euthanasia, and socioeconomic issues of food and shelter for all. His teaching recognizes the relationship between these social issues and the obligation to respect human life and dignity in all arenas. According to this principle, abortion and

### S'ter Says

The **"seamless garment of life"** refers to Jesus' robe, which legend has it, was seamless. In applying this ethic, one recognizes that protection of life is the basis for determining the morality of war, capital punishment, and abortion. In other words, under this ethic, it would be difficult to be in favor of capital punishment and against abortion.

euthanasia (pro-life issues) and social ethics (human rights, peace, social justice, and capital punishment) must all be viewed in the same light. In other words, Cardinal Bernardin's teachings ask for moral consistency in what he has called the *"seamless garment of life."* Let's take a look at each of these issues.

### Your Guardian Angel

If you are facing the death of a loved one, ministries to the dying are available in many parishes. You can locate them through your parish directory or speak to your parish priest and find out how to become involved with this ministry.

## Euthanasia: Say No to Dr. Death

Euthanasia comes from the Greek and means "good death." Today, we use it to refer to intentionally ending the life of a terminally ill person. Other terms used to describe euthanasia are mercy killing, assisted dying, and recently, aid in dying. The 1980 Vatican *Declaration on Euthanasia* defines it as "an action or omission which of itself or by intention causes death, in order that all suffering may in this way be eliminated."

The issue of euthanasia boils down to the difference between taking an action to bring about death versus allowing a person to die naturally. *Killing* is a human act carrying moral responsibility for causing death. *Allowing to die* refers to withholding or withdrawing treatment so that the illness can run its course, the outcome of which may be death.

The church teaches that one is not morally obliged to use "extraordinary means" to stay alive, for example, to have surgery, or chemotherapy, or radiation, or be force-fed, live on a ventilator, or seek a transplant. All of these can be seen as "extraordinary." One is only bound to the ordinary: shelter, comfort, and food and water if eating and drinking is possible. The capacity of modern technology to ward off death and the failure of individuals, their families, and their caregivers to accept death are factors that contribute to the choosing of extraordinary and often futile treatment.

The Catholic Church recognizes life as a precious gift, humans as mortal, and God as supreme. Euthanasia violates the sanctity of life and the sovereignty of God by assuming ownership over life. The church views the legalization of euthanasia as a threat to the common good. The church's teaching affirms the role of health care providers as stewards of healing and caring. It upholds the hospice movement as a model for health care. Hospice sends health care professionals into the homes of terminally ill people with the objective of making the people as comfortable as possible while they die a natural death without prolonging or hastening the process.

## Just War

The just war doctrine claims that, despite its destructive character, war is morally justifiable in certain circumstances and limitations. The doctrine has its roots in the

Hebrew Scriptures and the Greek and Roman world. Augustine formulated it in the 400s when he stated that war is love's response to a neighbor threatened by force. Thomas Aquinas in the 1200s claimed the legitimacy of war waged in self-defense. These teachings came before the rise of modern warfare.

The just war doctrine has two purposes: First, it is a reminder that war is always a moral matter, not simply a political one. It requires serious consideration. Second, although the doctrine can judge certain circumstances for war as just, violence must be limited. The doctrine recognizes that regardless of its justification, war is a serious matter and must be mourned.

The eight criteria used to determine a just war are the following:

➤ It must be a just cause. Traditionally, to be a just cause, a war must have as its goal the protection of people from unjust attack, the restoration of rights that have been taken away, or the restoration of just political order.

➤ It must be led by a competent authority, which means that declarations of war must be made by competent authorities following established criteria, or due process. This principle has recently come under scrutiny.

➤ It must be a last resort after all possible peaceful solutions have been explored.

➤ It must involve comparative justice to remind both sides that neither is absolutely just.

➤ Its ends must be proportionate to its means: Even a just war for a just cause cannot be pursued if the evils to be suffered significantly outweigh the good.

➤ It must have a right intention, which means it cannot be motivated by vindictiveness or hatred, but must be for the purpose of establishing a better and more peaceful existence.

### For Heaven's Sake!

No nukes! Church teaching about war has said that because of the enormity of the destruction, nuclear war is not to be used under any circumstances.

➤ There must be a probability of success; if there is no possibility of winning and many people will be killed in the process, then it cannot be a just war.

The just war doctrine includes an additional principle of right conduct within war. Justice must rule conduct within war. Attacks against civilians are forbidden, and there must be ethical treatment of the wounded or surrendered.

The just war doctrine has been an important part of Catholic moral teaching. However, because of the development of nuclear weapons of mass destruction, theologians are now questioning whether war can ever be justified. In 1983, a pastoral letter by U.S. bishops, *The Challenge of Peace: God's Promise and Our Response*, reaffirmed the just war doctrine, but with the additional comments that in no cases could nuclear war, even limited nuclear war, be justified.

The matter of establishing competent authority has also come under scrutiny. Many are unwilling to give the state the authority to determine whether justice is being served by war. Church teachers realize that governments are prone to interpret the situations in their favor, using the doctrine of just war to justify war. It falls to the church community as a dedicated and informed body to be a voice for peace against the strong cultural presumption of violence as a solution.

## Abortion: A Tough Choice

Few issues are more emotionally and morally charged than *abortion*. In this discussion, we're defining abortion as the intentionally induced termination of a pregnancy. Abortion is legal in some form in most countries in the world. The United States has the most unrestricted laws regarding abortions, having made abortion on demand both legal and available to any woman who can afford to pay for it.

**S'ter Says**

**Abortion** is the termination of a pregnancy. A spontaneous abortion is called a miscarriage. Clinical abortion means the intentional termination of a pregnancy to cause the death of the fetus.

The controversy surrounding abortion centers on identifying the time at which a new life is said to become human. At this time, there is no hard scientific agreement regarding this very important point. The church had found it to be the most reasonable and prudent position to accept conception, the moment when the sperm fertilizes the egg, as the beginning of human life. However, the church never attempts to baptize the aborted embryo or nonviable fetus after a miscarriage, nor does the church offer a funeral Mass for the deceased life.

The Catholic Church opposes unrestricted abortion for the following three reasons:

➤ The church sees God as the author of life and views the conception of a child as a gift to be welcomed into the community. The Catholic response to pregnancy is to care for both the mother and child.

➤ There is no clear scientific agreement to determine when life begins. The church has taken the stand that it begins at the moment of conception.

➤ Because life is sacred and because there is no reason to believe it does not begin at conception, the fundamental value of life must be awarded the soul in the womb.

The church believes no one possesses the right to take the life of the fetus. Although the right to choose is an important concept within the church, it exists only before conception. Cases of pregnancy due to rape or to coercion or ignorance pose difficult problems for church teaching; these issues have not been fully addressed. However, there are extenuating circumstances for abortion. Under a concept of the lesser of two evils, the church allows abortions when they are necessary to preserve the mother's life.

The church recognizes the difficulty of many women who are faced with the painful decision of whether to terminate a pregnancy. The "seamless garment of life" teaching about abortion would require that we address the social, cultural, and economic issues that affect the unequal status of women.

# Capital Punishment: A Call to Reconciliation

Catholic teachings hold to the sacredness of human life and teach that it must be respected from conception to death. Although Catholic teaching allows life to be taken through the just war theory and in cases of self-defense, church leaders have increasingly brought the wisdom of capital punishment into question. The growing sense of the image of God present in all people presents a distinct spiritual obstacle to taking a life, even where serious injustice has occurred. Arguments against capital punishment are based in the following religious principles:

➤ Jesus' command to love your enemies and to be reconciled to them calls on society to find spiritual solutions.

➤ The Gospels provide bountiful evidence of God's absolute love for every person. Jesus did not avoid sinners in his ministry, but focused on the abundant mercy and gracious forgiveness of God.

➤ There is a foundational Catholic belief in the potential for moral conversion present in all people, even the worst sinners.

**For Heaven's Sake!**

Be consistent! Catholic teaching has come to identify a "consistent ethic of life" that questions taking life in any circumstances, including abortion, just war, euthanasia, and capital punishment.

For these reasons, many Christian churches have denounced capital punishment as incompatible with Christianity. Although the Catholic Church has been reluctant to condemn it in principle, most of the recent popes and bishops have spoken out against its use. The pope recently made a strong social statement against capital punishment in St. Louis, where he personally met with the governor and requested that the sentence of a man condemned to die be commuted. His request was honored.

We've taken a look at the major teachings of the church and gained an understanding of the process of how church teaching evolves. In the next chapter, you'll learn more about the inside workings of the Catholic Church and about some of the career officers of the religious orders and the church hierarchy.

## The Least You Need to Know

➤ Church moral teaching has shifted to what you are doing to promote love away from what you are doing wrong.

➤ Current teaching about heaven and hell says that they are states of mind endured by separation from God, not physical places.

➤ Catholics are reconstructing their understanding of human sexuality and healing from some misunderstandings of the past.

➤ Catholics are urged to follow a consistent ethic of respect for all life in their teachings on abortion, euthanasia, capital punishment, social justice, and just war theories.

# Chapter 20

# The Church: Moving from Steeple to People

> ### In This Chapter
>
> ➤ How does the church structure work?
>
> ➤ What is a vocation? How would I know if I had one?
>
> ➤ Religious orders: Who does the work of the church?
>
> ➤ Can regular folks have vocations, too?

The Catholic Church is in the midst of change. It's moving from the hierarchical structure developed at the time of Constantine into a more communal model with shared power, one more representative of the church in its earliest years. Blueprints were drawn at Vatican II, and the changes have begun to take place. The church is moving from a centralized power base with authority at the top to a concept of hierarchical communion.

The Catholic Church is governed by the college of bishops with the Bishop of Rome, the pope at its head. It's one of the few churches that maintains a centralized authority, which means that almost every decision has to be cleared through Rome. As mentioned earlier, the pope exercises full authority over the church's teachings through the doctrine of papal infallibility. However, the new Vatican II blueprint assures that the pope teaches infallibly only when he consults with the college of bishops. Each bishop has the authority to teach in his own diocese. Rome restricts that power in only a few cases. The appointment of bishops is the big one.

## Blueprints for Change

The church is not one big corporation with joined assets. The Holy See administers its own funds, including money contributed by individuals around the world. These funds support 25 major administrative offices that employ more than 4,000 people. Collectively these offices are known as the *Roman Curia*. The Holy See does not administer any other property, other than in exceptional cases. Each diocese, which contains individual parishes, functions with a high degree of financial autonomy.

In the Catholic Church, the parishes are grouped under the guidance of a bishop. Each diocese is a complete unit. It makes local decisions but in conjunction with Rome.

The Church of Rome is like any other diocese, although its bishop, the pope, presides over the other dioceses. This structure is somewhat similar to the United States, with Washington, D.C. presiding over the other states. Washington, like Rome, is the seat of government, but each state has a governing structure and independence.

The hierarchical communion model of the Catholic Church is a union of churches expressed as "one." This expression of "oneness" happens through each diocese's connection to the diocese of Rome. There is a tension or balance constantly being struck between the federal government and state government, and in the church there is the same tension between diocesan control and the control of Rome. Depending on which party is in power, it can go either way.

We have shown this post-Vatican II structure with the diagram labeled hierarchical communion, which better describes the emerging notion of church. The old hierarchical pyramid of power is shown in the other illustration.

## The Roman Curia

Continuing our parallel between the church and the United States government, the Roman Curia would be similar to the president's cabinet, but with greater power. The Roman Curia is headed by cardinals who make decisions that affect the other diocesan churches. They handle such things as the appointment of bishops, regulation of worship, church missionary efforts, and oversee who teaches and what is taught. One of the major offices in the Roman Curia is the office of the Secretariat of State. Through this office, the Vatican maintains ambassadors to almost every nation in the world.

Many of the church's decisions about teaching come from the office called the Congregation for the Doctrine of the Faith. This office was originally started in 1542 as the Congregation of the Holy Inquisition. In 1908, the name was changed to the Congregation of the Holy Office. In 1967, it received its present name, the Congregation for the Doctrine of the Faith. The purpose of this office is to …

➤ Promote and safeguard the faith and morals of the Catholic Church by investigating writings that seem contrary or dangerous to the faith and issue warnings and admonishments.

➤ Respond to new initiatives in science and culture.

➤ Assist bishops in their role as teachers.

**Your Guardian Angel**

The church's authority is in flux. It has sustained the church through the years as an organization, and at the same time it has caused most of its troubles. The splits with the East and with the Protestants were over the issue of papal authority.

The relationship of the Curia to the pope is a hard one to nail down. The Curia makes many decisions that are never seen by the Pope. Some are specifically approved; others are allowed to be published under his name without his explicit approval. It differs with the issue being decided upon. Again, this can be compared to the authority given by the president to his cabinet members.

## Who's Who in the Church

As we've said, the new model is a hierarchical communion. The hierarchy still exists. All power is in the office of bishop. The pope is a "big bishop." He leads the bishops and is their spokesman. The hierarchical order of the church consists of the following offices:

➤ **The Pope.** The structure of the church begins at the top, with the pope, the bishop of Rome. The College of Cardinals elects the pope.

➤ **Cardinals.** The College of Cardinals is a group of approximately 120 bishops who have been elevated by the pope to the rank of cardinal. Membership in the College of Cardinals is divided between those who hold office in the Vatican (the Curia) and those who are bishops of major cities in the world. For example, the United States has eight cardinals from cities such as New York, Chicago, and Los Angeles.

➤ **Bishops.** Bishops are priests nominated by other bishops in their country and appointed to office by the pope.

➤ **Priests and deacons.** The bishop ordains priests and deacons.

Everyone below this level is considered part of the laity of the church. An unofficial hierarchy exists within the laity. It might be represented in the following way:

➤ **Seminarians.** Those who are in training to become priests.

➤ **Nuns.** Women in religious orders.

➤ **Brothers.** Nonordained men in religious orders.

➤ **"Lay" professionals.** Directors of Religious Education, pastoral ministers, ministers of music, and chaplains, for example.

➤ **All the rest of the folks.**

To a large degree, this unofficial hierarchy does not follow the teachings of Vatican II. Every person has a role in all the missions of the church, and none is more important than another.

# Vocation: No Family Is Complete Without One

The word *vocation* means calling. For Catholics, vocation has always been synonymous with a calling to church service, and a lot of pride and respect is connected with religious service. A big part of growing up Catholic means being open to the possibility of becoming a priest or a nun.

Vocation to religious service starts at baptism. The traditional use of the term *vocation,* however, describes a professional level of church service with special commitments. Those following a religious vocation give themselves completely to the service of the church as a full-time endeavor; they do not hold other jobs. A religious vocation is considered very important because this person will have influence over many people. Consequently, the time of preparation is lengthy and rigorous and can last from 5 to 15 years.

Religious vocations include becoming a *priest,* nun, or brother. We'll look at these vocations and different religious orders, including what characterizes them and the work that they do. We'll begin with the vocation to the priesthood.

**S'ter Says**

**Vocation** means "calling." It describes a profession for which one is particularly suited and has been specially trained. It comes from the Latin word *vocare,* which means "to call." The Catholic Church uses this term to designate God's call to the priesthood or religious life.

**Your Guardian Angel**

Consider yourself "called" if you've been baptized. For Catholics, baptism is a calling or vocation to life with Christ.

# Priests

The first choice a person entering the priesthood makes is whether to be a diocesan priest or join a religious order. Diocesan priests work directly for the bishop and often head up parishes as pastors. "Order" priests belong to specific religious communities and their jobs vary. Often they are teachers or missionaries.

The three ministries of the diocesan priest are preaching, teaching, and administrating the business of the parish. He celebrates Mass, administers the sacraments, visits the sick, marries, and buries. He is in charge of the buildings and finances and organizes the various parish ministries. He reports to the bishop. Priests promise celibacy and obedience to their bishop.

Order priests join a particular religious community and take vows to their particular religious order. A religious order is a group of people who have joined together to live in a religious community.

The concept of a leader with an identity separate from other members of the church did not develop until the end of the first century, when the church moved away from Judaism and began to form its own identity as a separate religion. In the beginning, the first leaders were called bishops. Later bishops delegated some of their duties, especially the celebration of the Mass, to people who were called priests.

The belief that priests had liturgical power to change bread and wine into the sacrament of the body and blood of Christ added to the priestly mystique and remains at the core of the priestly image today. Their relationship as members who lived in the community of the faithful diminished as their positions of power over the community became established. In the 1500s, the Council of Trent formally established church hierarchy, drawing clear lines of distinction between the priests and the people.

A popular image of the Catholic priest evolved in which he was seen as a man "set apart." He was a celibate person who was called to distinctive liturgical service. The priest's defining role involved the Eucharist and the Mass. These rituals in many ways define Catholicism. This privileged role remained in effect until Vatican II, an event that began a process of rethinking the priestly ministry in relationship to the ministry of the people as a whole.

**S'ter Says**

There are two kinds of **priests** in the Catholic Church: diocesan priests and religious order priests. Diocesan priests work directly for their bishop, and their job is to lead parishes throughout the diocese. Order priests belong to particular religious communities and serve the concerns of their order, such as teaching or missionary work.

**Your Guardian Angel**

Call your priest "Father" when speaking to him. The written form uses the title "Reverend" followed by his surname.

### Epiphanies

During its first 300 years, as it became established as the favored religion of the Roman Empire, the Catholic Church began to order itself on Roman organizational structure. In fact, Constantine, the head of the Roman Empire, helped establish the church structure. As the priesthood became an elevated position, responsibility began to shift to priests as the professionals while the responsibility of the people lessened.

Since Vatican II, a considerably different understanding of the priesthood exists. Vatican II reaffirmed that the entire community of the baptized is a priestly people and is able to relate directly to God, as Jesus taught. Vatican II brought Catholics back to a balance in the threefold ministries of the priesthood:

➤ Preaching and teaching

➤ Administering of the sacraments and community care

➤ Leading the people

The emphasis after Vatican II has shifted away from the priest as the one who presides over the Eucharist and toward the position of priest within the community. This new emphasis reaffirms the priest's position as being with the people rather than as having power over the people. The priest and the people are now seen as having a more equal partnership.

### Your Guardian Angel

The proper way of addressing a bishop is "Your Excellency." The written form uses the title, "Most Reverend."

## Bishops: Shepherds of the Flocks

In the rank and order of the church, a bishop is in charge of a diocese, which is made up of many parishes. He assigns priests to parishes and is the administrator of the business of the diocese. The parish priests report to him. As priests are pastors to their parish, he is the pastor to his diocese. His church is called the cathedral. From the cathedral, he presides over feast day Masses and special ceremonies. He travels to the parishes in his diocese to administer the sacrament of Confirmation and leads special events throughout the diocese, such as the dedication of a church or the installment of a new parish priest.

The bishop supervises all the charities and educational institutions within his territory. He represents the church in civic matters, and he is the principal teacher for his diocese. Just as the pope writes encyclicals to the whole church, the bishop writes letters that teach and direct his people. Bishops are nominated by a group of other bishops from the same country. Following an elaborate process to determine eligibility for the office of bishop, the pope makes the final approval of all bishops.

# Religious Orders: Know Your Players

Religious orders are groups of men or women living in separate communities where they practice a particular form of spiritual life. The Catholic Church has a number of religious orders. Most of them are celibate communities, in which the members join with the intention of staying for life, similar to the commitment others make to marriage.

Religious life focuses upon a community of prayer and service. Some orders live in seclusion from the world, even raising their own food, keeping a few animals, and making food products to sell. Other orders serve in the world by running schools, hospitals, and other social services. Orders have been a constant tradition in the church. Some date almost from the beginning of the church history; others have begun in this century.

### Epiphanies

Although other religions and Christian denominations have religious orders, such orders are probably more highly developed in the Catholic world. Religious life has traditionally been characterized by the vows of poverty, chastity, and obedience. Chastity means celibacy or virginity. Poverty generally means that all money is held communally. Obedience means the individual takes direction from his or her religious superiors regarding the nature of work assignments and living arrangements. Since Vatican II, the interpretations of the poverty and obedience vows have become less strict. Many members of religious orders keep some personal money, and many choose to live on their own.

There are two basic types of religious life: active and contemplative. Active religious members are characterized by their work in the world. Contemplative life describes the life of those who choose solitude, silence, prayer, and penance. The contemplative tradition goes all the way back to a second-century church movement called the Fathers and Mothers of the Desert. The contemplative tradition expresses values of prayer and work and is characterized by separation from the world. The spiritual focus of contemplative life is the earth. In living away from the world and worldly concerns, the members of contemplative orders are especially attuned to nature's rhythms. The essence of contemplative life is the chanting of the Liturgy of the Hours, where the passing of the day and night is marked by special prayers. (Chapter 14, "Catholic Prayers and Music: Tangible Poetry," has more information about the Liturgy of the Hours.)

**Your Guardian Angel**

Let yourself go at Christmas! In the old days, everyone bought their priest or nun a pair of black gloves or an umbrella for Christmas. Now it is okay to give money or even a gift of blue–chip stock.

After the renewal of Vatican II, religious life was updated. The church urged religious orders to reexamine their original connection to Christ and to live the Gospel and recapture the spirit that inspired the founding of their institutions. They were also asked to adapt to the contemporary world. This radical shift resulted in many leaving the orders. Now, many years later, new ways of forming religious communities have developed, and new ministries have formed that are more in tune with the times.

Today, much of the polarization between contemplative life and active life has been de-emphasized. Both are seen to have their own action. Where once the divisions between internal life and external life were seen to be very deep, the church now acknowledges that all expressions of religious life contribute to the wholeness of spiritual life. New religious movements and groups are increasingly open to single and married people. Several groups are embracing non-Catholic members.

The essential elements of religious life today are still rooted in a response to living the Gospel by following Christ and being in service to others. Religious life requires commitment to the community to which you belong, personal and communal spiritual development, prayer, and meditation.

## *Monks, Nuns, and Brothers*

Preparation to become a monk, nun, or brother begins with a one-year *novitiate*. This is a time of intense spiritual formation in which candidates learn about the order they are preparing to join and spend time assessing their call to religious life. This time is followed by a profession of the vows of chastity, poverty, and obedience made in accordance with the traditions of the community they are joining. At that time, the candidates make a permanent commitment to God, to the religious life, and to the community they are entering.

The term *monk* refers to any member of a male religious community who lives a solitary life of prayer and contemplation. The word means "one who lives alone." The Camaldolese, for instance, are members of a community that live in total silence.

Other orders of monks are the Benedictines and Cistercians, also known as Trappists. Some monks are ordained as priests, and some are not. Technically, all members of religious communities who are not ordained as priests are considered part of the laity of the church.

*Nun* is the term used to describe women in religious orders. There are many orders of nuns, and the traditions and rules of each order are different. Some orders are contemplative, meaning they live in seclusion from the world. This *cloistered* life is characterized by prayer and meditation, including a daily chanting of the Liturgy of the Hours. Other nuns are very much present in the world: they teach, care for the sick, and participate in a variety of social ministries.

Most orders of nuns call themselves *sisters*. The popular image of nuns presents women dressed in recognizable outfits called *habits* and living in homes called *convents*. Since Vatican II, many religious orders have modernized both their styles of dress and their interaction with the world. All orders of nuns are committed to living the spiritual values of the Gospel in some manner. Just how those values are adhered to differs with each order. There are more than 500 orders of nuns in the United States alone, including 83 orders of Franciscans and 11 different orders of Dominicans, among others.

Brothers are male members of religious orders who take the vows of poverty, chastity, and obedience. Like nuns, they are lay members of the religious community. The call for brothers is to live the Gospel in community, with a deep sense of commitment. In the post-Vatican II church, brothers, like sisters, have moved into a wide variety of ministries, especially in the area of peace and justice needs. Traditional arenas of education and health care remain at their core, and they have expanded their ministries to better meet the needs of the times.

**S'ter Says**

**Cloister** means a place of religious seclusion. Members of a cloistered order limit their interaction with the world, remaining behind closed doors for the most part, where they lead a life dedicated to prayer, fasting, and meditation.

**Your Guardian Angel**

Most Nuns take a new name when they enter the convent. It is correct to refer to a nun as "Sister" followed by her religious name, if you know it, or simply as "Sister" if you don't.

## Benedictines: Behind Closed Doors

The Rule of St. Benedict is the basis for thousands of Christians who belong to the monastic movement. As you may remember from earlier discussions, monasteries are places where people go to practice a particular form of spiritual life, and they are a part of most world religions. Benedict, a religious man in the late sixth century, wrote a set of rules governing monastic life that is so remarkable for its wisdom and clarity of language that it remains the practice of many religious orders even today.

The Rule of St. Benedict teaches basic monastic virtues such as humility, silence, and obedience, as well as directions for daily living. Benedict suggested times for common prayer, meditation, reading of sacred scripture, and manual labor. He recommended moderation for his monks, believing in principles of sound health. He imposed limits to the fasting and all-night prayer vigils that had become extreme in many monasteries. He recommended working with the hands about six hours a day and having leisure for reading and common prayer.

The Rule of St. Benedict remains the backbone of Christian monasticism today. Many religious communities follow it, if not by the letter, definitely in spirit. Its particular recipe for prayer, fasting, and service assures the values of the Bible are lived in a balanced way. Each Benedictine monastery is a local institution and has a high degree of autonomy. A person who joins the order usually remains in one place for life. Many monasteries were formed during the Middle Ages by nobility, but they began to wane at the end of the twelfth century when many newer orders, such as the Franciscans and Dominicans, developed. By the close of the eighteenth century, Benedictine numbers were very small. Over the next century, Benedictines experienced a revival.

Benedictine Sisters are a branch of the Order of St. Benedict and have been around since the 500s. This order was formed by St. Scholastica, Benedict's sister. Its works include agriculture, hospitality, education, skilled crafts, scholarship, counseling, and parish ministry. The Benedictine Sisters remain true to the Rule of St. Benedict by supporting one another. Many of the Benedictine monasteries observe strict seclusion. The Benedictine Sisters came to the United States in 1846 and are actively involved in education and justice service ministries. Benedictines have the initials O.S.B. (order of St. Benedict) after their names.

## The Rule of St. Francis

The Franciscan order is the common name of the Order of Friars Minor (O.F.M.). The members of this order follow the rule of life written by its founder, Francis of Assisi. The rule is rooted in the call to a life of poverty and models St. Francis's peaceful and gentle love of all, especially the poor. The rule was written in the early 1200s, and it embraces complete poverty not only for all its members, but also for the order itself. Over the years, Franciscans have negotiated a more moderate and practical interpretation of their rule, changing it to meet circumstances and pastoral needs more in tune with the times.

The Franciscan order originated in the late twelfth and thirteenth centuries along with many movements of lay people who were seeking to return to the life characterized by the early church of Jesus and his followers. The members were choosing to live simply to counter the emerging culture of the commercial towns of central Italy with their growing wealth and social status. The Franciscans supported themselves by whatever trades they knew, devoting their lives to living the Gospel in simplicity and preaching its message to others. The order became enormously popular, and it soon demanded a more sophisticated structure.

The Franciscan friars (the English pronunciation of the French word for brother, *frere*) largely abandoned their rural lifestyle and settled into urban monasteries known as friaries. The training schools for the orders, located in centers such as Paris and Oxford, produced some of the greatest masters of theology of the church. Franciscans have remained in the forefront of intellectual Catholicism and were the primary missionaries who brought the religion to the New World.

Two other orders descended from St. Francis's original followers are the contemplative nuns known as Poor Clares, founded by Clare of Assisi under the direction of St. Francis, and the lay movement later known as the Third Order. Today, these two orders have evolved into two different ways of life: the Secular Franciscans for laypersons and a large number of religious congregations of both men and women who follow the Third Order Regular Rule.

## Saints Preserve Us

### St. Clare, August 11, Patron of Television

St. Clare, born in Assisi, is said to be St. Francis's spiritual daughter because she very much followed in his footsteps. Born in 1193, she felt her calling from childhood. Under the guidance of St. Francis, she entered a Benedictine convent. She persisted in her desire to live an even more austere life, further separated from the world, and finally succeeded in founding the Poor Clares, or the Second Order of St. Francis. Her order soon spread across Europe. Clare inherited a great sum of money, which she gave to the poor, and she would accept no revenues for her monastery. She died in 1253 and was made a saint two years later. How and why this very unworldly woman became the patron of television is unknown.

The Franciscan Sisters, who are members of the Third Order Regular of St. Francis of Assisi, were founded in the nineteenth century. The spirituality of its members is akin to that of Francis and is characterized by peacefulness, compassion, poverty, and a deep love for all of God's creations. Many members wear the traditional brown or black habit associated with St. Francis.

Although the Prayer of St. Francis may or may not have been written by him, it captures Francis's spirit and the spirit of the Franciscans. It has been handed down over the ages and is a beloved prayer of Catholics and other Christians as well:

> Lord, make me an instrument of your peace;
> where there is hatred, let me sow peace;
> where there is injury, pardon;
> where there is doubt, faith;
> where there is despair, hope;
> where there is darkness, light;
> and where there is sadness, joy.
> Grant that I may not so much seek to be consoled as to console;
> to be understood as to understand;
> to be loved as to love;
> for it is in giving that we receive;
> it is in pardoning that we are pardoned;
> and it is in dying that we are born again in eternal life.

### For Heaven's Sake!

Don't think that all religious communities live isolated from the world. Many of them are active in the world and maintain a life of prayer as well. For example, the Dominicans and Franciscans practice both prayerful meditation and service in the world.

## Dominicans: Telling It Like It Is

The Dominican order, officially known as the Order of Preachers (O.P.), is a religious order of priests and brothers founded in 1216 by St. Dominic de Guz-man for the intention of teaching and preaching the Gospel message. The founder, Dominic, believed that in order to be effective as preachers of the Gospel, members must return to the "apostolic life," meaning the life as led by the apostles, where members lived in communities, free from worldly concerns such as maintaining property. They could then travel and preach without being caught up in their material responsibilities.

Traditionally, Dominicans lived a contemplative life in their communities, were dedicated to prayer and poverty, and were devoted to the study of the word of God. The order was further shaped by one of its well-known members, Thomas Aquinas, whose vision is best summed up by his words: "To gaze with love on God, and then to share what has been seen with others." Catherine of Siena (1347–1380) brought a social dimension to the order, infusing it with a concern for human rights. This concern is still very much a part of the Dominican life today. The Dominicans' outward focus is balanced by their strong tradition of inward-looking spirituality.

The Dominicans were established in the United States in 1805. Although they've undergone changes over the years, they continue to be characterized by a commitment to poverty, prayer, and study. After Vatican II, the order revised its constitution and renewed itself in the democratic spirit of its founder. Dominicans publish periodicals, conduct schools of theology, and work in dozens of parishes, hospitals, and universities all over the world. The order now includes cloistered nuns and nuns in active ministry. Although Dominican organizations function autonomously, they are united as the Dominican Family under the master of the order, who resides in Rome.

## Jesuits: The Pope's Foot Soldiers

Jesuit is the popular name for the Society of Jesus (S.J.), a religious order founded by St. Ignatius of Loyola in 1540. The Jesuits' motto is "For the greater glory of God." Ignatius, a military man, imbued the order with his fighting spirit. It was started with the purpose of engaging in an active ministry to "quell the heresies" of the day. The Jesuits went to Rome and put themselves at the disposal of the pope, declaring that they would not be "chanting Office," like the other religious orders. Instead of chanting, which represented to them a passive type of spirituality, they declared that their work would be action for the advancement of Catholic doctrine and life. They vowed to go anywhere in the world the pope chose to send them. In addition to poverty, chastity, and obedience, Jesuits have a special vow of obedience to the pope.

Like the Dominicans and Franciscans, the Jesuits have a social ministry and have established many orphanages and other agencies for social assistance. Because one Jesuit motto asks Jesuits to "see God in all things," this order is seen as more worldly than some of the other orders. Earlier in their history, they became explorers of the New World in both North and South America as well as Asia. They helped organize large numbers of American Indians whose communities were destroyed and whose land was taken through European expansion.

### Epiphanies

The Society of Jesus, popularly known as the Jesuits, is the largest religious order in the church. It numbers some 25,000 members on six continents and in 112 nations. Among these members are 18,000 priests, 3,000 brothers, and 4,000 men preparing for the priesthood. They serve under their general superior in Rome, who is immediately accountable to the pope.

Jesuit spirituality is grounded in its founder's spiritual exercises, which we described in Chapter 15, "For Catholics Prayer Is More Than Just Words," and the values he communicated. These values include the following:

➤ **The centrality of Christ.** Christ is the preeminent focus of Jesuit spirituality (compared, for example, with the Dominicans, who have a great devotion to Mary). The spiritual exercises are designed to deepen the bond with Christ within the person who practices them.

➤ **Collaborative action with God.** This principle is based in the belief that God is vigorously at work in the world and needs human help to accomplish his work.

➤ **Spiritual discernment in decision-making.** This principle means using the exercises to choose options that support collaboration with God.

➤ **Generosity of spirit.** The exercises were developed in Spain in an environment of chivalry and romance, and that spirit is expressed in the Jesuits' willingness to be of service.

➤ **Fraternity and companionship.** Early Jesuits called themselves "friends in the Lord," and this community bond is an important part of their practice.

➤ **Finding God in all things.** Spiritual integration is the primary theme of the Jesuits. This integration of prayer and service, contemplation and action, and effect and reason marks their spirituality.

**S'ter Says**

In Catholic terms, **lay** refers to church members who are not ordained. The status of the laity has been greatly enhanced since Vatican II.

# Lay Vocation: What About the Rest of the Folks?

We opened this chapter by saying that Catholics traditionally used the word vocation to talk about priests, monks, nuns, and brothers. Since Vatican II, the terms *lay vocation* and *lay spirituality* have worked their way into Catholic talk. The terms refer to the individual ways members live out their religion in their everyday life by elevating common endeavors to the status of vocation.

The common understanding of the word *lay* is "a nonprofessional." Catholics use the term to mean those who are not ordained. The old assumption was that the church was better than the world. A professional minister in the church, then, was on a higher spiritual plane than the rest of the community. All too often the role of lay spirituality has been understood to be less than the role of priestly, religious, or monastic spirituality. Vatican II documents have attempted to break down the dichotomy between church and world and challenge any notions of spiritual elitism that distinguish between the laity and clergy.

Christian spirituality is faith in action, and it takes many forms. It means living the Gospel values in whatever arena one is invited to enter by grace or the Holy Spirit. Post-Vatican II thinking is that full participation in Catholic life as a layperson exists side-by-side with the spirituality of the religious and ordained.

One of the primary focuses of Vatican II was on the call of the laity to bring Christ into the modern world. Historically, the laity had come to accept themselves as passive people who left the spiritual and religious matters to the clergy. The laity were expected to simply "pray, pay, and obey." A concerted effort has been made in the post-council church to redefine the role of the laity and encourage the idea of its shared responsibility as the people of God.

Our discussion will now focus on the ways the laity participates in their religious calling. We'll describe the responsibilities that the nonordained, nonvowed Catholics take in the church, specifically focusing on volunteer work. We'll also explore the revolution within the church that now allows the laity to take professional leadership positions.

## There Is a Job for Everyone

Although the church has always relied heavily on volunteers, the following ministries reflect a growing process of the people sharing in the sacramental ministry and the governing of the church:

➤ Eucharistic ministers are people who distribute communion during Mass as well as take it to the homes of the sick.

➤ Lectors read the first two readings of the Mass.

➤ Song leaders are members of the congregation who announce hymns, teach new songs, and lead congregational singing.

➤ Offertory gift bearers bring the bread and wine up to the altar.

➤ Altar servers are often young boys and girls who light the altar candles, hold the book for the priest to read from, ring the bells at the important times during the Mass, assist at communion, and in other ways help with the celebration of Mass.

➤ Parish council members are elected by the parish to serve on the advisory council to the pastor in the operation of the church. Council members head up committees, such as the finance committee, the committee for the liturgy, and more. Lay people also serve on diocesan pastoral councils.

**Your Guardian Angel**

Get active in your parish! It is a Catholic tradition to participate in service work, and there are many ways to do this at your local parish. Consider starting a new group that meets your needs and serves others. The main thing is to belong by being active.

➤ Social action enlists the aid of many volunteers. The parish may operate a shelter for the homeless, soup kitchens, or a food basket program. The parish might also spearhead education and social action on topics like capital punishment, abortion, peace, and justice.

The following represent traditional lay ministries:

➤ Ushers greet people as they enter the church, show them to their seats, take up the collection, and generally assist the congregation.

➤ Ministers of hospitality welcome new members to the church and arrange the refreshments and coffee following Mass.

➤ Catechists teach the Sunday school religion classes.

➤ Youth ministers organize and gather the adolescent members of the church for social outings and spiritual reflection.

➤ Ministers of care are assigned to visit the sick and homebound.

➤ Pray-ers are the faithful who often attend daily Mass and are called on by the parish when it has a particular prayer to offer.

In addition, volunteers do a myriad of jobs ranging from cleaning the altar on a regular basis to providing transportation for elder members.

### For Heaven's Sake!

Give everyone his or her due respect! No one's job is any better than anyone else's. Jesus was a carpenter, a day laborer. Peter was a fisherman. Luke was a doctor. Matthew was a tax collector. The women were homemakers, prepared food, and had leadership positions. Yet all had equal respect in the community.

## New Vocation: Transforming the World

The Jews have a word, *napesh,* which means how you are in the world. This word isa good definition for lay spirituality. Spirituality is how your spirit affects the world. Catholic laity is reclaiming its true vocation as the people of God in the world. A recent letter from the United States Catholic bishops called *Everyday Christianity* acknowledges Catholics' vocation in the world. "Catholicism does not call us to abandon the world," reads the letter, "but to help shape it. This does not mean leaving worldly tasks and responsibilities, but transforming them."

The kingdom of God moves forward by increments. People who join the Jesuit Volunteer Corp or go to India to work with Mother Teresa's house for the dying, for instance, certainly advance the kingdom. So do conscientious workers in all fields: bricklayers, mothers, musicians, trash collectors, and high school biology teachers. Faith sees God's presence in ordinary human interaction. It is played out in the midst of life's everyday hustle and bustle. The moment is rich with sacred potential; the holy is deeply contained in the ordinary.

For Catholics, transformation is enhanced by a certain spiritual sensitivity. It is developed through prayer and meditation and carried out into the world in everyday activities. Vatican II's embrace of the world encouraged the church to pay attention to this "spirituality of the mundane."

The Catholic lay spirituality is not dependent on job or position, but in the dignity you bring to the work and to the people you meet. Our spirituality shows in our jobs, families, and neighborhood interactions as we bring love, justice, integrity, and care into them. The laity is the heart and spirit of the church and shares its heart and spirit in the world. Lay vocation is not a vocation to the church, but a vocation to the world.

The vocation is lived through Catholics' engagement with the world as corporate executives, migrant farm workers, senators, welfare recipients, university presidents, parents, daycare workers, farmers, office and factory workers, union leaders, small business owners, teachers, scientists, bankers, salespeople, artists, and entertainers. All are called to partner in God's creative action in the world.

## Faith in Action

To reinforce the connection between church and world, some parishes have begun to hold ceremonies in which a person and their vocation is blessed. For example, during Mass one Sunday, the pastor called recent graduates of a nursing program to come forward. He prayed with them, saying: "God, you are the Great Physician, be present with these young people as they go about the work of healing. Bless these caps and stethoscopes, symbols of their service as a nurse." He then anointed the nurses' hands with holy oil.

One church has specified the following days as jubilee days for specific occupations to honor workers for their contributions to the life of the church and the world and to "reflect on the challenges these workers face in living the Gospel."

➤ **February 18.** Jubilee for artists

➤ **May 25.** Jubilee for scientists

➤ **May 29.** Jubilee for the military

➤ **June 4.** Jubilee for journalists

➤ **September 4.** Jubilee for building trades

**Your Guardian Angel**

Begin to think of your job as your spiritual vocation. You will be amazed at how much this thought can improve your attitude and your relationships with fellow workers. You are also more likely to receive the spiritual assistance or grace you need in overcoming difficult situations. Just try it for one day!

➤ **September 10.** Jubilee for teachers

➤ **November 5.** Jubilee for government employees

➤ **November 12.** Jubilee for agricultural workers

➤ **November 19.** Jubilee for police

As you can see, the trend in the church is toward more respect and equality within the ranks—moving from steeple to people. The church is beginning to recognize the laity as full participants. In the next chapter, we'll revisit the church's early years to gain a deeper understanding of its long history.

---

### The Least You Need to Know

➤ Vatican II drew the blueprints for a new model of church with shared power.

➤ Vocation is shifting from a call to privilege to a call of service.

➤ The new model of church empowers the laity.

➤ Ministry is becoming recognized as one's occupation in the world.

---

# Part 6
# The Church's History

*In this part, we look at how the story of Catholicism, the oldest tradition in Christianity, often parallels the story of the Western world.*

*This part of the book explains the different periods of history that shaped the church: how it was marked by its identification with the Roman Empire, how its centralized authority was established, how its concern with unity developed, and how it became a European church.*

*We'll learn about the two big splits in the church: the first between the Latin Church based in Rome and the Eastern Church based in Constantinople, the second resulting in Protestantism. We'll also see how Catholicism became further established in the United States through European immigration. We look at how the sons and daughters of these immigrants mainstreamed into life in the United States. We'll end the book with a look at some of the challenges that the church will meet in its third millennium and the resources it has to remain a vital church in the world of tomorrow.*

# Roman Establishment

Back in Chapter 6, "'It's Elementary, My Dear Watson,'" we left the story of the early church just as it was getting established. This chapter returns to those early days to describe some of the key players and important events in church history. We resume the story in the fourth century with a look at two remarkable men, one an emperor and the other a bishop, with two remarkable mothers.

## From Underdog to Top Dog

As you may remember from previous chapters, the early church was an outlaw religion. For the first 300 years of Catholicism, Catholics faced the very real threat of having to choose their religion over their life, and many of them died for their faith. Despite these dangers, however, an unusual and interesting thing happened: The church not only survived, but it also grew in numbers. The church's core message of liberation appealed to a growing number of people inside the Roman Empire.

As the church entered the fourth century, two men—and their mothers—would have a great impact on its development. The first was Constantine, the Roman emperor who gave his protection to the new church, effectively ending the persecutions. the early years, the church consisted of small communities of members who met in individual homes. Rituals were simple and intimate. This organization began to change when the important leader Constantine began to embrace the church.

The second man to strongly influence the emerging church was Augustine, who was active just a few years after Constantine. Soon after the scriptures were recorded, church leaders began to write down their thoughts and reflections, and Augustine was the most significant figure in this theological tradition. He was one of the great systematic minds, and he established the church's intellectual foundation.

# Constantine: The Church Gets a Break

In the year 312, Catholicism got its first big break. A man named Constantine from Gaul (which is modern-day France) took control of the Roman Empire and became its new leader. He then made a decision that altered the course of history. He legalized the Catholic Church and supported it personally.

Although Constantine himself was not baptized a Catholic until his death, two forces drove him to endorse this new religion. The first was the influence of his Catholic mother, and the second was a dream he had just before going into a battle. The dream revealed to him that he would win if he accepted the cross, Catholicism's major symbol. His subsequent victory in the battle thus became one of the most decisive moments both in the history of the Catholic Church and the history of Western civilization. Eventually, under his protection, Catholicism became the favored religion.

## Saints Preserve Us

### St. Helena, August 18, Patron of Converts and Divorced

St. Helena was born in England. She married Constantius, an officer in the Roman army, and gave birth to Constantine. Shortly after her husband was given the title of Caesar and took over the governing of Gaul and Britain, he divorced her to marry another. Helena later converted to Catholicism and influenced her son regarding his favorable treatment of the church. He made her an empress, and she used both her wealth and her power to help the poor and to build churches. At the age of 80, she built a church on Mount Calvary and went to Jerusalem to find the Holy Cross, the one upon which Christ was crucified. Legend says that she found it. She died in Rome in about 326.

Constantine affected both the external and internal structure of the church. First, his favors took the form of both land and tax incentives. Second, Catholics, no longer fearing persecution, stopped meeting in homes and started holding services in newly constructed church buildings. Finally, he influenced the church's internal structure by finding a way to settle disputes of faith.

### Epiphanies

Keep in mind that although the edict of toleration ended the Roman persecutions, the Catholic Church has been systematically oppressed in many other countries over its 2,000–year history. England in the sixteenth century, Ireland in the seventeenth, the United States in the nineteenth and the Soviet Union in the twentieth are just a few places where the property, rights, and even lives of Catholics were threatened. As we'll see, there have been times when the church has sanctioned similar behavior towards those who disagreed with it. The Declaration of Religious Freedom issued at Vatican II in 1965 held that religious freedom was both a natural and a civil right for all persons.

Constantine began the tradition of church councils, in which members assembled to discuss differences and make decisions by majority rule. This method assured that the church would always speak with one voice. Constantine was an administrator who was familiar with both military and political organization. He gave the church a political form, emphasizing the collective authority of the bishops. This structure gave the church the stability it needed in the early years, which enabled it to grow, but the structure also gave the church its authoritarian character, which has brought it much controversy.

Almost from the beginning, worldly considerations influenced church structure, and it gradually adapted to the Roman world around it. Within the next 100 years, household church communities became a thing of the past. The role of women in the church, once so apparent during the time of Jesus, was all but eliminated as its all-male structure developed. Rather than being associated with service, church office began to be associated with status and power.

Increasingly, church and state finances mingled, and the church became not just a vocation but a prosperous career for many people. Church leaders lived like members of the secular aristocracy, often enjoying wealthy splendor. The simple communal meal that once characterized Catholic communion gradually gave way to massive and ornate altars, where bread and wine were laid out ceremoniously. The separation between the priests and the people grew. In the centuries to follow, separation from the people, worldliness, and opulence would bring many problems to the church.

On the other hand, there were positive changes that stemmed from the church's relationship with the Roman state. The church was able to exert a more humane influence on the empire. The state began to apply a more Christian understanding of social responsibility by feeding the poor and taking care of the sick.

Although its decline had begun in the West, the Roman Empire was still vast and powerful, and Catholicism, now a favored religion, spread to its four corners. The church suddenly began to acquire many new converts. When a chief of a tribe of people within the Empire converted, his whole tribe came with him.

## Augustine: Lover and Loser

Like Constantine, Augustine was also greatly influenced by his mother. He was born in North Africa in what is now Algeria in 354 and grew up to become a writer, teacher, philosopher, and one of the most influential people in the church's early history. His father was a pagan and his mother, Monica, was a Catholic. Augustine had an inquiring mind and explored many of the philosophies and theologies of his time before being drawn to Catholicism. Once a very worldly man, he founded a religious community as a safe haven from what he called "the decadent world," where he prayed and wrote extensively. He was made a bishop and worked tirelessly for the church by preaching, writing, and administering. He believed in the power of education as a way to reclaim the soul's lost goodness. His vast body of writings on many subjects has been admired from his time through today.

### Saints Preserve Us

**St. Monica, August 27, Patron of Mothers and Widows**

St. Monica, the patron of mothers and widows, was born in 333. She married a pagan man described as having a "high temper." Her patience and gentleness influenced him, and he converted to Christianity before his death. Their son, Augustine, who was only 17 at the time of his father's death, was a bit of a playboy around old Algeria. Monica prayed long and hard and with great fervor for his conversion. When he left to go to Italy, she followed him and, along with St. Ambrose, the bishop of Milan, had a positive influence on him. However, it took another 15 years before he converted. In 387, she witnessed his return to God as he was baptized by his good friend Ambrose. Monica died soon afterward.

Augustine left Christianity a mixed legacy. His deep love of the church and of spiritual matters cannot be denied. He wrote beautifully and poetically about how the human spirit will only be satisfied when it falls in love with the will of God. On the other hand, he was highly influenced by Plato's understanding of human nature and was caught up in a belief of the time called Manichaeism. Manichaeism taught that matter was separate from spirit and was in fact evil. It went even further to imply that there were two gods, one of good and one of evil. Although he eventually abandoned this philosophy and returned to the church, he was never able to completely reconcile Manichaeism's dualism of good and evil. This led to Augustine's writings on original sin, which we discussed in Chapter 19, "The Teachings of the Church: More Than Just the Party Line."

Augustine's most influential book was called *The City of God*. In this book, Augustine's Platonic ideas show up in his views about the relationship between the Christian community and the larger world. Augustine was also writing in response to the sack of Rome in 407. For him, this world-shaking event demonstrated the frailty of human endeavor. Only the soul endures forever in Augustine's view. His dualistic thinking showed up in his understanding of the relationship between the Christian community and the larger world. He believed that the church should strive to form a "perfect society," a religious society separate from the material world around it. He believed humans' only purpose in life is to form this "City of God" on earth.

**Your Guardian Angel**

Read the creation story. The teaching on original sin is not explicit in the Bible. Augustine coined the term, original sin. Before that it was referred to as the sin of Adam.

Augustine's idea of the relationship of religion to the state greatly influenced how the church saw itself. It laid the foundation for medieval society, which was a society that was more concerned about the welfare of the soul than the welfare of the body. The difficulty resulting from Augustine's theories was the separation between the church and the world around it. The church adopted his beliefs on original sin and his views on separating spiritual matters from worldly concerns.

Even today, this dualistic view haunts Catholics as they sort their material and spiritual priorities. The redefinition of the relationship between the church and the world was one of the primary points of Vatican II. Since Vatican II, the church has made major efforts to improve its relationship with the culture around it.

# Christianity Comes to Your Hometown

For the most part, Western Europe of the 400s to the 800s was an unstable patchwork of towns, villages, and settlements, some of which were Roman and some of which were Germanic. The period was characterized by almost constant power struggles and fighting. Tribes coming from the northern and eastern areas of the world were pouring into the settled parts of Europe in search of land and riches. By this time, the old

Roman Empire had lost much of its power and no longer offered the people protection against the invading tribes. In the Roman Empire's absence, the Catholic Church became the stabilizing force in Western Europe. The religion prospered and was characterized by its missionary work, building an elaborate system of monasteries and convents. These places provided safety, education, and support in an unstable time.

### S'ter Says

**Missionaries** are religious workers who are sent to foreign countries to do religious or charitable work. At times, they have been criticized for imposing values and beliefs on other cultures without an open exchange of ideas. In recent time, missionaries offer medical and educational assistance while working within the cultural beliefs of the people they serve.

## Monasticism: Attraction Rather Than Promotion

Monasteries and convents brought Catholicism to non-Christian Europe. Monastic life is a tradition in the Catholic Church that goes back to the desert with St. Anthony and his followers in the third century. As we learned in Chapter 20, "The Church: Moving from Steeple to People," St. Benedict shaped monastic life under what is called the Rule of St. Benedict, which became the template for Western monasticism.

Monasteries and convents housed communities in which religious life developed. Men who belonged to these early church communities were often called monks; women were called nuns. From these communities came the *missionaries* who went out and lived among the tribes, helping to convert many tribal people to a new way of life.

The monasteries were cradles of art, sacred writing, and theological thought. As the invading tribes spilled down into Europe, the monasteries became safe harbors for the people and their culture. While continuing the work of conversion begun by the founding missionaries, some monasteries grew extremely wealthy and powerful. Their abbots (the name given to the head of a monastery) became some of the most influential figures in the area.

## St. Patrick: Three Cheers for the Irish

Missionary work was an important part of the early church. If ever there was a giant among missionaries, it was St. Patrick. He is called the "apostle of Ireland" and remains its patron saint. Dates of his birth differ between 432 and 456, and his death is given as 461 or 493.

One of the best-loved stories about him says he drove the snakes out of Ireland. This story may be a reference to converting Ireland from the Druid religion, because snakes were one of its sacred druidic symbols. He used the shamrock to teach about the Trinity, which is why it is the sacred plant of Ireland. The Druids burned ritual fires throughout the countryside as part of their spring rites. Another legend says St. Patrick lit the Easter fire in defiance of this pagan custom.

The story goes that St. Patrick was captured in his home in Britain by raiders from the sea when he was 16. He was taken to Ireland where he worked as a slave for the next six years. He eventually escaped and went back home to Britain. He became a priest and later a bishop. He was haunted by a dream in which he believed God was calling him back to Ireland. He eventually followed his dream and went back to the Irish and never left. He carried out massive missionary work, implanting the Catholic faith so widely and deeply in Ireland that it became one of the most Catholic of nations.

Many Christian texts were stored and copied in the monasteries of Ireland. For hundreds of years, the invading tribes from the "uncivilized" northern regions invaded Europe, eventually capturing and destroying Rome. Works of literature and art were hidden in the monasteries, thus preserving them from the invaders.

The term Celt has come to be associated with the Irish, but it refers to many of the people who lived across Western Europe. Their conversion to Catholicism was gradual. The old Druid religion existed side-by-side with Catholicism in most of the Celtic lands for many years. Catholic churches were built on the old holy sites of the Druids, and often the names and images of the old gods were carved into the stone walls. The Celts retained the holy days of the old religions and rededicated them to Catholic saints. Ceremonies to acknowledge the new holy days were often similar to the ceremonies of the deities they supplanted. They were celebrated with songs, dances, and ceremonies of the old religions. This process of appropriation was very common in the spread of Catholicism.

### Epiphanies

Did you know that the Irish are credited with saving Western civilization? Invading barbarians were destroying towns and villages throughout Europe, and the art and books of both the Greek and Roman civilizations were in danger of being lost. Many of them were hidden in the Irish monasteries, and so the boast has been made that the Irish saved Western civilization.

As the church replaced Druids with bishops and priests, the people transferred their love and loyalty to them. Some of the magical world of Celtic mythology was translated into the rich Catholic stories of the lives of the saints. The Celtic religion had many goddesses, such as the Great Mother called Anna who would eventually be found in different forms in the various Celtic cultures of Europe. In Christian times, she lived on through the veneration of St. Anne in Brittany, St. Non in Wales, and St. Brigid in Ireland.

As a rule, Celtic and other indigenous religions held the female principle in equal if not higher regard than the male. You'll often hear reference to the Catholic Church as the "mother church," both in everyday language and in official documents. This designation represents the feminine or nurturing aspect of God. It refers to the church as a womb in which the members grow and develop. The church is the spiritual home, and home is the domain of the mother. The spirit of the Celtic people infused Catholicism with a sense of story, a love of song, and a strong community spirit.

Celtic monasticism was characterized by an independence of spirit and generally had little or no use for the politics of the church in Rome. The clergy of the Celtic monasteries was able to get along well with the barbarian royalty. Their style was to mingle with the dignitaries, and they made every effort to respect local values. The intense era of Irish missionary activity throughout Europe lasted for roughly 100 years from approximately 550 until 670.

### Saints Preserve Us

**St. Brigid of Ireland, February 1, Patron of Dairy Workers, Nuns, and Scholars**

Sometimes called the second St. Patrick, St. Brigid of Ireland was born in 450. She established communities all over Ireland, which helped the growth of the church. Many miracles are attributed to her. One story says she once turned water into milk, which is why she is the patron of dairy workers. Her symbol, St. Brigid's Cross, is a straw cross, which is kept in the homes of Irish country people. This cross appears in pre–Christian art forms as well, giving substance to the idea that Brigid is an adaptation of the Celtic goddess, Brigit. Most likely, attributes of the pagan Brigit were transferred through folk memory to Brigid. Some scholars suggest that St. Brigid was the first bishop of Kildare, although this has not been proven. She is buried at Downpatrick with St. Patrick.

Two very different ideas of the Catholic Church existed side-by-side in Europe. The Celtic version was an independent and decentralized concept of Catholicism; the other Catholicism was a very Roman-centered church, which saw itself as the authority in religious matters.

## German Christianity

In the countryside that would eventually be known as Germany, people lived in small villages and settlements and practiced pagan religions. The Catholic Church was extending its missionary efforts into the area. Boniface, one of the leading missionaries of the time, was to Germany what Patrick was to Ireland a couple of hundred years earlier. He brought Catholicism to the German people.

**For Heaven's Sake!**

Don't think that all the clergy danced to Rome's tune. Many times the clan bonds were stronger than the bonds to the church in Rome. In Ireland, for example, the Irish clergy had very little to do with the Roman establishment.

Boniface was born about 680 in Devonshire, England, and from the age of 13, he was educated by monks in a monastery in Exeter, which he later joined. One of the stories about Boniface tells of an encounter he had with a pagan chieftain. Boniface felled a sacred oak tree that the people believed belonged to Thor, the thunder god. When he was not struck dead, as the local people believed he would be, many of them converted. He built a church out of the oak tree. However, the pagans may have had the final say. A few years later when traveling near the same place, he and his 52 companions were attacked and murdered by a band of locals. His grave soon became a sanctuary where many gathered to pay respects to him.

Earlier missionary activity in Germany had left converts to Christianity without the adequate support to maintain their faith in the outposts of civilization in which they lived. Boniface was able to bring support to these stranded Christians and bring many more converts to the church. He did this by establishing monasteries that were centers for the faith, in which people were educated and instructed in the ways of the religion. He and his female cousin, Leofgyth, instituted a series of monasteries, which became anchors for the faith. These monasteries lasted for over 1,000 years, and many of them are still in existence today. The church's missionary zeal did not confine itself to Germany, but was extended to Hungary, Russia, Denmark, Sweden, and all parts of Europe.

# From Rationality to Mysticism

The Roman world, influenced by the Greek culture, had carried many of the classical Greek thoughts and ideas into Europe. As the Empire ended, so did the time of classic learning. The period that followed, known as the Dark Ages, lasted until the 1100s. However, it's important to recognize that many things lumped together under this period's moniker are not necessarily "dark." Catholicism prevailed, for instance, to become the popular religion of the land despite constant power struggles and wars.

During this time, the church defined many of the practices and rituals with which it is so strongly identified today. For example, the Rosary was introduced, and statues and paintings of the saints sparked devotions. Feasts were celebrated with processions of colorful vestments, flags, and music. Morality plays and religious dramas were acted out publicly. Catholicism stabilized into the form it would keep for the next 1,200 years.

### Epiphanies

Just as Ireland has Patrick and Germany has Boniface, many European nations have a missionary saint who first established Catholicism within their borders. Here are a few such saints with the approximate dates they began their missionary work:

➤ St. Severinus of Austria, 470

➤ St. Columba of Scotland, 560

➤ St. Ansgar of Denmark, 830

➤ St. Cyril of Russia, 860

➤ St. Methodius of the Czech Republic, 870

➤ St. Sigfrid of Sweden, 1,000

### For Heaven's Sake!

Don't confuse the Holy Roman Empire with the church whose headquarters are located in Rome. The empire was a political structure. The Catholic Church and the kingdoms of Europe partnered for a thousand years, during which time the difference in roles between church and state was often unclear.

# A New Empire Is Born

Roman culture continued to influence both politics and the church's identity. Like the Roman Empire, the church was headquartered in Rome and developed a centralized power structure. In the absence of the Roman state, the church found itself existing as both a spiritual and often a civil authority, not entirely because it wanted political control, but because the people looked to it for leadership.

When Pope Leo III crowned Charlemagne emperor on Christmas in 800, the marriage between the church and state became official. Charlemagne was the leader of a tribe in central Europe called the Franks. As he was crowned, he accepted the role of protector of the church. The religious and political foundation for the later Holy Roman Empire was laid.

Let's summarize and clarify this important relationship between Catholicism and the Roman Empire. Initially, Catholics were outsiders and a threat to the Roman state. Then they became not only tolerated but also favored by Rome, which was losing its power to invading tribes at the time. The popes in Rome became the ones who could hold government together, and the church began to exercise both civil and religious authority.

When Charlemagne was crowned emperor, civil power and church power again became separated, that is to say, there were again two distinct leaders, the pope and emperor, but there was still one agenda: to build Augustine's City of God. This new child of the marriage between church and state, called the Holy Roman Empire, would last 1,000 years. For centuries to come, Christian Europe was torn by wars between kings and princes. Contrary to the church's intentions, the Holy Roman Empire never succeeded in bringing about the City of God.

By the time of the Dark Ages, the church had adopted an authoritarian model and was wedded to the state. Problems of money, power, and authority infiltrated its structure. In the next chapter, we will look at the corrupt practices that resulted from these problems.

---

### The Least You Need to Know

➤ The organizational structure of the church given to it by Constantine stabilized it and allowed it to grow.

➤ The indigenous tribes of Europe provided the church with a rich, colorful heritage rooted in the earth.

➤ Monasteries were stabilizing influences on European culture, and spread the values of Christianity throughout Europe.

➤ The problems of power, money, and authority came with the church's marriage to the Roman Empire.

# Chapter 22

# Division, Debauchery, and Reform: The Church's Second Millennium

The preceding chapter explained how the Catholic Church spread across Europe to become aligned with the major powers of the time. In this chapter, we'll look more closely at some of the problems that would haunt Catholicism for the next 1,000 years. We'll look at the reforms within the church that brought it into modern times.

As the new millennium dawned, trouble that had been brewing for some time was about to boil over. First, the Greek church split off from Rome over differences in politics, ritual, and language (Greek versus Latin). Then a couple of protesters, one of them a monk (Martin Luther) and the other a king (Henry VIII), turned against the church, taking big portions of Europe with them. These events finally forced the church to examine its practices and its role in the lives of the people. Although church leaders instituted major reforms, the church never again captured the unifying power it had. Let's take a closer look at these changes.

# Catholic and Orthodox: The Church's Y1K Problem

Although the first crack in Catholicism didn't occur until 1054, tension had been building for several centuries. The Catholic Church in the East, centered in Constantinople, and the Catholic Church in Rome argued over differences of language and theology. They quickly became locked in a power struggle. Rome's way of handling the problem was to excommunicate (expel) the entire Eastern church. In turn, the Eastern church excommunicated Rome, thereby breaking off from Roman rule. The Eastern church became known as the Orthodox Church and was centered in Russia, Greece, Ukraine, Romania, Turkey, and other parts of Eastern Europe.

Over the next 400 years, there were major attempts to mend this tear in the fabric of Catholicism. Essential practices and much of the theology of the churches remained the same, and today, it would be difficult to identify the differences between them. However, they remain distinct churches. Efforts to reunite the Orthodox Church and the Catholic Church continue. Pope John Paul II, the present pope, is from Poland, which borders on and is influenced by the culture of Orthodoxy. He has made the rejoining of the churches one of the aims of his rule.

### S'ter Says

**Crusades** were military expeditions undertaken by the Christians of Europe from the eleventh to the thirteenth centuries to reclaim the Holy Land from the Muslims. An **inquisition** is an official investigation by the church of suspected heresies. **Indulgences** were a partial remission of the punishment due for a sin after it had been confessed.

# Catholicism's Dark Side

Although the church felt the loss of its Eastern members, growth throughout the West more than made up for it, and the church remained a major power in the Western world. Due to some unhealthy developments, which we'll examine in this chapter, the church found itself rolling in money and basking in power. Such a combination was extremely damaging for an organization whose mission was to proclaim God's reign and to do good works. Over time, the church strayed far from its humble beginnings in the small towns of Galilee where Jesus walked the dusty roads with the people and taught about his Father's love. We'll look at three particular practices the church employed that took it further away from ministering to the people: the *Crusades*, the *Inquisition*, and the selling of salvation in the form of *indulgences*.

At the time of Christ, the church's liberating message called for an end to political oppression. Ironically, the Catholic Church conformed to the patterns of the society it was supposed to transform, the Roman Empire. In modeling the worldliness of the Roman

Empire, opulent displays of wealth became the norm for the church. Church leaders often lived like princes, holding court balls and hosting great banquets. Membership in the clergy carried privilege to the degree that church offices could be bought and sold, a practice called *simony*. The organizational structure of the church became a hotbed of infighting and jockeying for position. At one time, three different people claimed to be pope. The following sections take a look at practices that have caused problems for the church even into current history. Although it has made steps toward change, the church still struggles to come to grips with its past.

### Epiphanies

Simony refers to both the buying and selling of church offices (the office of bishop, for example). This practice was originally condemned in the Acts of the Apostles, when Simon Magus tried to buy the apostles' power of blessing through the laying on of hands. Despite repeated efforts by the church to extinguish this process, it was a recurring problem until the sixteenth century. Major offices of the church, such as appointment to the position of cardinal, were bought by wealthy and influential political figures who wished to control church decisions and finances.

## Crusades: Holy War or War on the Holy?

Crusades are the name given to the "holy wars" launched by the church mainly for the purpose of liberating the sacred places of Palestine from the Muslims, who are the members of the Islamic religion. Islam began to develop in Arabia under the direction of its founder, the prophet Muhammad. The spread of Islam after Muhammad's death in 632 has had no match in history. For the next 29 years, it expanded north of Arabia to Damascus and Jerusalem, east to Persia, west to Egypt, and further on to the northern coast of Africa. By 715, Islam had reached Spain. The spread of Islam left the great centers of Eastern Christianity cut off from the Roman Empire. Lines were eventually drawn, and a peace was established that lasted for some time.

By the middle of the eleventh century, Islamic leaders closed the Holy Land to Christian pilgrims. The pope saw this action as an opportunity both to unite the Catholic princes of Europe against a common enemy and to liberate the Holy Land. He called for the first of a series of Crusades that stretched from the late 1000s to the late 1200s. Although the first of the Crusades did open up the Holy Land for Christian pilgrims, the net effect of the Crusades was destructive. This section provides a quick look at some of them.

### Epiphanies

Did you know that Islam is the fastest-growing religion today, with about a billion believers? Its population centers are in Indonesia (161 million), Bangladesh (100 million), Nigeria (100 million), and India (100 million). Its name comes from the Arabic word *Salaam*, meaning peace. Membership requires surrender to God: "There is no God but Allah, and Muhammad is his prophet." This basic belief is accompanied by the practice of good deeds prescribed in their holy book, the Quran. Islam's history begins with Abraham of the Jewish scriptures, and is monotheistic. In this regard, Judaism, Christianity, and Islam are akin to one another.

The First Crusade lasted from 1097 to 1099. In it, Christian armies defeated Turkish armies, capturing the ancient city of Antioch and occupying Jerusalem. Their motto was *Deus vult*, "God wills it," and by this time, no one doubted it! Their victory, which was a complete slaughter, came at the expense of the inhabitants of the area, including Jews and Christians. The Second Crusade (1148–1149) failed. Jerusalem fell back into the hands of the Muslims about 40 years later. The most romanticized crusade, the Third Crusade (1189–1192), began when Europe's three most powerful rulers, Emperor Frederick Barbarossa of Germany, King Philip Augustus of France, and King Richard Coeur-de-Lion of England (Richard the Lion-Hearted) "took the cross." This phrase described the fact that the shields of the crusaders bore a cross. Tales of Richard became legend, but nothing much was accomplished. The Muslims kept Jerusalem, and Richard was stuck in an Austrian prison, waiting to be ransomed.

The Fourth Crusade (1203–1204) resulted in the complete sacking of Constantinople—a Christian city! After robbing, murdering, and raping the inhabitants, the out-of-control crusaders divided the spoils. The pope was furious at the crusaders.

The Children's Crusade in 1212 was perhaps the most bizarre one of all. Thousands of children followed a boy from Cologne who believed God wanted him to liberate Jerusalem. The main group was over 7,000

### For Heaven's Sake!

Don't think the Holy Wars were always holy. All too often they became excuses to attack and destroy any perceived enemies of the church. Although some of the crusaders probably had noble intentions, many saw the Crusades as an opportunity to get rich. Crusaders were allowed to keep the spoils of war, and this incentive attracted many who had no interest in religion.

strong. The Crusade failed, and while many of the children made it home, Christian merchants sold countless others into slavery and prostitution.

The church promised Crusaders rewards for their efforts. If they died in battle, their sins would be forgiven, and they were assured of going straight to heaven. If this inducement were not enough, they also were allowed to divide the booty of the war, an incentive that led to the pillaging and looting of property and the rape and murder of innocent people. These military expeditions put blood on the hands of the church, because tens of thousands of innocent people were slaughtered in its name.

## Good Out of Evil

Despite the negative consequences of the Crusades, there was an unintended positive by-product for the West. There was a reconnection to the great learning of the ancient world and an influx of new ideas from the Islamic world, such as astronomy and chemistry. The Islamic world gave the West the Arabic number system and introduced the concept of zero, which made higher mathematics possible. In fact, *algebra* is an Arabic word.

One of the major beneficiaries of the rediscovery of classical learning was Thomas Aquinas. Taking the previously lost works of Aristotle, one of the greatest thinkers of the Greek Classical period, Aquinas incorporated his logical method into the theology of the church. His methods of teaching, thinking, and talking about God have remained part of church education up to the present time.

### Saints Preserve Us

**St. Thomas Aquinas, January 28, Patron of Schools**

Thomas Aquinas (1225–1274) was born in Italy and was sent to the monastery of Monte Cassino at age five for education. He joined the Dominicans in 1244 and taught in Paris. He was named a saint in 1567. In 1880, Pope Leo XIII made him the patron of all the church's schools and required all seminary students to study his thought as the official philosophy of the church. He is acknowledged as the greatest master of church thought.

### S'ter Says

**Heretics** are people who engage in any deliberate, persistent, and public denial of some article of revealed truth of the Catholic faith. The church calls such false beliefs heresies. It does not tolerate heresy, and punishment for it has always been severe.

## Inquisition: Ask Me No Questions, and I'll Tell You No Lies!

People have questioned church teachings since the church began. Among the teachings that seemed to raise the most doubt were beliefs about the results of the fall from grace, original sin, heaven and hell, Jesus' divine nature, the virgin birth, and the real presence of Jesus Christ in the bread and wine of the Eucharist. The Church did not always deal well with questions or dissent. It felt that heresy threatened its duty to keep the teachings of Jesus pure. Alignment with the political sector gave the church the opportunity to use civil authority to employ physical force against dissenters, whom it branded as *heretics*.

The Inquisition was a court system set up by the church for the purpose of identifying heresies and punishing heretics. The word *inquisition* means "to question." At the same time, however, the Inquisition involved more than church authorities. Secular authorities had an interest as well. Both groups wanted to minimize dissent and disruption, and neither tolerated diversity. The Catholic Church was still smarting from the loss of the Orthodox Church, and its ideal of one faith. In an attempt to hold it all together, the church and the secular authorities joined to exert control over the world around them.

Priests of the Inquisition, mainly Dominicans, traveled throughout Europe preaching the faith. Following their sermons, they would ask the question: "Does anyone disagree with these church teachings?" People were encouraged to come forward to report any wrong thinking or wrongdoing they might know about. Usually, no one would admit that they had any doubts about the religion themselves, but quite often they would declare a neighbor or enemy a heretic. Under torture, those who were accused and found guilty by the Inquisition were fined, imprisoned, and their lands and goods confiscated. If they refused to renounce their false beliefs, and often even if they did, they were cruelly tortured and killed.

The courts of the Inquisition were church courts, and the crimes for which people were tried, specifically heresy and related offenses, were religious in nature. However, the power to punish was in civil hands. Those suspected of heresy by the church were handed over to the civil authorities for punishment. In so doing, the church attempted to absolve itself of the moral consequences.

There were three distinct Inquisitions, spanning hundreds of years. Unfortunately, historical accounts of the Inquisitions are affected by a religious bias that hinders the gathering of accurate data. The avowed purpose of an inquisition was to protect the faithful from heresy. Although the Inquisitions originally were launched against heretics, they later became directed against Jews and Muslims. In many areas of Europe, women became a favorite target of the Inquisition. In 1484, the pope issued an order that allowed an inquisition of those suspected of witchcraft.

> ## Saints Preserve Us
>
> ### Joan of Arc, May 30, Patron of France
>
> Joan of Arc was caught in both the politics of France and England and the Inquisition. Born on January 6, 1412 in France, she heard the voices of St. Michael and St. Catherine from an early age. When she was 17, the voices told her to go to the King of France and help him recapture his kingdom, lost to the English. She was captured in battle, and the French did nothing to save her. After many months of imprisonment, she was tried and found guilty of heresy, sorcery, and adultery. Joan was burned at the stake on May 30, 1431. She was only 19 years old. Thirty years later, she was exonerated of all guilt.

The most notorious of the Inquisitions was the Spanish Inquisition, which began in about 1480. Unlike the others, which were under ecclesiastical (church) control, the Spanish Inquisition was an instrument of secular power, the Spanish crown. The goal of the Spanish Inquisition was to search out converted Jews and Muslims suspected of practicing their "old" religions. The Spanish Inquisition was used against political opponents. The Inquisition lasted in Spain for almost 400 years until the 1800s. The Spanish conquistadors exported the tradition to the new world and used it against the native people. They demanded loyalty to Spain and to the church under penalty of torture and death.

> ## Epiphanies
>
> A remnant of the Inquisition called the Congregation for the Doctrine of the Faith exists in the church today. (We talked about this group in Chapter 20, "The Church: Moving from Steeple to People.") It safeguards and promotes authentic Catholic teaching throughout the worldwide church. It investigates controversy and holds extensive studies regarding questions surrounding matters of church doctrine. It evaluates theological opinions and may admonish those regarded as incorrect or harmful to Catholic teaching. It also examines books and provides the authors the opportunity to defend themselves.

**S'ter Says**

**Relics** are any part of the physical remains of a saint or items, such as clothing, that have touched the body of a saint. Bones and hair are classified as first-class relics. In October 1999, the bones of St. Térèse of Lisieux arrived in New York to tour the United States.

**S'ter Says**

A **Protestant** is any Christian belonging to a sect coming from those that seceded from the Catholic Church at the time of the Reformation. Lutheran, Episcopal, Methodist, and Baptist are some Protestant denominations.

## *Indulge Me, One More Time*

Nobody knows when the practice of selling indulgences began, but it blossomed during the 1400s and 1500s. *Relics* of the saints were often displayed for a price and sometimes sold. Relics were a popular religious sacramental of the time. They consisted of pieces of wood, said to be from the authentic cross, or pieces of cloth, hair, or bone that were believed to belong to one of the saints. Money from the sale of these goods was used to finance the building of the cathedrals and fund the extravagant lifestyle of the clergy.

*Indulgence* was a term that describes the remission of punishment due for sins. The church supported its belief of what was right and wrong with the idea of punishment in the afterlife. It assigned a spiritual value to certain practices or prayers. The performance of these practices or prayers is said to erase spiritual debt. If a sin were committed, an indulgence could balance the books. An indulgence is like a "get out of jail free" card from Monopoly. This practice went on until it was officially condemned in 1562, but not before it became the proverbial straw that broke the back of the Western church. Indulgences are still a part of the church today; however, they are not sold. They are a measurement of the spiritual value of prayers and good deeds.

## Problems, Protest, and Protestants

The church, having partnered with the state in the Inquisition, employed increasingly more authoritarian means to thwart any diversity of thought or question of its dogma. Its use of power and control, albeit for the intended end of protecting the teachings of Jesus, had taken it far from its original mission.

Against this backdrop of corruption, a sound could be heard, a tap, tap, tap in Wittenberg, a small town in Germany. The sound came from a hammer banging against the large cathedral door. When the sun rose on that October morning in 1517, it shone upon a large piece of paper known as the *95 Theses* on which were listed 95 complaints against the Catholic Church. The man who wrote the paper and nailed it to the door was Martin Luther. It was not long before the document was discussed all over Europe, and the *Protestant* Reformation was born.

On the heels of Luther's protest, Henry VIII, the king of England, broke with Rome and declared himself head of the church of England. The differences in the beginning were political rather than religious, a quarrel between the king and the pope, which was not unusual in the Middle Ages. However, this quarrel went on to result in a permanent schism. Let's take a look at both of these influential men and how their actions affected the Catholic Church.

## Martin Luther: The Hammer Heard 'Round the World

Martin Luther, a German monk, began the Reformation, which was the catalyst for many of the Protestant religions. He was an Augustinian priest who was sent on a mission to Rome in 1510 and returned indignant at the corruption and worldliness of the Catholic Church. The following year, he became a professor of theological studies, a position he held until his death. Luther's studies brought him to the belief that people are saved by faith alone. They could not earn salvation through actions or prayers. As a result, Luther was particularly outraged at the selling of indulgences, which violated this core belief. He attacked this practice and others in his *95 Theses*.

Luther followed his first list of complaints with his treatises of 1520, in which he questioned papal authority and other official church doctrines. He was excommunicated in a document issued by Rome, which Luther promptly burned in the public square. Soon, the emperor summoned him. Luther defended his beliefs eloquently and refused to recant. He was outlawed and sought refuge in the castle of Wartburg under the protection of Frederick, an official of the area. Luther translated the Bible into German. He also organized the Lutheran Church and wrote essays, sermons, catechisms, and hymns, including the famous Protestant hymn, "A Mighty Fortress Is Our God." The creation of the Lutheran Church, which was formed around the teachings of Martin Luther, resulted in the Catholic Church losing its followers in a major portion of Germany.

## Henry VIII: Love and Marriage

The man known as Henry VIII was not only one of the most colorful rulers in the history of England, he also maintains an important place in church history as well. Henry was more practical than idealistic; his actions were motivated by his desire to divorce his wife and marry another. The church refused to grant him the annulment he desired. Henry defied church doctrine and authority by

**Your Guardian Angel**

Although divorce is not a part of church practice, the church recognizes civil divorce. However, the divorced Catholics are not free to marry again. Annulment (discussed in Chapter 11, "Seven Sensual Sacraments") applies to cases where the marriage itself is invalid.

remarrying in 1533, and was duly excommunicated. In response, Henry instituted the Church of England and declared himself its head. As a result, Catholicism lost most of its English members. The Church of England, better known as the Anglican Church, still exists today.

In addition to the Lutheran Church and the Anglican Church, many other churches were founded in the 1500s in protest of the Catholic Church and its various practices. These splits weren't entirely about the selling of indulgences or the Catholic Church's prohibition of divorce. The emerging states of Europe were gaining power and wanted their independence. They resented the fact that church money was channeled into Rome. The church and the state were so intertwined that political independence had to come at the cost of religious independence, and many wars would be fought throughout Europe for centuries because of it. Further splits with the Catholic Church occurred in France, Switzerland, and other Northern European countries. Generally, the southern countries remained in Rome's fold.

# Trendy Trent: Going to Reform School

Both Martin Luther and Henry VIII packed a big wallop, and the Catholic Church felt the sting of its losses. It realized that it had better make some changes, or it was going to lose even more members. The birth of Protestantism gave the push for the reform that many had been urging for hundreds of years. The pope called the Council of Trent. During the years 1545 to 1563, bishops of the church met to clarify doctrines and to pass reforms that would redirect the course of the Catholic Church for the next 400 years. The results of this council essentially sounded the death knell for corrupt church practices, and church leaders got back to business—religious business.

## Scripture and Tradition Upheld

The Protestant Reformation sparked what is called the Counter-Reformation, in which the Catholic Church began to define its authority. It reaffirmed its stand that revelation is found in both written scriptures and unwritten traditions. The church had always claimed that a person couldn't interpret God's truth simply by reading the Bible. It has always believed God's revelation continues to unveil itself through the teachings of the church. This idea, which was completely unacceptable to the Protestants, allowed bishops to continue to formulate church teaching on more than just the Bible. In addition, they declined to approve new translations of the Bible that were in the people's everyday language. This seemed to justify the Protestants' claim that the Catholic Church was afraid to have people read the Bible. The gulf between Catholics and Protestants was widening.

By the time the Council of Trent closed in 1563, it had dealt with many of the abuses cited by the Protestant Reformers, and it ended the corruption in the Catholic Church. The changes included a prohibition on the sale of indulgences, a crackdown on simony, a reformed liturgy, the establishment of seminaries for the proper training of priests, and more local control given to bishops.

The Council of Trent did not, however, address the important issue of the nature of the church's relationship to the world. As you've seen, that subject became the focus of the most recent council, Vatican II.

## Lines Drawn: Them and Us

The church began to define itself over and against Protestantism. Catholicism was no longer the only game in Christendom, and by the end of the Council of Trent, firm boundaries were established between the Catholic Church and Protestantism. There were five primary differences between them, and these differences remain in effect even today:

**For Heaven's Sake!**

Be careful about how you use the word Protestant. This is a generic term Catholics (and other non-Protestants) often use to refer to non-Catholic Christians. Baptists, Presbyterians, or Episcopalians, for example, would not refer to themselves as Protestants, but instead use the specific name of their denomination.

➤ Catholics maintain that moral authority comes from both scripture and tradition. Remember, the Catholic Church bases its authority to declare truth both in scripture and in its interpretation of the scripture, which it calls tradition. Protestants believe that the scripture alone holds moral authority.

➤ Catholics hold that Christ is truly present in the consecrated bread and wine of the Eucharist. Protestants, for the most part, see the Eucharist as a symbolic memorial of Christ's last supper.

➤ For Catholics, the Sacraments are celebrations of the salvation achieved by Jesus Christ, which God offers us as a gift. Sacraments are Catholics' participation in this reality. Protestants believe that salvation comes through faith in Biblical scripture alone.

➤ Catholics keep the traditional seven sacraments: Baptism, Reconciliation, the Eucharist, Confirmation, Holy Orders, Marriage, and Anointing of the Sick. Protestants for the most part believe in two sacraments: Baptism and the Eucharist.

➤ Catholics believe in mediation, the establishment of a relationship between one person and God through the efforts of another person. The mediator can be a priest or a favorite saint. It can be other persons who pray for them. They themselves can be mediators, as they pray for others, the souls in Purgatory, for example. Mary is the favorite Catholic mediator. Protestants believe in an immediate and direct relationship with God, and shun intermediaries, for the most part.

# The Church Turns Its Face to the New World

The Protestant Reformation caused much of Germany and England to leave the Catholic Church. The result was that the Catholic Church lost its position as the primary religion. While the Catholic Church was losing its hold on Europe, a Catholic country, Spain, was opening up a new world. The New World provided an opportunity for the Catholic Church to establish the "City of God" one more time. That's what we'll discuss in the next chapter.

---

### The Least You Need to Know

➤ The ideal of one religion for all was shattered with the separation of the Orthodox Church.

➤ The involvement of the church in money and power caused a loss of identity and integrity.

➤ The Protestant revolt spurred the reform of the Catholic Church.

➤ The Catholic reformation assured the church's survival as a religious institution and brought it into modern time.

# Chapter 23

# The Birth of the Church in the New Land

---

### In This Chapter

➤ The conquistadors meet the Aztecs

➤ Christianity in the Americas begins with an apparition

➤ A new race is born: the brown face of the Catholic Church

➤ Mexican–American Catholic heritage

---

In 1492, a Catholic Italian explorer named Christopher Columbus claimed America for Spain. Well, that's almost true. Actually, Columbus claimed America for both Spain and for God, because in 1492, Spain's official religion was Catholicism. In that way, both Catholicism in America and America itself share a common birthday.

Spain had just ended hundreds of years of war against Islam and was determined to solidify its kingdom. The Spanish believed in the unity of church and state, and a strong alliance had been forged between the crown and the cross. In this arrangement, the church sanctioned the activities of the state, and the state promoted the authority of the church. This unity, combined with a high degree of military expertise, became Spain's double-edged sword, and explorers carried this sword with them into the New World.

In this chapter, we'll take a look at the drama that was the establishment of Catholicism in the Western Hemisphere. We'll look at the religions that were already here and the effect that Catholic missionaries and soldiers had in the spread of Catholicism. This story involves missionaries, apparitions, exploitation, poverty, discrimination, and new beginnings. Indeed, a lot happened to Catholics and for Catholicism after October 12, 1492.

### For Heaven's Sake!

Don't assume that colonization always meant progress! Time has taught us to examine the ambiguous character of colonization and the role that the church played in it. All too often, colonization was carried out by brutal military force, and all too often, the church was the beneficiary of these violent actions.

### S'ter Says

A **conquistador** is a Spanish conqueror of Mexico, Peru, and other parts of the New World in the sixteenth century. **Colonialism** is a process by which one country exploits another for economic purposes. In the Americas, churches were a central part of this colonialism, thanks in large part to the work of missionaries.

# Colonization: Ready or Not, Here We Come!

We often think of the New World as comprised of New England first and then the rest of the United States. However, the term *New World* describes the continents of South America and North America, including Central America and the Caribbean. Therefore, the story of Catholicism in America begins in Mexico. Catholicism was exported from Europe on the same ships that brought the conquistadors. *Conquistadors* were the soldiers who were sent by Spain to conquer the people of the New World and establish European rule, which included European religion.

The indigenous people of the New World were architects of beautiful cities. They built canals, temples, and observatories. They knew mathematics and had accurate tools by which they measured the movement of the stars. They had a high degree of technological, artistic, religious, and scientific development. What they did not have, however, were the sophisticated tools of war that the Spanish and Portuguese brought with them. The finely tuned European war machine eventually overwhelmed the indigenous people of the Americas.

It is impossible to separate the spread of the Catholic religion from the effects of exploration and *colonialism* on the native cultures. Franciscan missionaries accompanied the soldiers into the New World. The soldiers and the priests each had their own agenda: to find gold for Spain and to baptize converts for Catholicism. This era of European expansion lasted for hundreds of years. During this time, the ideas, economies, and religion of Europe were transplanted to the New World.

## Europe Comes to Mexico

The first areas of the New World conquered by the conquistadors were the Caribbean islands, Mexico, and the countries of Central America. Critics of European conquest cite many incidences of inhumane treatment of the native people. Massacres and, in some cases, the complete annihilation of whole cultures occurred. The arrival of the Europeans and the imposition of their civilization left many of the original inhabitants poor, hungry, and suffering from the many illnesses brought by the explorers.

For the most part, the church turned its back on the atrocities of the armies, accepted the legitimacy of conquest, and apparently had no trouble combining the practice of slavery with the practice of Christianity. It seems as though the church was satisfied with the belief in the "natural" superiority of the Europeans to these strange, apparently "barbaric" pagans.

At the same time, Mexican historians have noted that it was the missionaries who extended the few acts of kindness and who challenged military practices. It seemed that although the "big" church was indifferent—and by its indifference was a partner in the atrocities—the "little" church took a stand against the prevailing practices.

One of the ways the missionaries attempted to assist the people was through the establishment of missions. Missions were like small villages containing schools, churches, infirmaries, and shelter. Native language, customs, and religious beliefs were replaced with European language, manners, and values. In theory, the missions provided safe havens and were an attempt to socialize the native people into European culture. Many missionaries made little effort to understand the beliefs of the native people, to learn their language, or to engage their culture in any positive way. However, some missionaries did learn the language of the people and even adopted many of their ways.

### Saints Preserve Us

**Blessed Bartolomé de las Casas (1484–1566)**

Born in Seville, Spain, he was a missionary to Latin America and the first priest to be ordained in the New World (1512). He was a Dominican who worked to improve conditions of indigenous people and to end their enslavement. The king of Spain named him Protector of the Indians. Bartolomé's efforts influenced the pope to declare that American Indians were rational beings with souls and their lives and property should be protected. His efforts led to the "The New Laws" adopted to protect the native peoples in Spanish colonies. He was the first bishop of Chiapas. A scholar and historian, he has been called "the father of anti-imperialism and anti-racism." He knew Columbus and edited his journal. He is called Blessed, a step on the way to sainthood.

# The Beliefs of the Indigenous People

Europe met three main cultures in the New World: the Mayans, the Incas, and the Aztecs. According to historian and theologian, Virgilio P. Elizondo in La Morenita, the Mayans had a well-developed culture and were great traders. The Incas had a closely knit society that insured the equal redistribution of goods throughout the empire. The Aztecs were ruled by a monarch and had a hierarchical society. All three cultures were polytheistic, with both male and female deities, including an Earth Goddess and a Sun God. The concepts of an underworld and an afterlife were present, and human sacrifice featured in all, to a greater or lesser degree. The Mayan pantheon was particularly interesting, the dual nature of their deity represented the duality of life and death, with stories of death and resurrection figuring prominently.

In the indigenous religion, Ometéotl, the name of "Great Spirit," was both the Lord and Lady of all creation. Ometéotl's feminine aspect was known by many names. She was the mother of earth, mother of the gods, mother of wisdom, and the heart of earth.

### For Heaven's Sake!

Don't make the mistake of thinking that all indigenous cultures are alike or that they are inferior to European culture. Mexico was the location of one of the greatest Indian civilizations on the North American continent: the Mayans. They developed a calendar that is more accurate than the one we use today and were skilled in mathematics and astronomy. Their culture was at its height between 300 and 900 B.C.E.

The indigenous religions had many similarities to the Catholicism of Europe, which, after all, had roots in the practices of the old tribal people. For example, both the religion of the Indians and the religion of the missionaries had sacred ritual, a calendar of religious feasts, and a sacred language in which to speak to their God(s), a well-defined priesthood with vestments, temples, and processions. The Indians also expressed their religious beliefs through poetry, song, and symbol. In the Indian religion, Elizondo explains, "Nothing is unrelated." As we saw in the Old World, Mary intertwined with symbols of existing deities. The feminine aspect of the Indian's Great Spirit, Ometéotl, resurfaced in the coming of Christianity to the New World, as we will see later in this chapter.

The Aztec religion had some similarities to the religions of the Mayans and Incas, but the Aztec culture had a different social and economic structure. They believed in private property, and they owned slaves. Their well-developed society posed a formidable challenge to the conquering Europeans, but a particular practice of their religion pushed the already overzealous military to the point of destruction. The Aztecs believed in human sacrifice, and practiced it much more freely than did neighboring cultures. This shocked the Spanish soldiers. They were convinced that the Aztecs were savages, and on this point, the missionaries agreed. Together, they waged war against them.

# Spanish America

Even though the Aztecs did not possess the essential tools of war that the Spanish had, such as horses, steel weapons, and guns, they could have been a formidable force. However, it only took six years for Spain to conquer this major civilization. Three factors contributed to the success of the Spanish leader Cortés and the demise of the Aztec leader, Montezuma.

### Epiphanies

Hernán Cortés (1485–1547) was a Spanish explorer and conqueror of Mexico. In 1519, he was welcomed into the Aztec capital by Montezuma II (1466–1520), the last independent Aztec emperor. Montezuma mistook Cortés for the incarnation of the Aztec god Quetzal-cóatl, whose return had been prophesied. Four years later, Montezuma was fatally wounded in a battle against the army of Cortés.

The first factor was the same one that had turned the Spanish against the Aztecs, the Aztec practice of extensive human sacrifice. Many subject Indian tribes felt that the Aztecs' use of human sacrifice was a corruption of the religion of Quetzalcóatl, which was based on the dignity of life, simplicity, and prayer. Other groups of Indians disliked the Aztecs, who used brutal methods to hold their empire together, and they joined the conquistadors in a popular uprising against them.

The second factor giving Cortés an advantage over Montezuma was a religious one. In both the Mayan and Aztec cultures, the prophets had read many signs and had begun to prophesy the end of their civilization. The end had been predicted to occur in 1517 and 1519. In a very powerful coincidence (or perhaps as the fulfillment of their prophecy), Cortés landed on the Yucatan Peninsula in 1517 and arrived in their land in 1519.

### For Heaven's Sake!

Don't think Christians are the only ones whose God talks of simplicity and peace. Quetzal-cóatl, a central spiritual figure in the religion of the Central Americans, was a teacher/priest/king whose message was essentially to live a peaceful, simple life.

A further prophecy given to the Indians by their priests predicted the return of Quetzalcóatl, a spiritual figure central to the religion of many Central American cultures. The prophecy foretold that he would come as a bearded white man out of the East. When the Indians saw Cortés, bearded and white, approaching from the East, many of them believed they were seeing the return of their god, and they began to follow him.

After Cortés took over the Aztec capital, the Franciscan priests met with the Aztec priests for a brief period of time. After the Catholic priests examined the religion of the native people with its blood sacrifices, they concluded that the religion should be destroyed. So Cortés and the soldiers not only brought down Montezuma, but they also plundered the temples. In their frenzy, they caused the massive destruction of all aspects of the Central American culture. Towns were destroyed, women were raped, and subjection and slavery were instituted. In the wake of the conquest, the oppression of the native people would last a long time.

The Incas and Mayans experienced similar fates. When the conquistadors arrived in modern-day Peru in 1532, they betrayed and murdered the Inca emperor, and were able to wipe out all resistance in just five years. The Mayan civilization was in an advanced state of decay by the time of the conquistadors, yet they still held out against the technologically superior Spanish for nearly 20 years (1527–1546), defeating them on several occasions. After they were overcome, both cultures suffered the same treatment the Aztecs had received.

## Missions and Conversion

As we stated earlier, the relationship of the missionaries to the people tended to be different from that of the conquistadors. The missionaries' underlying belief was that all people should have access to God. They believed the God of Jesus was the true God. However, they respected the people and defended them against the soldiers whenever they could. The native people came to see that the missionaries were sincere, simple men who literally walked barefoot among them. The missions became "sanctuaries" against the soldiers, and the missionaries protested the military's brutal treatment to the civil authorities.

### Epiphanies

The Spaniards founded the first university in North America, the University of Mexico in Mexico City in 1551. Also, the famous Texas landmark called the Alamo was once a Spanish mission.

*Frailes e Indigenas, A Representation of the Comparison of the Bible and the Aztec Codex (the Aztec's sacred writings) by Spanish and Aztec Holy Men. Federico Cantú 1959.*

*(Courtesy of CONACULTA—I.N.B.A.—PINACOTECA VIRREINAL, Mexico City)*

However, in spite of an improved relationship between the missionaries and the natives and despite the missionaries' most zealous efforts, the missionaries still were unable to convert the Indian people to Catholicism in any significant numbers after 10 years. Broken and powerless, the native people still weren't buying into the new religion!

# A New People Emerges

Although the church failed at first in its efforts to convert the masses, some remarkable developments changed the face of Catholicism in the New World forever. Many who have examined the details of these happenings believe that they were a new incarnation of Christ. Let's take a look at these amazing events.

## The Brown Lady of Guadalupe

On December 12, 1531, a native peasant named Juan Diego had a religious experience that profoundly affected the development of the Catholic Church in the New World. It occurred as he hurried up Tepeyac Hill just outside of Mexico City on his way to Mass at a Franciscan mission. Suddenly, a vision of the Virgin Mary appeared before him. In his vision, she was a young Indian woman, brown and pregnant. As he saw her, she stood in front of the sun, but she did not obliterate its light. Rather, it glowed all around her, illuminating her. Her face radiated compassion, and she spoke to Juan, telling him she was the holy virgin mother of the true God. She spoke in Nahuatl, the Indian language of the conquered people. She told him that she wanted a temple to be built in her honor on the very spot on which she appeared. From the temple, she would help the people. She then sent Juan to the bishop to tell him of her request.

Juan went to the bishop with the message the Virgin gave him, but he was refused admission and sent away. He left feeling sad about failing in his important task. He went back to the hill where he had seen the Virgin, and to his surprise, she came to him again. Juan asked her to please find another more important man to deliver the message, because the bishop would not see him. The Virgin assured him that he, "the smallest of my children," was the one she wanted to bring this powerful message.

Juan went back to the bishop, and this time he was finally granted an audience. The bishop asked him many questions, and he told the story of the Virgin, right down to the smallest detail of his experience. The bishop did not believe him and asked for a sign that would prove it was the Virgin who had sent him.

Juan went back to the hill, where Mary appeared to him once again. He explained that the bishop wanted proof in the form of some kind of a sign. She told him to come back the next day and promised to give him proof. The next day Juan was detained due to the illness of his uncle. He was rushing to get the priest, and in his hurry, decided to not stop at the place where he had seen the apparition. As he passed by the place, Mary called out to him. He was embarrassed, but he stopped. She told him that his uncle would recover and that she would have a sign for him at the top of the hill. He went where she directed him to go and was astounded by what he found. There were exquisite roses where they should not be growing at this time of year. She told him to gather the roses inside his cloak and to show no one but the bishop.

**Your Guardian Angel**

Apparitions of Mary are often accompanied by flowers and music. It is believed that these things are the supreme, most perfect means of communicating the presence of God. Likewise, honor is paid to Mary by bringing her flowers and through playing music, such as the many versions of the Ave Maria that have been composed for her.

He went to the bishop, and at first his servants ignored Juan. Eventually, the aroma of the roses began to spread throughout the office, and they went to tell the bishop something unusual was happening. Juan was invited in, and the bishop asked to see what he was holding inside his cloak. As Juan opened his cloak, beautiful roses of many varieties and colors spilled out onto the floor. The bishop was amazed. But perhaps even more astonishing was the exact image of the Virgin that had been imprinted on Juan's cloak. The bishop fell to his knees in prayer.

Elizondo tells us the appearance of the Virgin Mary had profound importance for the Indian people. In discussing the symbolic meaning of the appearance, he goes on to say that perhaps most important of all was that the mother of God came to them not as a Spaniard but as one of their own. Her skin was brown, the exact color that the conquerors told them was "inferior." Unlike the typical European images of her, the Virgin was obviously an Indian woman of native Mexican heritage.

It was significant to the Indian people that she stood in front of the sun. The Sun God was the main god in their pantheon. Her position in front of it showed that she came as a new representation of the divine, growing out of that which came before her. In this way, she connected the symbols of the old religion to the new religion of Christianity.

There were further symbols, as well. The Lady's dress was a pale red, the color of the blood sacrifices of the old religion and the color of the blood of the people that had been spilled by the conquerors. Red is also the color of the East, and it represented new beginnings to the people. Her blue mantle told them she was of royal descent, possibly a deity. The stars in her mantle echoed the prophecy given 10 years earlier that told of a comet signaling the end of their civilization. Perhaps most significant was the black maternity band stretched across her belly, in the center of which was the Aztec cross. The Lady was clearly offering her child to the New World. This vision would come to be understood as a new incarnation of Christ in the Americas.

Word of the Lady's appearance spread rapidly across the land. Crowds began to gather at the bishop's home to see the cloak that held her image. It was placed above the cathedral altar and later in the shrine that was built on the site of her appearance, as she had requested. The "Brown Lady" became the new symbol of the Mexican people and a new symbol for Catholicism as well.

The image of Our Lady of Guadalupe, as she is called, fused European Christianity with the spirit of the native people. Because the Indian people could see themselves in her, their own spirituality could translate into Christianity. To this day, the image remains brilliant in the Basilica in Mexico City, which was built on the site of the original appearance of the Lady. Millions of people visit this site every year.

As brilliant as the image hanging in the Basilica is, it lives even more brilliantly in the hearts of the people. The merging of symbols in this image—the Aztec Sun God and the God of the Christians in the womb of the Virgin Mary—transformed both Catholicism and the indigenous religions. For the Indians, the new religion of Catholicism was no longer seen as something foreign, but as something growing out of their own religion. They believed they had entered the next phase of their spiritual story. Rather than seeing the end of their civilization, they saw a new beginning. For Catholicism, this image offered an opportunity for renewal.

## La Nueva Raza: The New Race

In the beginning, the church opposed what they referred to as the Guadalupe incident, fearing that it was a ploy by the native people to reinstate their own religion. Although the grassroots Franciscan missionaries understood the importance of the devotion to Guadalupe, the Franciscan intelligentsia fought it vehemently. However, the archbishop reaffirmed his official support of the devotions. He had ordered the building of the basilica, and he was convinced of the importance of the image.

*A picture of Our Lady of Guadalupe as imprinted on the cloak of Juan Diego in 1531.*

*(Norberto Mujica)*

### S'ter Says

**La Nueva Raza,** the new people, is a Spanish phrase that describes both the mixing of the Spanish, African, and Indian blood, spirituality, and culture, and the resulting new culture which was produced.

In the long run, the church could not deny the remarkable effects the Lady of Guadalupe had on its mission to spread the word of Christ to the people. Unlike the first 10 years of the Spanish presence in the New World, the second 10 years were marked by the conversion of a phenomenal number of Indian people to Catholicism. It was as though the Mexican culture sprang back to life. Festivals, pilgrimages, and dances are still a huge part of Mexican Catholicism today. A mingling of cultures amongst the Spanish, the African slaves they brought over, and the indigenous Indians occurred. From this mixture, a new race of people was born called *La Nueva Raza.*

The "official" church waited many years before ruling on the miraculous nature of Juan Diego's vision. In 1754, a little over 200 years after the vision, the pope knelt in front of a painting of the Virgin and declared Our Lady of Guadalupe the patroness of Mexico. He instituted a Mass and prayers in her honor. What this meant to the people, in effect, was that the Virgin's appearance had become "dogma."

### Saints Preserve Us

**St. Martin de Porres, November 3, Patron of Hairdressers**

St. Martín de Porres (1579–1639) was born in Lima, Peru, the son of a Spanish gentleman and a freed African slave. He is one of the few saints of color recognized by the church. At age 15, de Porres became a Dominican lay brother and became known for his rugged humility. God worked extraordinary wonders through him. He spent his life in service to his community both as a barber and a farm laborer. It was said that God rewarded Martín for his humility with the gift of great spiritual wisdom. Bishops sought his advice, and he resolved many theological problems of the day. St. Martín de Porres became the patron saint of hairdressers because hairdressing was one of the duties he performed for his brothers in the friary to which he belonged.

# Cultural Contributions to Today's Catholicism

Firmly planted in the New World, the Spanish and Portuguese culture flowered, as did the church. The scope of the lands these countries would come to control was immense. It stretched thousands of miles from the tip of the South American continent, across Central America, the major islands of the Caribbean, and from Florida across the South and Southwest to the western shores of California. The heritage of these Catholic lands continues to exist today in place names such as St. Augustine, San Antonio, Santa Fe, and San Francisco.

This heritage goes beyond names on a map. Today, Catholicism exists in large numbers among Hispanic Americans who, as this century ends, are estimated to comprise nearly 50 percent of the total United States Catholic population. As the number of Latin American Catholics increases, the face of Catholicism in the United States is changing. The Catholic Church, once dominated by Europeans, struggles today to understand the hearts and minds of these "new people." Communal by nature, and still remembering the poetic-symbolic religion of their ancestors, these people embody a spiritual aspect of religion that offers balance to the more "rational" side of the European Catholic Church.

The Hispanic people have a strong sense of family and family values. They bring particular religious and cultural practices to the United States Catholic Church in the form of *liturgical rituals* that strengthen family values.

*Percent of total United States Hispanic population by region and state with a population of 500,000 or more.*

*(Source: U.S. Bureau of Census, 1991)*

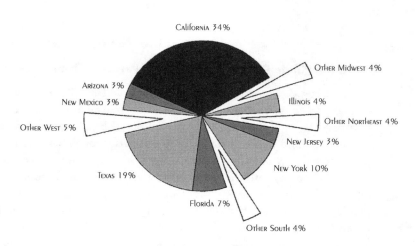

PERCENT of TOTAL HISPANIC POPULATION by REGION and STATE with 500,000 or MORE

California 34%

Other Midwest 4%

Illinois 4%

Arizona 3%

New Mexico 3%

Other Northeast 4%

Other West 5%

New Jersey 3%

New York 10%

Texas 19%

Florida 7%

Other South 4%

### S'ter Says

**Liturgical rituals** refers to all church services and ceremonies, including readings at Mass, communion, the sacraments, prayers, and celebrations.

The *Posadas* is a ritual enacted at Christmas in many Mexican-American parishes in Texas, Chicago, California, New Mexico, and elsewhere. It involves a house-to-house procession in which a couple, playing the role of the two Galileans, Joseph and Mary, walk through the streets, knocking on doors seeking shelter. Over and over again, they are refused. After the young couple has been rejected a number of times, someone finally listens to what they are saying and offers them a place to stay. As they are received into a home, there is much joy and celebration.

The two key themes of this Gospel re-enactment are the rejection of the poor and the joy that comes to those who open their home and heart to those whom others have rejected. In a remarkable connection, this faith ritual relates beautifully to the current Mexican-American experience. Risking their lives by crossing the border to find work to feed their children, Mexicans meet rejection. Like the holy couple who is carrying the child Jesus, the hope of the future, with them, they do not give up.

As in the ritual enactment of the *Posada,* the second important part of this real-life Mexican *Posada* involves a request to the people of the United States to open the border, share their wealth, and receive the gift of joy that is the completion of the ritual.

In this chapter, you've met some of the indigenous cultures that were living in the area now known as Central America and Mexico and have heard how Catholicism arrived in the New World. In the next chapter, you'll see how Catholicism spread in the North through European immigration.

**S'ter Says**

**Posada,** the Spanish word for "shelter," is used to describe a house-to-house procession at Christmas time in which the drama of the Galilean couple Joseph and Mary is enacted.

## The Least You Need to Know

➤ There were well-developed cultures on the American continent when the Europeans arrived.

➤ The colonization and evangelization of North America and South America was accomplished with pain, death, and a great loss of native culture.

➤ The appearance of Our Lady of Guadalupe transformed the European assault into a new revelation of the face of God.

➤ Mexican-American Catholics play an important role in shaping the new face of the Catholic Church in the United States.

# Chapter 24

# Catholics Earn Their Citizenship

In this chapter, you'll see what happened north of the border in the New World. At first, the 13 colonies of New England barely noticed Catholicism. Soon, however, following an enormous wave of immigration, Catholics became major players in the construction and expansion of the United States. The reaction of the established Protestants to the immigrants was not altogether favorable, and Catholics suffered a great deal of prejudice and discrimination. They reacted by building a fortress church and developing a strong Catholic identity of separatism.

As time went on, their prosperity in the middle of the twentieth century allowed them to become part of mainstream America and to become champions of democracy. The reward was the election of one of their own, John F. Kennedy, as president. Before they were able to bask in this new glory, however, his assassination, the Vietnam War, the cultural revolution, and Vatican II's redefinition of Catholicism put American Catholics in a tailspin. This chapter explores these developments.

# Catholicism and Colonial America: There Goes the Neighborhood!

Catholicism's journey took a very different route north of Mexico. The first English colonists were Protestant, Puritan, Quaker, and Anglican, not Catholic. At the time of the American Revolution in 1776, the proportion of Catholics in the British Colonies was estimated to be less than 1 percent. Slowly but surely, however, Catholicism entered mainstream American life.

## *Breaking into the Protestant Club*

The colonial adventure began in 1607, when a small number of colonists, mostly from England, settled in the new land. They had endured the difficult migration across the Atlantic and survived the challenges of the first years of homesteading. Houses had been built, and the village church had been roofed. The essentials for life in the New World had been secured.

Put yourself into this picture and imagine that you and your family were living there. The hard hours you had spent in your small candle-making business in downtown Boston had begun to turn a profit. Life was good. The promise of America stretched out in front of you like the vast sea you had recently crossed, and it was filled with hope and expectation.

You were part of a group of Protestant reformers who left Europe to come to a new land free of the trappings of the Old World religion. You saw this land as a "New Jerusalem," "A City on the Hill" that would be both politically and religiously free from the Old World and its Roman ways. Here was the definitive break from Rome, both the state and the church.

All too soon, word began to reach you and the other colonists that the Catholic colonists from Spain were advancing northward, stretching out across the plains. So much for keeping the Puritan New World to yourselves!

At the same time, another situation was all too rapidly becoming apparent in the marketplace of Boston and other ports along the eastern seaboard: a marked increase in the number of French Catholic traders selling furs. All over the coast of eastern Canada and northern Maine, French trappers and their families were arriving, bringing their version of the Catholic story with them. They brought Catholicism to the northern regions where they trapped and moved down the trade route of the Mississippi River to the port of New Orleans. Like the Spanish in the southern part of the continent, the French intermarried with the native population.

### Saints Preserve Us

**Blessed Kateri Tekakwitha**

Kateri Tekakwitha (1656–1680) had a Christian Algonquin mother, and her father was a chief of the Mohawk. She converted to Catholicism and was rejected by her people. She ran away to the Christian Indian village of Sault Ste. Marie, near Montreal. She dedicated herself to Christ and led a life of holiness and austerity. She died at the early age of 24. She was known as "Lily of the Mohawk," and the faithful have credited her with many miracles. She has been beatified, meaning that she is called "blessed," which is a step in the process of becoming a saint.

No doubt, the British Protestant population felt the squeeze of these two sets of unwanted "invaders," the Spanish and the French. In this unfriendly and somewhat hostile environment, Catholicism, for the most part, was met with prejudice, fear, persecution, and eventually laws of discrimination. Indeed, discrimination and prejudice against Catholics were to have a long history in Britain's original colonies and throughout much of modern American history. The Protestants were there first, and the Catholics were forced to earn acceptance, to say nothing of respect. For instance, early copies of the basic school reader for the colonies, the *New England Primer,* were filled with images that would persuade any young reader that the Catholic Church was the Devil incarnate.

### S'ter Says

The **New England Primer** was a commonly used textbook in the colonies. Printed in 1690, it was still in use in 1900. Intended to help teach children to read, it used religion to teach subjects such as the alphabet: A (In ADAM'S fall, we sinned all) to Z (ZACCHEUS, he did climb the tree, our Lord to see). Its illustrations presented anti-Catholic images.

## Catholics and the Revolution

Back home in England, in an effort to civilize the Irish and rid the country of its popish religion, Britain had strengthened its Penal Laws. These laws discriminated against Catholics, even to the point of forbidding the celebration of the Mass. England extended these laws to its colonies in America. Catholics, although few in number, were forbidden to own land or hold office in the New World. Without land, they could not build churches or schools. In

**343**

### For Heaven's Sake!

Don't think the New World was a hot bed of religious liberty! For instance, the colony of Maryland was founded in 1632 as a haven for persecuted English Catholics. Twenty years later, Puritans seized control of it and ended religious toleration for them. It took many years for the Catholic religion to be secure in the colonies.

spite of the prejudice they faced in colonial America, Catholics joined their Protestant neighbors in the revolution. They had a specific interest in it because their religious survival was being threatened. They became fervent supporters of independence.

With the winning of the Revolutionary War and the ratification of the Constitution in 1789, the Catholic Church was able to officially establish its first diocese, which it did in Baltimore, Maryland. The Catholic Church then elected the first U.S. bishop, John Carroll.

As Catholics began to own land and start businesses, they came to be regarded as good citizens, and as a result, their Protestant neighbors more readily accepted them. For the first time, Catholics felt welcome in the new United States. All that would change, however, during the nineteenth century, when Catholic immigrants began to arrive in record numbers, upsetting what had been a delicate balance.

## Coming in Droves: The Immigrant Experience

The words *foreign, Catholic,* and *poor* became synonymous in the minds of the original Protestant settlers. If you think of how the host body fights to reject foreign matter that enters it in biological life, you can imagine the relationship of "native" Protestants to "foreign" Catholics entering the United States in the nineteenth century.

The story of immigration is found in the population statistics. During the century after 1790, the Catholic population grew from a mere 1.1 percent to a significant 14.4 percent. Most of these immigrants were Irish or German, and they tended to congregate in the cities. The number of foreign-born Catholics in major U.S. cities was staggering:

➤ Philadelphia: 30 percent

➤ New York: 49 percent

➤ Chicago: 50 percent

➤ St. Louis: 60 percent

Catholic Hispanics, French, Irish, and Germans immigrated to the United States in significant numbers during the first part of the 1800s. Italy, Poland, and Eastern Europe sent even more Catholics at the end of the 1800s and the beginning of the 1900s.

**344**

Over two million Italians and more than a million Poles and Eastern Europeans came to the United States between 1900 and 1925. These immigrants formed ethnic neighborhoods and parishes often staffed by the clergy and nuns who accompanied them in their migration. They built schools, convents, hospitals, and orphanages. These neighborhoods still characterize cities such as Chicago, St. Louis, and New York.

Due to the U.S farmers' need for harvesters between the 1920s and 1960s, Mexican Catholics increased their migration to the United States. In the 1970s and 1980s, Catholic refugees from Vietnam, Cambodia, Laos, Guatemala, El Salvador, Nicaragua, and Haiti came to the United States as a result of political unrest in their home countries.

**Your Guardian Angel**

You can still visit ethnic neighborhood churches in most United States cities. These churches will often be dedicated to a saint that was part of the people's religious history. St. Boniface in St. Louis is an example of a parish for the German community.

## Potatoes, Poverty, and Discrimination

The Irish potato crop failures in the late 1840's sent huge waves of Irish, most of whom were Catholic, to the United States. In a relatively short period of time, Ireland's population was reduced by half. Thousands died of starvation at home, and many more died in the "coffin" ships that brought them to America. Over five million Irish have emigrated to the United States.

If you were living in New York in 1840, imagine how you would react to the dirty, disease-ridden ships as they pulled into the harbor and disgorged their cargo of impoverished, illiterate, and often desperate people onto the streets in staggering numbers. Barely able to hold on to their lives, much less a job, these immigrants created an incredible strain on the existing population, posing a real threat to social stability and the economy. The reaction of the citizens to this overwhelming situation was unfortunate but predictable.

Political cartoons, rampant discrimination, derogatory literature, and even physical assaults occurred. By the end of the century, acts of political and economic discrimination were prevalent. For a time in Philadelphia, the bishop had to close all the Catholic churches, dispensing people from their Sunday obligation in order to protect his flock from physical harm. Protestants were attacking and burning the churches primarily in reaction to the Catholics' challenge of the use of the Protestant version of the Bible in the city's schools.

In New York, the bishop armed his Catholic flocks with stones and brickbats for some of the first and most severe urban riots the United States has ever experienced. The sheer numbers of Irish Catholic immigrants, their poverty, and the perceived threat to the Protestant Bible laid the groundwork for the next century of prejudice.

### Epiphanies

After the Protestant Reformation, English-speaking Protestants used their translation of the Bible known as the King James version. As we discussed in Chapter 7, "The Bible," the Protestant Bible differs somewhat from the Catholic version. Public schools of the day used the King James Bible and prayed Protestant prayers, sang Protestant hymns, and required attendance at Protestant services. This situation made Catholic children feel like second-class citizens.

A national political party, popularly known as the Know-Nothings, was formed in the middle of the nineteenth century to oppose Catholics and other foreigners. Their standard-bearer, Millard Fillmore, was a former president of the United States. Several state legislatures had a significant number of Know-Nothing representatives who passed many laws discriminating against Catholics and their schools. One of the most notorious of these laws was the Convent Inspection law. This law required nuns to open their doors to state-appointed committees to ensure that no woman was being held there against her will. During the immigration of Italians and Poles at the turn of the century, the infamous Ku Klux Klan widened its scope to include anti-Catholicism.

Despite the difficult situations the Irish faced in settling in their new home, they survived and strongly influenced the character of the Catholic Church in America, not only by their sheer numbers, but also by their indomitable spirit. They brought a love of family, a sense of humor, and a deep respect for the clergy. Since they lacked other political representation, they elevated their priests to the status of the old tribal chieftains of their beloved homeland.

## Sauerkraut and Sausages: Germanic Education and Liturgy

German Catholics also had a strong influence on the course of Catholic history and culture in the United States. At one time, the German immigrants instituted a movement whose purpose was to make German a second language in the public schools. When this movement failed, they turned to an alternative. They began to promote and champion what was then only a small movement, the Catholic school system, to preserve their language and culture.

An abiding question for the church during this time of growth and adjustment was just how much it should participate in the dominant Protestant U.S. culture. There were those who favored assimilation and those who fought to keep the church separate. The hierarchy spent much time in its national meetings debating the "school question," that is, whether or not Catholic children could be educated and retain the Catholic faith in the "common" or public schools. By the end of the century the question was decided at the Third Council of Baltimore. With German agitation and support from Rome, the council decided that every parish had to build a Catholic school and that parents had to send their children to the Catholic school under the sanction of mortal sin.

As the twentieth century began, the only question Catholics had about their schools was how good they could make them. As Garry Wills points out, the decision of Baltimore III had many implications: It meant that a poor body of immigrants would make great sacrifices to build their own school system, and with no support from the taxes they paid to build the public school system. It meant that a massive work force of religious nuns and brothers would be recruited and trained, not to be contemplatives or instructors of the upper classes as in Europe, but to be teachers of all classes. It meant that nuns would have as much if not more formative influence on young Catholics as priests did. It meant that U.S. Catholicism would be child-centered with a feminine piety. And, most significantly, it meant that the church would concentrate most of its resources on this system.

For the first two thirds of the twentieth century Catholicism could be described as "the Church that was a School." The Irish-dominated hierarchy granted an important concession to German immigrants and to other non–English-speaking Catholics who longed to hear the sound of their faith expressed through the prayers and hymns of their mother tongue. They permitted the establishment of *national parishes,* which are parishes based on ethnicity rather than geography. Germans and other non–English-speaking Catholics were able to keep their language both in the schools and in the churches.

If you were a German-speaking Catholic, you were allowed to become a member of a German-speaking parish, which might lie outside the normal parish boundaries for your home. By 1912, there were more than 1,600 national parishes: 346 German, 336 Polish, and 214 Italian. Today, as a remnant of this policy, you might find two Catholic churches standing side by side: one that served an English-speaking Catholic congregation and the other that served a German-speaking one.

Another contribution made by the German Catholics are the monasteries in the heartland of Indiana and Minnesota, where the vibrant Catholic liturgy was kept alive for this country. The German tradition of monasteries goes back over 1,000 years to the time of St. Boniface.

**S'ter Says**

A **national parish** is a parish that is not based on geographic boundaries, but which belongs to an ethnic group. Such parishes, where English was the second language, were common in the United States during the years of immigration.

### For Heaven's Sake!

Don't think the term *mixed marriage* always meant a marriage between a Catholic and a non-Catholic. Indeed, in the 1860s, Catholics would have called the joining of an Irish Catholic and German Catholic a mixed marriage.

# Poles, Pierogi, and Patriotism

Large-scale Polish immigration to the United States began in the 1870s. The early settlers attended Irish or German Catholic parishes until they could found their own. Soon however, they established lay committees to raise funds and lobby the bishops to provide Polish parishes and schools. With the parish came other Polish organizations providing insurance for illness and death, promoting Polish religious observances, and sponsoring youth activities.

Polish financial contributions were among the highest in the U.S. Catholic Church. In 1870, there were about 15 Polish parishes; by 1930, there were more than 800. By 1920, there were more than 400 Polish American Catholic schools, and more than two thirds of Polish American children attended them. The role of the Polish priest was that of the undisputed religious and civic leader. He was spiritual leader, temporal leader, teacher, legal counselor, business advisor, and mediator between the immigrant and American society. In the parish schools, classes were generally taught in Polish, and English was taught as a foreign language.

U.S. church authorities exercised strict control over national parishes. They demanded title to all property and the authority to assign priests. This denial of lay participation in decision-making conflicted with the Polish experience of Catholicism back home. It also conflicted with their dreams of American democracy. A foreign, mainly Irish, clergy and hierarchy controlled the most important Polish institution in America, the parish church. Despite Polish pleas for the appointment of Polish American bishops, it was not until 1908 that the first Pole was ordained. He was an assistant bishop to the archbishop in Chicago.

By 1904, however, several Polish priests and parishioners had seceded from the Catholic Church and formed what later would become the Polish National Catholic Church, which does not accept the pope as its head. This church immediately began to celebrate Mass in Polish, added "the word of God, heard and preached" as a sacrament, and permitted priests to marry. Currently, this church has four dioceses in North America with more than 150 parishes. This was the first schism, or independent movement, in the U.S. Catholic experience. Presently, talks between the Polish Catholic Church and the Roman Catholic Church are underway in the hope of possible reunification.

Although the overwhelming number of Polish American priests and parishioners remained members of the Catholic Church, Poles, perhaps more than any other ethnic group, saw the mission of the church as the transmission of a Polish identity to an increasingly Americanized and secularized group of Polish immigrants. In 1980, only

38 percent of German national parishes were still functioning, but more than 75 percent of Polish national churches were. Today, Poles are the fastest growing immigrant group in Chicago and continue to swell the ranks of U.S. Catholicism.

## Italians, Pasta, and Festa

In 1870, Rome, the last vestige of the papal states, fell, and the pope retaliated by forbidding Italian Catholics to participate in national politics. The Vatican denied recognition to the kingdom of Italy. With the accompanying political, social, and economic unrest, millions of Italians left their homeland. By 1900, more than 100,000 Italians were migrating annually to the United States. Four fifths of these immigrants were from southern Italy, and 75 percent of those who came were working-age males. For the most part, these immigrants were poor and illiterate.

### Saints Preserve Us

**St. Frances Xavier Cabrini, November 13, Patron of Immigrants**

Born into a farming family in Italy, the youngest of 13 children, St. Frances Xavier Cabrini (1850–1917) founded a religious order called the Missionary Sisters of the Sacred Heart of Jesus. She sailed to New York with Italian immigrants in 1898 and opened Columbus Hospital there. She became a citizen in 1909 and took her works of mercy to all parts of the United States. At the time of her death, 3,000 of her nuns lived in 70 convents. She founded more than 50 hospitals, schools, and orphanages. She is the first American citizen to be canonized a saint, and she is the patron of immigrants.

The Irish-dominated church in the United States saw as its task to make these Italian immigrants into church-going, law-abiding Catholics who would demonstrate to U.S. Protestants the compatibility of Catholicism and American patriotism. Their aim was assimilation. Few Italian priests migrated to the United States, and those who did were generally not accepted by the American bishops, who regarded them as incompetent and avaricious. It wasn't until 1954 that the first Sicilian-born bishop was ordained in the United States. It was mainly the Italian religious orders, such as the Franciscans and the Scalabrini Fathers (a special order that was founded in 1887 to minister to immigrants), who served as missionaries to the Italian Americans.

### Your Guardian Angel

You can attend the annual **festas,** commemorations of the patron saints of particular villages or areas of Italy, in many United States cities. They are popular citywide celebrations. Perhaps the best known is the feast of San Gennaro in New York, which runs for 11 days in September, and attracts over three million visitors.

### For Heaven's Sake!

You make a mistake if you think that Africa hasn't played an important role in the Catholic Church from the beginning. Sts. Augustine, his mother Monica, Benedict the Moor, Moses the Black, Cyril of Alexandria and Simon of Cyrene who helped Jesus carry his cross were all African. So were three popes!

The assimilation goals of the U.S. Catholic Church succeeded with the Italian immigrants. They stand in marked contrast to Italians in Italy, who are not regular churchgoers and are at times downright anticlerical. They take great pride in the many Italian American Catholic men and women who serve the United States as mayors, governors, cabinet members, and members of the Supreme Court.

## African Americans, Soul Food, Clapping, and Justice

Catholicism is the largest religion in the world for people of African descent, and there are more than 200 million black Catholics worldwide. However, Catholics make up less than 6 percent of the population of African Americans. Presently, there are 2.3 million black Catholics in the United States. The history of African American Catholics goes back to the oldest Spanish settlement in the United States: St. Augustine, Florida in 1565.

The church's relationship with its African American members has not always been ideal. The church's position on slavery was disturbingly conservative and cautious. For example, the bishop of Philadelphia during the time just before the Civil War stated that he regretted the consequences of slavery, but at the same time, he cautioned his church members that the public law must be obeyed. Catholic landowners, including priests, owned black slaves as early as the 1600s. The practice was not widespread, but it continued until the end of the Civil War. On the positive side, the pope sent missionaries to the United States from England to open the schools and seminaries to black membership. Also, some bishops, like the bishop of Cincinnati, used his religious authority to call for emancipation.

By the late 1800s, the black Catholic population was approximately 200,000 out of a total black population of 7 million. There were 20 churches, each with its own primary school, and 65 other schools. The schools were staffed primarily by two orders: the Oblate Sisters of Providence in Baltimore, Maryland, founded by Elizabeth Lange, and the Sisters of the Holy Family in New Orleans, Louisiana, led by Henriette Delille and Juliette Gaudin.

Father Patrick Healy, Ph.D., born in 1830 of an Irish father and a mother who was an emancipated slave was the first free-born African American priest. This remarkable man became the president of Georgetown University in 1868. Born in 1854, Father Augustine Tolton was the first slave-born priest in the United States. Because no American seminary would permit his entrance, he was educated and ordained in Rome. Upon completion of his studies, he was supposed to be sent to work in Africa. In a surprise decision and possibly to test the United State's claims of being an enlightened nation, Rome sent him to America. He served in a parish in Quincy, Illinois and later in Chicago.

Today, although still under-represented in the Church hierarchy, African Americans are visible in all areas of the U.S. Catholic Church. There are 14 African American bishops in the United States, and about 500 priests. Their presence, and the presence of many other black leaders (deacons, sisters, seminary professors, and heads of religious communities), has created many positive results. Their lively liturgies are a joyful expression of the African soul. Their commitment to justice is a living example of the church "walking its talk" on a variety of social issues. The emergence of an effective cadre of Black Catholic scholars has resulted in the following contributions:

➤ Insights about black culture and black theology have been introduced into mainstream scholarship.

➤ Ministry to black parishes and social programs has increased.

➤ A new emphasis on black lay leadership and spiritual formation has developed.

➤ Strides to end racism in the church have been made.

As a result of the efforts of these black scholars and others working for racial equality in the church, a hymnal entitled *Guide Me: The African-American Catholic Hymnal* was published in 1987. That same year, the first Black Catholic congress in the twentieth century was held in Washington, D.C. Shortly afterward, Catholic bishops issued a pastoral letter on racism called "Brothers and Sisters to Us," and the black bishops issued their own pastoral letter on evangelization, "What We Have Seen and Heard."

Perhaps the ministry valued most by the African Americans is the church's commitment to inner-city Catholic schools. Big-city dioceses heavily subsidize education for African Americans who make great sacrifices to enroll their children. Religious affiliation is not a requirement of acceptance into these schools. In fact, the number of Catholics enrolled is under 30 percent in some schools. Nor are these schools seen as a means of Catholic proselytization. These schools are a perfect fit between a Catholic Church that values good teaching and African Americans who value good education.

# Infallibility in the Land of Liberty

The nineteenth century, the intense time of Catholic immigration, was a difficult time for the church in Europe. The monarchies of Europe began to fall as governments transformed into modern nations. The mutually beneficial relationship between

**S'ter Says**

**Modernism** was a heresy condemned by the pope in 1907. The term refers to the church's condemnation of modern scientific thinking that said truth changed. The church believed truth was eternal and unchanging. Up until 1967, Catholic priests were required to take an oath against modernism.

church and state, which Constantine had formed with the church way back in the 300s, was long gone. The key question for the church became how to exist in the age of democracy and nation-states. What would its new relationship to the world be?

Since the Council of Trent in the mid-1500s, the church had less and less influence in the world of politics. It went its way, and the culture went another. The world looked to science rather than religion for truth. The church reacted by dismissing the progress of the world. It wouldn't accept new ideas, scientific developments, or the fact that its own truth and doctrine evolves. It was protesting against what it called *modernism*. Modernism is a term used to describe the fact that people had turned to the world rather than religion to solve their problems; they became self-sufficient.

The church took a strong stance against the modern culture, especially on any of the emerging notions of religious freedom. It developed a defensive attitude.

This stance came to a head in a declaration of papal infallibility in 1870 at the First Vatican Council. This teaching said that the pope has the special protection of the Holy Spirit and cannot err when he officially defines a doctrine of the faith or moral behavior.

In sharp contrast to Rome, many of the U.S. bishops opposed the definition of papal infallibility. For over 100 years, the U.S. bishops had carefully woven relations with their Protestant neighbors to prove that Catholicism was not contrary to democracy. Papal infallibility would only lend fodder to the feelings of anti-Catholicism that were just beginning to tone down.

Due to the threat of war in Europe at that time, several bishops sailed home early from the council and did not register their votes before leaving, so the true extent of disagreement may never be known. Fifty-five bishops signed a letter to the pope saying they would absent themselves in order to avoid voting against it. However, two negative votes were cast. One was by the bishop of Little Rock in the United States. The headlines at home read: "Little Rock Attacks Big Rock." "Rock" refers to Jesus' statement to Peter, "Upon this Rock, I will build my church," which is the scripture passage on which Catholics based the supremacy of the pope.

The doctrine of infallibility gave the church a feeling of internal security and perhaps the sense of regaining some of its lost power. However, it further alienated the church from a secular world that generally found such a position totally untenable. As Catholicism came kicking and screaming into the twentieth century, the church became trapped by its own absolutism. The transforming event of Vatican II was yet to come. It would teach the church to embrace the world's development and accept change as a fact.

# A Checkered Church Solidifies

If you look at a penny, you'll find imprinted upon it the Latin phrase *E Pluribus Unum*, "one people out of many," which became the motto of the United States. If the Catholic Church in the United States minted its own pennies, they might read *E Pluribus Unum Catholicum*: "one Catholic Church out of many people." The U.S. Catholic Church faced a major challenge, namely to maintain an essential Catholic identity characterized by oneness under Rome within a culturally diverse America. This Catholic identity was fed by a diversity of ethnic customs, with an emphasis on emotional practices and devotions of the faith, such as celebrations of Mary, feast days of saints, novenas, public processions, and benedictions. Immigrant Catholicism was characterized by dependency on clerical authority and strong ties to Rome.

**For Heaven's Sake!**

Don't think sheer numbers created a Catholic culture in the United States. By 1850, the Catholic Church was the largest single denomination. However, the character of the culture in the United States remained Protestant well into the twentieth century.

The Catholics' first experience in the United States was a positive one. In the American Revolution, they won their freedom of religion and the right to own property. They ended the nineteenth century in great numbers, but rejected by the larger society. The Catholic reaction was to develop a siege mentality and form a cultural fortress within the cities. The Irish had broken the ground of immigration in the new country. The next waves of immigrants, the Germans, the Italians, the Poles, and the Eastern Europeans, benefited from this groundbreaking, but they also inherited the anti-Catholicism that was so strong in this century.

# Immigrant Catholics Dig In

By the 1920s, Catholics made up 25 percent of the U.S. population, and this figure remains the same today. In the first half of the century, the church focused on securing its internal structures, unifying its practices, and firming up its relationship with its new home, the United States.

Catholics, who had been persecuted in the last century, now became champions of what America could become and what a Catholic immigrant could become in America. Catholics and Protestants had resolved some of their differences, having bonded in the foxholes of World War I. Protestants and Catholics, who might have had differences at home, found themselves fighting side by side. Catholics, whose patriotism had been doubted, proved by their action in war that they were true Americans. The war had the effect of leveling differences between Americans.

Protestants, still the majority, began to open economic and social doors to Catholics, and Catholics saw in America the best chance for the church since Jesus told the apostles to go out and baptize all nations. It seemed that the seeds that Jesus planted were coming to fruition in the United States.

## 353

### Epiphanies

Al Smith, a Democrat, was governor of New York. In 1928, he became the first Catholic to run for the presidency. He lost to Herbert Hoover in a campaign marred by anti-Catholic bigotry. The slogan "A vote for Smith is a vote for the Pope" was frequently heard. Born on the Lower East Side of Manhattan, Smith used to joke that he graduated from the Fulton Fish Market. Smith made a commitment to religious liberty and freedom of conscience.

## Roots of Anti-Communism

Many of the immigrants who came to the United States after World War I came from a Europe that was birthing Communism. The church found itself face to face with an ideology that rejected all religion. For almost 400 years, the Catholic Church had withdrawn from the world, distancing itself from the needs of the common people. Communism rose to fill that void, and it had no use for God or the Catholic Church. In the first papal letter in modern time dealing directly with social issues, the pope called the church back to the needs of the people. He proposed a Catholic stand on the conditions of the working class that contrasted with Communism.

### Your Guardian Angel

Pray for world peace! Since the 1950s, there had been a Catholic practice of praying three Our Fathers, three Hail Marys, and three Glory Bes for the conversion of Russia. The formal practice ended, but you might keep world peace in your prayers.

## Catholic Prosperity

Although Catholicism prospered, it still remained separate from the mainstream. Instead of merging into the public American world, Catholics built a parallel world of Catholic-run hospitals, orphanages, and welfare agencies that provided food, heating fuel, clothing, and money. There were homes for the aged, schools from elementary through university levels, professional organizations, social charities, and even cemeteries.

During the 1950s, a Catholic building boom exploded across America. Catholic churches and schools filled the land from Maine to California. In numbers never before experienced in the history of the church, Catholic parents sent their sons and daughters into religious service as priests, sisters, and brothers. They became the work force that built the strong identity of the Catholic tribe in the United States. Upwards of 70 percent of Catholics attended church every Sunday, and one half of all Catholic children were educated in parish schools. In the evenings, families across the country gathered around their radios to listen to Father Peyton broadcast the family Rosary. Bishop Sheen delivered his weekly TV message to millions of Catholics and Protestants. The Catholic Church was comfortable in the 1950s.

**Your Guardian Angel**

The family that prays together stays together! This phrase was made popular in the 1950s by Father Patrick Peyton's radio program, during which the Rosary was broadcast.

## "Perfect" Catholic Citizens

Every Catholic classroom in the United States displayed an American flag, a picture of the president of the United States, and a picture of the pope. Class began with prayers, followed by the Pledge of Allegiance and four verses of "My Country 'Tis of Thee." Students were taught that good citizenship was an important part of good Catholicism. There was an optimistic spirit and a sense of well-being that went with being a Catholic in America. An entire generation had climbed out of the poverty of the immigrant years and could now put money away for their children to attend Catholic colleges. The spirit of the day seemed to say to Catholics that they surely were in the right place at the right time. It fostered their belief that they were citizens of the one true country and that they held the one, true faith.

## The Loss of Innocence

In 1960, in a history-making event, John Fitzgerald Kennedy was elected to the highest office in the land, which further fanned the fires of Catholic faith. The odds of Kennedy, a Catholic, winning the nomination and then the presidency of the United States were poor to say the least. Anytime a Catholic aspired to public office, anti-Catholicism showed itself to be lurking just below the surface. Although Catholics had certainly achieved a respectable number in the population, they could not elect a president by themselves. Any candidate would have to win a considerable Protestant vote to make that happen. Protestants feared that a Catholic's allegiance to the church in Rome superceded allegiance to the United States Constitution.

In a famous speech to the Houston Ministerial Alliance, candidate Kennedy convinced his audience that this fear was unfounded. He was elected by the most narrow of margins, showing the world that Catholics had "made it," even if just barely. Kennedy was bright, attractive, and promised Americans that life would be good. In so doing, he redeemed a generation of older Catholics from the humiliation of Al Smith's brutal defeat in 1928.

Bubbling beneath the surface of society, however, were stewpots of unrest. As those pots began to boil over in the decade of the 60s, the certainty of the 1950s gave way to questions for all Americans. This experience would ultimately affect Catholics as well. The changes during this decade challenged accepted notions of what it meant to be a United States citizen and what it meant to be a Catholic.

Kennedy's assassination after just 1,000 days in office, along with the assassinations of other political and religious leaders—Martin Luther King Jr., Robert Kennedy, and Malcolm X—in the years that followed, abruptly ended the innocence of the time and set the nation spinning. For Catholics, it was an especially tough time. The changes in society seemed to go against every tenet of their faith: the use of drugs, protest against the government's involvement in Southeast Asia, the sexual revolution, the advent of the birth control pill, and the possible legalization of abortion. Their identification as the new carriers of America's promise to become the "New Jerusalem" was being sorely tested.

# Catholics Come of Age

Jack Kennedy broke through the religious barrier and seemed to free Catholics' access to higher office. If you examine the lists of the candidates nominated for president or vice-president during the '60s, '70s, and '80s, it seems that it was almost a requirement to include a Catholic on the ticket: Tom Eagleton, Sargent Shriver, James Miller, and Geraldine Ferraro are all examples of prominent Catholic candidates. The numbers of Catholics in the president's cabinet continued to grow, and their leadership in Congress increased.

Social research showed that Catholics were among the best-educated people in the United States. They were capturing major executive positions in business, and they were moving to the suburbs. What had been a poor, immigrant, illiterate, disempowered minority who had built a Catholic fortress was now truly becoming an organization of the first citizens of the land.

In the 1960s, however, Catholics received a double whammy. Vatican II was called to take a serious look at the definition of church. It created questions in the minds of many Catholics. In so doing, it knocked out a major pillar they had come to rely on: the notion that their church was the perfect church, the one true church. In the political arena, anti-war and anti-patriotic demonstrations in the form of burning flags and draft cards knocked out another pillar that held up many citizens: the idea that the United State was the perfect state. These two blows shook the U.S. Catholic identity. The 30 years since the crumbling of these pillars has been a tough time of reconstruction.

# Movin' on Up

For Catholics, moving into the suburbs meant moving away from the tight-knit, ethnic neighborhood parishes. In the suburbs, Catholics lived side by side with "other"

Americans. Often, the parochial school did not follow them to their new suburban parishes. This happened for a couple of reasons. Although Catholic wealth increased dramatically, the cost of building new schools increased even more dramatically. In addition, the suburban public schools that served these Catholics were extremely well-financed and clearly superior to the schools in the cities from which the Catholics had come. Catholics who now had their sights set on upward mobility would turn to these public schools for the sake of socially and financially bettering their offspring. It became clear that post-Vatican II Catholicism would no longer be primarily fostered in a Catholic classroom.

At the time of Vatican II in the 1960s, there was a massive system of primary, secondary, and higher education with the Catholic University of America in Washington, D.C. as the capstone. By the 1990's, however, enrollment had dropped from its high water mark of 5.5 million grade and high school students to 2.5 million children, reflecting Vatican II's openness to the culture.

## The Transference of Leadership: The Baton Is Passed

Not only did the profile of parishioners change in the 30 years following Vatican II, but so, too, did the leadership. The council introduced a new word to Catholicism: ministry. In the 1960s and 1970s, as the clerical and religious leadership began to digest Vatican II, they saw a new opportunity to serve in the church. Nuns, whose work had largely been confined to education and health care, went back to school and retooled themselves for work as *pastoral ministers,* rather than schoolteachers. In their absence, both the teaching core and the leadership of Catholic parochial grade schools and high schools shifted to the control of the lay members of the church.

Throughout the church's history, walls had existed between the clergy and the people. Vatican II seriously challenged this division between the sacred and the secular. Consequently, a great number of priests and sisters re-examined their state in life and the basis on which they had made the choice to "leave the world." Priests left the priesthood, and sisters and brothers left the religious life in great numbers. The post-Vatican II climate affected the new supply of leadership coming into the church as well. Enrollment in seminaries by the end of the 1960s plummeted in a more dramatic fashion than the stock market crash of 1929. In 1960 there were 41,000 U.S. seminarians. By 1995, that number was down to 4,500. On the other hand, while in 1960 there were few lay people preparing for professional ministry, in 1985, there were 10,500, and by 1996 that number had almost doubled.

**S'ter Says**

**Pastoral ministers** is the term used in the Catholic Church since Vatican II to describe church workers who have taken on various roles that once were filled by priests.

Vatican II gave the Catholic Church a new character. For the first time in its history, it was forced to find ways to tolerate dissent. This change took place during the information age, which meant that every move of the council was reported around the world. Lifting the veil of secrecy from a church council allowed everyone to see the significant amount of debate and contention that goes on when leaders deal with the word of God. The openness and the intensity of the debates at Vatican II confirmed that dissent was not only possible, but also invigorating.

Although dissent might seem like a negative result, just the opposite was true. Today, the Catholic Church, especially in the United States, is more vibrant and alive than ever. As to parish leadership, a 1990s survey showed that more than 20,000 lay people and sisters are now functioning in professional, pastoral roles that in the 1960s would have primarily been filled by priests. The nonordained serve at the level of diocesan leadership as well as in such positions as chancellor (manager of the bishop's office), chief financial officer of the diocese, and judges in diocesan church courts. Women comprise more than 85 percent of this leadership. Administrative and pastoral responsibilities in the post-Vatican II church in the United States have become virtually female arenas.

The Catholic Church represents a broad spectrum of beliefs today. There are those small groups that tenaciously reject the changes, but a Gallup Poll survey of Catholics in the 1990s provides the following data:

➤ Eighty-seven percent believe the church should end the ban on artificial birth control.

➤ Sixty-seven percent favor the ordination of women to the priesthood.

➤ Eighty percent favor ordination of women as deacons.

➤ Seventy percent would allow priests to marry.

Several polls show that opinions among Catholics are not very different from those of Protestants on the issue of abortion, but are opposed to the position taken by Rome.

## Catholicism's Emerging Identity

Catholic identity is less and less defined by specific practices such as abstaining from meat on Friday, going to weekly confession on Saturday, or attending Mass every Sunday. Catholics are continuing these practices out of choice, not obligation. Present-day Catholic identity is shaping itself in a myriad of ways. Catholicism is no longer the "one-size-fits-all" model of the past. There is much greater personal liberty in moral decision-making. Both liberal and conservative activism is much more pronounced. The spirit of religious freedom from Vatican II has for the most part ended the notion that only those who accepted the Catholic Church as the one true faith could be saved. Church authorities are no longer seen as the final word. Today's dissenters do not leave the church; they stay on their own terms.

For many in this country, the post-Vatican II church captured a spirit of justice and gave voice to hope. Idealism among Catholic youth today finds its outlet not just in the few who might enter religious life. A large number of Catholic young people join programs such as the Peace Corps, Jesuit Volunteer Corps, and hundreds of other volunteer programs sponsored by the church and religious orders. It is typical for these young people to spend a year or two living a life of poverty in service to the community. They feed the hungry, work with the homeless and jobless, teach skills to inner-city children, and become a witness for justice and civil rights in many arenas. The Jesuit Volunteer motto, "Ruined for Life," is an apt description of the countercultural transformation that these young people undergo. As they reenter the culture from which they came, they do so with a value system that is remarkably different than the norm.

In the spirit of Vatican II, the U.S. bishops reorganized themselves as a national body. Since Vatican II, they have met in sessions one or even two times each year. A primary focus of the sessions is the internal operation of the church, but the sessions have become a platform for *prophetic* teaching as well. Prophetic teachings from the bishops' councils include the pastoral letter on peace and nuclear warfare and the pastoral letter on the economy, to name just two.

In the years following Vatican II, however, a return to centralization has been noticed. This centralization seems to be in conflict with the Vatican II call for a sharing of power. Present church leadership seems intent on restoring the old model of authority. Many of the decisions in the years since Vatican II have reversed the directives to share control, especially with the bishops in their various countries and cultures.

**Your Guardian Angel**

Traditional prayers and practices such as fasting and abstinence from meat on Friday during Lent are still very much a part of the religion. However, private expressions of the faith are also being encouraged.

**S'ter Says**

**Prophetic** tradition has its origins in the Bible with the prophets of the Old Testament. They were people in the community who warned others about the consequences of their actions. Some of the prophets were Isaiah, Jeremiah, Amos, and Micah.

At times even the simplest of issues, such as the use of inclusive language in the English translation of the Mass, have had to go back to the top at Rome rather than being decided locally where the Mass is being said. Seemingly, Rome is reversing Vatican II through its appointment of bishops. As the progressive bishops who served at Vatican II retire, conservative bishops who work from the top-down model of decision-making replace them. For the most part, the Catholic Church is a revitalized church, with more participation at deeper levels than ever before, perhaps since its very earliest days with Jesus.

We've seen how the church was brought to the United States with the immigrants, how it became accepted, and how it eventually became mainstream. In the next chapter, we'll look at some of the challenges the church faces and opportunities it offers in the new millennium. We'll address the question of what will the church look like?

---

### The Least You Need to Know

➤ An American checkered church characterizes the growth of Catholicism in the United States.

➤ Immigrants from Ireland, Germany, Italy, Poland, Mexico, and many other countries have contributed their cultural traditions to the United States Catholic Church.

➤ *E Pluribus Unum Catholicum:* One church out of many people would be a good motto for the Catholic Church in the United States.

➤ The results of Vatican II are more participation in the church by greater numbers of people.

# Chapter 25

---

# Face to Face in the Third Millennium: The Church Looks to the Future

We've looked at the church from its very earliest years up to the present time. We've seen how it is both a product of the culture and an instrument to transform it. Each age presented different situations, and the church had to grow and change to maintain itself as an effective institution in the world. The new millennium has its own set of challenges. In this chapter, we'll take a look at some of them and identify resources within the church that can be used to respond to these challenges creatively.

## Recap: Past, Present, and Future

First, let's quickly recap the 2,000-year history of the Catholic Church, highlighting some of the major events we've covered in the book. The Catholic Church began with the experiences of a small group of people around Jerusalem who followed Jesus. Two thousand years later, it now has over one billion members located in every country of the world. The church has experienced dramatic and profound changes: expulsion from Judaism, persecution, and then expansion and growth into Europe. We have seen how the church succumbed to the temptations of power in the "good times," which led to its corruption and the painful splits of the Orthodox and Protestant churches, followed by its own reformation. We've seen how the Catholic Church lost its political stronghold as the monarchies of Europe fell to more modern governments. We've seen how the church came to the New World and how democracy has begun to shape the church.

Democracy's influence on the church became clear when Vatican II set the task of looking to the culture to learn from it. As we enter the third thousand years of Catholicism, and the church follows that directive, what are the lessons or challenges the society will be offering it?

There are several issues on the forefront. Today, we hear the term *globalization* in almost every area of life. We hear about global education, global communication, and global economy to name just a few. How will the church respond to globalization and the diversity it brings?

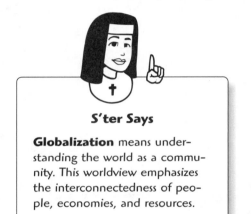

**S'ter Says**

**Globalization** means understanding the world as a community. This worldview emphasizes the interconnectedness of people, economies, and resources.

In the United States, women have moved into the mainstream in almost every political and social sector, with the notable exception of the Catholic Church, where the key positions of leadership remain unavailable to women. How will the church respond to the inevitable feminization of this previously all-male bastion?

As church membership moves away from defining itself by adherence to tightly bound beliefs and strict rules of behavior, it moves toward a more spiritual understanding of the human journey. Indeed, 4 out of every 10 people in the United States meet at least monthly in some sort of a small group that defines its purpose as a spiritual quest. This is a startling shift from a few years ago, representing a transformation not only of our sense of community but also of our sense of the spiritual. As people take more responsibility for their spirituality and become more personally involved, self-motivated, and self-directed, they will challenge the church to look at the relationship between religion and spirituality. What resources does the church have to meet these needs?

The ultimate survival of the church, of course, depends on the generations to come. As we close this book, we'll look at what the church of the future might be like as it meets the challenges of the next generation.

# The Paradigm Shift

Underlying the challenges and changes we have just described is a cultural shift that is as powerful as a shift in Earth's geological plates. It is one of those major events that happen periodically throughout history after which nothing is the same. The 1960s brought a new phrase into common vocabulary, the *paradigm shift*. A *paradigm* is a way of doing things; it is an organizing principle upon which a society is formed.

For example, the dominant paradigm for education in U.S. culture is to send children to school. In tribal societies, children learn by their association with their elders. That is the paradigm for education in those societies.

There are paradigms, or models, for education, economics, politics, and even religion. A paradigm shows how a whole culture is organized. For example, we talked about how our society is organized on a hierarchical paradigm. You might remember the illustration we used of a ladder and the alternative paradigm we gave of a circle in Chapter 6, "'It's Elementary, My Dear Watson.'" Each paradigm meets certain needs, carries certain values, and creates an identity.

For a very long time, the church had an identity as "The City of God." When it thought of itself this way, it exhibited certain values. For example, it felt it had to be above the world, which it considered to be less perfect. It assumed a position as better than the other cultures or societies around it. It saw itself as the teacher and the people as the learners. As we have seen, in this paradigm or core identity, the church often found itself pitted against the culture.

## Church as "The People of God"

As we discussed in Chapter 5, "The '60s: Seeds of Revolution," Catholicism took a new direction. It shifted from seeing itself as the only means of salvation and began to view all humanity as "the people of God." This new approach represented a paradigm shift in the church and with this shift came different values and different ways of relating to the world.

The old paradigm, from which both the church and the culture are moving away, involves the model we inherited from Greek thinking. This model understands matter and spirit as separate. It sees the church as separate from the culture. In this model, the world is nonspiritual, which is why it's also called a mechanical worldview. *Mechanical* means that the material world has no spirit or Godliness; it runs like a machine, for example, a clock that is wound up and then runs on its own. In that model, God exists outside the human experience and outside of the world. In the mechanical worldview, creation is an object, existing as a creation of God, but without containing God's spirit.

In the old paradigm, humans are a unique creation. Their material bodies have been infused with a soul, or God's spirit, which exists separate from the body. Because humans are the only creatures with spirit in this worldview, they have power over everything that is not human.

**Your Guardian Angel**

Prayer is an equal opportunity event! According to Vatican II, the new image of the church challenges any notions of spiritual elitism, which have been fostered by differences in clergy and lay people. The spirituality of the common people is not to be considered in any way lesser than priestly, religious, or monastic spirituality.

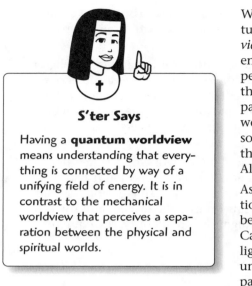

We are calling the new paradigm or worldview quantum, in contrast to mechanical. This *quantum worldview* understands the universe as an indivisible field of energy in which all creation is connected and interdependent. Things are not separate, as we have perceived them to be in the mechanical worldview, but are all part of a whole. In the quantum view, the material world is not separate from the spiritual; the human soul is one with the body and connects with everything. The spirit of the Creator is infused in creation. All is one.

As the church changes its identity, it changes its relationship to creation, and it ends the separation it built between itself and the world. Let's call it "Quantum Catholicism." In Quantum Catholicism, science and religion, matter and spirit, and body and soul are again united. The following are some of the values that were part of the pre-Vatican II church and the values that make up the post-Vatican II church.

| Pre-Vatican II Church | Post-Vatican II Church |
| --- | --- |
| Absolutist | Relative |
| Hierarchical | Mutual |
| Autocratic | Democratic |
| Differences | Likeness |
| Separation | Connection |
| Power over | Empowerment |
| Uniformity | Diversity |

In the quantum paradigm, separation disappears. Differences and diversity are celebrated. In the quantum paradigm, ranking disappears, too. One idea, one cultural group, or one person is not seen as higher than another is. Within the quantum paradigm, as within a circle, all the realms of creation exist like spokes of a wheel. All have a position of value, and all connect in the middle.

As the church moves further into its new identity, it recognizes diversity as a quality celebrating God's unbounded powers of creativity and the *omnipresence* of God's spirit. The Catholic Church is moving off the hierarchical ladder, which places it as superior to the culture, to a circular connection of oneness. In the new model, no one group or any one set of ideas has innate superiority over others. The unifier in the new model is God's presence throughout all of creation. Oneness is not accomplished through beliefs or practices imposed from the outside, but it is already present in creation. As the people of God turn to face the world, they are meeting God's creation with a deeper sense of belonging. We'll now look at four ways that the church's new paradigm engages the culture.

# The Global Village

The global village is a concept that describes a way of perceiving ourselves in relationship to the rest of the globe. It recognizes our oneness or unity with the rest of the world in economic issues, use of Earth's resources, and the sharing of knowledge. It looks at the common experiences among the people of the world, rather than their differences. Scientists, economists, ecologists, and theologians from many traditions are coming together and recognizing interconnectedness. To think of any one community's actions as not having an effect on other communities has become a thing of the past.

**S'ter Says**

**Omnipresence** is a traditional Catholic belief that God is everywhere. In other words, omnipresence is a Catholic concept that God's spirit exists throughout all of creation.

When explorers arrived in the New World, they had a profound effect on the cultures they visited as they carried ideas and goods from sea to sea. Today, we are instantly connected to both the ideas and products of cultures that are on the other side of the globe. With instant communication and travel accessibility, we truly are experiencing the globe as one village. In this global village, a thought can be transmitted around the world in four seconds. It is almost as though we are speaking face to face while living 10,000 miles apart.

How do we participate in the global village? What style of relationship will we be using? The world is moving toward a mutual relational style where we meet each other eye to eye in an open forum in which ideas are exchanged. As we have seen, from the beginning, the church has pursued a vision of unity. The quantum worldview brings with it the potential for realizing that vision.

## Missionaries and the Global Village Church

Although the Catholic Church began in Jerusalem, it quickly headquartered in Rome and spread to Europe, where it became the dominant influence in Western culture. Today, what was once an essentially European church now finds itself surpassed in size by the church in Africa, Asia, and the Americas. As we have seen in Chapter 2, "The People: Many Faces, Many Flags," one billion of the world's six billion people are Catholics. Of this population, Africa represents 11 percent, Asia 10 percent, the United States and Canada 7 percent, Mexico and Central America 14 percent, and South America 28 percent. Together these other parts of the world represent 72 percent of the Catholic population, leaving Europe with 28 percent. Catholicism is no longer a predominately European church.

The church has always thought of itself as one; it has held the vision and preached a message of unity from the beginning. In the quantum paradigm, the vision of unity is realized through the recognition of the presence of God in all people. The quantum perspective invites the people of God into new levels of intimacy with creation.

The church already exists beyond the boundaries of state or country or continent or hemisphere, and it has its own well-developed common culture with common ideals. As the world moves toward quantum consciousness, it is creating a common identity, a bond. The church can stand as a sacred symbol, a sacrament of a common identity, as it recognizes that we are all the people of God.

Global missionary work has long been a big part of the church. Catholics have set up schools and hospitals and created diplomatic alliances all over the globe in an effort to bring the church to other cultures. However, in so doing, Catholic missionaries often went to other countries to convert people to the church's way rather than learning the ways of the people.

### Epiphanies

Countries and continents have patron saints to watch over them. For example, Moses the Black is the patron of Africa along with Our Lady, Queen of Africa. Canada's patrons are St. Joseph and St. Anne. Central and South America share a patron saint, St. Rose of Lima. St. Joseph watches over China. St. Benedict of Nursia, St. Cyril, and St. Methodius all shepherd Europe. Mexico's patron is Our Lady of Guadalupe, who is also the patron of all of North America. The United States is under the protection of the Immaculate Conception of Mary.

The new quantum church is truly global because it interacts with other cultures from a position of mutuality. As the church builds relationships with other countries, it does so with a greater respect for the culture's autonomy. Native people now comprise an increasing number of the ordained clergy. Bishops and archbishops are then selected from their ranks. Missionaries adapt their life to the culture they have come to serve. New religious orders that are organic to the culture are founded. Rather than instilling European values, these new religious orders are founded out of the particular needs of the people in the new land and connect to the values, experiences, and stories of the people.

Celebration of the Mass becomes a celebration of the culture. Colors, fabrics, flags, and other sacramentals relate to the symbols of the indigenous people and are not European symbols. Church architecture is no longer imported from Europe; instead, churches are made of local materials and look like local buildings, matching the culture of the country. The same is true of church music and prayers. The Gospel message is grounded in the political, economic, social, and spiritual realities of the local area, rather than those of Europe.

# Partnership: From Power over to Empowerment

Quantum Catholicism is a partnership approach that has a new understanding of power. As the church shifts from the mechanical world to the quantum world, it is shifting from the hierarchical model to relational power. In the relational style, many groups are included in decision-making.

The old model separated the leaders from the people. Because they were separated from the people, they often knew very little about the people's lives. Leaders didn't have essential information when they made the decisions. The new model of church is based in partnership.

**Your Guardian Angel**

Look up the word "power" in your dictionary. Power is often thought of as control over others. However, the preferred dictionary definition of power is the best one. It says power is the ability to do or act.

## Absolute No More!

We all know the famous saying: "Power corrupts, and absolute power corrupts absolutely." As we've seen, the church's highly centralized idea of power and its absolutism has gotten it into trouble more than once.

The traditional objection from within the church to a shift in the flow of power is: "The church is not a democracy." This is true. However, as we have seen, the church fashioned its hierarchical model on the Roman Empire precisely because that model was part of the culture of its time. This structure stabilized the newly developing institution and clarified its beliefs.

As the church heads into the next millennium, it is modifying its structure to include both a way of talking with the people and a way of listening. This feedback loop will make decisions more communal.

## Sharing and Healing

The church has a powerful resource within its tradition to accomplish partnership. This resource is Jesus, the man who came out of Galilee 2,000 years ago and gathered together communities for healing and sharing. In every action, in every word, in every way, he told his followers that they had the power. "The Kingdom of God is within you," he said.

Jesus showed the people how to honor the "kingdom within." As he taught them to go within and connect with the God in them, he changed the rules of how power flows. It flows through God, through us, and through all creation.

Jesus also changed the flow of power in another significant way. He turned the church structure upside down, creating a bottom-to-top model of sharing power. He did not direct his teaching to the authorities. He did not tell them they should treat the people differently; he told the people to understand themselves differently. The challenge to build partnership models in the church of the next millennium is a challenge to the people, rather than to the leaders. As the paradigm within the church shifts, the challenge to its members is to accept their power and take responsibility as full partners.

# "Male and Female He Created Them" (Genesis 1:27)

As we move toward creating full partnership, the roles of both men and women and the way they relate to each other are being redefined. Strides are being made toward more equality in education, the workplace, the government, and in all segments of society. One thing is certain as we move ahead into the next era in history: Issues of gender will continue to be examined and restructured. This issue presents the church with an important opportunity to step into the lead as society searches for religious values to determine the right action in this regard.

## *Regaining Women's Voices*

Although it was contrary to the culture of the day, Jesus made women a central part of his life and work. Many stories in the Bible show women's involvement in his ministry, but two particular events tell the story. One is the faithful presence of the women at the crucifixion. They remained with Jesus until the end. Second, the resurrected Jesus first appeared to women. He said, "Go and tell the others …" The church began with women and men working and praying together in equal partnership. Over time, the role of women was gradually reduced. The early church was adopting the patriarchal structure of the society around it. By the time of the first council, women were locked out of the positions of leadership in the church. This inequality persisted for the next 1700 years. The results of this shift continue today. As we've seen, the church developed as an all-male structure. Women were excluded from the official ministries, governing structure, or any significant leadership, which was in line with the politics of the culture, but not in accord with the church as Jesus had modeled it.

From its first council in 325 C.E. to the present time, the church has held 21 councils in which beliefs and policies for all its members have been established. However, no woman has ever had decision-making authority at any of these councils. Strides toward partnership were made after the council of Vatican II, and women have been allowed to participate in several official ministries. However, ordination is not one of them. Papal statements since Vatican II have continued to uphold the ban against women's ordination.

To gain insight into the issue of women's exclusion from partnership in the decision-making process, let's use the power of the imagination. Imagine a woman is the pope of the Catholic Church. The entire College of Cardinals is composed of women; all the bishops are women; and all the priests, deacons, and seminarians are women. Let's imagine that only recently have men been allowed to be altar girls.

Imagine that this all-female decision-making body has had enormous power in the society in which you live and over your soul as well for 2,000 years. Imagine how disconnected this organization's decisions would be from a man's needs. How would such a structure be fair to men?

As you experience this exercise, you are able to see what it is like from the other side. The point of the gender concern is not a shift in who is the dominant one, but a call for a new paradigm of partnership. Let's use our imagination again to gain insight into how a partnership model might function. Imagine men and women working side by side to make decisions that reflect the true nature of being human. In this model the concerns of all are considered; participation is based on the Biblical reminder, "In his image … male and female, he created them."

**S'ter Says**

Pop John XXIII used the phrase **"signs of the time"** when he addressed the opening of Vatican II. He was telling the church, which had turned away from the world, to look at the world and to learn from it.

As we move toward full partnership, it is helpful to remember that at one time in history the exclusion of women met a societal norm. In the present time, this is no longer the case, at least not in the United States. The culture provides the church with a transforming opportunity to follow the instructions of Vatican II, which was to look at the *"signs of the time."*

## Women in the Wings

The church has a powerful resource for female leadership in the nuns. For many years, nuns have been the CEOs (chief executive officers) in three major arenas: the educational system, the health care system, and the governing of their religious orders. In this regard, the church has been ahead of the culture. If you were to look at college and university presidents in the 1950s, you would find very few females, but those you would find would very likely be Catholic nuns.

There was a noticeable difference between leadership in the public grade schools and high schools and church-operated schools. Although the teachers were mainly women in both systems, public schools almost always had a male principal. In most Catholic schools, women were the principals. For years, women owned and administered many Catholic hospitals across the country. They not only managed the health care, but also supervised doctors and trained nurses.

From the early years of the church when convents and monasteries first developed to the present time, there has been a strong Catholic tradition of religious women, which is a testimony to female leadership. These women have always made their own decisions and set their own policies, making Catholic women among the first women in Western culture to occupy executive roles.

Today, women remain a primary resource for the continuing life of the church. They are in the forefront of religious scholarship. For example, the majority of students in the ministry programs at Catholic Universities are females. At many Protestant seminaries, Catholic females make up an increasingly large proportion of the student body. They are studying in the fields of theology, pastoral ministry, chaplaincy, and religious education. They are in every way preparing to be leaders and decision-makers in the church. Thousands of parishes in the Catholic Church today are without a priest, and women are pastoring them.

As Catholics approach the third millennium, they find well-trained women theologians, teachers, and pastoral ministers who are ready to become partners with men in leadership. However, ordination is the only gateway to decision-making. As these women prepare to take ministerial responsibilities in a variety of areas, some are preparing for ordination. At this time, the doors of the Catholic seminaries, and therefore ordination, remain closed to them. In the past, when the U.S. Catholic Church refused to admit black students to the seminaries, the Vatican opened Roman seminaries and ordained them. The church does have precedents and resources for dealing with change regarding cultural inequities.

**Epiphanies**

Sister Mary Madeleva, C.S.C., president of St. Mary's College in Notre Dame, Indiana, was a champion of women's education in the church. In 1949, she presented a groundbreaking paper in which she proposed an educational reform program for American nuns. Until this point, they had been put into the burgeoning Catholic schools before they had a chance to finish their own education. The pope called the major superiors of religious women to Rome and urged them to offer programs of professional education and spiritual formation before sending sisters to their assignments. This movement changed the identity and set the direction of Catholic nuns, making them some of the best-educated women in the country.

# Quantum Spirituality: Matter and Spirit as One

As the twenty-first century dawns, there is a tremendous interest in spirituality in the culture at large. There was greater material consumption in the twentieth century than in all the rest of the centuries put together. Yet as it ended, the call to spirituality had never been heard more loudly. People who would not have imagined ever joining a church or belonging to a formal religion found themselves on a spiritual quest. Go into any bookstore and look at the shelves of material being written about spirituality. Retreats, seminars, and workshops on spirituality abound. Coursework at any given Catholic university shows a decided proliferation of classes on inner growth and self-discovery.

Previously, there were two specific camps regarding spirituality. One group did not believe in it at all. They thought it was too "churchy," a holdover from an antiquated worldview. For them, the only thing that was real was the material world. The other camp saw spirituality as "otherworldly." The people in this group believed that the spiritual would be found later in heaven. The world was a distraction, a temptation to be avoided. They saw God as outside of the world of matter.

The once great distance between these two camps is now just a stone's throw. They are meeting in an understanding that matter and spirit are one and the same thing. As these two opposite worldviews connect, both are sensing the presence of the spiritual in the everyday. With this growing sensitivity, there is an awareness of connectedness. We have coined the phrase *quantum spirituality* to describe this, because quantum is about realizing that there is one field of energy unifying both matter and spirit.

Quantum spirituality is a celebration of our partnership with God's creative will in the universe. Through it, we are called to embrace the world and its creative process. Redemption is seen as part of divine creation, not as necessitated by sin. Quantum spirituality's origins are in the ancient spiritual traditions, especially the matriarchal and indigenous societies whose cultures modeled the solidarity among nature, human-kind, and the divine. Current expressions of this spirituality are mending the dualism of Western spirituality that sees these as separate. Quantum spirituality is incarnational because it proclaims the divine presence in both matter and spirit.

### S'ter Says

**Quantum spirituality** is a spirituality that calls us to recognize the holiness of the world and be involved with it creatively, as Jesus did in becoming human with us.

This emerging spirituality is not concerned with dogma, rules, and church rituals. People are experiencing spirituality in nature, in relationships, in communities, and as they reach out to help others. In so doing, spirituality is located less in beliefs and traditions and more in the everyday interactions in the world in which we live in perceiving our interrelatedness. Those who follow quantum spirituality say it is about recognizing life's mystery. It creates for them a mystical awareness of being alive and a sense of the goodness of life.

## *From Religion to Spirituality*

For a lot of people, church rituals have lost their original meanings. Having been so tightly locked into form, they have lost their spiritual sensitivity and have become disconnected from the lives of the people. In past generations, people went to church because of fear of punishment. Much of the practice of the religion was about avoiding consequences, whether it was guilt, damnation, or just a stern look given by an irate sister, pastor, or parent. Today, most people no longer find themselves motivated by fear and punishment. They are looking for connection and a sense of oneness that they feel is spirituality, and they are going wherever they can find it.

## *Back to Our Roots in the Earth*

The new spirituality draws church members back to their Catholic identity in the sacraments. As they reconnect to their sacramental roots in the elements—earth, air, fire, and water—their consciousness of the presence of the sacred in all creation is awakened. As their senses are sharpened, they are reminded that Christ is here now, as always, and is present in the world. Quantum Catholicism retrieves the Catholic understanding of the sacredness of life.

A revitalized church imagines sacraments in a new way. For example, a group of people might gather on a Saturday night for a communal dinner. They bring ingredients and spend time together baking bread. As the dough is kneaded, rolled, and punched, the kitchen becomes dusty with flour, and stories are shared. "I remember when I was a kid …" "The smell of the bread reminds me of …" "This is just like the time when …" They connect. As the bread is ready and they sit down to dinner, they might break it ceremoniously, giving thanks for the grains of wheat and the warmth of friends gathered together around the table that will nourish them. They experience Eucharist.

Likewise, a family outing to the lake can become the occasion to have an intimate relationship with baptismal waters. Paddles dip into cool water as the canoe slides across a still lake. A child trails her fingers in the water, mesmerized by the small wake it creates. A paddle bounces across the water and drops, splashing the children. Catching an opportunity for a game, one of them splashes back. Laughter rings out across the lake, and the worries of the week are washed away. A moment in time has been made holy. Later in the evening, as the parents sit by the water's edge, they reflect over the experiences of the day. They feel the intensity of being alive and the goodness of it all. They are overcome with gratitude, the kind that spontaneously wells up from a deep place inside when you give it the time and space to do so.

At Mass on Sunday, the Eucharistic bread now tastes different because of the spiritual connection between baking bread on Saturday night with friends and receiving communion on Sunday morning. The priest's sprinkle of the holy water has a renewed meaning. A day on the lake with the family is a blessing, a baptism in which all are renewed. The spiritual connection between the sacraments and the world tells Catholics that God is present. Quantum spirituality connects us.

# The Next Generation

As we conclude our story of the church, there is a chapter yet to be written, and only time can write it. It will unfold as we move forward into this millennium, as it is lived by the generations to come. Let's take a look at the young people who bring the new Catholicism.

Although we have been faithful to history in presenting the story of the church, including its Biblical origins, the first millennium's growth, and the second millennium's splits, the prism that we have used to focus on the story is Vatican II. No one can tell the story of Catholicism's future, but we do know it lies in the hands of the next generations. Popular culture has described the current generation of young adults in the United States with two images: Generation X and Generation Ñ (pronounced *EN-yay*). Let's see who these folks are.

## *Generation X*

Generation X is largely made up of the descendants of the European immigrants. They are roughly in their 20s and 30s. In an article in the July 1999 issue of *U.S. Catholic* they're described as the first generation of "latch-key children" who learned early to fend for themselves in day care and after-school programs. Many Generation X'ers are seeking family and beyond that, a community. They have spent far less time with their parents than the generation before them, so for many of Generation X, family is a matter of shared commitments, not shared blood. Community is formed around a common spiritual purpose and commitment. Their description of the ideal community is not unlike the New Testament family whom Jesus identified when he was asked who his brothers and sisters were. He replied, "Those who hear the word of God and do it."

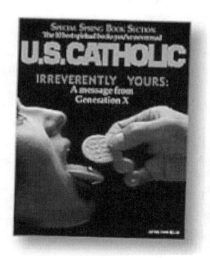

*Generation X'er receiving communion.*

*(Courtesy of Tom Wright)*

This generation has a healthy irreverence and skepticism of all institutions, including the church. They recognize God's presence in the broadest sense. To them God is present in all communities, in all religious traditions, in all races. Their God is not bound to one sexual identity. This generation is more comfortable crossing cultural barriers than any of its predecessors.

Indeed, diversity may be the most common bond the people of Generation X share, and tolerance is their ethic. They are at home on many spiritual paths: Catholic, Protestant, Hindu, Buddhist, Jewish, Muslim, and Native American. They move in and out of many cultures: Black, Caucasian, Asian, Latino. They do not define people by their sexual preference or political alignment: gay, lesbian, straight, Republican, or Democrat.

For them, church is not an end in itself, and they refuse to idolize it. If they believe in it at all, they believe that church exists not for its own sake, but as a sign of God's reign. Religion is not about words; it's about love in action. They want the church to be a role model and live out its beliefs.

This generation has not been schooled in religious education in the traditional ways. For example, many of them are unfamiliar with the Catechism, and their heroes and role models are not found in the lives of the saints. They are unfamiliar with the history of the church. Although they may attend Mass and partake of the sacraments, they do so without a deep connection to the traditional meanings.

Rather than drawing on the established religious symbols and interpretations, the symbols for their spirituality are drawn from the pop culture, which is a major system of meaning for their lives. It rivals family and church. Life's meaning is conveyed to them through music, movies, sitcoms, and comic book characters. A large portion of this pop culture, by Generation X'ers' own admission, is meaningless, yet a part of it does carry meaning and even creates inspiration. Generation X'ers seem to be asking for the church to help them in sorting out the mix.

One Generation X'er described his idea of church in the following way, "The church in the next millennium will welcome all, as did our role model in the first century Palestine, regardless of their physical and social situations. Church is not an institution for dispensing grace. Church is people who have accepted grace and are striving to live in harmony with each other and creation."

# Generation Ñ

The term *Generation Ñ* was coined and copyrighted by Bill Teck and was used in a July 1999 issue of *Newsweek*. It is used to describe young Hispanics who, like their counterparts in Generation X, are in their 20s and 30s, but feel that the phrase "Generation X" does not completely describe them. They come from as many as 22 different countries of origin. Many are white, some are black, and most are in between. They are a global culture. Some of their families have been in the United States for centuries; some have only recently arrived. They are the descendants of the conquistadors and the Indians of the New World culture.

More than being simply bilingual, they are rediscovering their roots and inventing a new bicultural identity, meaning that they move freely in both worlds without losing anything in the process. They weave a complex web of relationships with their elders, the others in the United States, Euro-culture, and with one another. Yet this generation shows no signs of assimilation or "Americanization." Rather, their strong identity influences the culture.

### Epiphanies

The terms *Hispanic* and *Latino* are used interchangeably to define a diverse people. The terms refer to Mexicans, Caribbeans, Cubans, Puerto Ricans, Dominicans, the Andean people, and people from the American Southwest. The diversity of the Hispanic community is its strength. The religious spirit of these people blended with the Catholic faith. Their spirituality is expressed in love of God, love of neighbor, and love of self; this love binds the people together fashioning *el pueblo de Dios*, the people of God.

For the most part, they are Catholic. Like Generation X, their faith is more unstructured. As one member of Generation Ñ put it, "We respect and honor Catholic traditions, yet are not bound to the old practices." Their Catholicism is cultural as well as religious, and it is integral to their Hispanic identity. They are aware they come from a rich culture and history, and they want to celebrate it. Like Generation X, they are less tolerant of the male dominance over females than the previous generation. Both Generation X and Generation Ñ believe in religion, but the affluence of their lives has reduced their dependence on it. In a marked contrast to Generation X, Generation Ñ draws a strong part of its religious values and identity from its family. The people in Generation Ñ often grew up living together with aunts, uncles, cousins, and grandparents, all attending church together.

## Quantum Generation: Generation Q

As the church enters the new millennium, it does so with a new identity in which all things are connected. These changes bring a new set of challenges to a new generation that we call the Quantum Generation. As we've just seen, they are already carrying the values it will take to create the new church in the next millennium. They embody a globalized vision of what it means to be human. They have crossed the cultural boundaries that once restricted their elders. The conflicts around sexuality and gender that haunted their parent's generation seem to be healing. They are not overly concerned with dogma, yet they are not superficially religious. They seek guidance, question established religious practices, and ask for integrity from their religious leaders. They value spiritual connection, often understanding it in a more integrated way than generations before them.

The third millennium will contain major challenges for the Catholic Church. Although this book ends here, the story does not. It will be lived and written by the church's greatest asset: the next generation. From our point of view, it is in good hands.

## The Least You Need to Know

➤ The church's new identity brings a new structure and new values.

➤ The church of the future will have a broader power base and include more people in the decision-making process.

➤ The new church will be less "religious" and more spiritual.

➤ The present generation already is carrying the values for the transformation of the church.

# Glossary

**abortion, clinical**   Intentionally bringing about the termination of a pregnancy to cause the death of the fetus.

**absolution**   The power the priest has through the sacrament of Reconciliation to extend God's forgiveness to contrite people.

**altar**   From the Latin *altare,* akin to Latin *adolere,* which means to burn up, an altar is a raised structure or place on which sacrifices are offered or incense is burned in worship.

**angels**   Purely spiritual creatures with intelligence and free will, acting as messengers and protectors in service to God.

**Ascension**   Jesus' return to heaven after his death and resurrection to be reunited with God and to prepare a place for his followers.

**Assumption**   When the Blessed Virgin Mary's earthly life was completed, she was taken up body and soul into heaven, where she shares in the glory of her son's resurrection.

**baptismal font**   Large container of water often made of marble and placed at the entrance of the church that is used in the sacrament of baptism.

**base communities**   Small groups led by laity who gather together for scripture reading, discussion, communion services, and community action; this movement started in Latin America.

**belief**   An expression of faith accepted as true even in the absence of proof; it may or may not be part of official church teachings (see *dogma*).

**Bible**   The sacred texts of both the Old Testament (or the Hebrew Scriptures) and the New Testament, which is the material written after the time of Jesus.

**Bible vigil**   Post-Vatican II church ceremony during which the Bible is honored on the altar and passages are read and reflected upon.

**bishop**   The highest order of ordination in church hierarchy; this person is ordinarily in charge of a group of parishes called a diocese.

**canon** (Biblical)   The word used to designate those writings that came to be accepted as authentic Biblical texts.

**Canon Law**   The rules governing the church. One refers to church law as Canon Law.

**capital sins**   Not actual sins, but thoughts and behaviors that the church has determined to be the human conditions that are dispositions toward sinning. They are pride, covetousness, envy, anger, lust, gluttony, and sloth.

**catacombs**   A system of tunnels beneath the ground outside of Rome and other ancient cities often used by early Catholics as hiding places when they were being persecuted. Many saints are buried there, and they are visited as sacred sites.

**Catechism**   The book containing the official teachings of the Catholic Church for the instruction of children or adults interested in the Catholic faith.

**cathedral**   From the Greek *cathedra,* meaning bishop's chair or throne, cathedrals are churches in which a bishop ordinarily celebrates the sacraments.

**Catholic**   The word *catholic* means universal. It refers to the fact that the Catholic Church is a church for all, and all its believers follow a set of common beliefs and practices.

**celibacy**   Promise made by those entering religious service to abstain from sexual relationships.

**ceremony**   A formal practice or custom established as proper to honor a special occasion.

**Christ**   The Greek word for "anointed"; Kings were anointed in the Old Testament. Applied to Jesus as the anointed one of God.

**Christian**   Term first used (disparagingly) to describe the followers of Christ in Damascus as early as 40 B.C.E. Later adopted by these followers in the second century.

**church**   A specific community of the faithful, usually determined on a territorial basis, local or regional, that carries on the mission of Christ in the world to reconcile humankind to God.

**cloister**   Place of religious seclusion for prayer and meditation.

**college of cardinals**   A group of select bishops that offers counsel to the pope, elects new popes, and governs in times between popes. They are the chief administrators of the church. They are the bishops of major dioceses and/or head up the various church agencies. They are appointed by the pope.

**Colonialization**   A process by which one country occupies another for the purpose of economic exploitation.

**communion of Saints**   An expression of unity linking all the people of God, living or dead, through all ages, into one eternal community.

**conquistador**   A Spanish conqueror of Mexico, Peru, and other parts of America in the sixteenth century.

**contemplative**   A meditative form of prayer developed in the monasteries.

**co-redeemer**   An unofficial but popular title celebrating Mary's part in the Redemption.

**council (ecumenical)**   A world-wide assembly of bishops called together by the pope for the purpose of setting policy and making decisions.

**covenant**   A bi-level agreement used in the Old Testament to describe the relationship between God and the people. It establishes that God will not abandon the people even if they fail to live up to their side of the agreement.

**creation**   The unfolding of all God's plans. Creation is in a state of movement toward an ultimate perfection as destined by God.

**cross**   Two planks of timber, one placed across the other; an instrument of execution in Roman times. Jesus was put to death on a cross.

**crucifix**   A cross that holds the image of Jesus crucified, used for devotion in Catholic churches and homes.

**Crusades**   Military expeditions undertaken by the Christians of Europe in the eleventh to the thirteenth centuries for the recovery of the Holy Land from the Muslims.

**dogma (doctrine)**   A formally stated official belief of the Catholic Church concerning faith or morals.

**ecclesial** or **ecclesiastical**   Pertaining to the church.

**encyclicals**   Letters written by the pope to instruct the people.

**epiphany**   A sudden intuitive perception or insight into the essential meaning of something.

**Epiphany**   The feast when the kings or wise men visited the Christ child in Bethlehem. It is celebrated January 6. The birth as well as the baptism of Jesus are considered epiphanies.

**Eucharistic ministers**   Parishioners who assist the priest in the distribution of communion during Mass.

**evil**   That which motivates or results from morally bad or wrong choices.

**excommunication**    Ecclesiastical censure excluding a Catholic from participation in the sacramental life of the church and from the exercise of any church office.

**Existentialism**    Twentieth-century philosophical movement emphasizing man's radical aloneness, personal freedom, and personal responsibility for decisions in one's existence.

**Extreme Unction**    Former name of the sacrament now called Anointing of the Sick. "Extreme" refers to the deathly condition of those who are receiving it, and "Unction" means anointing with oil.

**faith**    Our belief in the basic goodness of God's plan for us. In faith, we believe and act as if what we hope for will be granted. It also refers to the acceptance of church teachings or the content of those teachings.

**First Communion**    Reception of the sacrament of the Eucharist for the first time.

**free will**    The human experience that governs our actions and gives us the freedom to make choices regarding our full expression of God's love.

**globalization**    Understanding the world as a community and seeing the interconnectedness of people, economies, and resources.

**God**    The supreme divine being, the creator of all that is, the fullness of being and of all perfection. God is without beginning and without end. God is love, the binding force in all that is.

**Gospel**    The good news that Christ has come. The Gospel is taken from the Biblical books of Matthew, Mark, Luke, and John.

**grace**    The gift of God's life in our souls, which guides us toward right choices.

**heaven**    State of fulfillment of our souls as they rest in God's presence for eternity.

**hell**    State of our existence without God; once understood as the eternal fires in which the damned suffered forever.

**heretics**    Catholics who engage in any deliberate, persistent, and public denial of some article of revealed truth of the Catholic faith.

**Holy Orders**    The process by which a man becomes a deacon, priest, or bishop. Priests minister to people's spiritual needs and safeguard the rules and regulations of their parish.

**Holy Spirit**    The third person of the Trinity—Father, Son, and Holy Spirit. It describes God's eternal presence to us as it opens our hearts and minds, guides us in our actions, and otherwise assists us on our journey.

**Homily**    A sermon, especially one centering on scriptural text.

**host**    One of several names for the Eucharistic bread. From Latin *hostia,* meaning "victim," it recalls that Christ was sacrificed for us.

*Humanae Vitae*   Latin for "of human life," this is the letter written by Pope Paul VI continuing the ban on the use of artificial birth control.

**Immaculate Conception**   Dogma that Mary was conceived in her mother's womb free from original sin to enable her to be a pure vessel through which Jesus would be brought into the world.

**immanence**   God's presence here and now that can be experienced by humans.

**Incarnation**   The event in which God took human form and entered the human journey.

**indulgences**   Penitential prayers or actions that remit the punishment for sins.

**infallibility**   A dogma stating that the pope speaks without error, on behalf of the church, in union with the bishops when he proclaims an article of faith or morals.

**Inquisition**   Official investigation by the church of suspected heresies.

**intercessor**   Christ's function as the mediator between God and the people. This term is also applied to his mother, Mary, because she was a necessary link in God's plan to send his son as an intercessor. Saints act as intercessors, too.

**Jesuits**   A religious order established in the 1500s by St. Ignatius of Loyola, dedicated to work for the pope. The official name is the Society of Jesus.

**Jesus**   Hebrew name meaning "God saves," expressing both the identity and the mission of the Son of God born of the Virgin Mary.

*La Nueva Raza*   Spanish phrase, "the new race," describing the mixing of the Spanish, African, and Indian blood, spirituality, and cultures through which all of the cultures are changed.

**laypeople**   From the Greek word *layos,* meaning "the people." Church members who are not ordained.

**liberation theology**   An array of theologies that articulate the faith journey from the perspective of the people's experience of their struggles.

**liturgical practices**   Church services and ceremonies, readings at Mass, communion, the sacraments, prayers, rituals, and celebrations.

**liturgy**   The prayers and rituals of the church.

**magisterium**   The church's teaching function.

**martyrs**   Those killed for their faith. Martyrdom automatically results in sainthood. That is to say, a martyr's soul goes directly to God.

**Mary**   The mother of Jesus, the Son of God.

**miracle**   An event that breaks the laws of nature; an extraordinary happening that gives us a glimpse of God at work in the world.

**missionaries**   Religious workers sent to foreign countries to do religious or charitable work.

**missions**   Agencies such as schools and hospitals established and maintained by the church to assist people to meet their everyday needs.

**modernism**   A heresy condemned by the pope in 1907 referring to modern scientific thinking, which believed that truth changes.

**monasticism**   Tradition of taking oneself away from the mainstream of society for the purpose of developing spiritual practice.

**monstrance**   Ornate golden vessel containing the Blessed Sacrament under the form of bread, pressed between two pieces of clear glass. It sits on the altar for Eucharistic devotions.

**moral** (noun)   What we believe is right or wrong.

**moral law**   A sense of right and wrong that is part of an inborn and informed conscience. It is based in the understanding of a rational order established by the Creator that gives us guidance in making moral choices.

**mysteries**   Beliefs taken on faith, which can never be fully understood.

**mystic**   From the Greek meaning "mystery," this term describes a person who engages in the practice of meditation from which he or she experiences a relationship with God and gains spiritual insight.

**mysticism**   Going within yourself to a quiet place where it is possible to experience the mystery of God.

**myth**   A story that tells the beliefs of a group of people regarding their origins, history, and destiny. Myths transmit truths.

**national parish**   A parish not based on geographical boundaries, comprised of an ethnic group.

**natural law**   The way the natural world works. It makes itself known to us by our awareness of the natural order of things. It represents a common-sense understanding of the world.

***New England Primer***   A commonly used textbook in the American Colonies. It was printed in 1690 and was in use until 1900. It was used to help students learn to read by using religion and Biblical verses. It included anti-Catholic images and cartoons.

**novena**   From the Latin *novem,* meaning "nine," this is a devotion repeated nine successive days.

**omnipresence**   One of the characteristics used to describe God; it describes God's presence everywhere.

**ordination**   Entrance rite into the order of deacon, priest, or bishop.

**original sin**    An inherited state of reduced power that we endure because of being separated from our original state of unity with God. It is part of being human.

**Orthodox**    Describes the Greek or Eastern churches that are not under the direction of the pope.

**parish council**    A post-Vatican II development in the church's governing structure made up of church members who are elected or chosen to plan and secure the resources for the parish.

**parochial schools**    Elementary and high schools supported by the parish, which provide a general education and instill Catholic ethics and values.

**pastoral ministers**    Church workers who have taken on various roles that once were filled by priests.

**Pentateuch**    The "book of the five scrolls" known as the Old Testament Torah. Moses commanded that the Torah law be placed in the Ark of the Covenant to be kept safe during the wilderness journey of the Hebrew people.

**Posada**    From the Spanish for shelter, this term describes a house-to-house procession at Christmas in which the drama of Joseph and Mary is enacted.

**priests**    The ordained clergy of the church.

**prophetic tradition**    Old Testament warnings about the consequences of actions. Some of the prophets were Isaiah, Jeremiah, Amos, and Micah.

**Protestant**    Any Christian belonging to a sect that seceded from the Catholic Church at the time of the Reformation. Lutheran, Episcopal, Methodist, and Baptist are some Protestant denominations.

**pulpit**    From the Latin *pulpitum*, this is a staging platform from which the priest proclaims the Gospel reading of the Mass and preaches the homily.

**purgatory**    A state of the soul after death in which it progresses toward its final union with God. The soul in purgatory can be aided in this journey through prayers and good works of the living.

**quantum spirituality**    The call to recognize the unity of the world and be involved with it creatively.

**quantum worldview**    An understanding that everything is connected by way of a unifying field of energy. It is in contrast to the mechanical worldview that perceives a separation between the physical and spiritual worlds.

**RCIA**    Stands for the Rite of Christian Initiation of Adults. It is a process of entrance into the Catholic Church.

**real presence**    A dogma that Christ is present in the sacrament of the Eucharist, physically and spiritually feeding the body and soul.

**reason**   Our ability to know the existence of God with certainty through our hearts and minds.

**Reconciliation**   The sacrament by which sins are forgiven and we are reconciled with God and absolved from guilt.

**relics**   Any part of the physical remains of a saint or items such as clothing that have touched the body of a saint.

**religion**   From the Latin *religare,* meaning "to bind back," religion is concerned with making connections between the sensate world and that which exists beyond. Religion operates from a faith basis rather than reason.

**religious liberty**   A Vatican II doctrine affirming the natural right to be free of coercion in one's religious beliefs.

**Renaissance**   The rebirth in Europe of the classic Greek and Roman architecture, painting, sculpting, music, and literature during the fourteenth, fifteenth, and sixteenth centuries.

**Resurrection**   The faith event of Jesus' rising from the dead on the third day after his crucifixion, demonstrating his victory over sin and death and eternal life that is available to people.

**revelation**   A source of knowledge existing beyond the ability to reason; it is divine insight or inspiration by which God speaks to people of the divine plan.

**ritual**   See *ceremony*.

**Roman Curia**   Bureaucracy that assists the pope in administering his duty of governing the Catholic Church.

**Roman Ritual**   Liturgical book containing special rites and blessings commonly performed by the clergy. Since Vatican II, this book has been called the *Book of Blessings*.

**sacramentals**   Objects used to connect Catholics to spiritual experiences. Rosaries, candles, bells, and statues are common Catholic sacramentals.

**sacred scripture**   The sacred writings of the Old and New Testament that are believed to be inspired by the Holy Spirit and written by human hand.

**salvation**   God's loving action through Jesus that guides us and moves us toward what is good for us and away from that which would harm us.

**seamless garment of life**   An ethic recognizing all created things are connected to and by the Creator in a whole and unbroken relationship. It requires a consistent ethic of respect for the value of life across the board in the areas of access to food, shelter, health care, and education; capital punishment; war; abortion; and euthanasia.

**"signs of the time"**   Phrase used by Pope John XXIII in opening Vatican II that told the church to look at the world and to learn from it.

**simony**   Refers to both the buying and selling of church offices.

**sin**   Behaviors or intentions that are against God's will for us. It has been described as "missing the mark" or falling short of our potential.

**social justice**   A state in which all members are free to participate fully and receive the just benefits in the society in which they live.

**soul**   Our individual spiritual self, the breath of life, the indwelling of the Holy Spirit. Not separate from the body, but integral to it, it connects us to God, to one another, and to all of creation. Our souls live on when our physical lives are finished.

**spiritual director**   One trained to work with people spiritually, much like a psychologist works with someone emotionally.

**tradition**   Church teachings that have developed over the years based on the teachings handed down from Christ and the apostles.

**Triduum**   The liturgy celebrated on the three days prior to Easter Sunday: Holy Thursday, Good Friday, and Holy Saturday.

**Trinity**   The mystery of faith expressing one God in three persons. The divine persons, the Father, Son, and Holy Spirit, do not share the one divinity among themselves, but each of them is God whole and entire.

**Viaticum**   Latin meaning "on the way with you," the name of communion when it is being given to a dying person.

**virginity**   In ancient times, a state of independence or autonomy, referring to a woman who made her own decisions. When used to describe Mary, it means she said yes to God of her own free will, acting independent of any influence or coercion.

**virtues**   Right ways of acting, habits that guide us in the way of good sense and good faith and govern our relationships with others.

**visit**   Catholic custom of stopping in to the church for a few minutes during the day to say a quick prayer.

**vocation**   From the Latin *vocare*, meaning "call," this term refers to a calling to the priesthood, religious life, or other spiritual paths.

**vows**   Binding promises made when one goes into a religious order. The principal three are poverty (giving up private ownership to the community), chastity (giving up the right to marry and have an intimate sexual relationship in order to devote oneself to the church), and obedience (submitting to the authority of one's superiors for assignments).

**Western world**   Lands west of Istanbul, Turkey. Lands to the east of Istanbul are called the Eastern world.

# Recommended Readings

*The American Catholic Catalog,* by Bernard Hassan

*Barrios and Borderlands: Cultures of Latinos and Latinas in the United States,* by Denis Lynn Daly Heyck

*Bare Ruined Choirs: Doubt, Prophecy and Radical Religion,* by Garry Wills

*Catechism of the Catholic Church*

*Catholic Almanac*

*Catholicism,* by Richard P. McBrien

*Catholicism Today: A Survey of Catholic Belief and Practice,* by Matthew Kohmescher

*Celtic Christian Spirituality: An Anthology of Medieval and Modern Sources,* by Oliver Davies and Fiona Bowie

*A Church at Risk: the Challenge of Spiritually Hungry Adults,* by Marcel J. Dumestre

*A Democratic Catholic Church: The Reconstruction of Roman Catholicism Edited,* by Eugene C. Bianchi and Rosemary R. Ruether

*The Essential Mary Handbook: A Summary of Beliefs, Practices, and Prayers,* edited by Judith A. Bauer

*Galilean Journey: The Mexican—American Promise,* by Virgilio P. Elizondo

*Growing Up Catholic: An Infinitely Funny Guide for the Faithful, the Fallen and Everyone In-Between,* by Mary J. F. C. Meara, Jeffrey A. J. Stone, Maureen A. T. Kelly, and Richard G. M. Davis

*How to Save the Catholic Church,* by Andrew M. Greeley and Mary Greeley Durkin

*La Morenita,* by Virgilio Elizondo

*Why Do Catholics?: A Guide to Catholic Belief and Practice,* by Sr. Charlene Altemose

# Internet Resources

**Catholic Worker Home Page**
www.catholicworker.org/

**Catholic Information Center on Internet Home Page—Catholic.Net**
www.catholic.net/

**Catholic Resources on the Net**
www.cs.cmu.edu/~spok/catholic.html

**The Holy See**
www.vatican.va/

**Religious Orders**
maple.lemoyne.edu/~bucko/orders.html

**SisterSite**
www.geocities.com/Wellesley/1114/

**Woodstock Jesuit Theological Center**
www.georgetown.edu/centers/woodstock/

# For In-Depth Reading

## Encyclopedia and Catechisms

*The Companion to the Catechism of the Catholic Church*

*The Encyclopedia of American Catholic History,* edited by Michael Glazier and Thomas J. Shelley

*The HarperCollins Encyclopedia of Catholicism,* by General Editor Richard P. McBrien

*The Modern Catholic Encyclopedia,* by Michael Glazier and Monika K. Hellwig

*New Catholic Encyclopedia*

## Catholic Beliefs and Practices

*The Catholic Myth: The Behavior and Beliefs of American Catholics, by* Andrew Greeley

*The Catholic Thing,* by Rosemary Haughton

*A Catholic Vision,* by Stephen Happel and David Tracy

*The Gospel in History: Portrait of a Teaching Church: The Origins of Christian Education,* by Marianne Sawicki

*The Great Work: Our Way into the Future,* by Thomas Berry

*Guadalupe: Mother of the New Creation,* by Virgilio P. Elizondo

*Quantum Theology: Spiritual Implications of the New Physics,* by Diarmuid O'Murchu

*Seeing the Lord: Resurrection and Early Christian Practices,* by Marianne Sawicki

*Understanding Catholicism*, by Monika K. Hellwig

*Understanding the Old Testament (Third Edition)*, by Bernhard W. Anderson

*Virtual Faith: The Irreverent Spiritual Quest of Generation X*, by Tom Beaudoin

# Catholic History

*American Catholic: The Saints and Sinners who Built America's Most Powerful Church*, by Charles Morris

*The American Catholic Experience*, by Jay P. Dolan

*Catholicism Confronts Modernity: a Protestant View*, by Langdon Brown Gilkey

*Celtic Christian Spirituality: An Anthology of Medieval and Modern Sources*, by Oliver Davies and Fiona Bowie

*The Chalice and the Blade: Our History, Our Future*, by Riane Eisler

*The Church That Was a School: Catholic Identity and Catholic Education in the United States Since 1790*, by Robert T. O'Gorman

*Contending with Modernity: Catholic Higher Education in the Twentieth Century*, by Philip Gleason

*Hidden Women of the Gospels*, by Kathy Coffey

*The History of Black Catholics in the United States*, by Cyprian Davis

*Mary of Magdala: Apostle and Leader*, by Mary R. Thompson

*Reclaiming Spirituality: A New Spiritual Framework for Today's World*, by Diarmuid O'Murchu

*The Sacred World of Celts: An Illustrated Guide to Celtic Spirituality and Mythology*, by Nigel Pennick

*The Survival of American Innocence: Catholicism in an Era of Disillusionment, 1920–1940*, by William M. Halsey

*Tomorrow's Catholic: Understanding God and Jesus in a New Millennium*, by Michael Morwood and Thomas Groome

# Catholic Culture

*American Catholic Arts and Fictions: Culture, Ideology, Aesthetics*, by Paul Giles

*Building the Great Cathedrals*, by Francois Icher

*Catholics and American Culture: Fulton Sheen, Dorothy Day, and the Notre Dame Football Team*, by Mark Stephen Massa

*El Dia de los Muertos*, The Institute of Texas Cultures San Antonio 1991 video tape

*Gregorian Chant: Songs of the Spirit,* edited by Huston Smith, David Wakely, Thomas Moore, and Ismael Fernandez De La Cuesta

*Integrated Healing Arts,* by Mary Faulkner

*Three Catholic Writers of the Modern South,* by Robert H. Brinkmeyer

*The Woman's Dictionary of Symbols and Sacred Objects,* by Barbara G. Walker

## Catholic Prayers and Saints

*Alone of All Her Sex: The Myth and the Cult of the Virgin Mary,* by Marina Warner

*Dictionary of Saints,* by John J. Delaney

*The Directory of Saints: A Concise Guide to Patron Saints,* by Annette Sandoval

*The Essential Mary Handbook: A Summary of Beliefs, Practices, and Prayers,* edited by Judith A. Bauer

*Favorite Prayers and Novenas,* edited by Marianne L'Trouve

*Ignatius Loyola: Spiritual Exercises,* by Joseph A. Tetlow

*The Life of Saint Theresa of Ávila By Herself,* translated by J. M. Cohen

*The Little Flowers of St. Francis of Assisi Edited and Adapted,* by W. Heywood

*Lives of the Saints for Every Day of the Year,* by Hugo Hoever

*Mary: Art, Culture, and Religion Through the Ages,* by Caroline H. Ebertshäuser

*Queen of Apostles Prayerbook,* by James Alberione

*The Rule of Benedict: Insights for the Ages,* by Joan D. Chittister

*Saints and Sinners: The American Catholic Experience through Stories, Memoirs, Essays and Commentary,* by Greg Tobin

*Teresa of Ávila: Mystical Writings,* by Tessa Bielecki

# Chart of Symbolic Elements

This chart shows how the religious symbols that are the basis of the rituals in the Catholic Church connect through time to Europe's old religions.

| Elemental Symbol | Corresponding Symbols | Symbolic Meaning | Implied Meaning | Catholic Beliefs and Practices |
|---|---|---|---|---|
| Earth | Winter; night; north; black | Death and gestation; nurturing; physicality; creativity; female | What appears to be dead is gestating and will be reborn; food and shelter; Earth as sacred; physical body as sacred; wisdom; the mystery of life | Jesus' physical presence on Earth; Jesus' birth in the manger; Mother Mary; Jesus' healing ministry (feed the hungry, heal the sick, raise the dead); Jesus' death on the cross and burial in earth; altar; holy oil; ashes (dust to dust); sacraments: Holy Eucharist, Anointing the Sick, Marriage (procreation) |

*continues*

*continued*

| Elemental Symbol | Corresponding Symbols | Symbolic Meaning | Implied Meaning | Catholic Beliefs and Practices |
|---|---|---|---|---|
| Air | Spring; morning; east; white; green | Birth; life and breath; new beginning; movement; promise; mind/meaning; male | The gift of life; hope; renewal; communication; thoughts as sacred | Incense; bells; prayers, songs, and chants; Declaring the Word; Holy Spirit as dove; preaching and teaching; hope reborn; resurrection; Sacrament: Holy Orders (as preaching and teaching) |
| Fire | Summer; noon; south; red; orange | Passion; action; clarifying; celebration; male | Transformation; strengthening the will; in the action world; willing into being; fruition and abundance | Candles; sanctuary lamp; Holy Spirit as fire; zeal; missionary work; Catholic action (do the right thing); Christ's Passion; Use of miracles; sacraments: Holy Orders and Confirmation |
| Water | Fall; evening; west; blue | Inner depth; quieting; soothing; waters of the womb; emotions; female | Cleansing; initiation; reflection; fulfillment; universal solvent | Holy water; blessings; mediation; contemplation; intuition or doorway to wisdom; sacraments: Baptism and Reconciliation |

# The Poop on Popes

There have been over 260 bishops of Rome since St. Peter, with dozens more antipopes (pretenders claiming to have that title) in the nearly 2,000-year history of the church. They have been a mixed bag, some extraordinary, some unremarkable, some great, and some just plain awful. What follows is a baker's dozen of past popes.

**St. Linus** (66–78). Hardly anything is known about St. Linus, who was St. Peter's, the first pope, immediate successor. He may be synonymous with the Linus mentioned in the Second Letter from Paul to Timothy. If so, he has the distinction of being the only other pope other than Peter to be named in the New Testament.

**St. Damascus I** (366–384). Described as a charming but forcible, even arrogant, man, St. Damascus's distinction is that he saw Christianity proclaimed the state religion of the Roman Empire and Rome established as the head of the church. He worked to enhance the appeal of Christianity to the Roman aristocracy. He believed in converting the women, with the expectation that they would soon bring their husbands over as well. The opulence of his reign left a bad taste in the mouths of some, and he was not without his critics. At one point, his enemies accused him of adultery, a charge he was acquitted of by a synod of 44 bishops.

**St. Leo I** (440–461). One of only two popes to be referred to as "the Great." He defined the doctrine that each pope inherited his authority directly from St. Peter and thus could not be tainted by the questionable acts of a previous pontiff. The emperor confirmed the pope's authority over other bishops. He is probably best remembered for his confrontation with Atilla the Hun in 452, when he successfully persuaded him to withdraw his armies and not invade Rome. He was successful in further negotiations with Vandal leaders and lessened the damage caused by their invasions.

**St. Gregory I** (590–604). The first monk to rise to the papacy, Gregory criticized the lack of discipline he saw in his fellow bishops and urged the need for higher moral standards, especially with regard to clerical celibacy. He was the first to use the term *ex cathedra* to define the bishop's authority to speak on matters of doctrine. He sent missionaries to Anglo-Saxon England and is probably best known today for the chant that bears his name (although he may have had nothing to do with its composition).

Times had changed for both Rome and the papacy. The empire that provided structure and order was now falling. Somebody had to fill the void. Gregory organized plague relief and the disbursement of food to the hungry. To deal with invading Lombards, he also arranged for the city's defense, paying the troops out of the church's treasury and eventually negotiating a peace.

Gregory began his life as an aristocratic civil servant and rose to the position of prefect of Rome. But then he became a monk and, reluctantly, pope. He was, however, the right man for this role. Although not necessarily a great intellect, he was an administrator *par excellence*. It is in this role as a temporal ruler that Gregory most clearly shaped the future of the papacy.

**Stephen VI** (896–897). Stephen was about as bad a pope as could be imagined. He was apparently motivated by equal parts political favoritism and a bizarre need for revenge. He exhumed the body of an earlier pope, Formosus, and put the corpse on trial for imagined misdeeds. The body was dressed in papal vestments, and a deacon was forced to provide the voice. After the corpse was found guilty, the three fingers that the dead man had used to administer blessings were cut off, and the body was delivered to a cemetery for the homeless. A couple of days later, it was thrown into the Tiber River.

Unrest in Rome, partly due to his horrifying behavior, soon led to Stephen's imprisonment. While in prison, he was strangled. Assassination and violent death were all too frequent dangers to the popes of this era, and Stephen died in a manner befitting the way he had lived.

**Sergius IV** (1009–1012). About the only thing Sergius, the son of a shoemaker, is remembered for is establishing the tradition whereby the pope chooses a new name upon his election. In the past, a pope might take a new name under special circumstances (for example, he might have a given name of a pagan deity, such as Mercury), but in the nearly 1,000 years since Sergius, only two have retained their original names. Sergius seems to have had two reasons for changing his name. His given name was Peter, and Peter would be a rather presumptuous handle for any pope to merit. In addition, he probably wanted to have a new name so people would stop using his nickname of "Pig-nose."

**St. Gregory VII** (1073–1085). A stubborn, forceful individual, Gregory fought hard for his ideals. He pushed ardently for church reform, especially clerical celibacy. He battled with the Holy Roman Emperor over the buying and selling of church offices (simony) and the power of lay rulers to name bishops within their own territory.

Gregory lost the battle and was driven into exile, where he eventually died. The emperor seized Rome and installed his own antipope. However, Gregory won the war. In 1122, the Concordant of Worms cemented the principles for which Gregory had struggled.

**Adrian IV** (1154–1159). The only English pope, Adrian (also known as Hadrian) probably owed his accession to the influence of the English King Henry II, the most powerful monarch in Europe. It was common for both local (Roman) and European politics to have a powerful effect on papal elections. In a document, he urged Henry to subdue Ireland and reform the Irish Church. Whether this document meant giving Ireland away to the English crown forever is a matter of some debate, but it was the catalyst to the violence that still affects that island today.

**Alexander VI** (1492–1503). Alexander certainly was the most notorious of the popes. His uncle, an earlier pope, made him a cardinal at the age of 25. He used lavish bribes to secure his election as pope. A Borgia, he fathered at least nine illegitimate children, the most infamous of whom were his daughter Lucretia and his son Ceasare (whose exploits inspired Machiavelli).

Alexander's reputation for extravagance was exaggerated to X-rated proportions by generations of later Protestant critics. He greatly extended the practice of selling indulgences, particularly when he declared a Jubilee Year in 1500 in order to increase the number of pilgrims and donations flowing into Rome. He used these monies to finance his son's military adventures.

Despite his immodest behavior, Alexander is also remembered as a great patron of Renaissance artists and a capable administrator. He neatly divided the New World between Spain and Portugal (favoring his fellow Spaniards) simply by drawing a line on a map. Although his death was probably due to fever, the old legend that he accidentally consumed the poison he had arranged for a rival cardinal cannot be discounted.

**Adrian VI** (1522–1523). Adrian was the last non-Italian pope prior to the election of John Paul II in 1978. He had three daunting challenges in front of him when he assumed power: Lutheranism, the Ottoman Empire, and reforms needed in a church whose leadership viewed him as an outsider to begin with, and which was determined to hold onto its many perks. Adrian's acknowledgement that the Roman Court had been the fountainhead for all corruption in the church won him no allies. He died after only 20 months, but 20 years probably would not have been enough to accomplish these tasks.

**Pius IX** (1846–1878). Pius was considered liberal when compared to his immediate predecessor, who, for example, considered railroads to be an invention of the devil. Pius was forced to deal with the inevitable crisis of the modern age. His reign saw the loss of the papal states and a corresponding loss of the temporal power that had been a part of the papacy for 15 centuries. Pius's reaction to this occurrence was to insist on absolute authority in the spiritual realm. He declared the doctrine of papal infallibility. His 32-year pontificate is the longest in history.

**John Paul I** (1978). The penultimate pope, John Paul was pontiff for only 33 days. He seemed to promise a breath of fresh air, and his first two acts suggested a new pope for a new era. Upon his election, he broke precedent and chose a dual name to honor his two predecessors, Paul VI and John XXIII. Typical of this man's humility, he refused the traditional crown of the popes and instead wore only a bishop's miter. During his short reign, his charming personality earned him the nickname of "the smiling Pope." His unexpected death, so shortly after his accession, shocked the world and gave bogus ammunition to conspiracy theorists everywhere.

And the ever popular ...

**Pope Joan** (855 or 1087?) No list of popes would be complete without the mythical Pope Joan. As the thirteenth-century legend has it, Joan was a devout and learned woman who disguised herself as a man and earned the admiration of all for her keen intellect and holiness. After the death of the preceding pope (either Leo IV in 855 or Victor III in 1087, depending on which version you believe), Joan was elected pope, taking the name John. It was said that she ruled wisely and well for a couple of years, but her secret was revealed in disastrous fashion. One day while walking through the streets of Rome with her cardinals, she gave birth. Her legend was enjoyed for centuries, and no amount of Vatican denials could stifle it. The story was especially popular with Protestant reformers, because it seemed to prove the debasement of the papacy. The myth wasn't thoroughly disproved until the seventeenth century, and even today she is still better known than the vast number of real popes.

# Index

## A

A.D. (Anno Domini), 81
Aaron, 84
Abba, 103, 131
abbots, 308
abortion, 12, 280-281, 377
   cultural shifts, 12
   protests, 4
Abraham, 91
absolution, 269
abstinence, 276-277
   birth control, 275
abstinence from meat, 359
abuses of power, 243
acceptance as a candidate, 240
Act of Contrition, 150, 152
active religious life, 289-290
activism, 33
Acts of the Apostles, 97
Adam, 159
Adam and Eve, 81
administrative offices
   (Roman Curia), 284
adolere, 221
adoration prayer, 186
Adrian IV, Pope, 395
Adrian VI, Pope, 395
Advent, 182
   vestments, 118
Advent calendars, 178
Advent wreaths, 177-178
Africa
   base communities, 258
   demographics, 29
   influences, 350
African Americans, 23-24,
   350-351
African-American Catholic
   Hymnal, The, 351
aggelos, 208
Agnus Dei, 219
agricultural communities, 24-25
agricultural workers, jubilee for,
   300
aid in dying, 278
AIDS, 12
Alexander VI, Pope, 395
All Saints Day, 23
altar bells, 217
altar servers, 223, 297
altars, 222
   candles, 111

American Revolution, 343-344
Americas
   Aztecs war, 331-333
   colonization, 328-329
   demographics, 26-28
   Hispanic influences on
      Catholicism, 337-339
   Incas war, 332
   indigenous people, 330
   La Nueva Raza (The New
      Race), 336
   Mayans war, 332
   missions, 332-333
   Our Lady of Guadalupe
      (Virgin Mary), 333-336
   United States, see United
      States
Amos, 63
Ananias, 94
Angelica, 39-40
angels, 208-209
   hierarchy, 208-209
   prayer, 209
Angelus, 118-119
Anglican Church, 323-324
Anno Domini, 81
Annunciation, 162, 168
Anointing of the Sick, 380
Anselm, 252
Ansgar of Denmark, St., 312
Anthony, 10
Apocalypse, Bible, 97
Apostles' Creed, 217
apostolic succession,
   ordination, 148
apparitions, 165
   Mary
      Fatima, Portugal, 166
      Guadalupe, Mexico,
         166-167
      Lourdes, France, 165-166
Aquinas, St. Thomas, 123, 319
   Dominican order, 294
   Just War Doctrine, 279
   original sin, 266
Archangel Gabriel, 208
archangels, 209
archbishops, 49
archdioceses, 49
Arianism, 248
Aristotle, 251
Arius, 248
Ark of the Covenant, 84
arrangers, Bible, 94
art, 7
artemesia, 161

Artemis, 161
   Council of Ephesus, 163
articles of faith, 165
artists, jubilee for, 299
ashes, palm ashes, 180
Asia
   base communities, 258
   demographics, 29
assisted dying, 278
Assumption, 168-169
attire
   church, 222
   clergy, 14-15
Augustine, 17, 258, 304-307
   just war doctrine, 279
   original sin, 266, 307
Australia, demographics, 29
authority of tradition, 246
authors, Bible, 94
Aztecs, 330-333

## B

B.C. (before Christ), 81
B.C.E. (before the common era),
   81
Baltimore Catechism, 250
baptism by blood, 141
baptism by desire, 141
baptism by water, 141
baptismal font, 138
baptismal pools, 139
baptisms, 138-140
   abortions, 280
   assisting, 140
   attending, 140
   origins, 140-141
   presiding over, 139
   types, 141
Baptists, 322
Bartolome de las Casas, 329
base communities, 256-257, 259
   origins, 258
Basilica of Notre Dame, 50
basilicas, 50
beatitudes, 52-53
Belgium, demographics, 28
beliefs, 8, 247
   Bible, 98
   Jesus, 108
   personal responsibilities, 9
bells, 118-119
Benedictines, 291-292
Benediction, 225-226
Berrigan, Daniel, 32-33
Berrigan, Philip, 32

# M

# W

# Y-Z

# A Little Knowledge Goes a Long Way ...

# Check Out These
# Best-Selling
# COMPLETE IDIOT'S GUIDES

Understanding Catholicism

0-02-863639-2
$16.95

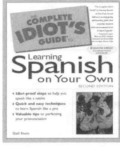

Learning Spanish on Your Own
SECOND EDITION

0-02-862743-1
$16.95

The Bible

0-02-862728-8
$16.95

Feng Shui
SECOND EDITION

0-02-864339-9
$18.95

Playing the Guitar
SECOND EDITION

0-02-864244-9
$21.95 w/CD-ROM

Personal Finance in Your 20s & 30s

0-02-862415-7
$18.95

Creating a Web Page
FIFTH EDITION

0-02-864316-X
$24.95 w/CD-ROM

Digital Photography
SECOND EDITION

0-02-864235-X
$24.95 w/CD-ROM

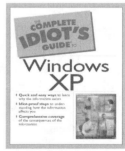

Windows XP

0-02-864232-5
$19.95

# More than *400 titles* in *26 different categories*
# Available at booksellers everywhere

ALPH